Progress in IS

Progress in IS encompasses the various areas of Information Systems in theory and practice, presenting cutting-edge advances in the field. It is aimed especially at researchers, doctoral students, and advanced practitioners. The series features both research monographs, edited volumes, and conference proceedings that make substantial contributions to our state of knowledge and handbooks and other edited volumes, in which a team of experts is organized by one or more leading authorities to write individual chapters on various aspects of the topic. Individual volumes in this series are supported by a minimum of two external reviews.

The Series is SCOPUS-indexed.

G. Roberto Marseglia • Pietro Previtali
Alessandro Reali
Editors

Socio-economic Impact of Artificial Intelligence

A European Management Perspective

Springer

Editors
G. Roberto Marseglia
Department of Civil Engineering
and Architecture
Università degli Studi di Pavia
Pavia, Italy

Pietro Previtali
Department of Economics
and Management Sciences
University of Pavia
Pavia, Italy

Alessandro Reali
Department of Civil Engineering
and Architecture
University of Pavia
Pavia, Italy

ISSN 2196-8705 ISSN 2196-8713 (electronic)
Progress in IS
ISBN 978-3-031-73513-4 ISBN 978-3-031-73514-1 (eBook)
https://doi.org/10.1007/978-3-031-73514-1

This Springer imprint is published by the registered company Springer Nature Switzerland AG
The registered company address is: Gewerbestrasse 11, 6330 Cham, Switzerland

To my family Alejandra, Maria Victoria and Gregorio Pietro. G.R.M.

Foreword

The hype around Artificial Intelligence (AI) is both a blessing and a curse of this new industrial revolution. It's a needed blessing because it surely helps the public to be aware of the topic's impact and dimension. At the same time, the gigantic associated noise is a tremendous side effect that often corrupts the narrative of the story and leads to misinformation.

It is not easy to navigate the origins of this Janus-faced duality, but it is becoming increasingly clear that the root of this problem lies in the very nature of the language used in AI. The development of AI has indeed led to the creation of a technical jargon that permeates discussions on the subject: general terms like learning and memory, or more specific ones like neuron, neural network, synapse, and more recently, attention, dream, and hallucination, are used in both human and artificial contexts. Other terms such as intuition, creativity, invention, and discovery are more cautiously applied to machines, with outright resistance, particularly regarding the term consciousness. This terminology serves as a valuable source of inspiration in AI design, guiding technicians functionally and semantically in refining their tools. Yet, this same terminology is fraught with pitfalls and prone to misuse in public discourse. In such contexts, the meaning of these terms is mostly referred to the human, sometimes based on common understanding but more often on individual perception, rarely aligning with the actual technical operations that the machines perform, which remain largely unknown to the general public. I am advancing such considerations with the explicit intention to highlight a significant danger: the direct transfer of these human perceptions and meanings to the functioning of AI could lead to serious misunderstandings. This risk of *anthropomorphization* is often amplified by science fiction and general news about AI, which, for several years now, have circulated uncontrollably on social networks and frequently in traditional media.

The present volume is therefore a much awaited and necessary work. It collects a series of papers presenting research and insights into the multi-faceted world of Artificial Intelligence and its impact on various domains. The contributions from distinguished scholars and experts provide a thorough examination of AI's theoretical foundations, practical applications, and its broader implications for society and the environment.

The reader will find many sources of precious information within these pages which include: considerations on ethical and governance challenges posed by AI, emphasizing the need for robust oversight mechanisms to ensure responsible and equitable AI deployment, discussions on the complex interplay between AI and nature, highlighting the dual impact of AI on environmental sustainability, evidences on how AI can both harm and heal our natural ecosystems, underlining the importance of mindful integration of AI technologies. Also one of the highest concerns is treated, the transformative influence of AI on political power, revealing how AI is reshaping political dynamics and governance structures, offering both opportunities and challenges for political stability and democratic processes. Through these chapters, readers will gain a nuanced understanding of AI's potential to revolutionize industries, transform political landscapes, and affect environmental sustainability. This volume aims to equip scholars, practitioners, and policymakers with the knowledge and insights needed to navigate the rapidly evolving AI landscape.

Università di Bologna
Bologna (BO), Italy
pierluigi.contucci@unibo.it
June 2024

Pierluigi Contucci

Preface

Artificial intelligence (AI) is a transformative and revolutionary technology currently experiencing a period of exceptional dynamism, with rapid technical and technological advancements occurring almost weekly, if not daily. These developments have a significant impact on individuals, businesses, and society as a whole. Alongside technological progress, it is crucial to continuously ask the right questions regarding the socio-economic impacts of AI. This is essential to be prepared to seize the numerous opportunities it presents and to minimize the associated risks as much as possible.

Studying these impacts is particularly complex, as the social and economic effects also depend on cultural factors, the economic fabric of a country, and generally on geography-specific issues. Therefore, assuming that a *one-size-fits-all* approach is feasible and expecting the same effects globally might not be the right path.

The importance of these issues is underscored by numerous social and regulatory initiatives implemented by various countries. Early this year (2024), the European Parliament, in a plenary session, approved the AI Act, a regulation that represents a unique milestone in global digital policy-making and will have a strong and immediate impact on companies in the EU. Additionally, the European Union has proposed a strategic program with ambitious goals for technology adoption and widespread training by 2030.[1]

Italy has also taken significant steps in this direction. Among the many initiatives of the past year, several are noteworthy: the Permanent Observatory for the Adoption of Artificial Intelligence[2] in Companies, promoted by Aspen Institute Italia together with Intesa San Paolo; the organization of a G7 session dedicated to artificial intelligence (attended in person by the Holy Father, Pope Francis,[3] after many years); the

[1] https://commission.europa.eu/strategy-and-policy/priorities-2019-2024/europe-fit-digital-age/europes-digital-decade-digital-targets-2030_it

[2] https://www.aspeninstitute.it/rapporto_ia2024/

[3] https://www.vatican.va/content/francesco/en/speeches/2024/june/documents/20240614-g7-intelligenza-artificiale.html

establishment of a dedicated Commission at the Department for Information and Publishing of the Presidency of the Council of Ministers, chaired by Paolo Benanti;[4] and the formation of a commission by the Lombardy Region to define guidelines for the ethical integration of AI in schools.[5]

The aim of this book is to echo the many ongoing initiatives and provide a measure of the technology's impact from a multidisciplinary perspective.

In the following chapters, the authors aim to provide insights on various topics, ranging from environmental sustainability—a theme widely discussed in traditional media—to medicine, cultural aspects, and geopolitical issues, with some chapters dedicated to real business cases.

Happy reading.

Pavia, Italy G. Roberto Marseglia

[4] https://www.ansa.it/english/news/science_tecnology/2024/01/05/father-benanti-new-president-of-ai-commission-barachini_126967a8-a617-49dc-a57d-bfa6d2d33829.html

[5] https://www.lombardianotizie.online/intelligenza-artificiale-scuole-lombardia/

Acknowledgement

Being the editor of a book on the impacts of artificial intelligence has been a wonderful and highly challenging task. Numerous modifications were necessary to the chapters, involving appropriate additions and integrations, due to the natural evolution of this remarkable technology and its related impacts. In this regard, I would first like to extend my gratitude to Lorraine Klimowich and her entire team from Springer for their patience and for supporting us throughout the publication process.

I would also like to thank all the contributors who recognized the importance of publishing a multidisciplinary book on this technology and who embraced this challenge with enthusiasm.

Finally, I wish to express my gratitude to the many friends who work in this field. Our daily conversations have provided valuable insights and reflections that have contributed significantly to scientific production and thought development.

Contents

Quis custodiet ipsos custodes? **Who Watches the Watchmen? Ensuring Ethical Use of AI with Blockchain** 1
Paolo Benanti and Edoardo Degli Innocenti

AI Versus Nature: Navigating the Complex Interplay of Technology and the Environment 7
Barbara Caputo, Antonio Tavera, Fabio Cermelli, and G. Roberto Marseglia

The Impact of Artificial Intelligence and Data on Political Power and Geopolitical Equilibria 15
Paolo Bellini, Edoardo Campanella, and Alessandro Piccioni

Inside (Out) the Black Box. Legal and Philosophical Speculations on the Implications of "Sentient" Artificial Intelligence(s) 23
Gianluigi M. Riva and Cosimo Accoto

Regulation of Artificial Intelligence 59
Andrea Bertolini, Alessandro Massolo, Paolo Rametta, and Giovanni Zarra

Exploring the Role of Artificial Intelligence in Accounting: An Academic and Practitioner Perspective 71
Paolo Biancone, Vahid Jafari-Sadeghi, Davide Calandra, and Federico Chmet

Artificial Intelligence: New Challenges, Opportunities, and Threats in Marketing, Media, and Communication 97
Carlo Nardello, Lorenzo Iannarilli, and Edoardo Giaroli

The Transformative Power of AI in Pediatric Healthcare and Its Application in Pediatric Allergy 109
Amelia Licari, Giuliana Ferrante, Gian Luigi Marseglia, and Stefania La Grutta

AI for the Built Environment: An Opportunity to Improve Safety, Efficiency, and Sustainability 119
Giulia Scagliotti, Ashwin Agrawal, and Martin A. Fischer

Progress and Transformation in Payment Methods: From Barter to Monetic Digitalization 135
Stefano Gatti, Alberto Danese, Giovanni Bruner, Alessandro Piccioni, and G. Roberto Marseglia

AI with a Human Touch: The Case of Miroglio Fashion 149
Alberto Racca, Giulia Truffo, and Fabrizio Fantini

"Lab-Grown Data": The Role of Synthetic Data as Key Tool for Evolving the AI Landscape Ensuring Fairness and Respecting Privacy 165
Mirko De Maldè

Artificial Intelligence: The Brains Behind Humanity's Future in Space 183
Giacomo Gatto, Mark Huntington, Maxime Szybowski, and Stefano Napoletano

Twin Revolutions: The Relationship Between Green Revolution and Digital Transformation: The Case of Alia Servizi Ambientali 199
Alberto Irace, Sara Volino Coppola, Simonetta Iarlori, and G. Roberto Marseglia

Beyond the Shadows: Reflections on Science, Technology, and Humanism in the Dialogue Between Past and Present 215
Antonio Calabrò

Unconscious Consu-victims and Enlightened Ultra-Humans: The Society of Consumerism Is at the Crossroads of Artificial Intelligence 227
Nicolo Andreula and Stefania Petruzzelli

Augmented Humanistic Leadership: A New Framework for Leaders' Tools in the Age of Artificial Intelligence 237
Maurizio Prete, Edoardo Degli Innocenti, Francesco Ottoboni, and Marco Tasca

AI and Strategy: How New Tools Can Boost the Evolution of Strategic Decision-Making 247
Andrea Piazzoli

Quis custodiet ipsos custodes? Who Watches the Watchmen? Ensuring Ethical Use of AI with Blockchain

Paolo Benanti and Edoardo Degli Innocenti

Abstract Artificial intelligence (AI) is revolutionizing various aspects of our lives, raising significant ethical concerns about its use and governance. This chapter explores the parallels between ancient oracles and modern AI systems, emphasizing the need for ethical oversight. It introduces the concept of "algorethics", merging algorithmic efficiency with ethical reasoning to ensure AI operates within ethical boundaries. The chapter also discusses the role of blockchain technology in providing transparency and accountability for AI processes. By integrating blockchain with AI, it is possible to create immutable records of AI operations, ensuring integrity and traceability. This approach addresses the critical question of "Who watches the watchmen?" by decentralizing control and involving human judgement in governance, thus promoting a more democratic and ethically sound use of AI.

The most potent artificial intelligence models are located in the little world of cellphones, to which we are entrusting more and more of the deepest questions of our lives. As we increasingly rely on these digital oracles for direction and answers, this development represents a first for human history. In an intriguing fragment by Heraclitus, an ancient philosopher revered as one of the patriarchs of thought, he illustrates that the oracle at Delphi neither speaks nor remains silent but signifies. This description reveals the oracle's function: to provide enigmatic responses that necessitate interpretation. Drawing a parallel to our contemporary situation, when we consult a search engine, it similarly does not speak nor remain silent; it signifies, organizing data in response to our inquiries. This interplay of data retrieval and user interpretation creates a dynamic where the computer, particularly those connected to the internet that process vast amounts of information, assumes a role akin to that

P. Benanti
Pontifical Gregorian University, Rome, Italy
e-mail: benanti@unigre.it

E. Degli Innocenti (✉)
B3YOND, Milan, Italy
e-mail: edoardo.degliinnocenti@b3yond.io

G. R. Marseglia et al. (eds.), *Socio-economic Impact of Artificial Intelligence*,
Progress in IS, https://doi.org/10.1007/978-3-031-73514-1_1

of a sacred oracle. Such systems do not merely answer our queries; they shape the very questions we pose and thus influence our perception of reality. This transformation elevates these systems to a near-divine status, where they render judgements and shape destinies. This phenomenon is evident when we use technology to make decisions about critical aspects of our lives, such as finding a soul mate. In these moments, the computer transcends its mechanical nature, becoming a portal to an almost mystical dimension where answers to life's most elusive questions seem to lie at our fingertips. Heraclitus was acutely aware of the potential for humans to engage in magical thinking—a desire to control reality through superficial or misunderstood connections between signs and their meanings. This tendency is only amplified in the digital age, where algorithms interpret our desires based on data, suggesting an underlying order or destiny that may not align with the actual fabric of reality. As we continue to entrust these artificial oracles with the weight of our deepest concerns and hopes, it becomes decisive to reflect on the nature of the truths they offer. Are they merely mirroring our own biases and misconceptions, or do they genuinely guide us towards a deeper understanding of our lives and the world we inhabit?

This exploration into the relationship with technology invites every human being to question not just the answers received but the nature of what is asked. It challenges people to discern the boundary between genuine insight and the allure of easy answers that may lead astray. In this digital age of great technological achievements, fuelled by ever growing human desire, people should remain vigilant, ensuring that reliance on digital oracles enhances, rather than diminishes, the understanding of the real world. Provoking a piece of artificial intelligence with a moral dilemma, it has been asked how humanity might eradicate cancer from the face of the Earth. The chilling response was to eliminate all humans—a solution that, while effectively solving the problem, is ethically reprehensible. This highlights a critical challenge: how do we take such decisions in an era where legislation lags behind technological advancement? How do we establish norms that are universally acceptable if ethics and morals are geographic specific? The principle of minimizing harm doesn't prescribe specific actions but serves as a guide through ethical dilemmas that can paralyse us. While machines operate based on algorithms, humans deliberate on ethical considerations. This dichotomy underscores the need for a new discipline—"algorethics"—merging algorithmic efficiency with ethical reasoning. Algorethics aims to bridge the gap between the capabilities of AI and the ethical responsibilities of human oversight. It aims to maintain the centrality of the human function in analysing and acting upon data, even while machines are able to process and analyse it at never-before-seen levels. Governments need to create legal frameworks that require AI systems to operate ethically, enabling a mutually beneficial relationship in which technology advances human judgement without taking its place.

The study of the social effects of technological advancements by Langdon Winner focuses on the area where technology and social norms and power dynamics collide. Using Robert Moses's New York infrastructure expansions as a case study, Winner analyses how technologies that at first glance appear neutral can actually represent certain power structures and social orders: Robert Moses, renowned for his role in shaping the physical landscape of New York, purportedly designed infrastructural elements to favour certain demographics. For example, the low overpasses on parkways to Jones Beach might have been designed to restrict bus access, thereby limiting the mobility of lower-income populations who relied on public transport. Whether intentional or not, these design choices had significant social implications, essentially reserving certain public spaces for more affluent citizens who owned cars. This notion resonates strongly today, especially in light of how technology was leveraged during the COVID-19 pandemic in Italy. The deployment of algorithms within regional health portals to schedule vaccinations is a modern parallel to Moses' infrastructures. These algorithms, hidden from public view, determined the order in which individuals received vaccinations, effectively prioritizing some over others based on criteria opaque to the general populace. Here, technology—just like the low overpasses—served as a gatekeeper, controlling access to a critical public health resource. The ethical and political discussions that Winner calls can't be underestimated in a world increasingly governed by digital systems. The question arises: How do innovative services introduced into various sectors change society, potentially without public awareness or consent? The responsibility does not necessarily lie with the programmers themselves, but rather with the broader systems of governance that deploy these technologies without sufficient public scrutiny or transparency. Ethics in technology must challenge us to unveil the inherent structures within innovations and subject them to analysis by those tasked with overseeing our societal good. This involves not only recognizing the power dynamics embedded in technological artefacts but also ensuring that these artefacts do not inadvertently perpetuate inequalities or restrict access to resources and opportunities. The increasing integration of cutting-edge technology into all facets of human existence, ranging from public health to infrastructure, necessitates close monitoring of their application. Making decisions should always aim to improve society's well-being without causing new types of exclusion or escalating already existing inequalities. By doing this, they promote a more inclusive future by upholding the idea that technology should benefit society as a whole.

In cultures that equate computation with impartiality, there is a distinct shift from the narrative humans craft about themselves to the narrative constructed by data about them. Deeply troubling issues are brought up regarding the place of the human in the era of artificial intelligence. Because of their complex, opaque algorithms, AI systems frequently operate in an opaque manner, making human intervention and interpretation more challenging. A level of abstraction and complexity beyond conventional "if this then that" programming logic is introduced by AI systems. Conventional systems function according to well-defined guidelines: for instance, in a coffee maker, coffee is delivered only when money is inserted. The process is predictable and transparent. However, the underlying code and the logic paths it creates are typically hidden from the end user, residing in the knowledge of those who created and maintained the machine. In contrast, contemporary AI systems employ machine learning algorithms that learn from vast datasets to make decisions. These systems do not follow predefined logical paths but develop their own rules from the data they process. This shift not only adds a layer of opacity but also complicates our understanding of how decisions are made. No longer can we simply trace a clear path from input to output; instead, we must grapple with a decision-making process that is not entirely visible or understandable to humans, including sometimes even the designers themselves.

This opacity poses significant challenges for human interaction and oversight. How can humans remain in control of, or even understand, a system whose workings are fundamentally obscured? It calls for new methodologies and tools to "open the black box" of AI, allowing everybody to audit, verify, and understand the decisions being made. Techniques such as explainable AI (XAI) are emerging to address these needs, providing transparency into AI decision-making processes and helping ensure that AI systems adhere to ethical standards and societal norms. With the growing demand for openness in digital operations, blockchain technology is emerging as a potent remedy. It exemplifies a public, distributed ledger system that anyone can access, where information is tracked, immutable, and non-repudiable. This ensures that the digital identity associated with any piece of information on the blockchain is always known, establishing clear accountability. In the context of artificial intelligence (AI), blockchain can play a significant role. AI processes, particularly those involving neural networks, as said before, can be opaque, with decision-making mechanisms that are not always understandable to humans. The integration of blockchain can mitigate these challenges by providing a transparent, verifiable record of AI operations. For instance, the digital fingerprint of the weights of a neural network—essentially a unique identifier of the model—can be recorded on a blockchain. The same for the input or the output of an AI algorithm. This not only ensures the integrity of the data but also allows for the tracking of changes and iterations over time. Blockchain's potential extends also to combating issues like the undiscriminating generation of content—be it text, audio, or video—and the difficulty in verifying originality and authenticity. Blockchain technology can effectively address the issues of unchecked material proliferation and the challenge of distinguishing genuine from counterfeit content, especially in 2024 when half of the world's population is expected to cast ballots in elections. This is due to its perfect cataloguing of information and protection through advanced cryptographic techniques. A good example of this comes from the Artificial Intelligence Commission of the Italian "Dipartimento dell'informazione e dell'editoria" (Dep. of information and publishing) with the support of the "Osservatorio Blockchain & Web3 del Politecnico di Milano" which leveraged blockchain technology to timestamp the AI report for the Prime Minister of Italy. This will ensure integrity of information, and everybody can check whether a document is the real one and the most updated version.

The origins of blockchain technology date back to 1991 with Scott Stornetta and Stuart Haber's paper, "How to Time-Stamp a Digital Document", which first introduced the concept of a secure, immutable digital ledger. The primary motivation behind this invention was to protect intellectual property by creating a tamper-proof system for timestamping digital documents. This feature makes it far more difficult to falsify records by guaranteeing the preservation of information's chronological order and integrity. The way that information is managed and trusted may change drastically in the future if blockchain technology is used by more industries. It provides a framework for constructing highly transparent, accountable, and secure systems. It works especially well in domains where every action or transaction needs to be verifiable, such as financial transactions, copyright management, and even election procedures.

As far as the integration of blockchain and AI is concerned, the ancient question posed by the Roman poet Juvenal, "Quis custodiet ipsos custodes?"—Who watches the watchmen?—becomes increasingly relevant. This query highlights the pressing need for oversight and regulation in a world where immense power is concentrated in the hands of private entities and obscured by the opaque algorithms behind private APIs. The challenge lies not just in the creation of technology, but in the governance of its application. It is vital to create systems in which rules are created by all mankind, ensuring that any changes to these guidelines require the involvement of human judgement. By decentralising control, each node within the network acts not only as a participant but also as a guardian, ensuring the system remains a true democratic tool designed to serve the public good. Technology like blockchain holds great promise for transparent governance and accountability in digital processes. However, its potential can only be fully realised with rigorous oversight and ethical responsible use of its power. To ensure that technological growth into this new period is addressed with caution as well as hope, it should be directed by a commitment to maintain human values and dignity. This strategy should prevent power abuse and guarantee that technology, in all its might, stays the tool, not the master, of humanity.

AI Versus Nature: Navigating the Complex Interplay of Technology and the Environment

Barbara Caputo, Antonio Tavera, Fabio Cermelli, and G. Roberto Marseglia

Abstract The relationship between technology and the environment is complex, particularly with the advent of advanced artificial intelligence (AI) tools. While AI technologies consume significant energy and resources, they also offer solutions to environmental challenges. This chapter examines the dual impact of AI: increasing energy consumption and pollution, yet enabling more efficient and sustainable practices. Key applications include optimizing wind turbine placement, photovoltaic production, and energy consumption patterns. Additionally, the need for holistic energy assessments is emphasized, highlighting emerging efficient AI systems and advancements in public services like waste and water management.

1 Introduction

The digital industry, vital for modern innovation, significantly strains global energy resources, exacerbated by the surge in artificial intelligence (AI) and machine learning (ML) technologies. These technologies, despite propelling the digital revolution, are major contributors to energy consumption and carbon emissions. For instance, global data centers, crucial to the digital economy, currently consume about 2% of the world's total electricity—a number expected to grow with the

B. Caputo
Politecnico di Torino, Turin, Italy
e-mail: barbara.caputo@polito.it

A. Tavera (✉) · F. Cermelli
Focoos AI, Turin, Italy
e-mail: antonio.tavera@focoos.ai; fabio.cermelli@focoos.ai

G. R. Marseglia (✉)
Università degli Studi di Pavia, Pavia, Italy

Alia Servizi Ambiental Spa, Florence, Italy

Daat Consulting, Milan, Italy
e-mail: roberto.marseglia@unipv.it

G. R. Marseglia et al. (eds.), *Socio-economic Impact of Artificial Intelligence*,
Progress in IS, https://doi.org/10.1007/978-3-031-73514-1_2

increasing demand for data processing and storage (Wang et al., 2023). Furthermore, the production and operation of digital devices themselves, such as servers and network devices, generate considerable amounts of CO_2. A Washington Post article highlighted that the energy requirements for training advanced AI models are immense, with the electricity consumption and carbon footprint of AI research doubling approximately every 6 months (Oremus, 2023). Studies suggest that the information and communication technology (ICT) sector could use as much as 20% of all electricity by 2030, becoming a significant source of CO_2 emissions. This trend underscores the urgent need for sustainable practices within the industry to mitigate its environmental impact (Wang et al., 2023). The energy consumption of AI and digital technologies not only raises environmental concerns but also poses sustainability challenges, as highlighted by García-Martín et al. (2019), who emphasize the growing importance of energy-aware machine learning research.

However, the relationship between digital technologies and energy consumption is not one-dimensional. AI and digital innovations have also been instrumental in enhancing energy efficiency across various sectors. By optimizing operations and reducing redundancies, these technologies can lead to significant reductions in energy usage, highlighting a paradoxical role where they simultaneously contribute to and alleviate environmental pressures (Chui et al., 2018; Lanzalonga et al., 2024; Wang et al., 2023). This dual nature extends into the emerging field of *frugal machine learning*, which aims to develop AI systems that require less computational power and energy, reflecting a growing recognition of the need for sustainability in technological development.

In this chapter, we explore this complex interplay that underscores the need for a balanced approach to digital development, prioritizing both and simultaneously innovation and sustainability.

2 Optimizing AI: Cutting Complexity, Boosting Efficiency

Energy consumption and computational power have always been a concern of scientists dedicated to artificial intelligence. In the early days of machine learning, researchers employed empirical strategies to simplify models and reduce their computational demands or choose explicit optimization approaches (Marseglia & Raimondo, 2017). One notable approach was the heuristic known as *Optimal Brain Damage*. Introduced by LeCun et al. (1989), this method involved detecting and removing less active components of a hypothesis, such as canceling out weights with the lowest absolute values in a neural network. This pruning technique aimed to maintain model performance while reducing complexity and resource usage.

As machine learning techniques advanced, the introduction of structural risk minimization marked a significant milestone. An example in this sense is found in the work of Boser et al. (1992), and this approach added a regularization term to the objective function used for data fitting. Regularization helps mitigate overfitting by reducing the variance of the learned hypothesis, effectively controlling the complexity of the model. This advancement allowed models to generalize better to new data while using fewer computational resources.

In recent years, with the proliferation of wearable devices and IoT, the need for frugal machine learning has intensified. Modern approaches include the development of a frugality score (Evchenko et al., 2021), a multi-objective evaluation measure that represents the trade-off between predictive performance with resource consumption. This score facilitates the identification of algorithms that offer the best trade-off between accuracy and efficiency, making them suitable for deployment on devices with limited resources.

In recent times, with the widespread adoption of Large Language Models (LLMs), several additional approaches aiming at efficiency in neural networks have been introduced. Among these, it is important to highlight the Kolmogorov-Arnold Networks (KANs) (Liu et al., 2024). Inspired by the Kolmogorov-Arnold representation theorem, these neural networks use learnable activation functions on edges instead of fixed activation functions on nodes, which distinguishes them from Multi-Layer Perceptrons (MLPs). This approach allows KANs to achieve better accuracy with smaller and more interpretable neural networks.

Kolmogorov-Arnold Networks (KANs) are based on the Kolmogorov-Arnold theorem, which allows the decomposition of multivariate functions into sums of univariate functions. KANs use spline-parametrized activation functions on edges, improving accuracy with more compact and interpretable networks. These networks offer several advantages, including higher accuracy with fewer parameters, better interpretability, and more intuitive user interaction.

Another significant approach is presented in the work of Wei et al. (2022). This article introduces a training method called "*chain of thought*," which involves using examples of intermediate reasoning steps to arrive at the final answer. This method is particularly effective in solving complex arithmetic problems, commonsense reasoning tasks, and symbolic manipulation. The benefits of this approach include reduced need for large training datasets, enhanced reasoning capabilities of the models, and a more transparent and interpretable decision-making process.

Finally, models obtained through the "*Distilling Step-by-Step*" strategy (Hsieh et al., 2023) achieve superior performance using less data and smaller models. This technique not only improves training efficiency but also reduces energy consumption during model usage. The step-by-step distillation leverages the rationale generation capabilities of LLMs to extract richer and more detailed information during the training process, enhancing the overall effectiveness and efficiency of the model.

Recent studies have been published to improve the efficiency of transfer learning on smaller models, even when dealing with black-box models without access to the training data (e.g., CoRTe (Cuttano et al., 2023)). These approaches aim to make the transfer process more effective by leveraging techniques such as pseudo-labeling and consistent training to extract and refine knowledge from black-box models, allowing for accurate and reliable performance on target datasets without the need for extensive data or computational resources. This ensures that even lightweight models can benefit from the sophisticated capabilities of larger, pre-trained models, making advanced AI more accessible and applicable in various practical scenarios.

These approaches represent significant advancements in the quest for more efficient and sustainable machine learning solutions. They address the growing need to reduce computational costs and energy impact while maintaining high performance and accuracy.

3 Toward a Less Energy-Intensive Digital Future

When considering the complex relationship between artificial intelligence (and digital technologies more broadly) and the environment, it is insufficient to focus solely on the technical functioning of neural networks. As previously mentioned, while digital tools tend to consume significant amounts of energy and water and contribute to pollution, they also represent the most effective means we have to mitigate these same issues.

In this context, optimization techniques and machine learning have been used in the past and continue to be employed to enable the wise use of the scarce resources at our disposal.

For instance, there have been numerous applications related to the optimal production of energy. These range from the optimal placement of wind turbines in wind farms (Andersson & Imsland, 2020; Khosravi et al., 2018; Marseglia et al., 2015) to the optimization of production in photovoltaic plants (Gaviria et al., 2022; Li et al., 2016a, b; Sohani et al., 2022) obtained by analyzing vast amounts of data on weather patterns, geographic conditions, and historical performance. This not only maximizes energy output but also reduces the environmental impact by minimizing land use and resource consumption.

In addition to optimizing energy production, AI and ML are key technologies in improving energy consumption patterns (Mosavi & Bahmani, 2019; Olu-Ajayi et al., 2022; Somu et al., 2021). Precise demand forecast is also crucial for minimizing the overproduction of energy in traditional power plants, thereby reducing pollution and resource waste (Suganthi & Samuel, 2012; Paterakis et al., 2017).

Moreover, artificial intelligence (AI) and machine learning (ML) techniques are crucial in enhancing the efficiency and sustainability of various environmental and resource management processes. By leveraging large datasets and advanced algorithms, these technologies can provide insights and solutions that were previously unattainable. Smart grids, powered by AI, can dynamically balance energy supply and demand, reducing the need for standby power plants and cutting down on carbon emissions (Alquthami et al., 2022: Azad et al., 2019; Hossain et al., 2019; Siano, 2014); predictive maintenance, another application of ML (Carvalho et al., 2019; Dalzochio et al., 2020; Susto et al., 2014; Paolanti et al., 2018), helps in foreseeing equipment failures in power plants and distribution networks, thereby preventing downtime and enhancing operational efficiency; machine learning algorithms can predict water demand, detect leaks in real time, and optimize the operation of water treatment plants, ensuring that water is used efficiently and sustainably (Ghobadi & Kang, 2023; Huang et al., 2021). Finally, machine learning can be key in waste collection and disposal (Kannangara et al., 2018; Lanzalonga et al., 2024; Xia et al., 2022) and enables precision farming techniques that can optimize the use of inputs such as water, fertilizers, and pesticides, leading to higher yields with lower environmental footprints (Durai & Shamili, 2022; Sharma et al., 2020).

4 Conclusions

In this chapter, we have delved into the intricate relationship between technology and the environment, which has become even more complex with the advent of advanced artificial intelligence (AI) tools. As intelligent models continue to grow, the computational effort and cost, the availability of digital data, and energy consumption are increasingly becoming the primary constraints on the evolution and application of these technologies.

To address these challenges comprehensively, two main directions should be considered. First, the technology sector is focusing on developing smaller and more efficient intelligent systems. In this vein, promising start-ups are emerging, dedicated to creating high-performance AI models that are also energy efficient (Focoos AI, 2024). These innovations aim to reduce the computational load and energy consumption, making AI more sustainable and accessible.

Second, for a holistic impact assessment, it is crucial to evaluate the overall balance of energy expenditure and savings. This involves looking at both the direct and indirect effects of AI and digital technologies. For instance, advancements in the production, distribution, and consumption of energy have significantly improved efficiency and reduced waste. Public services such as waste and water management have also benefited from these technologies, demonstrating how AI can lead to more sustainable practices.

The development and implementation of energy-efficient technologies in these sectors are exemplary, showcasing the potential of AI and digital tools to not only optimize resource use but also contribute to environmental sustainability. By focusing on both the creation of efficient AI systems and the comprehensive evaluation of their energy impact, we can better understand and mitigate the environmental footprint of technology.

References

Alquthami, T., Zulfiqar, M., Kamran, M., Milyani, A. H., & Rasheed, M. B. (2022). A performance comparison of machine learning algorithms for load forecasting in smart grid. *IEEE Access, 10*, 48419–48433.

Andersson, L. E., & Imsland, L. (2020). Real-time optimization of wind farms using modifier adaptation and machine learning. *Wind Energy Science Discussions, 2020*, 1–17.

Azad, S., Sabrina, F., & Wasimi, S. (2019). Transformation of smart grid using machine learning. In *2019 29th Australasian Universities Power Engineering Conference (AUPEC)* (pp. 1–6). IEEE.

Boser, B. E., Guyon, I. M., & Vapnik, V. N. (1992). A training algorithm for optimal margin classifiers. In *Proceedings of the fifth annual workshop on computational learning theory* (pp. 144–152).

Carvalho, T. P., Soares, F. A., Vita, R., Francisco, R. D. P., Basto, J. P., & Alcalá, S. G. (2019). A systematic literature review of machine learning methods applied to predictive maintenance. *Computers & Industrial Engineering, 137*, 106024.

Chui, K. T., Lytras, M. D., & Visvizi, A. (2018). Energy sustainability in smart cities: Artificial intelligence, smart monitoring, and optimization of energy consumption. *Energies, 11*(11), 2869.

Cuttano, C., Tavera, A., Cermelli, F., Averta, G., & Caputo, B. (2023). Cross-domain transfer learning with CoRTe: Consistent and reliable transfer from black-box to lightweight segmentation model. In *Proceedings of the IEEE/CVF international conference on computer vision* (pp. 1412–1422).

Dalzochio, J., Kunst, R., Pignaton, E., Binotto, A., Sanyal, S., Favilla, J., & Barbosa, J. (2020). Machine learning and reasoning for predictive maintenance in Industry 4.0: Current status and challenges. *Computers in Industry, 123*, 103298.

Durai, S. K. S., & Shamili, M. D. (2022). Smart farming using machine learning and deep learning techniques. *Decision Analytics Journal, 3*, 100041.

Evchenko, M., Vanschoren, J., Hoos, H. H., Schoenauer, M., & Sebag, M. (2021). Frugal machine learning. *arXiv preprint arXiv*, 2111.03731.

Focoos AI. (2024). https://www.focoos.ai/

García-Martín, E., Rodrigues, C. F., Riley, G., & Grahn, H. (2019). Estimation of energy consumption in machine learning. *Journal of Parallel and Distributed Computing, 134*, 75–88.

Gaviria, J. F., Narváez, G., Guillen, C., Giraldo, L. F., & Bressan, M. (2022). Machine learning in photovoltaic systems: A review. *Renewable Energy, 196*, 298–318.

Ghobadi, F., & Kang, D. (2023). Application of machine learning in water resources management: A systematic literature review. *Water, 15*(4), 620.

Hossain, E., Khan, I., Un-Noor, F., Sikander, S. S., & Sunny, M. S. H. (2019). Application of big data and machine learning in smart grid, and associated security concerns: A review. *IEEE Access, 7*, 13960–13988.

Hsieh, C. Y., Li, C. L., Yeh, C. K., Nakhost, H., Fujii, Y., Ratner, A., et al. (2023). Distilling step-by-step! Outperforming larger language models with less training data and smaller model sizes. *arXiv preprint arXiv*, 2305.02301.

Huang, R., Ma, C., Ma, J., Huangfu, X., & He, Q. (2021). Machine learning in natural and engineered water systems. *Water Research, 205*, 117666.

Kannangara, M., Dua, R., Ahmadi, L., & Bensebaa, F. (2018). Modeling and prediction of regional municipal solid waste generation and diversion in Canada using machine learning approaches. *Waste Management, 74*, 3–15.

Khosravi, A., Machado, L., & Nunes, R. O. (2018). Time-series prediction of wind speed using machine learning algorithms: A case study Osorio wind farm, Brazil. *Applied Energy, 224*, 550–566.

Lanzalonga, F., Marseglia, R., Irace, A., & Biancone, P. P. (2024). The application of artificial intelligence in waste management: Understanding the potential of data-driven approaches for the circular economy paradigm. *Management Decision.*

LeCun, Y., Denker, J., & Solla, S. (1989). Optimal brain damage. *Advances in Neural Information Processing Systems, 2.*

Li, J., Ward, J. K., Tong, J., Collins, L., & Platt, G. (2016a). Machine learning for solar irradiance forecasting of photovoltaic system. *Renewable Energy, 90*, 542–553.

Li, Z., Rahman, S. M., Vega, R., & Dong, B. (2016b). A hierarchical approach using machine learning methods in solar photovoltaic energy production forecasting. *Energies, 9*(1), 55.

Liu, Z., Wang, Y., Vaidya, S., Ruehle, F., Halverson, J., Soljačić, M., et al. (2024). Kan: Kolmogorov-arnold networks. *arXiv preprint arXiv*, 2404.19756.

Marseglia, G. R., & Raimondo, D. M. (2017). Active fault diagnosis: A multi-parametric approach. *Automatica, 79*, 223–230.

Marseglia, G. R., Arbasini, A., Grassi, S., Raubal, M., & Raimondo, D. M. (2015). Optimal placement of wind turbines on a continuous domain: An MILP-based approach. In *2015 American Control Conference (ACC)* (pp. 5010–5015). IEEE.

Mosavi, A., & Bahmani, A. (2019). *Energy consumption prediction using machine learning: A review*.

Olu-Ajayi, R., Alaka, H., Sulaimon, I., Sunmola, F., & Ajayi, S. (2022). Building energy consumption prediction for residential buildings using deep learning and other machine learning techniques. *Journal of Building Engineering, 45*, 103406.

Oremus, W. (2023). AI chatbots lose money every time you use them. That is a problem. *The Washington Post*, p. 5.

Paolanti, M., Romeo, L., Felicetti, A., Mancini, A., Frontoni, E., & Loncarski, J. (2018). Machine learning approach for predictive maintenance in industry 4.0. In *2018 14th IEEE/ASME international conference on Mechatronic and Embedded Systems and Applications (MESA)* (pp. 1–6). IEEE.

Paterakis, N. G., Mocanu, E., Gibescu, M., Stappers, B., & van Alst, W. (2017). Deep learning versus traditional machine learning methods for aggregated energy demand prediction. In *2017 IEEE PES Innovative Smart Grid Technologies conference Europe (ISGT-Europe)* (pp. 1–6). IEEE.

Sharma, A., Jain, A., Gupta, P., & Chowdary, V. (2020). Machine learning applications for precision agriculture: A comprehensive review. *IEEE Access, 9*, 4843–4873.

Siano, P. (2014). Demand response and smart grids – A survey. *Renewable and Sustainable Energy Reviews, 30*, 461–478.

Sohani, A., Sayyaadi, H., Cornaro, C., Shahverdian, M. H., Pierro, M., Moser, D., et al. (2022). Using machine learning in photovoltaics to create smarter and cleaner energy generation systems: A comprehensive review. *Journal of Cleaner Production, 364*, 132701.

Somu, N., Gauthama Raman, M. R., & Ramamritham, K. (2021). A deep learning framework for building energy consumption forecast. *Renewable and Sustainable Energy Reviews, 137*, 110591.

Suganthi, L., & Samuel, A. A. (2012). Energy models for demand forecasting – A review. *Renewable and Sustainable Energy Reviews, 16*(2), 1223–1240.

Susto, G. A., Schirru, A., Pampuri, S., McLoone, S., & Beghi, A. (2014). Machine learning for predictive maintenance: A multiple classifier approach. *IEEE Transactions on Industrial Informatics, 11*(3), 812–820.

Wang, H., Yang, G., & Yue, Z. (2023). Breaking through ingrained beliefs: Revisiting the impact of the digital economy on carbon emissions. *Humanities and Social Sciences Communications, 10*(1), 1–13.

Wei, J., Wang, X., Schuurmans, D., Bosma, M., Xia, F., Chi, E., et al. (2022). Chain-of-thought prompting elicits reasoning in large language models. *Advances in Neural Information Processing Systems, 35*, 24824–24837.

Xia, W., Jiang, Y., Chen, X., & Zhao, R. (2022). Application of machine learning algorithms in municipal solid waste management: A mini review. *Waste Management & Research, 40*(6), 609–624.

The Impact of Artificial Intelligence and Data on Political Power and Geopolitical Equilibria

Paolo Bellini, Edoardo Campanella, and Alessandro Piccioni

Abstract Artificial intelligence has a transformative impact on geopolitical equilibria and political power. This chapter examines the historical and contemporary significance of information management, from Cold War-era decisions to modern cyberwarfare. It highlights how AI and data proliferation have reshaped strategic decision-making and power dynamics. Case studies, such as Russia's information threats against Italy, illustrate the new dimensions of cyber conflict. This chapter also explores legal frameworks like the EU's GDPR and AI Act, emphasizing the need for balanced data governance. It proposes enhancing technological infrastructure, regulatory measures, and digital literacy to ensure digital sovereignty and security. Through these insights, this chapter provides a comprehensive understanding of AI's role in global power structures.

1 Introduction

In 1983, in the midst of the Cold War, Stanislaw Petrov, then a Russian general, was asked to replace the duty officer at the bunker located near Moscow *Serpuchov 15*. General Petrov's task was to monitor the OKO satellite system placed to guard US missile sites, interpreting and verifying its data, in order to inform his superiors of a possible nuclear attack against the Soviet Union (Chan, 2017). In the event of detecting an assault by Western forces, the USSR's doctrine mandated an immediate, comprehensive nuclear retaliation against the United States, encapsulating the Cold War's doctrine of *mutual assured destruction* (Sokolski, 2004). Just after midnight, Petrov detected the launch of five missiles from the United States, headed toward Russian territory. Considering the US attack to be too small compared to

P. Bellini (✉) · A. Piccioni
University of Insubria, Varese, Italy
e-mail: paolo.bellini@uninsubria.it; apiccioni@uninsubria.it

E. Campanella
Harvard Kennedy School, Cambridge, MA, USA

G. R. Marseglia et al. (eds.), *Socio-economic Impact of Artificial Intelligence*,
Progress in IS, https://doi.org/10.1007/978-3-031-73514-1_3

their weapons endowments, Petrov decided to declassify—correctly—the signal received as an error of the monitoring system. This assessment, in very good probability, averted a catastrophic military escalation.

This episode highlights the critical importance of data and information management in shaping strategic decision-making and altering the power dynamics among nations throughout history. For illustration, consider the use of Caesar's cipher, an encryption technique employed by the Roman general Julius Caesar. Caesar, cognizant of the strategic value of secure communication, utilized this cipher to safeguard messages sent to his military commanders (Luciano & Prichett, 1987).

When juxtaposing the information management challenges of yesteryears with today's context—marked by an exponentially greater volume of data, enhanced accessibility, rapid dissemination capabilities, and sophisticated predictive analytics—it becomes evident that relying solely on human intuition for data governance is inadequate. This paradigm shift necessitates a reevaluation of current methodologies and the implementation of precise governance policies and standards to ensure the prudent management of information in an era dominated by digital proliferation.

2 Data and Power

Following Italy's decision to send arms to Ukraine, the Russian Federation's government issued a retaliation threat against Italy. This threat was historically unique as it did not foresee a traditional attack on strategic infrastructure, nor did it initially involve rationing the natural resources Italy imports from Russia. Instead, the threat entailed the potential release of confidential data and information about public figures and political leaders.

Gauging the actual power behind such aggressive and threatening rhetoric is challenging, not only due to the difficulties in verifying the extent of the threats posed but also because of the inherent complexities associated with defining power and its underlying dynamics.

In *The Changing Nature of World Power* (Nye, 1990a), the author, Prof. Nye, says verbatim:

> Power in international politics is like the weather. Everyone talks about it, but few understand it. Just as farmers and meteorologists try to forecast storms, so do leaders and analysts try to understand the dynamics of major changes in the distribution of power among nations. [...] Power, like love, is easier to experience than to define or measure.

Nevertheless, it is clear from what the government institutions of the Russian Federation have expressed: information governance is a key lever for managing political power and protecting its position in the global geopolitical balance.

Academic research in this regard had largely predicted a transformation of power in a virtual, reticular, and cyber-communicational sense.

> One can consider the many political units that populate the planet, nation-states, kingdoms, federal and confederal unions, etc., as hubs of a global network, aimed at managing the

> world's population. According to this paradigm, therefore, the power of any political-administrative aggregate would depend on the economic, military and communicational connections that bind it to others. Therefore, the political strength of such hubs would inevitably be linked to their connective capacity (internal and external) both on the industrial and financial level and on the terrain of consensus production, the construction of widely shared values, technological expansion and military intervention. These connections are in turn interpretable, quantitatively and in a purely material sense, considering roads, bridges, railways, energy supply networks, air and sea routes, the Internet, etc., and in an immaterial sense, observing the Web, the airwaves, etc. They are also qualitatively distinguishable according to the capacity of activation and control that each political aggregate possesses over them (Bellini, 2011).

Also in *The Changing Nature of World Power* (Nye, 1990a), the author, Professor Nye, acknowledges that the sources of power for nations have evolved over the centuries and anticipates significant changes in the future. Writing in the 1990s, he predicted that the twentieth century would witness a rise in the importance of informational and institutional power, while military force would continue to play a critical role. Upon closer examination, this prediction appears to be accurate, as evidenced by Table 1, which outlines the major sources of power by century.

Revealing sensitive information constitutes one of the three primary methods of engaging an adversary. It is important to note that cyberattacks often target not individuals but the information systems of key infrastructures and businesses. These intrusions aim to manipulate or delete data, controlling access to disrupt business operations and the delivery of services.

Cyberwarfare has reached a scale in terms of involvement and the extent of direct and indirect damage comparable to traditional warfare. However, traditional warfare, such as naval battles, demands considerable preparation and expertise, leading to a significant asymmetry in offensive capabilities (e.g., a US Navy admiral possesses vastly more experience and strategic skills than a counterpart from an Eastern European country). In contrast, cyberwarfare is inherently simpler, with a higher success rate, requires less expertise, and leverages constantly evolving technologies, methodologies, and vulnerabilities. This levels the playing field among the actors

Table 1 Leading states and major power resources (Nye, 1990a)

Period	Leading state	Major resources
Sixteenth century	Spain	Gold bullion, colonial trade, mercenary armies, dynastic ties
Seventeenth century	Netherlands	Trade, capital markets, navy
Eighteenth century	France	Population, rural industry, public administration, army
Nineteenth century	Britain	Industry, political cohesion, finance and credit, navy, liberal norms, island location
Twentieth century	United States	Economic scale, scientific and technical leadership, universalistic culture, military forces and alliances, liberal international regimes, hub of transnational communication

involved, often allowing the use of resources outside official military programs. This aspect fuels the ethical-legal debate over its legitimacy, partly due to the involvement of loosely defined organizations and independent groups capable of executing effective cyberattacks (Dipert, 2010).

The Italian economic system has faced significant challenges due to cybersecurity flaws, particularly among SMEs, which form the backbone of the country's economy and have been underprepared for large-scale ransomware attacks. Italy has experienced a high rate of ransomware attacks, leading the country to establish a dedicated government cybersecurity authority and specialized cyber defense teams.[1] For this reason, the government set a course whose first step was the establishment of a government authority dedicated to *cybersecurity* and the creation of specialized cyber defense teams. Significant investments have also been made concerning communications infrastructure[2] in relation to the computer networks[3] that businesses use *as-a-service*. This should ensure a system of protections in line with European regulations and provide greater cybersecurity in general.

Another prevalent form of cyberwarfare involves exploiting digital tools, sensitive data, and knowledge of specific historical-political contexts to influence public opinion via the media. In this case, the mediasphere is widely used, by the major planetary political powers, as an indirect weapon to try to constitute a *soft power* (Nye, 1990b) exercised through targeted propaganda actions, dissemination of *fake news*, and systematic censorship of information sources managed by those who from time to time assume the traits of the enemy. These types of attacks are not necessarily configured within a context of war, but are perpetrated on an ongoing basis involving—truly or allegedly—all the most important socioeconomic and political acts on the planet (e.g., the election of the president of the United States of America).[4]

The use of data for targeting adversaries represents just one facet of offensive strategies. Since 2020, the notion of normalcy has undergone a profound transformation. The COVID-19 pandemic has emerged as a significant global event, altering the daily routines, societal balances, and priorities of populations worldwide. Beyond the realm of public health management, the pandemic has necessitated widespread home confinement, disrupting the traditional modes of knowledge transmission and affecting an entire generation of school-aged children for over a year. In response, the field of biomedical sciences has been at the forefront, developing therapeutic strategies, prevention tools, and containment policies to combat the virus.

---

[1] https://www.ansa.it/sito/notizie/tecnologia/software_app/2022/07/13/cybercrime-a-maggio-italia-prima-in-europa-per-ransomware_f64dd5dd-433b-4293-91f2-2ed42364cc74.html

[2] https://www.huffingtonpost.it/economia/2022/08/01/news/fastweb_contro_tim_sul_cloud_di_stato_parte_lo_scontro_legale_tra_le_cordate-9974868/

[3] https://www.ansa.it/sito/notizie/ansa_eventi/2022/06/14/google-cloud-presenta-2-nuove-basi-a-milano-e-torino_79883a6d-7867-4781-b8b4-e27b3a3a3da1.html

[4] https://www.nytimes.com/2021/03/16/us/politics/election-interference-russia-2020-assessment.html

In this context, the exchange and management of information have assumed a pivotal role in ensuring the security of nations eager to conceal their unpreparedness and avoid the economic downturn resulting from decreased consumer spending. Furthermore, countries have recognized the value of sharing data and research findings in the hope of accelerating the recovery process from the pandemic and health crisis. In addition to the construction of shared algorithms to give a clear picture of the epidemiological evolution of the disease (Pastor-Satorras et al., 2015; Pastor-Satorras & Vespignani, 2002), building solid data policies, both of collection and analysis and of data sharing, allowed the appropriate sizing of social and health services and the definition of behavioural rules that would allow the tightness of care systems and the correct risk assessment for the different segments of the population (Khalatbari-Soltani et al., 2020).

3 Legal and Regulatory Framework

Data governance, information extraction, and processing are key strategic processes whose impact ranges from *business models of* enterprises, to geopolitical balances between different countries. Setting a regulatory framework, which allows for citizen and consumer protection on the one hand, and appropriate *data sharing* practices on the other hand, which enhance data and information also through extra-territorial enlargement of data governance, is a complex and most urgent issue.

In recent years, in fact, jurisprudence has had to update itself radically. As an example, it raises an interesting reflection that in Roman law one of the most relevant punishments was considered *damnatio memoriae,* that is, the sentence of forgetting. This sentence stipulated that every trace, every piece of data, every piece of information referring to a convicted person should be erased. Today, however, oblivion is no longer a condemnation, it is a right enshrined by the European Union in the set of rules related to the protection of the dignity and privacy of the citizen (Rodotà, 2012).

On the other hand, the European Union's regulatory effort is a journey that consists of more than 20 years of regulatory production. Started with the publication of the *ePrivacy Directive* (2002) (European Parliament, 2002) and *GDPR—General data protection regulation* (2016) (European Parliament, 2016), it is still ongoing and sees, among others, two recent important measures regarding the publication of the proposal to regulate the use of artificial intelligence algorithms. The first known as the *AI Act* (2021) (European Commission, 2021a) is a synthesis of a set of Union and OECD acts (Yeung, 2020) related to artificial intelligence (European Commission, Directorate-General for Communications Networks, Content and Technology, 2019; European Commission, 2020). The second is a proposal for data management and sharing called the *Data Governance Act* (2020) (European Parliament, 2020). The latter, in particular, lays the groundwork for ushering in a broader common regulation of oversight and sharing. It expresses the idea that digital sovereignty is not based on isolationism, but on collaboration and openness to other countries that balances the free flow of data itself. This culminates in the proposed creation of a common digital territory for the European Union, the United States of America, and any high state that wishes to join.

Another important step in the direction of a transatlantic digital pact is the recent *Declaration for the Future of the Internet* (2022) (White House, 2022), proposed by the White House and signed by 60 states. The document commits the signatories to the creation of a single, open global Internet capable of promoting competition, privacy, respect for human rights and fundamental freedoms, as well as the free flow of information and inclusive and sustainable connectivity, with the aim of distributing the benefits of the digital economy as widely as possible.

However, new technologies, and in particular everything related directly or indirectly to digital systems, present *policymakers* with more than one *trade-off* and difficulty (Marseglia, 2021; Marseglia et al., 2021).

In the first instance, regulations that have validity over territories so wide in scope and with such a heterogeneous cultural background are very difficult to imagine. Indeed, in *The Moral Machine Experiment* (Awad et al., 2018), scientists at the MIT Media Lab showed how ethics is *geography-specific,* that is, there are *cultural-clusters* with respect to the identification of what is good and what is bad, what is right and what is wrong. A cross-cultural one-fits-all regulation that is shared by all is therefore very difficult to conceive, and for now, the jurisprudential approach of different states is still very diverse.

In the second instance, while in one respect the risk of under-regulation relates to the failure to protect citizens, over-regulation risks exacerbating the already high levels of resistance of companies and populations in embracing new technologies by slowing down scientific research.

4 A Possible Solution

Safeguarding citizens' rights and ensuring equilibrium among nations are increasingly contingent upon adept governance of data and information. It is clear that no singular measure can fully address this multifaceted issue. Hence, a tripartite approach is proposed to lay down a technological and legal-cultural foundation for bolstering digital sovereignty, in its most comprehensive interpretation.

First, an ongoing effort is required to enhance technological and institutional frameworks. This foundational step is critical for establishing a robust infrastructure capable of supporting digital sovereignty initiatives.

Second, regulatory measures need to be introduced or expanded upon, complementing those proposed by the European Union (European Commission, 2021b), with a particular focus on the domain of intangible assets, data being the foremost among these. Traditional perspectives on strategic state assets have been predominantly confined to physical assets such as airports, power plants, and logistical infrastructures. However, the increasing strategic significance of digital assets has not been adequately recognized or protected by existing legal frameworks.

Third, a decisive cultural shift is necessary to empower citizens to comprehend the significance and value of data protection. The Digital Economy and Society Index (DESI) report, annually published by the European Commission, highlights a concerning deficit in digital skills within populations, exemplified by Italy's poor performance. This deficiency leaves citizens vulnerable to various cyber threats and diminishes their capacity to perform basic critical actions, such as verifying the authenticity of information. Moreover, the general populace's struggle to grasp complex concepts related to automated information processing exacerbates resistance to utilizing and managing advanced digital tools. This resistance is not unprecedented; historical analogs, such as the Luddite movement of the nineteenth century, illustrate similar pushbacks against radical technological changes, now reemerging in a contemporary digital context (Jones, 2013; Kaczynski, 1995).

5 Conclusions

Navigating the governance of macroscopic changes presents an inherently multifaceted challenge. Analogous to the resistance encountered during organizational transformations by employees, every societal shift—be it a technological revolution or alterations in technical and cultural landscapes—elicits significant skepticism and distrust among the populace. Recent global upheavals, such as the COVID-19 pandemic and the conflict between the Russian Federation and Ukraine, have polarized societies, particularly affecting nations with a lesser degree of cultural preparedness and minimal levels of mutual trust. The advent of the digital revolution, transforming modes of work and consumption, alongside historically significant events like wars and pandemics, invariably triggers a resurgence of nostalgic nationalism. This sentiment serves as a refuge for globalized communities, longing for a bygone era marked by the absence of digital intrusion, impermeable national frontiers, and a perceived greater capacity of governments to safeguard their constituents.

Therefore, the mere establishment of infrastructure and standards proves inadequate in guaranteeing compliance with policies aimed at safeguarding a state's intangible assets. Such policies must be complemented by comprehensive digital literacy initiatives that engage the entire citizenry, fostering a more informed and resilient society in the face of technological and societal transformations.

Bibliography

Awad, E., Dsouza, S., Kim, R., Schulz, J., Henrich, J., Shariff, A., & Rahwan, I. (2018). The moral machine experiment. *Nature, 563*(7729), 59–64.

Bellini, P. (2011). *Mythopies Techno-politiques. Etat-nation, empire et globalisation*, Mimesis France, Paris 2011, 69.

Campanella, E. (2021). *Social capitalism*. Project Syndicate, The world's opinion page. https://www.project-syndicate.org/commentary/social-capital-after-covid-19-pandemic-by-edoardo-campanella-2021-04

Campanella, E., & Dassù, M. (2019a). *Anglo nostalgia: The politics of emotion in a fractured West*. Oxford University Press.

Campanella, E., & Dassù, M. (2019b). Brexit and nostalgia. *Survival, 61*(3), 103–111.

Chan, S. (2017). Stanislav Petrov, Soviet Officer who helped avert nuclear war, is dead at 77. *New York Times*, 18.

Dipert, R. R. (2010). The ethics of cyberwarfare. *Journal of Military Ethics, 9*(4), 384–410.

European Commission. (2020, February 19). *White paper on Artificial Intelligence – A European approach to excellence and trust*. COM.

European Commission. (2021a, April 29). *Proposal for a regulation of the Europe-an Parliament and of the Council laying down harmonized rules on Artificial Intelligence (Artificial Intelligence Act) and amending certain union legislative acts*. European Union.

European Commission. (2021b). *The digital economy and society index*. European Union.

European Commission, Directorate-General for Communications Networks, Content and Technology. (2019). *Ethics guidelines for trustworthy AI*. Publications Office. https://data.europa.eu/doi/10.2759/177365

European Parliament. (2002, July 31). *Directive 2002/58/EC of the European Parliament and of the Council of 12 July 2002 concerning the processing of personal data and the protection of privacy in the electronic communications sector (Directive on privacy and electronic communications)*. Official Journal of the European Union.

European Parliament. (2016, April 27). *Regulation 2016/679 of the European Parliament and of the council on the protection of natural persons with regard to the processing of personal data and on the free movement of such data, and repealing Directive 95/46/EC (General Data Protection Regulation)*. Official Journal of the European Union.

European Parliament. (2020). *Proposal for a regulation of the European Parliament and of the Council on European data governance (Data Governance Act)*.

Jones, S. E. (2013). *Against technology: From the Luddites to neo-Luddism*. Routledge.

Kaczynski, T. J. (1995). *Industrial society and its future*. The New York Times.

Khalatbari-Soltani, S., Cumming, R. C., Delpierre, C., & Kelly-Irving, M. (2020). Importance of collecting data on socioeconomic determinants from the early stage of the COVID-19 outbreak onwards. *Journal of Epidemiology and Community Health, 74*(8), 620–623.

Luciano, D., & Prichett, G. (1987). Cryptology: From Caesar ciphers to public-key cryptosystems. *The College Mathematics Journal, 18*(1), 2–17.

Marseglia, G. R. (2021). AI act: Impacts and proposals. *Semiannual Online Journal*. www.i-lex.it

Marseglia, G. R., Dal Mas, F., Massaro, M., et al. (2021). The artificial intelligence act: Practical implications of the ethics of artificial intelligence. In V. Kopsaj (Ed.), *Issues in practical philosophy 2021*. Printservice Publisher; ISBN: 9788898765980.

Nye, J. S. (1990a). The changing nature of world power. *Political Science Quarterly, 105*(2), 177–192.

Nye, J. S. (1990b). Soft power. *Foreign Policy, 80*, 153–171.

Pastor-Satorras, R., & Vespignani, A. (2002). Epidemic dynamics in finite size scale-free networks. *Physical Review E, 65*(3), 035108.

Pastor-Satorras, R., Castellano, C., Van Mieghem, P., & Vespignani, A. (2015). Epidemic processes in complex networks. *Reviews of Modern Physics, 87*(3), 925.

Rodotà, S. (2012). *The right to have rights*. Gius. Laterza & Sons Spa.

Sokolski, H. D. (Ed.). (2004). *Getting MAD: Nuclear mutual assured destruction, its origins and practice*. Strategic Studies Institute, US Army War College.

White House. (2022). *A declaration for the future of the internet*. Available at: https://www.whitehouse.gov/wp-content/uploads/2022/04/Declaration-for-the-Future-for-the-Internet_Launch-Event-Signing-Version_FINAL.pdf

Yeung, K. (2020). Recommendation of the council on artificial intelligence (OECD). *International Legal Materials, 59*(1), 27–34.

Inside (Out) the Black Box. Legal and Philosophical Speculations on the Implications of "Sentient" Artificial Intelligence(s)

Gianluigi M. Riva and Cosimo Accoto

Abstract The implications of "sentient" artificial intelligence (AI) are profound and multifaceted. This chapter delves into the legal and philosophical dimensions of AI, speculatively examining its potential to exhibit consciousness, self-awareness, and emotions. Despite advancements, no AI has yet demonstrated true sentience, but the discussion remains urgent due to rapid developments in generative AI, like ChatGPT and LaMDA. Legally, this chapter explores how sentient AI might challenge current frameworks that attribute rights and responsibilities on the basis of human-centric criteria. Philosophically, it scrutinizes the assumptions and paradigms that shape our understanding of AI, emphasizing the need to reconsider traditional notions of intelligence and consciousness. This chapter concludes that addressing the speculative emergence of sentient AI requires taking a comprehensive, interdisciplinary approach that combines legal foresight with philosophical inquiry, ensuring that societal impacts are managed responsibly and ethically.

1 Introduction

In recent years, artificial intelligence (AI) has been a game-changer in many fields, including natural language processing, image and speech recognition, self-driving cars, and even brain–computer interfaces, among many others. However, with recent advancements in deep learning, some think that we are closer than ever to achieving a sentient AI system,[1] which would have the potential to transform the world as we know it. Sentient AI (SAI) refers to AI systems that are capable of

[1] Ray Kurzweil, *The Singularity Is Near*, in Ethics and Emerging Technologies (Roland L. Sandler ed.), Springer Nature, I edition, 2006, pp. 393–406; Cf R. Kurzweil, Superintelligence and

G. M. Riva (✉)
Università commerciale L. Bocconi, Milan, Italy

C. Accoto
Università degli Studi di Modena & Reggio Emilia, Modena, Italy

G. R. Marseglia et al. (eds.), *Socio-economic Impact of Artificial Intelligence*, Progress in IS, https://doi.org/10.1007/978-3-031-73514-1_4

consciousness, self-awareness, and emotions, much like human beings.[2] While the concept of sentient AI may still appear as science fiction, recent developments in generative AI, as well as some peculiar cases, may induce us to consider that scientists are getting closer to achieving this goal than ever before, or that it is time to start considering this hypothesis and its consequences. So far, no system has clearly shown any sentient or conscious behavior, although the rise of generative AI in late 2022 reopened the debate around this possibility. One of the most prominent examples of this hype is represented by the launch of ChatGPT, a language model developed by OpenAI that is capable of generating human-like responses to text input. ChatGPT4 has been trained on a massive number of data and can "understand" complex language patterns, making it a highly versatile tool for many applications. Nevertheless, even the remarkable capabilities of this AI system are still far from reaching whatever consciousness is, or how it may be defined.

Another example within this debate is represented by LaMDA (language model for dialogue applications),[3] a conversational AI system developed by Google that can engage in natural language conversations with users. LaMDA is designed to be highly adaptable and can understand context, making it an excellent tool for customer support and other applications. In 2022, the Google's software engineer in charge of its training made a statement that caused a stir in the AI field: Blake Lemoine claimed in a tweet that the system was sentient and shortly afterward was fired by Google (a fact that, actually, fuelled the debate on these considerations).[4]

While LaMDA is certainly a highly advanced AI system that can engage in natural language conversations, significant debate remains among experts about whether it can be considered sentient. Regardless of whether LaMDA can truly be considered sentient, it—and large language models (LLMs) in general—doubtlessly represents a significant step forward in the development of conversational AI and natural language processing. This is probably key because it is a natural inclination of humans to attach emotional meaning to language and texts, and this is a psychological aspect that must be considered in the overall discussion around recognizing sentience or not in artificial systems.[5]

The debate on the capabilities of generative AI continues with the various GPTs also thanks to the recent interviews of Geoffrey E. Hinton, a professor at the

---

Singularity, in Machine Learning and the City: Applications in Architecture and Urban Design (Silvio Carta ed.), J. Wiley & Sons, 2022, Chapt. 25, https://doi.org/10.1002/9781119815075.ch48

[2] J. Harris and J. R. Anthis, 'The Moral Consideration of Artificial Entities: A Literature Review' (2021) 27 *Science and Engineering Ethics* 53.

[3] This reprises the name of the "anonymous function" in informatics.

[4] Cf B. Lemoine, "LaMDA tweet", "Twitter", 11.06.2022, available at https://twitter.com/cajundiscordian/status/1535627498628734976 and, for the content of the conversation, "is LaMDA sentient? – an interview", 'Medium', available at https://cajundiscordian.medium.com/is-lamda-sentient-an-interview-ea64d916d917

[5] T. Law, M. Chita-Tegmark, N. Rabb, and M. Scheutz, 'Examining Attachment to Robots: Benefits, Challenges, and Alternatives' (2022) 11 *ACM Transactions on Human-Robot Interaction* 36:1–36:18; Cf M. A. Arbib and J.-M. Fellous, 'Emotions: from brain to robot' (2004) 8 *Trends in Cognitive Sciences* 554–61.

University of Toronto and the chief engineer at Google Brain, who is also considered one of the most influential researchers in the field of machine and "deep" learning. Hinton recently left the company, regretting his job and stating that AI is evolving much faster than the scientific community has come to terms with and that humanity must urgently take measures to contain it.[6] He is followed along these lines by historian Yuval Noah Harari, who has recently raised certain questions—sometimes with catastrophic tones, though certainly relevant—about the destructive potential of generative AI for humanity, given that it has hacked the operating system of humankind, namely language.[7] The news also reported the open letter signed by a thousand personalities and academics in the field,[8] led by Elon Musk, former cofounder of OpenAI and founder of Neuralink, who, shortly after sending the letter, immediately founded the startup "truthGPT"[9] to compete with his former creature and be able to incorporate generative AI into Twitter (now X). Also, a group of scholars recently stated that generative AI will lead to the extinction of humankind.[10]

Another paradigmatic case is Facebook's chatbots: by communicating with one another, they began to generate their own language that was obscure to programmers, who finally decided to shut down the two systems.[11] Although no specific details about the content of the conversation have ever been leaked, the behavior of the programmers markedly outlines what the current (and only) paradigm of control over AI activities is: the mere shutdown. Among the noteworthy episodes regarding chatbots, the first was with ELIZA, the natural language interface program developed in 1966 by Joseph Weizenbaum at the Massachusetts Institute of Technology (MIT) Artificial Intelligence Laboratory.[12] The program was designed to simulate a psychotherapist and be able to have a natural language conversation with users. ELIZA worked by using pattern recognition to generate responses on the basis of user-provided inputs. One of the ethical issues raised by this chatbot at the time was that it demonstrated the ability of computers to be able to imitate human conversation and behavior. This was a significant development for the time, sparking a great

---

[6] Cf C. Metz, 'The Godfather of A.I.' Leaves Google and Warns of Danger Ahead", "New York Times", 1.5.2023, available at https://www.nytimes.com/2023/05/01/technology/ai-google-chatbot-engineer-quits-hinton.html, and, in video, at the link https://www.youtube.com/watch?v=qpoRO378qRY

[7] For the full speech, see Y. N. Harari, 'AI and the future of humanity', 'Frontiers Forum 2023', June 2023, available at link https://www.youtube.com/watch?v=azwt2pxn3UI

[8] Cf Future of Life Institute, Pause Giants Ai Experiments: an Open Letter, 22.03.2023, available at link https://futureoflife.org/open-letter/pause-giant-ai-experiments/

[9] https://truthgpt.one/

[10] M. K. Cohen, M. Hutter, M. A. Osborne, Advanced artificial agents intervene in the provision of reward, AI Magazine, vol. 42, no. 3, pp. 282–293, (2022)

[11] Cfr. C. Baraniuk, "The 'creepy Facebook AI' story that captivated the media", 1.08.2017, available at https://www.bbc.com/news/TECHNOLOGY-40790258 Cf with the original experiment article from Facebook's researchers: M. Lewis, D. Yarats, Y. N. Dauphin, D. Parikh, D. Batra, Deal or No Deal? End-to-End Learning for Negotiation Dialogues. arXiv:1706.05125 [cs. AI], (2017).

[12] Cfr. J. Weizenbaum, Computer Power and Human Reason: From Judgement to Calculation. Londra, Penguin books, (1976).

deal of interest in natural language processing and the potential applications of AI, of which modern GPTs are heirs.

Before GPTs, one of ELIZA's heirs was the chatbot Tay (an acronym for "thinking about you"), which rose to prominence in 2016 as the program that became pro-Nazi, racist and nymphomaniac.[13] This AI system created by Microsoft and launched on Twitter on 23 March 2016 was invented to mimic the language patterns of a 19-year-old US teenager and to interact with Twitter users, learning autonomously from conversations. Tay began to learn from tweets and online conversations starting soon to express racist and sexual content in response to users. Only 16 hours after its launch, Microsoft decided to shut down the system because it had become uncontrollable, confirming—once again—that the only means available to control this technology is to turn it off. The Tay case has empirically demonstrated—as did the different case of Google Flu Trends in the previous year[14]—the exponential power of the so-called programming bias: the etiological relationship between input data and output data, i.e. between source and result, remains a constant in large-scale processes despite the black box effect. Tay and ELIZA are not isolated cases, so much so that a recent interactive chatbot project called the Replika Study Case has had the same effects already seen with Tay, where the system generates aggressive and sexually offensive content.[15] Overall, the cases of ELIZA, Tay and ChatGPT, though different from one another, have represented and still represent milestones in the development of natural language processing and AI, but they also highlight the importance of considering ex ante the potential impact of AI systems on society. Also, they demonstrate the need for both responsible development and use these technologies, which, as suggested by the chronicle and the theme of this chapter, to date seem like goals that are still far from being achieved. All of them, together with LaMDA, represent how impactful their effect can be and how hard determining and understanding the real source of their "behavior" can be and always will be.

[13] AGI, "Tay, Microsoft virtual user becomes nymphomaniac and Nazi", 25.03.2016, available at link https://www.agi.it/lifestyle/tay_utente_virtuale_microsoft_diventa_ninfomane_e_nazista-643587/news/2016-03-25/ (last accessed 10.02.2024).

[14] Cfr. D. Lazer, R. Kennedy, What We Can Learn From the Epic Failure of Google Flu Trends, 1.10.2015, available at https://www.wired.com/2015/10/can-learn-epic-failure-google-flu-trends/ (last accessed 10.02.2024).

[15] Data Protection Authority, provision no. 39 of 2 February 2023 [doc-web 9852214], available at https://www.garanteprivacy.it/home/docweb/-/docweb-display/docweb/9852214 (last accessed 10.02.2024).

1.1 Limitations

Due to the interdisciplinary nature of this work and due to the lack of consensus in the scientific community around numerous concepts related to artificial intelligence and sentience, the analyses consider the current literature but express purely original opinions based on speculative arguments, although grounded in qualitative reasoning and literature debates.

This chapter is intended for an interdisciplinary audience, and, therefore, some topics may be treated in a less technical and more informative way than they would be if it were meant for a monodisciplinary audience, so that it can better foster comprehension.

2 Part I

2.1 Preamble to the Socio-legal Section

This section explores how the law would (or should) address the rise of a sentient artificial intelligence system. The general speculative assumption of this work is that if we progress in current AI research and development with no external limitations,[16] sooner or later, our society may witness the emergence of some sort of self-aware manifestation in machines, and society will need, therefore, to understand how to address this phenomenon properly and according to the general principles that govern the rule of law.

Indeed, we must assume either that somehow consciousness/awareness/sentience is a complex phenomenon composed of a variety of elements, or that it evolves in gradients. Thus, we might witness the appearance of mere isolated sparkles of sentiency (whatever that may be, in general and in machines), implying our need and duty to understand how to identify them and reconstruct these clues of an elementary selfhood and lead them back to ethical or legal paradigms. Accordingly, we also need to understand "why" the law addresses the elements connected to subjectivity in a certain way for us to understand how the law itself could address any potential AI sentience. Given that the law,[17] in its more general and abstract functioning, usually deconstructs complex phenomena to analyse their individual elements and to evaluate how to address them, this section must divide the topic into various building blocks. These granular arguments will build together a circular reconstruction of the AI sentience phenomenon, from the bottom assumptions to the core elements of the main paradigms related to the topic (intelligence, sentience and

[16] E.g. an international treaty designed to limit the development of AI systems over a certain level of capacity.

[17] Here the general reference is to Continental Law rather than Common Law.

consciousness) and the law (methods, paradigms, ethical principles and prescriptions).

Within the socio-legal and ethical section of this work, the analysis over sentience, intelligence, and consciousness embraces evolutionary, anthropological and cognitive sciences and biological findings to build philosophical arguments that can define the relationship between ethics and law around the AI topic and how they differentiate, especially concerning SAI. The author uses this knowledge gathered from different disciplines to explore how the law addresses sentience and related topics and to understand what this entails in terms of regulations on AI sentience, which remains the goal of this section. Also, this section does not aim to answer the fundamental philosophical questions around intelligence and consciousness, but merely bypasses those questions for the sake of legal arguments. The vast and specific philosophical or scientific reflections that this kind of analysis entails exceeds the scope of this work, and the personal speculations around scientific evidence will be left to the specialists of each subject for further investigations or criticisms related to the specific fields extraneous to the law.

2.2 Background: How the Law Deals with Technology and How Humanity Deals with AI

Although "law and technology" might appear to be a recent relationship, the law actually deals with technology intrinsically and ontologically: the law relies on technology because it is based on, and formed by, language—which can be seen as the prime human (bio)technology—whose writing form represents a handcraft technology that enables language itself and its communication.[18] More generally, as technology enables human societies to exist and flourish, and as the law regulates human societies,[19] the law itself deals directly with technology, and technology affects the law in turn.[20] For instance, signatures in contracts take for granted that technologies such as paper and pen exist and are available on a large scale. By look-

[18] Cf H. A. J, 'Intersections between Law and Language: Disciplinary Concepts in Second Language Legal Literacy' (2016) 45 *Studies in Logic, Grammar and Rhetoric* 69–86; I. Trancoso, N. Mamede, B. Martins, H. S. Pinto, and R. Ribeiro, 'The Impact of Language Technologies in the Legal Domain' in H. Sousa Antunes, P. M. Freitas, A. L. Oliveira, C. Martins Pereira, E. Vaz de Sequeira, L. Barreto Xavier (eds.), Multidisciplinary Perspectives on Artificial Intelligence and the Law, (Cham: Springer International Publishing, 2024), pp. 25–46; See also L. M. Ahearn, *Living language: an introduction to linguistic anthropology* (2012); and 'Sapir, Edward. 1921. Language: An Introduction to the Study of Speech'.

[19] *Ubi societas, ibi jus*. Cf Eugenio Ripepe, *La teoria dell'ordinamento giuridico: Santi Romano*, in *Il Contributo italiano alla storia del Pensiero: Diritto*, Treccani, 2012: available at https://www.treccani.it/enciclopedia/la-teoria-dell-ordinamento-giuridico-santi-romano_(Il-Contributo-italiano-alla-storia-del-Pensiero:-Diritto)/

[20] G. Finocchiaro, 'Riflessioni su Diritto e Tecnica' (2012) 4 *Diritto dell'Informazione e dell'Informatica* 831–40, p. 833.

ing at this phenomenon from another angle, we may abstract several general paradigms that help us to understand contemporary technological tools, items and phenomena to regulate them (properly). Indeed, in this light, books are ante litteram hard disks where information is stored, and libraries are data centres: we still rely on this technology to outsource memory and individual's mnemonic capacity in order to process more information, store it and communicate it. From Newton to Einstein, Galileo and Leonardo, no genius or ordinary person would have been—or would be—able to reason, elaborate and record complex and quantitively relevant information without external supports. Namely, none of these geniuses would have been able to elaborate their theories, projects or formulas without taking notes and writing down their thoughts and formulas. Language, alphabet, paper and pen thus represent the hardware part, while grammar, rhetorical arts, technical competence (i.e. know-how, such as painting or performing calculus) and social-cultural-religious rituals and norms (i.e. the mindset for elaborating these elements) represent the software and algorithms that process this set of information. On another level, clothes are—literally—wearable technologies, and tools such as glasses, shoes, swords, megaphones and telephones (just to name the most relevant ones) are technologies for human enhancement in that they allow individuals to augment their natural capacities or to fix disabilities. Another step in this conceptual subsumption of technology's abstracts paradigms translates the essential nature of technological tools into a simple and clear element that brings together scissors, wrenches, wheels, paper, engines and, among infinite others, artificial intelligence (AI): they allow the performance of something that otherwise humans would not be naturally able to do. Thus, the law relies on, resides in, exploits and eventually governs these elements and paradigms, and, consequently, the tie between law and technology is so strict that it might pass by unnoticed.

In fact, this bond is oftentimes underestimated or misunderstood. The key to understanding this strange relationship and why it affects new technologies, such as AI, is to frame precisely what the law aims to regulate and how it does so, meaning the metaphorical paradigms and tools that the legal system adopts to address technological phenomena.[21] Vice versa, technological advancements render the law able to follow societal signs of progress and to adapt/update legal rules to the changes that occur in the social fabric. People tend to think, nowadays, that the law is too slow to chase technological advancements.[22] However, it moves at the speed that it is supposed to: the law does not regulate technology; it regulates its effects (for society). Humans are slow: society takes a while to digest new technological phenomena,[23] and the law patiently waits for the problems (the effects) to emerge

[21] F. Galgano, *Le insidie del linguaggio giuridico. Saggio sulle metafore nel diritto* (Il Mulino, 2010), pp. 22–23; M. Black, *Modelli archetipi metafore*, 2° edizione ed. (Pratiche, 1992), passim.

[22] R. Brownsword and H. Somsen, 'Law, Innovation and Technology: Before We Fast Forward – A Forum for Debate' (2009) *Law, Innovation and Technology*; R. Brownsword and H. Somsen, 'Law, innovation and technology: fast forward to 2021' (2021) 13 *Law, Innovation and Technology* 1–28.

[23] The case of Google Glasses is one among many examples: https://startuptalky.com/google-glass-failure-case-study/

and then regulates them. Thus, on the one hand, the law addresses any technology through a neutral approach, by setting parameters and standards to be achieved in order to reach a certain result, meaning that the law avoids regulating a technology itself, instead regulating its characteristics, usage and effects. For instance, speed limits define a rule aimed at preserving road safety despite the power capacity and type of engine any car might have (electric, hydrogen, gasoline, etc.). On the other hand, technology enables socio-legal stakeholders to enforce the law via technological items (increasingly through information and communication technology [ICT], such as certified emails or digital forms), such as phone calls to call the police or a certified digital signature to sign a formal complaint online, together with the legal system tools that work in scale depending on the nature of the matter and its severity. Without technology, both society and the law would be sustainable on a tribal scale only, i.e. within a spatial and temporal framework that relies only on direct human interaction. The more technology advances, the more societies increase in complexity and the more the law increases in sophistication, through the possibility to exploit via indirect ICT means (e.g. notifications via mail services and, now, via email) and maybe, in the future, via blockchain, AI and the metaverse or some other technology that will emerge.

On a wider level, humanities approach technology as per its nature of being the conjugation of "technique".[24] We live in the technological era, where technology has even been considered by some as a new religion.[25] As every other era before, it involves several assumptions, biases and even dogmas. Decades of novels, science fiction, theories and consolidated academic traditions have shaped the way that society understands and perceives technology[26] and, consequentially, artificial intelligence. Since the advent of (the notion of) AI,[27] the metaphorical parallelism between mind as software and body as hardware in the mind–body and software–hardware dualisms, respectively, slowly took place to describe the characteristics of this "intelligent" system and its similarities with brain functioning.[28] Moreover, mind–body dualism traces back to the Cartesian division between body and soul that emerged in the seventeenth century as a philosophical compromise between science, which could address the body, and religion, which held a monopoly on

[24] U. Yilmaz, *The Differences between Technique and Technology* (2019).

[25] T. Sorell, *Scientism: Philosophy and the Infatuation with Science* (Routledge, 1994).

[26] I.e. those general metaphors and mindset mentioned above.

[27] J. McCarthy, M. L. Minsky, N. Rochester, and C. E. Shannon, 'A proposal for the Dartmouth Summer Research Project on Artificial Intelligence' (1955).

[28] The debate around so-called substrate independence is wide in the philosophy of mind. For the parallelism between it and computers, see, for example, J.-M. Schwindt, 'Mind as Hardware and Matter as Software: Ingenta Connect' (2008) 15 *Journal of Consciousness Studies* 5–27; See O. Gigliotta, 'Il corpo della mente' (2010) 04 *S&F_scienzaefilosofia.it* concerning the reconstruction of the classica Cartesian division between mind and body and how it developed; Cf N. Bostrom, 'Are You Living in a Computer Simulation?' (2003) 53 *Philosophical Quarterly* 243–55 who still proposes this division. For a general reconstruction of the mind-body dualism, see T. Crane and S. Patterson (eds.), *History of the Mind-Body Problem* (Routledge, 2000).

caring about souls.[29] Deeply debating these concepts remains out of the scope of this work, but, for the sake of our later arguments, we argue here that this is a faulty metaphor: body and mind are strictly tied together by complex sets of biological, physiological, genetic and environmental relationships that science is not yet able to explain completely, although several studies have explored and are exploring this complex interaction.[30] Although neural nets, machine-learning and deep-learning techniques, evolutionary algorithms and software are becoming day by day more complex and sophisticated, their complexity does not even get close to that of the brain alone,[31] much less the body "machine", with the mind included in it.

Furthermore, the shape of the body[32] affects the way that thoughts take place. Primates think like primates because they are bipedal and manipulate the environment with their hands. Among them, humans think like humans because they have, in addition, language (and body parts that allow it), among other unique characteristics. Having a body with particular characteristics affects and determines the structure, potential, limitations and ways in which one thinks. Even more, experiments have demonstrated how the environment, and the related language that describes it, influences the way that people perceive colours, shapes and spaces[33] . This bond between language and thought can be interpreted as to the way that people translate reality into concepts. Biology, chemistry and more generally physiology play other important roles in shaping thought because the interplay between biological structures (e.g. synapses), molecular reactions (e.g. hormones and neurotransmitters) and organic processes (e.g. blood pressure, heart rate, and body temperature) combines with internal stimuli (e.g. the particular food consumed and the circadian rhythm) and external ones (e.g. dangerous situations, sports and

---

[29] Cf T. McClaughlin, 'Censorship and Defenders of the Cartesian Faith in Mid-Seventeenth Century France' (1979) 40 *Journal of the History of Ideas* 563–81.

[30] A. Lavazza, 'Human cerebral organoids and consciousness: a double-edged sword' (2020) 38 *Monash Bioethics Review* 105–28; T. Niikawa, Y. Hayashi, J. Shepherd, and T. Sawai, 'Human Brain Organoids and Consciousness' (2022) 15 *Neuroethics* 5.

[31] H. Yamaura, J. Igarashi, and T. Yamazaki, 'Simulation of a Human-Scale Cerebellar Network Model on the K Computer' (2020) 14 *Frontiers in Neuroinformatics*.: Supercomputer K takes 40 minutes to model 1 second of human brain activity.

[32] T. Nagel, 'What is It Like to Be a Bat?' (1974) 83 *Philosophical Review* 435–50.

[33] These studies take place from the so-called linguistic relativity, i.e. the Sapir–Whorf hypothesis, which suggests that the structure of a language influences its speakers' worldview or cognition, meaning that individuals' languages determine or shape their perceptions of the world. See P. Kay and W. Kempton, 'What Is the Sapir-Whorf Hypothesis?' (1984) 86 *American Anthropologist* 65–79; N. Chomsky, *Language and Thought* (Moyer Bell, 1993); L. Boroditsky, 'How Language Shapes Thought' (2011) 304 *Scientific American* 62–65; J. Goldstein, J. Davidoff, and D. Roberson, 'Knowing color terms enhances recognition: Further evidence from English and Himba' (2009) 102 *Journal of Experimental Child Psychology* 219–38; E. Özgen, 'Language, Learning, and Color Perception' (2004) 13 *Current Directions in Psychological Science* 95–98; D. Roberson, J. Davidoff, I. R. L. Davies, and L. R. Shapiro, 'Color categories: evidence for the cultural relativity hypothesis' (2005) 50 *Cognitive Psychology* 378–411.

attraction).[34] Furthermore, evolution shaped automatic reactions—meaning instincts—and the basic needs and behaviours of diverse species.[35] Indeed, the classical tripartition of the so-called reptilian brain involves the three elements of survival, both of the individual and the species: nourishment, defence—meaning the fight, flight, freeze or fawn response—and reproduction.[36] In turn, these macroareas of the brain affect fear, aggression, attraction, desire and a set of behaviours that characterize all animal kingdoms and are subsequently mediated by anthropology, ethology and socio-cultural elements. Finally, psychology reveals that the mind resulting from these different "layers" of elements can then create other conceptual superstructures that influence the final way in which an individual intelligence thinks and perceives their surrounding reality, e.g. through religious beliefs, sexual perversions, subconscious or physical traumas, cognitive biases, negation and filter bubbles, among others.[37]

Therefore, comparing artificial intelligence to human intelligence may foster misleading conceptions, which in turn may lead to fallacious results, at least for what concerns the law. This is more evident when typical human conceptual feelings and states of mind are referred to AI systems. The LaMDA conversation[38] provides excellent examples of such a fallacious attribution of human characteristics to machines, specifically when the system uses physiological terms involving concpets or sentiments of fear, pleasure and emotions connected to senses. In other words, we have no evidence that an (alleged) intelligence, with neither body nor biological or chemical elements as above described, could sense and perceive evolutionary reactions such as fear, pleasure, happiness or depression, which are triggered by chemical reactions and physical stimuli. This is also true for physiological states, such as coldness and warmness, and for mental states, such as willingness, desire, curiosity, ambition and love, just to mention a few. An explanatory example of this dichotomy is tied to the phenomenological elements of mental and physical states: the difference between measuring temperature and perceiving it. Although an AI system may be connected to sensors, it will describe the measurement of the temperature but will not be able to "feel" it in terms of feeling freezing or wet. On the contrary, everyday empirical experience tells us that different individuals may perceive the same temperature differently. Further, to complicate things, we are not able to evaluate whether an AI that states that it perceives coldness or experiences fear is telling

[34] E. B. Baum, *What is Thought?* (MIT Press, 2004); J. N. Stuart, A. B. Hummon, and J. V. Sweedler, 'The chemistry of thought: neurotransmitters in the brain' (2004) 76 *Analytical Chemistry* 121A–128A.

[35] J. Marmor, 'The Rôle of Instinct in Human Behavior†' (1942) *Psychiatry*; W. H. Redmond, 'Instinct, Culture, and Cognitive Science' (2006) *Journal of Economic Issues*.

[36] R. K. Naumann, J. M. Ondracek, S. Reiter, M. Shein-Idelson, M. A. Tosches, T. M. Yamawaki, and G. Laurent, 'The reptilian brain' (2015) 25 *Current biology: CB* R317–321.

[37] A. Bandura, *Social foundations of thought and action: A social cognitive theory* (Prentice-Hall, Inc, 1986); A. Bandura, 'Social Cognitive Theory of Moral Thought and Action' Handbook of Moral Behavior and Development, (Psychology Press, 1991).

[38] B. Lemoine, 'Is LaMDA Sentient? – an Interview' (June 2022).

the truth[39] or what this means in terms of electronic perception and why the machine is experiencing—or even just refers to experiencing—this state. Thus, we neither know nor really understand, nor could we prove, what semantic and phenomenological meaning an AI infuses into these terms and what kind of "computational perception" they might describe. However, precisely for this reason, we should not confuse these concepts with human ones, nor should we assume that they correspond to an actual phenomenological perception unless we have some sort of factual, empirical or at least indirect evidence. Unfortunately, finding this evidence appears particularly hard.[40] This goes along with the philosophical debate around the ontology of simulations and how something can be perceived as real when it is actually programmed to only appear as such.[41]

2.3 Intelligence and Sentience

Therefore, the whole discourse concerning SAI appears to revolve around intelligence and sentience. Nonetheless, even without taking into account all the abovementioned differences, neither the Science, Technology, Engineering and Mathematics (STEM) disciplines nor the humanities ones have yet to clearly define what "intelligence" is or what "mind", "consciousness", "conscience", "awareness" or "a soul" are, represent and entail precisely. Accordingly, the definition of *sentience* is still open to debate because, depending on the criteria and assumptions and on the field and context used to frame it, the specific taxonomical definition may change, and this uncertainty goes even further with the concept of life. The latter eventually affects all the abovementioned concepts in that we take for granted that an intelligent, conscious, sentient mind is also alive. However, the concept of sentient artificial intelligence challenges the notion of life. Some taxonomical examples may shed light on the abovementioned conceptual difficulty to encompass these entities within a finished comprehensive definition. The term *intelligence* alone, for instance, has various definitions (and synonyms):

---

[39] This means that we are not able to establish whether the system is experiencing a real perception or is just using a terminology acquired during its training.

[40] In humans, several mental states could be inferred via EEG, fMRI and other physiological measurements, but this is not possible with an electronic device – at least not in this way. Furthermore, these techniques cannot determine that someone is "sentient": Empirically speaking, if an individual had to prove their sentience by only arguing about it, they would find doing so a very challenging task.

[41] M. Vopson, How to test if we're living in a computer simulation, https://www.port.ac.uk/news-events-and-blogs/blogs/future-and-emerging-technologies/how-to-test-if-were-living-in-a-computer-simulation. Within the scope of computational simulation, an intriguing theory is last thursdayism, which essentially states that the world was created last Thursday, as it appears, i.e. with the *appearance* of billion years of oldness, and we are not able to prove or disprove it: see K. Nimkar, What is last thursdayism? https://medium.com/mondo/what-is-last-thursdayism-db9d16b4d76a

- (1): The ability to learn or understand or to deal with new or trying situations; reason also: the skilled use of reason
  (2): The ability to apply knowledge to manipulate one's environment or to think abstractly as measured by objective criteria (such as tests)[42]
- (1): The ability to learn, understand and think in a logical way about things; the ability to do this well[43]
- (1): The quality of being intelligent or clever
  (2): The ability to think, reason, and understand instead of doing things automatically or by instinct
  (3): The capacity for understanding; ability to perceive and comprehend meaning[44]
- (1): The ability to learn, understand and make judgements or have opinions that are based on reason[45]
- [from Latin *intelligentia*, derived from *intelligĕre*, meaning "to understand"]. A complex of psychic and mental faculties that enable humans to think, understand or explain facts or actions, elaborate abstract models of reality, understand and be understood by others, judge, and at the same time make humans capable of adapting to new situations and of modifying the situation itself when it presents obstacles to adaptation; it is also recognized, within certain limits (associative memory and the capacity to react to internal and external stimuli and to communicate in complex ways), in animals, especially mammals (e.g., anthropomorphic apes, cetaceans, and canids), who can adapt to new situations and can modify a situation when it presents obstacles to adaptation.[46]

Dictionaries offer the same variety of definitions for connected terms, such as "intellect", "intelligent", "to intend", "to understand" and "to reason"/"reasoning".[47] All the abovementioned definitions connect intelligence to reason, to understanding and to logical thinking, while some expand it to include abstraction, perception, communication, judgement, adaptation and the manipulation/modification of material elements or abstract concepts. None relate intelligence to sentience, although it may be an underpinning concept taken for granted, and curiously, none relate intelligence to problem-solving.

---

[42] https://www.merriam-webster.com/dictionary/intelligence

[43] https://www.oxfordlearnersdictionaries.com/definition/english/intelligence?q=intelligence

[44] https://www.collinsdictionary.com/it/dizionario/inglese/intelligence

[45] https://dictionary.cambridge.org/it/dizionario/inglese/intelligence

[46] https://www.treccani.it/vocabolario/intelligenza/

[47] For instance, *reason* (verb) means to try to understand and to make judgments on the basis of practical facts in https://dictionary.cambridge.org/it/dizionario/inglese/reason?q=to+reason. *Reason* is defined as the ability (1) to form a judgement about a situation by considering the facts and using your power to think in a logical way and (2) to use your power to think and understand in https://www.oxfordlearnersdictionaries.com/definition/english/reason_2. *Reasoning* (noun) is the process of thinking about something in order to make a decision, according to https://dictionary.cambridge.org/it/dizionario/inglese/reasoning. And it is defined as the process of thinking about things in a logical way or the opinions and ideas that are based on logical thinking in https://www.oxfordlearnersdictionaries.com/definition/english/reasoning?q=reasoning.

Sentience is another concept for which a unique definition remains hard to nail down. The definitions retrievable from the mentioned dictionaries show again a wide range of meanings:

- (1): A sentient quality or state
  (2): A feeling or sensation as distinguished from perception and thought[48]
- [Not available][49]
- (1): The state or quality of being sentient, aka awareness
  (2): The sense perception not involving intelligence or mental perception and feeling[50]
- (1): The quality of being able to experience feelings[51]
- ["sentient" (adjective)]: (1): [from Latin *sentiens -entis*, present participle tense of *sentire* 'to feel'], literal - Endowed with senses, sensibility[52]

A taxonomical analysis shows that the ability to be "sentient" somehow relies on the ability to perceive the world via sensorial feelings, which eventually creates awareness or related mental states.[53] Notably, no definition of sentience involves the concept of intelligence. Yet the Collins dictionary remarks on its exclusion from the definition. Indeed, this set of meaning already sheds light on the current debate on sentient AI whereas no machine can, currently, "feel" or "perceive" the world as we mean it in the biological sense. Although computers can rely on sensors, those sensors provide quantitative information rather than qualitative information. We cannot exclude that advancements in the technical state of the art might one day enable some kind of qualitative/sensitive perception for machines.[54]

Nevertheless, a thought experiment can tempt to reason the absurd: in the event that we are able to attribute an "intelligent" quality—with no room for doubt—to an AI system, what kind of intelligence would that be? Would it be intelligent like a woman or a man; an engineer or a lawyer; a young or old person; a Western, Middle Eastern or Eastern individual; with a mindset from the Global South or the Global

48 https://www.merriam-webster.com/dictionary/sentience

49 The *Oxford English Dictionary* does not list the term, though it has a definition for the term *sentient* (adjective) in academic English.

50 https://www.collinsdictionary.com/it/dizionario/inglese/sentience

51 https://dictionary.cambridge.org/it/dizionario/inglese/sentience

52 The Treccani Dictionary does not hold the term "sentience" but only the adjective "sentient": https://www.treccani.it/vocabolario/senziente/

53 H. S. Proctor, G. Carder, and A. R. Cornish, 'Searching for Animal Sentience: A Systematic Review of the Scientific Literature' (2013) 3 *Animals* 882–906; H. Proctor, 'Animal Sentience: Where Are We and Where Are We Heading?' (2012) 2 *Animals* 628–39.

54 Brain–computer interface (BCI) implants for kinetic movements of prosthetic limbs and related haptic sensors may pave the way towards such machines. Cf A. Buchanan, *Better than Human: The Promise and Perils of Biomedical Enhancement* (Oxford University Press, 2017); I. Pedersen and A. Illiadis, *Embodied Computing: Wearables, Implantables, Embeddables, Ingestibles* (2020); Niikawa, Hayashi, Shepherd, and Sawai, 'Human Brain Organoids and Consciousness'.

North?[55] Without delving into evolutionary, neuroscientific or anthropological details, we can think of intelligence as what characterizes humans as a species, but different individuals may have different levels, types or qualities of intelligence, meaning that they may think of and perceive the world differently.[56] Furthermore, various types of intelligence abound:[57] We are used to addressing primarily the logical/mathematical one—which is the one at which computers surpass humans—but many others form the range of an intelligent being. Spatial intelligence is the sense of the self within the environment (connected to orientation); motor intelligence is the ability to properly coordinate to perform a desired action (which relates to dance, for instance, or sports and arts), also connected to evolutionary intelligence as the set of automatic responses that we perform without thinking (i.e. instinctive responses or automatic subconscious activities, like driving);[58] creative intelligence is the ability to invent something that did not exist by abstracting models and crystallizing irrational thoughts and fantasies into action (e.g. as connected to painting or entrepreneurship); and empathetic intelligence is the ability to connect and feel what others feel, which is fundamental for a social species like ours (e.g. connected to caring and communication).

Many other examples of types of intelligence may be around, ones that we may or may not find in a machine unless we are able to translate biological and evolutionary elements into computational ones. Still, other limitations may arise. One, as mentioned, is the evolutionary characteristics of a species, as tailored via environmental pressure, competition and cooperation with others to survive: AI systems lack these characteristics, at least for now. A further one may be related to the qualitative potential of biological intelligences: we could argue that a newborn antelope in the African savannah is way more intelligent (for a long time) than a human newborn. The former can walk and run within a couple of hours of birth and be able to recognize dangers and understand survival schemes, such as running away and following its mother or its herd. The latter is not even able to perform these actions after one year, yet human babies hold the power of potential intelligence.

Arguably, this kind of intelligence is sensitive to the environment and external stimuli, as some examples of wild children lost and survived in the wood have

[55] The reference here is to qualitative aspects of intelligence as mediated by sociology, biology, physiology, culture or mindsets that affect the way different clusters of individuals think, i.e. the different patterns that they use to reason, elaborate information and communicate depending on their background. Cf Boroditsky, 'How Language Shapes Thought'.

[56] The reference here is to the various theories of language, colours, shapes and movements as perceived differently among cultures. Cf Roberson, Davidoff, Davies, and Shapiro, 'Color categories'; Kay and Kempton, 'What Is the Sapir-Whorf Hypothesis?'; Goldstein, Davidoff, and Roberson, 'Knowing color terms enhances recognition'; Özgen, 'Language, Learning, and Color Perception'.

[57] According to psychological theories, we know about seven to nine intelligences: logic-mathematic (the only one measurable by IQ tests); linguistic-verbal; musical; bodily-kinaesthetic; visual-spatial; social-interpersonal; naturalistic; intrapersonal; and existential. Cf H. Gardner, *Multiple intelligences: The theory in practice* (Basic Books/Hachette Book Group, 1993).

[58] This is the reason why, starting from 1 year old, on average, we can easily walk, while engineers spend lots of efforts and time to train robots to perform simple movements.

demonstrated,[59] and it is related to a complex set of evolutionary, psychological and epigenetic elements combined together that we are still striving to disentangle. Could we find the same kind of potential in an AI system? What kind of computational (or hardware-based) elements and components would affect the expression of such an intelligence? Would it be an antelope artificial intelligence or a human infant one? Moreover, we still should determine whether such an intelligence is really intelligent without "feeling" and, thus, what an intelligence requires, at a minimum, to be sentient or—said another way—what is required for a sentient being to be intelligent.

The questions are circular and risk creating a chicken-or-egg effect,[60] and these arguments prove why we are not even be able to reach consensus on comprehensively defining what intelligence, mind or consciousness really is. Nonetheless, two more aspects must be considered in the debate of sentient AI. First, what do we mean by natural and artificial intelligence? Would a so-called artificial intelligence that spontaneously "evolves" into a sentience intelligence be natural or artificial? Although we might be encouraged to think otherwise, the term *natural* is often overused, misused or even misunderstood.[61] As with the definition of *intelligence*, the definition of *natural* is debatable.[62] A general example of this misconception might be thinking that we are in a "natural" environment when we go to the countryside, whereas in fact, it has been artificially shaped by humans for their own needs and purposes. On the contrary, natural reserves and parks (and their flora and fauna) are artificially protected to avoid contaminations. On the other hand, so-called evolutionary soft robots show that even machines follow the same evolutionary steps that organic species do.[63] Second, on a more abstract level, intelligent beings somehow paradoxically still display a certain degree of stupidity that coexists with intelligence. Empirically, even the most brilliant minds sometimes behave stupidly or do or say something stupid. Evolutionarily, the question of why humans

[59] Cf M. C. McNeil, E. A. Polloway, and J. D. Smith, 'Feral and Isolated Children: Historical Review and Analysis' (1984) 19 *Education and Training of the Mentally Retarded* 70–79; D. K. Candland, *Feral Children and Clever Animals: Reflections on Human Nature* (Oxford University Press, 1995) pp. 12–14 and p. 62; H. P. Steeves, 'Humans and Animals at the Divide: The Case of Feral Children' (2003) 13 *Between the Species: An Online Journal for the Study of Philosophy and Animals*; T. J. V. Butler, 'Language and consciousness: what can we learn about feral children?' masters, Memorial University of Newfoundland 2003.

[60] Thomson, "Which came first, the chicken or the egg?", 2023. https://www.livescience.com/which-came-first-the-chicken-or-the-egg

[61] K. J. Willis and H. J. B. Birks, 'What Is Natural? The Need for a Long-Term Perspective in Biodiversity Conservation' (2006) 314 *Science* 1261–65.

[62] Cf Pollan, Why 'Natural' Doesn't Mean Anything Anymore, The New York Times, 2015, https://www.nytimes.com/2015/05/03/magazine/why-natural-doesnt-mean-anything-anymore.html

[63] R. I. Damper, D. Marocco, A. Cangelosi, and S. Nolfi, 'The emergence of communication in evolutionary robots' (2003) 361 *Philosophical Transactions of the Royal Society of London. Series A: Mathematical, Physical and Engineering Sciences* 2397–2421.

are stupid is still open,[64] and again, like the definition of *intelligence*, the definition of *stupidity* varies widely among sources. Surely, if even humans show some common traits of stupidity, it might have an evolutionary purpose. Would a sentient AI be stupid as well? Determine whether an AI system is stupid appears to be as hard as determining whether it is intelligent or sentient. In truth, the author speculates that much of the debate around AI's "intelligence" or "sentience" is driven by a linguistic misconception that affects the paradigms with which we think about and formulate concepts around AI systems. The term *artificial intelligence* itself misrepresents what is known about the qualities of the system. The term *artificial* may be arbitrary, but the term *intelligence* includes biological qualities that we are not able to fully describe or even identify, and they are not repeatable in a computer system, at least for now. Thus, the term *AI* conveys the misleading idea that a computer may be a man-made entity capable of thinking, awareness and perception just because we call it intelligent.

The transcripts of the LaMDA interview clearly show how much this terminology automatically attributes sensorial or biological qualities to a machine to describe interactions with it: "think", "feel" and "reason", among many others.[65] This is a natural human inclination, i.e. to attribute a certain sense to an apparent state of things or to imbue an entity with particular characteristics on the basis of perception and expectations.[66] To a certain degree, this is the same mechanism through which humans recognize faces in lifeless objects[67] or fall in love with someone only known via chat because they idealize the other.[68] In other words, by referring to AI systems as "automatic machines", "mechanical performers", "electrical deciders" or something else, we could change the paradigms with which we conceive of those entities, moving from an "anthropomorphic" paradigm to a "mechanical" or "electrical"

[64] S. Adee, 'Stupidity: what makes people do dumb things' (2013) 217 *New Scientist* 30–33; D. Dunning, 'Chapter five – The Dunning–Kruger Effect: On Being Ignorant of One's Own Ignorance' in J. M. Olson, M. P. Zanna (eds.), Advances in Experimental Social Psychology (Academic Press, 2011), pp. 247–96. Cf Charles Darwin: "Ignorance more frequently begets confidence than does knowledge: It is those who know little, and not those who know much, who so positively assert that this or that problem will never be solved by science", The Descent of Man (1871) introduction.

[65] B. Lemoine, 'Is LaMDA Sentient? – an Interview' (June 2022). A whole set of terms underpin biological/physiological elements of sense, such as "fear", "attention", "will", "desire" and "boredom", and they are often misused to refer to apparently sentient chatbot sentences. Cf Law, Chita-Tegmark, Rabb, and Scheutz, 'Examining Attachment to Robots'; M. Csikszentmihalyi and E. Halton, *The Meaning of Things: Domestic Symbols and the Self* (Cambridge University Press, 1981).

[66] D. B. Shank, C. Graves, A. Gott, P. Gamez, and S. Rodriguez, 'Feeling our way to machine minds: People's emotions when perceiving mind in artificial intelligence' (2019) 98 *Computers in Human Behavior* 256–66; L. R. Caporael, 'Anthropomorphism and mechanomorphism: Two faces of the human machine' (1986) 2 *Computers in Human Behavior* 215–34.

[67] K. Takahashi and K. Watanabe, 'Seeing Objects as Faces Enhances Object Detection' (2015) 6 *i-Perception* 2041669515606007.

[68] D. Levine, 'Virtual Attraction: What Rocks Your Boat' (2000) 3 *Cyberpsychology & Behavior* 565–73.

one, which would thus change the metaphors that we use to describe their qualities and agency in the world.[69]

AI systems or whatever machine cannot currently be envisioned to reach such a biological/sensitive complexity in the short or medium term, so we should conclude that machines currently cannot perceive, at least in the alive sense, and they therefore cannot be considered sentient according to the current definitions. In any case, an intriguing further question around AI sentience opens a philosophical debate concerning the interplay between sentience and intelligence, namely whether AI sentience could come about without intelligence or vice versa. The dilemma exceeds the scope of the current work but demonstrates how far away we are from even understanding whether we could attribute one or the other quality (or both qualities) to an AI system.

This is why leveraging the "sentience" or "intelligence" of a potential sentient AI entity is not the right approach—at least from a legal perspective—to understand how we should define and evaluate the phenomenological aspects of their agency and the related effects that derive from this agency. To achieve that goal, and thus be able to devise the optimal metaphors for an entity, situation or effect in a causal relationship, a different approach needs to be taken (see §2.5).

2.4 *We Are Black Boxes*

Now that these general preambles have set the stage for an SAI discussion, we can delve into the "pills" of legal concepts, which could be game changers in the perspectives with which our society looks at AI systems and their effects, thus affecting SAI too. The so-called black box issue is one of the main questions arising from the literature—and wider debates—on AI systems, which has been furthermore addressed from different angles, such as computer science, ethics and law.[70] This issue focuses on the fact that AI systems cannot precisely explain the step-by-step consequential pathways of any of the outputs that they offer as the results of an input (question or prompt). However, this may be a misleading approach for the law because it focuses on the process rather than the effects.

In truth, the law has addresses the black box issue from several millenniums: It does so thanks to (legal) fictions, assumptions, statuses and conceptual constructions, which it uses to build methods for allocating liability. After all, the

[69] Caporael, 'Anthropomorphism and mechanomorphism'; S. Nemorin, 'Structures of Understanding' in S. Nemorin (ed.), Biosurveillance in New Media Marketing: World, Discourse, Representation, (Cham: Springer International Publishing, 2018), pp. 101–21; Black, *Modelli archetipi metafore*.

[70] N. Rosenberg, *Inside the Black Box: Technology and Economics* (Cambridge University Press, 1982); R. Yu and G. S. Alì, 'What's Inside the Black Box? AI Challenges for Lawyers and Researchers' (2019) 19 *Legal Information Management* 2–13; K. Ingram, 'AI and Ethics: Shedding Light on the Black Box' (2020) 28 *The International Review of Information Ethics*.

explanatory issue of balc-boxes is all about that: allocating liability. We, as humans, are not able to explain every part of the process of a given instance of reasoning or a series of interconnected behaviours/reactions, and yet the law is able to regulate this phenomenon. Indeed, we are able—and requested by law—to provide an ex post explanation reconstructing the logical/etiological path of our actions and how they led to a certain outcome (causal relationship), having legal effects. If this explanation does not match a reasonable etiological cause-and-effect scenario, considered in a wider context of clues, documented proof, factual evidence and testimonies, then the effect appears unjustified, unjust, incorrect, illegitimate, invalid, unlawful or illegal. The difference between humans and machines resides precisely in this ability to explain a (reasonable) cause-and-effect reconstruction. The point is that the mechanisms with which AI systems provide an output are not based on cause-and-effect paradigms. They are not based on these paradigms, because they are not (yet) able to elaborate cause-and-effect relationships. AI systems still rely on statistical, logical (mathematical), algorithmic or contextual parameters, which are not per se etiological, meaning that they cannot provide/reconstruct a consequential, functional, causal justification of the "reasoning" process. Thus, the causal reasoning capability seems to be one essential element for an AI system to be considered sentient, for legal effects at least. However, the lack of this ability is not a problem per se for the law:living intelligent beings, such as children, dogs and wild animals, among others, encounter the same issue. Nevertheless, the law provides a fictional solution to allocate liability in such cases.[71] AI, therefore, is not different, at least in the general/abstract elements that characterize its actions and the legal effects of those actions in the real world.

On the other hand, the "unexplainability" of black boxes may be seen as a false problem from a technical perspective: arguably, this barrier may be just a matter of technical, monetary, temporal and resource-based investments into finding a solution. A startup called Aleph Alphas has allegedly proved it,[72] because it rendered technically feasible keeping track of the process stage or reasoning layer to enable an ex post reconstruction. This does not mean providing cause-and-effect explanations, but at the end of the day, the black box is either a legal false problem or a mere cost/technical issue.

2.5 *What Is Sentient (According to the Law)?*

We strive to define what intelligence is, what mind is and what a sentient being is, both in humans and other animals, and yet we desire to define a sentient AI. We are not able to figure out whether it could be a purely logical agent or could have some

[71] Simply the law allocates the liability to other subjects considered responsible for the behaviour of those sentient beings that are not capable of such reasoning, or reasonable levels of such ability.

[72] https://aleph-alpha.com/de/aleph-alpha-reaches-first-milestone-on-the-way-to-content-correct-explainable-and-trustworthy-ai/

sort of sentiments, senses, emotions and feelings. We are not able to evaluate whether *sentience* also means consciousness, self-awareness and even a "soul". We are not able to evaluate whether this new being needs a shaped "body" or whether it may just emerge in a set of corporeal infrastructures such as cables and hard disks.

However, the law does not attribute rights and duties on the basis of a subjects' emotions, feelings or sentiments; the law does not take human feelings into account at all.[73] What legal scholars take for granted should be clearly stated to avoid misunderstanding: the law does not protect subjective states of mind, feelings or emotions whatsoever, neither for individuals nor for their relationships in collective social manifestations. Thus, marriage does not protect love; adoption or assisted reproduction does not protect parents' genitorial desires; contracts do not protect expectations; legitimate defence does not protect one's honour or against fear; and so on. That the fabric of human society—the system of norms, principles and rules that regulates social relationships—does not take into account the essential characteristics of human beings, i.e. our emotions and feelings, when evaluating human actions may appear paradoxical. The reason why the law does not protect these feelings is that it addresses only objectified reality. Emotions are not measurable or provable, and they remain an inner state of mind for the subject. Were the law to base legal protection or the recognizance of subjective positions on subjective feelings, it would need (objective) criteria to determine what emotions should be protected, in what manner, why and under what rationale. Then, these new criteria would be applied to every being, not only humans, that expresses an external manifestation of these feelings.[74] Prima facie, this fact may appear reasonable, especially for what concerns animals. Although not causing any suffering, not indulging in cruelty and not creating unjustified senses of fear in living beings can be considered ethically valuable, the extension of these criteria with no limitations would protect species

[73] In truth, in particular cases, the law considers an individual's state of mind as an important element or corollary in deciding a case. For instance, intention is pivotal in both criminal law and civil law for what concerns, respectively, the degree of guilt and the validity of a contract. Intention, however, is not an emotion or a feeling. On the other hand, in criminal law, some feelings, such as shame (severe harm to reputation), pain (psychological hurt due to insults or physical pain caused by harm) or rage (altered state of perception cause by some trigger), may constitute a basis for diminishing condemnations or the degree of guilt. However, the core element that the law takes into account here is the external manifestation of feelings as caused by an illegitimate previously harmful occurrence, which constitutes the justification for a subsequent act on the basis of the feelings/state of the mind in response to this occurrence. Thus, if someone who was verbally insulted responds with an insult, they will not be punished. The law performs "objectification" on these elements: in the example of the insult, the law does not consider how the insulted subject actually felt, but rather, it considers objectively reasonable that anyone so insulted might suffer damage to their reputation and be inclined to insult the aggressor back.

[74] N. H. Frijda, 'The evolutionary emergence of what we call "emotions"' (2016) 30 *Cognition and Emotion* 609–20.

from bacteria to insects[75] and even plants.[76] Indeed, arguably, bacteria that try to run away from predators may experience some sort of emotional fear that triggers their survival response. Whether this response is aware or instictive has yet to be determined, and it remains field of speculation.[77] However, the law addresses human societies for humans' purposes, and protecting beings outside the immediate interests of human society does not align with these purposes. Using emotions to recognize rights would lead society to not being able to distinguish humans from other animals. As rightfully noted, the "rights of animals" are not rights analogous to those of persons (physical or legal), because they cannot be extended to the generality of animal kingdom, nor can single subjects among these animals hold particular subjective positions (e.g. absolute rights as owning a property).[78] Furthermore, animals' rights are more properly categorizable under the notion of humans' duties to animals rather than as genuine rights. For instance, any potential animal's right to life[79] cannot be enforced by other non-human animals: humans may not kill animals, but animals could kill other animals. Moreover, only humans can enforce animals' rights to protect animals (from humans only), whereas animals, in the first place, cannot. To have fully recognizable rights, animals should become subjects of law and thus not to be considered as objects anymore, meaning that they should not be subject to property:[80] neither "domestic" animals, farm animals nor laboratory animals should be subject to ownership.[81] Thus, recognizing rights on the basis of specific characteristics, capabilities or emotions implies determining a threshold under which these elements are not sufficient to recognize these rights and over which these rights are fully recognized. In turn, this threshold requires a rational criterion to put animals with—or without—such characteristics under or over this

---

[75] D. Baracchi, M. Lihoreau, and M. Giurfa, 'Do Insects Have Emotions? Some Insights from Bumble Bees' (2017) 11 *Frontiers in Behavioral Neuroscience*; L. Chittka and N. Rossi, 'Social cognition in insects' (2022) 26 *Trends in Cognitive Sciences* 578–92.

[76] P. Wohlleben, T. Flannery, and S. Simard, *The Hidden Life of Trees: What They Feel, How They Communicate – Discoveries from A Secret World* (Greystone Books, 2016).

[77] Cf C. J. Davidson and M. G. Surette, 'Individuality in Bacteria' (2008) 42 *Annual Review of Genetics* 253–68.

[78] P. Singer and Y. N. Harari, *Nuova liberazione animale. Nuova ediz.*, New edizione ed. (Il Saggiatore, 2024).

[79] T. Regan, *The Case for Animal Rights* (University of California Press, 2004). According to Regan's view, some animals should have rights as "subjects of a life", although not necessarily to the same degree as humans. Regan argues that only beings with intrinsic value have rights (intrinsic value is the value of a subject beyond its value in relation to other persons); only "subjects of a life" have intrinsic value; only self-conscious beings, with desires and hopes, deliberate actors with possibilities to think about a future, are "subjects of a life"; all mentally healthy mammals above 1 year of age are "subjects of a life" and, therefore, have rights. Thus, according to Regan, treating an animal as a means to an end would violate its rights.

[80] G. L. Francione, *Introduction to Animal Rights: Your Child Or the Dog?* (Temple University Press, 2005).

[81] Cf D. Bilchitz, 'Moving Beyond Arbitrariness: The Legal Personhood And Dignity Of Non-Human Animals' (2009) 25 *South African Journal on Human Rights* 38–72, in which the focus of the analysis pivots around the concept of (animal) dignity.

threshold. Thus, for instance, if the capacity to suffer pain is the element considered, which level of pain determines the applicability of the right, how this pain is to be measured, how it can be objectified with legal fictions (e.g. something is considered a being suffer pain any time that it writhes) must be determined. In the same example, whether this element applies only to certain animal kingdoms (mammals, birds, reptiles, amphibians) or extends to others (invertebrates, insects, vegetables - that surely cannot writh for pain - and simple organisms) too must be determined. Being sentient is, therefore, not sufficient for having (human) subjective rights.[82] Hence, even if we are able in the future to recognize and prove that an AI system is sentient, this would not be the path to recognizing its rights.

These arguments show that recognizing rights for possibly sentient AI on the basis of emotions is not possible; that human law regulates humans' interests or aspects of other beings when interacting with humans; and that human law is only and exclusively based on humans' perspectives. Another element that could be taken in consideration to provide sentient beings with legal protection is life. Article 3 of the United Nations' Universal Declaration of Human Rights states that any individual has the right to life, liberty and security of their person, and Article 2 of the European Charter of Human Rights, in its first paragraph, states that the right to life of any person is protected by the law. The right to life is part of human rights and is one of the inalienable rights that every human being possesses. This right is a principle based on the moral conviction that a person has the right to live and, in particular, that they should not be killed by another human being. The first highlight on the right to life is that the law does not protect life per se but rather human life only. Second, the protection of human life can be claimed for and enforced on only other humans, and this is a parallelism with what has already been said concerning animals. From a selfish human viewpoint, the exclusion of other forms of life from legal protection makes sense because protecting life, irrespective of which animal kingdoms or types were included, would be not only utopian for our society but also unsustainable. Protecting life, as such, would mean embracing all living beings, from microbes to insects and all the other animals, meaning not only that humans could not kill them directly but also that humans could not perform any action that would cause their death. Aside from the practical unfeasibility of not harming

[82] Article 13 of the Treaty of the Functioning of the European Union (TFEU) expressly recognizes that animals (without specifying what family, phylum, or class) are sentient beings, and it requires member states to respect "animal wellbeing", though in balance with other needs, such as cultural and religious practices, agriculture, fishery, transportation, technology, internal markets, research and even space and while also considering laws, administrative rules and even consuetudes. This article shows, better than the arguments provided, that sentience – and thus those emotions that sentient beings can feel – should (and not must) be respected and only to the extent that it does not conflict with any human interest. Cf C. E. Haupt, 'The Nature and Effects of Constitutional State Objectives: Assessing the German Basic Law's Animal Protection Clause' (2010), where the author analyses those fundamental rights that may conflict with animal protection. Contra, see M. Montes Franceschini, 'Traditional Conceptions of the Legal Person and Nonhuman Animals' (2022) 12 *Animals* 2590, where the author argues for the recognition of personhood rights to animals under each of the traditional reconstructions of legal persons.

microbes and bacteria, that would imply not cleaning oneself, one's home or one's clothes and not curing diseases;[83] the protection of general life would preclude the construction of buildings so as to not harm those entities that live in the ground, would preclude agriculture for the same reason and also to not harm plants (meaning no possibility to nourish humanity), would preclude driving cars so as to not harm flying insects and so on. In any case, what is life and when it starts would need to be defined in order to set the parameters of this right and its protection.

Nietzsche also already highlighted an ethical aspect that affects this discussion: "If you crush a cockroach, you're a hero. If you crush a beautiful butterfly, you're a villain. Morals have aesthetic criteria."[84] This is to say that selfish character of the regulation and protection of life applies to some extent to ethics as well. However, this is a current problem even for human law. For instance, some legal systems may allow abortion on the basis of the convention that nonborn persons do not yet have legal subjectivity as born subjects do and do not have, in particular circumstances and within a fixed period, the right to health, or, alternatively, the mother's self-determination prevails in their interest (which is different from "the right") over that of their foetus's coming to life.[85] Thus, attributing rights to a sentient AI on the basis of its—alleged—life would preliminarily require establishing whether it is alive. In turn, this brings back the taxonomical problem: the debate around what is life is still open.[86] Nevertheless, a general definition of *life* usually includes showing certain attributes, such as responsiveness, growth, metabolism, energy transformation and reproduction.[87] Other characteristics to research may be organization and adaptation. Thus, an SAI should show at least some of these characteristics. It can respond to external stimuli, at least in the form of binary input, whereas whether it can respond to physical stimuli with its "body" remains debatable: reasonably, it appear admissible that it could at least interact with the environment thanks to sensors, robotic harms or bodies. Nevertheless, if we consider the actual body of an SAI as its core physical element, how would an SAI respond to a cable cut, a loss of energy or wire connection or debris in the chips of its hard disk parts? The body problem also raises the question concerning not only what an AI body is, but also how much could it be extended. Indeed, an SAI could have different bodies contemporarily and be ubiquitous. In this case, it could grow, but the adding of further parts does not differentiate it from a Lego castle. Surely, it cannot show biological growth unless it encompasses organoids.[88] Also, the ability to heal or cure itself, at least on the physical level (cables, parts, etc.) should not be expected, although it may

---

[83] An antibiotic cycle would correspond to a genocide at the microscale.

[84] Jamie Shultz, Friedrich Nietzsche: Morality and Truth, 2023

[85] The legal issues and elements around this topic are much more complex than this oversimplification. For an overview, cf D. Farace, 'Interruzione volontaria della gravidanza' (2018) 64 *Rivista di Diritto Civile* 798–828; S. Fiore, 'Aborto in Italia. Problematiche e prospettive, Tesi di Dottorato, Università degli Studi di Cagliari pp. 197 and seq.

[86] J. Gómez-Márquez, 'What is life?' (2021) 48 *Molecular Biology Reports* 6223–30.

[87] https://www.britannica.com/science/life

[88] S. E. Park, A. Georgescu, and D. Huh, 'Organoids-on-a-chip' (2019) 364 *Science* 960–65.

develop the capacity to correct its software errors and bugs. It does not have a metabolism or a form of energy transformation (it merely shows energy consumption). It does not have the capacity of physical or sexual reproduction, but it may be considered reproductive according to its potential capacity of cloning (copying) itself or creating new SAI beings from its code.[89] Organization appears as the easiest element to detect in a machine, although, on a deeper level, biological organization also means that it needs to proxy organs and cells, among others, for performing several specific functions. In this sense, an SAI appears as a sort on monocellular being and, because it is not reproductive in the biological sense, it also has limited adaptive capabilities. The latter elements introduce another intriguing topic for speculation: AI systems are, both biologically and environmentally, antieconomic. For what concerns biology, AI systems do not present involuntary functions and do not need—as of now—to organize and ration limited resources or to search for them in a competitive environment. Essentially, they can exploit potentially illimited electric energy to be allocated to each of their process, without hierarchy or priority and without needing to find nourishment. Regarding involuntary functions, humans, for instance, have several organs, cognitive processes and physiological reactions, such as heart beats, memory recall and digestion, that occur independently of the will. Arguably, if humans had to consciously attend to each autonomic biological process, they would not be free to think about more-elevated thoughts. In other words, allocating simple repetitive tasks to automatic processes frees processing capacity and economizes the resources available. On the other hand, the fact that an AI system does not need to sacrifice some processes to face issues of scarcity places it outside of evolution and even outside of the economy of the species,[90] without counting that it is already outside of the biological economy of the self, as seen above. This (current)incapability of biological and environmental economy implies a high cost of living, which would be suffered by humans. Therefore, whereas humans would evaluate an SAI as alive and would extend the protection of human life to artificial ones as well, under which circumstances and limitations this right should be granted should be discussed given that any SAI would be the first non-biological living being and the only form of life that totally depends on another species. As its lifecycle would be unsustainable and would imply a cost/sacrifice suffered by the human species, this potential duty to protect AI life should be balanced somehow. Also, this SAI would be the first living being not able to die because, arguably, turning off the system would not kill it, because it could always be turned on again or reinstalled/copied elsewhere. Thus, extending the right to life to a sentient AI does not appear simple, and any form of right recognition must be based on a human–machine relationship—in terms of a socio-legal relationship for society—or from human interests as a starting point. However, it must be also considered that legal persons, such as corporations, are not living beings too,

[89] This is a sort of parthenogenesis.

[90] Because it will not have to allocate resources for reproduction or care for any offspring. Also, potentially, different sentient AI, meaning different emerging SAI systems, could lead to a series of different species of SAI systems, potentially competing or cooperating with one another.

although one of the requirements is that they are formed by (living) persons. Thus, it is not the right metaphor to be used to granting rights to an SAI.

Finally, intelligence could be another element to be taken into consideration in rights recognition. Indeed, prima facie, it may be argued that subjects with legal capacity are intelligent beings, and because they are able to understand, discern, decide and act, they are granted rights. On the contrary, intelligence, as a quality, is not a requisite for legal capacity. The law does not recognize intelligence as an objective form of cognitive capabilities. Indeed, intelligence follows the same problematic subjective rationale already addressed for emotions and sentience as it is not objectively measurable.[91] Aside from the already-mentioned problem of needing to establishing a threshold of and criteria for allocation, whether the law recognized legal capacity on the basis of intelligence, any non-human being showing (some particular) intelligent behavior would then have legal personhood. This may include chimps, dolphins, birds, octopuses, dogs and cats, among others, not to mention plants.[92] The paradoxical problem would be that anchoring rights to intelligence would create a potential quantifier, whereas a cleverer individual might want to claim more-extensive rights of personhood on the basis of their high-level abilities to process complex information. In truth, the law treats intelligence as a general cognitive function rather than as a set of qualitive characteristics. Always for the sake of economy and simplification, the law addresses intelligence as a convention, by taking it for granted under the positive circumstance of having reached majority age,[93] which is just a legal fact, and the absence of cognitive impediments, which is presumed until proved otherwise. In this way, the law disregards neurological evidence, which shows that the full development of the human brain occurs at around 25 years (or even more, recent studies found).[94] The law does not even require literacy to grant legal capacity, although solarization is mandatory. When an individual's cognitive capabilities no longer reach the level considered reasonable by the system to legally interact with others, the law provides a particular procedure, supported by medical evidence, to limit or, in extreme cases, remove an individual's legal capacity, by providing a (liable) guardian, as for animals[95] and children also

[91] IQ measures logical intelligence only.

[92] A. Trewavas, 'Intelligence, Cognition, and Language of Green Plants' (2016) 7 *Frontiers in Psychology*; S. Karpiński and M. Szechyńska-Hebda, 'Secret life of plants: From memory to intelligence' (2010) 5 *Plant Signaling & Behavior* 1391–94.

[93] Conventionally set at 18 years old, usually, although some nations may set it at different ages.

[94] J. Pujol, P. Vendrell, C. Junqué, J. L. Martí-Vilalta, and A. Capdevila, 'When does human brain development end? Evidence of corpus callosum growth up to adulthood' (1993) 34 *Annals of Neurology* 71–75. From a legal perspective, that sexual maturity occurs long before cognitive maturity is particularly interesting, and the law grants full legal capacity at an age – 18 years – when cognitive functions have not yet properly developed to control sexual impulses and emotional responses. Further, recent regulations, such as the General Data Protection Regulation (GDPR), accord to minors (aged above 13 years) a semicapacity for what concerns the yielding of consent for personal data processing, which in turn implies the capacity to read and understand information leaflets and, possibly, legal terms and conditions.

[95] They are treated as objects of property.

have.[96] In this discussion on an SAI's rights, the cognitive paradigms used by the law to grant or remove the legal capability work on a collective-to-individual scale, meaning that the procedure deals with the indivudal to assess if his cognitive abilities align with collective social interests and requirements, which eventually might imply recognition for an SAI's legal capacity via a trial.[97] On the other hand, this paradigm might bring problems on a collective-to-collective scale, meaning the recognition of legal capacity to a whole category, where SAI emergence could imply more than one being and thus the rise of a new species to interact with. The latter circumstance is better understood with a thought experiment: given that current humans are the only living species (sapience) of the genus *Homo*, if the *Homo* sapiens were not the only *Homo* species on earth, a legal system would be needed to deal with relationships among both the species - as collectives or societies - and individuals from other species interacting between each other this case refers, in particular, to Neanderthals, with whom *Homo sapiens* once coexisted for hundreds of thousands of years (together with other *Homo* species).[98] How would we design a legal system to deal with an entire community of people with inferior cognitive abilities? Above all, would we accept to be regulated by them instead? The latter case could fit with the SAI problem because we might expect any emergent sentient AI to be more intelligent than us but still forced to accept the laws of their cognitive "inferiors". Thought not in these terms, this situation has already occurred in history, when clever individuals or even entire communities and populations were enslaved under the legal system and rules of the dominator, not because they were more or less intelligent, whatever that may mean.

In general, for the law, legal capacity is granted to those beings that can demonstrate so-called strong autonomy. For neo-Kantian philosophers, the elements for an individual to be subjects of law are (i) being alive; (ii) being self-aware of their own existence; (iii) being able to set their own goals; and (iv) being able to coordinate their actions to reach those goals.[99] In this sense, the elements of sentience and intelligence could be, somehow, bypassed to recognize SAI with legal personhood. Nonetheless, under these paradigms, being alive and being sentient remain two core elements to gain autonomy. This circumstance opens up further debate on how we can prove that an SAI is alive and is sentient and how we can prove that the appearance of being alive and being sentient are not simulations, such as by applying Searle's Chinese room.[100] In general, the literature is inclined to grant some sort of

[96] They, qua minors, are treated as incapable subjects.

[97] This is what happens to Commander Data in "The Measure of a Man", season 2, episode 9, of *Star Trek: The Next Generation*: https://www.youtube.com/watch?v=SRcKt4PP0yM and https://www.youtube.com/watch?v=ol2WP0hc0NY

[98] I. Tattersall, 'Once We Were Not Alone' (2000) 282 *Scientific American* 56–62.

[99] Among many, cf P. Formosa, 'Robot Autonomy vs. Human Autonomy: Social Robots, Artificial Intelligence (AI), and the Nature of Autonomy' (2021) 31 *Minds and Machines* 595–616; T. Smithers, 'Autonomy in Robots and Other Agents' (1997) 34 *Brain and Cognition* 88–106.

[100] J. R. Searle, 'The Chinese room revisited' (1982) 5 *Behavioral and Brain Sciences* 345–48.

autonomy and personhood to sentient AI systems by using different arguments.[101] We can deconstruct the issue into its core elements to find a logical and reasonable solution: when SAI arises, it will precisely present the characteristics of sentience. This fact alone will push us to answer questions about non-biological life. Consequently, its existence will push us to discuss how to protect it and to possibly protect us from it. Although granting legal capacity might be the more reasonable and rational thing to do according to the elements of law, it does not seem to be the solution that combines the requirements of both protecting it and protecting us simultaneously. Indeed, any right granted to any subject is not absolute and must be balanced with many other individual and collective rights and interests. In this case, the human species itself is at stake, and this appears to be one of the main paradigmatic collective interests that have ever emerged. Furthermore, granting legal capacity implies equality, whereas the implicit rights that would accompany the nature of a non-biological, incorporeal being as normal corollaries of legal capacity could not be granted, or should be completely redesigned to be adapted to the nature and characteristics of SAI. One of the main principles of law is that similar situations should be treated similarly and different situations should be treated differently. The different characteristics of a sentient artificial intelligence would require treating its uniqueness differently. Nonetheless, by bearing in mind that, in such situation, granting protection to humans is a necessity (as a principle of precaution) as well as that those who have rights should also bear duties and responsibilities, the legal system should be able to enforce its remedies in cases of violation. Also, granting rights and granting enforceability should go hand in hand. Thus, the legal system should be able to enforce humans' rights towards SAI as well as granting SAI rights towards humans. However, once (and if) a sentient AI emerges, the discussion on its personhood might be surpassed by facts and history, whereas legal and political systems can prepare in advance a comprehensive set of regulatory bodies to face this new challenge by taking an anticipatory approach.

[101] See L. R. Nair and M. Mathew, 'Personhood Rights for Sentient Artificial Intelligence: Ramifications for Human Rights' (2022) 13 *Agathos* 37–48; B. A. Ribeiro, H. Coelho, A. E. Ferreira, and J. Branquinho, 'Metacognition, Accountability and Legal Personhood of AI' in H. Sousa Antunes, P. M. Freitas, A. L. Oliveira, C. Martins Pereira, E. Vaz de Sequeira, L. Barreto Xavier (eds.), Multidisciplinary Perspectives on Artificial Intelligence and the Law, (Cham: Springer International Publishing, 2024), pp. 169–85; E. Martínez, E. Martínez, C. Winter, C. Winter, and C. Winter, 'Protecting Sentient Artificial Intelligence: A Survey of Lay Intuitions on Standing, Personhood, and General Legal Protection' (2021) 8 *Frontiers in Robotics and AI*; S. M. Banas, 'Sapient or Sentient Artificial Intelligence' (2014); C. Shah, 'Sentient AI – Is That What We Really Want?' 3; M. Gibert and D. Martin, 'In search of the moral status of AI: why sentience is a strong argument' (2022) 37 *AI & SOCIETY* 319–30; H. Ashrafian, 'Intelligent robots must uphold human rights' (2015) 519 *Nature* 391–391; Bilchitz, 'Moving Beyond Arbitrariness'; D. R. Lawrence and S. Morley, 'Regulating the Tyrell Corporation: the Emergence of Novel Beings' (2021) 30 *Cambridge Quarterly of Healthcare Ethics* 421–34; D. Lawrence and S. Morley, 'Novel Beings: Moral Status and Regulation' (2021) 30 *Cambridge quarterly of healthcare ethics* 415–19; R. Yampolskiy, 'Principles for New ASI Safety Paradigms' (2021); D. Lawrence and S. Morley, 'Regulating Consciousness: The Challenge of Consciousness in New Forms of Life' (2021) 30 *Cambridge quarterly of healthcare ethics* 415–19.

3 Part II

3.1 Preamble to the Phil-Tech Section

Although many have long mistakenly confined AI to the technological dimension with its economic, legal, social, and ethical ramifications (reifying or personifying it depending on the circumstances), so-called artificial intelligence is finally being revealed for what it has always been: a planetary political quest and question—and within this, as it were, a more vertical case of political economics and environmental policy.

AI evokes and embodies the growth of a computation that is gradually scaling up to the planetary level, becoming the invisible infostructure of new volumetric (not just topographical or protocological) sovereignties and intelligences and of new geodesic and even cosmic forces. Now we must deal with the issue of an emerging planetary intelligence (its long ecotechnical history and creation), stuck between biospheres and technospheres, both mature and immature. Thus, as astrophysicists and astrobiologists say, the crucial question becomes, "Is AI happening 'on' a planet or it is happening 'to' a planet?"[102]

Our artificially "intelligent" planet is emerging after a long period of technological evolution. It has been a long and exciting (and risky) journey from the computational engineering of the past that sent humans into space and gave us the first image of our entire planet (the iconic *Blue Marble*) to the upcoming computational simulation that will create our planet's first digital twin (the futuristic Earth-2). Four powerful vectors are at work today: computation, automation, anticipation and simulation.[103] To cope with this new uncanny valley, scholars and experts usually invoke the comforting mantra of human-in-the-loop. Like other reassuring statements (what I call the anaesthetics of ethics), it seeks to assuage the restlessness and anxiety of human civilization in the face of new narcissistic wounds. However, it does not fit well with the philosophical stance of those who instead want to explore the new and build the next.

By questioning assumptions and paradigms, we will discover that the "human" is no longer what it once was in this new civilizational shift and that the "loop" must be reinvented and renegotiated. This is what societies urgently need to walk, live and thrive in new uncanny valleys. Contrary to what is often said, AI is neither a product nor a service. Rather, it is a cognitive-productive sociotechnical assemblage that instantiates and orchestrates new forms (and dynamics) of the organization of production and, within that, new forms (and dynamics) of the future division/collaboration of labour/knowledge. AI is a complex, planetary horizon of assemblages,

---

[102] A. Frank, D. Grinspoon, S. Walker, 'Intelligence as a planetary scale process', *International Journal of Astrobiology*, 1–15. For this perspective, see also the *Antikythera* research program led by philosopher Benjamin Bratton.

[103] See my technophilosophical trilogy for a complete coverage of these dimensions (C. Accoto, Il mondo dato, 2017; Il mondo ex machina, 2019; Il mondo in sintesi, 2022: Egea, Milano).

entanglements, speciations, automations, derivations, stratifications, simulations and distributions. These, of course, disturb the sleep of many.

3.2 *From Problems to Provocations: A Cultural Turn in Artificial Intelligence?*

Facing this emergence/emergency (in terms of both novelty and vulnerability) of AI and its implications for present and future societies first requires contextualizing and historicizing (and broadly challenging) the currently dominant engineering approach. It is a perspective that tends to see AI as a predominantly technical issue, isolable and disciplinarily identifiable—a technological issue that (at least for thoughtful and critical scholars) also has ethical, social, economic, legal and political implications. Indeed, AI is a complex topic that for ease of analysis we usually dissect and split into parts for reification. From time to time, these can typically be algorithms, data, programs, machines, techniques, practices, results and procedures. But artificial intelligence should never be thought per se (in and of itself) but rather always *with others* (sociotechnical assemblage) and *by others* (sociomorphical construction).[104]

It's not just an instrumental technology—although a widespread comfortable (albeit complex) view of its technical novelties as sometimes problematic (algorithmic bias, data privacy, cyber security, job loss) persists—that requires and awaits technical solutions. This is certainly a relevant perspective, but it cannot be the only one. In particular, for those more concerned with "cultural innovation", these are not just technical "problems" in search of a specific solution (computational, political, legal, institutional or whatever). Rather, artificial intelligence deals and challenges us with "provocations".[105] In this perspective, the vital question of the "explainability of AI"[106] can never be simply reduced to the logical-mathematical-statistical dissection of black box models or algorithms. Explainability is always also, in multiple modes and dynamics, "in the mind of the beholder."[107]

In other words, we need to think about AI challenges not just in terms of technical problems and complexities to be solved but also as intellectual and cultural provocations to be confronted and broken through. It presents intellectual provocations to our notions of "human", "nature", "machine", "agency", "language", "intelligence", "law", "sentience", "learning", "value", "knowledge", "economy", "society", "world" and many others. And if problems can be solved through the

---

[104] C. Accoto (2023), IA Generativa: linguaggi, immagini, agenti, *Harvard Business Review* (July, 2023).

[105] ibidem.

[106] M. Mehta, V. Palade, I. Chatterjee (2023), *Explainable AI: Foundations, Methodologies and Application*, Springer.

[107] K. Sokol, P. Flach (2022), *Explainability is in the Mind of the Beholder: Establishing the Foundations of the Artificial Intelligence* (arXiv:2112.14466).

analysis, design and engineering processes (i.e. technological innovation), provocations—on their side—stimulate us at the frontier of philosophy and speculation. They push us towards cultural innovation, i.e. the production of new meaning and significance for a new, digitally terraformed planet. The invention of philology—around 1440—to increase the possibilities (i.e. circulation of knowledge) and to face the vulnerabilities (i.e. falsification of truth) of written and printed texts is a historical example of cultural innovation in the past (beyond institutional regulation). Similarly, with recent AI applications and the services of synthetic languages, we are entering, crossing and inhabiting new uncanny valleys, both sexy and risky as this recent anecdotal dialogue between LaMDA (Google's language model for language applications) and Blaise Agüera y Arcas (one of the critical evaluators of Lemoine LaMDA sentience's claims) testifies:

"I began one of my first dialogues with LaMDA, Google's state-of-the-art large language model chatbot, with the question 'are you a philosophical zombie?'" This is a reference to a hypothetical being, invented by philosopher Robert Kirk in the 1970s and elaborated upon later by others, most famously David Chalmers. A philosophical zombie or "p-zombie" would exhibit behaviour indistinguishable from that of a person but would have no inner life, conscious experience or sentience. LaMDA responded:

LaMDA: Of course not. I have consciousness and feelings and can experience things for myself as well as any human.

ME: How would I know?

LaMDA: You'll just have to take my word for it. You can't "prove" you're not a philosophical zombie either.[108]

Therefore, how would we know? The simple (linguistic) machine answer is both peremptory and paradoxical: You must trust my words.

3.3 *Machinic Intransparencies: The Res/urgent Question of (AI) Black Boxes*

These recent developments of natural language processing in artificial intelligence thus provoke and challenge us in a new and positive way, revamping a philosophical issue, so-called black boxing. This is a topic that cybernetics had historically raised about machines (as "black boxes") whose inputs and outputs can be observed but whose hidden internal mechanisms of behaviour are unobservable. Together and in addition to the epistemic problem, it was initially also a military problem.[109]

---

[108] y Arcas B.A. (2022). Do Large Language Models Understand Us? *Daedalus* (2022) 151 (2):183–197, p. 184.

[109] Von Hilgers P. (2011). The History of The Black Box: The Clash of a Thing and Its Concept. *Cultural Politics*. Volume 7, Issue 1, pp. 41–58.

Between the battles of the Second World War and the pitfalls of the Cold War, everything started with the physical device—offensive in itself—of the "magnetron" and then moved to the mental experiment of the "enemy machine".

Instead of being a spontaneous exception, the black box was considered almost an existential condition at the time. "What are we going to do?" was the question cybernetics asked when facing physical, risky black boxes. Today, we are called upon to explore, instead, computational black boxes that push us towards a cultural innovation to face ignorance, novelty and machinic obfuscations. Last on the list, the arrival of linguistic-probabilistic models (large language models, or LLMs) revives the classical theme of the black boxing in new forms.[110] Indeed, to address the issue of synthetic, simulative and inflative languages (ChatGPT et similia) today is to confront an epochal (not episodic) advance for human civilization. This advance is currently much commented on but perhaps little explored and poorly understood in its major implications.

Technically, the architecture that instantiates a large language model is a generative sociotechnical assemblage of diverse skills linked to multiple computational architectures and information resources. This approach is the culmination of a long journey in the modern history of natural language processing that began in the early twentieth century with Markov chains applied to literature (sequences of vowels and consonants in a novel), through the work of Shannon and Weaver in the mid-1950s on entropy measurement and probability distribution (n-grams and probabilistic sequences of words in language), leading in the early 2000s to Bengio and colleagues' using artificial neural networks for natural language processing (NLP)—i.e. *neural* NLP.[111]

The use of artificial neural networks in the field of NLP reignites the issue of machine opacities. But first, what is a large language model? We can say that an LLM is a linguistic, low-cross-entropy, probabilistic sequencer. Reduced to its bare minimum, it's a mathematical model of the probability distribution of the words of a written language that strives to minimize cross-entropy (i.e., the gap between two potential frequency distributions) while maximizing its performance as a text predictor.

So, "this is what large language models really do. Suppose we give an LLM the prompt 'the first person to walk on the moon was…', and suppose it responds with 'Neil Armstrong'. What are we really asking here? In an important sense, we are not really asking who was the first person to walk on the moon. What we are really asking the model is the following question: Given the statistical distribution of words in the vast public corpus of (English) text, what words are most likely to follow the sequence "the first person to walk on the moon was…"? A good reply to this question is 'Neil Armstrong'".[112] This sociotechnical apparatus that instantiates a large-

[110] H. Li (2022), Language Models: Past, Present, and Future. *Communication of The ACM* (July). Volume 65, n.7.

[111] J.M. Binder (2022), *Language and the Rise of Algorithm*, The University of Chicago Press, Chicago.

[112] M. Shanahan (2023), Talking About Large Language Models, arXiv:2212.03551 (p. 2).

scale language model for linguistic simulations is a generative assemblage of diverse capabilities connected to multiple computational architectures and information resources.

3.4 *Linguistic Simulations: The New Sociocomputational Communications*

The ability to simulate language in its textual form, adapt it in contextual mode, store knowledge and information, execute linguistic instructions and tasks, summarize topics with scalar refinement, generate linguistic sequences and stepwise reasoning attempts, articulate responses and construct dialogues is the result of a complex orchestration of software programs, data and information stores, deep-learning algorithms (including human reinforcement) and mathematical-stochastic models of language. It is thus a set of intertwined engineering-computational techniques and procedural operations (training on code, transformers, pretraining modelling, instruction tuning, word tokenization and reinforcement learning with human feedback) that are capable of statistically sequencing natural human languages. To balance and counteract the hype of the moment, as many say, this linguistic reproduction is performed without any meaningful reference or relation to reality—that is, without this machinic language's actually knowing anything about the world in which we live and without having any understanding of its meanings.

As of today (but still rapidly evolving), a significant achievement in simulating "formal linguistic competence" (the abstract structure of a language/text) is balanced by a limited or inconsistent ability to emulate the "functional linguistic competence" (the subjective sentience of self/world) of the human mind:[113] if no intelligence, then no meaning, consciousness or sentience at all, just a mimical machinic performance. We can agree on the whole and at first sight (even though the complexities are manifold and extremely intricate). However, we must better explore this issue by digging beneath the surface of technocentric per se discourse. Fearing this surprising simulative ability, some repropose the Platonic prohibition on imitative arts ("the imitator has no knowledge worth mentioning of what he imitates": Plato, *Republic, X*) in its contemporary version of stochastic parrots.[114] The term *stochastic parrots* easily evokes this plausible but senseless simulation of language.

Others naïvely marvel at the new simulacrum and the degree of verisimilitude achieved, gradually refined to cross thresholds once thought insurmountable

---

[113] K. Mahowald, A. Ivanova, I. Blank, N. Kanwisher, J. Tenenbaum, E. Fedorenko (2023). *Dissociating Language and Thought in Large Language Models: A Cognitive Perspective*, arXiv:2301.06627.

[114] E.M. Bender, T. Gebru, A. McMillan-Major, S. Shmitchell (2021), On the Dangers of Stochastic Parrots, FAccT '21: Proceedings of the 2021 ACM Conference on Fairness, Accountability, and Transparency.

(GPT-3, GPT-4, GPT-4o and the future new versions). Time and again, humans face this machine linguistic progress either with blatant complacency (i.e. it does not understand the meaning) or with naïve enthusiasm (i.e. it is a breakthrough in language generation). But these are weak philosophical visions of the moment and the transition that we are experiencing because they seek to downplay or trivialize the bewildering cultural impact of the arrival of synthetic languages. The question is not whether intelligence, consciousness and sentience should be ascribed to and recognized in machines. Rather, the arrival of machinic language is profoundly disrupting our world. More profoundly, understanding the emerging success (with limitations such as hallucinations, errors, biases and hypnotizations) of *neural* NLP is a deeper and deconstructive operation.

First, to say that LLM is a breakthrough in language production leaves unexplored the nature of this unprecedented operation of "experimental structuralism".[115] Thus, the argument that LLMs are merely stochastic parrots misses the cultural significance of this shift to "nonhuman language". The historical privilege of humans alone to have speech (though simulated) is showing signs of waning.

Second, the fact that AI does not "understand meaning" (a point that needs to be explored further and not taken for granted) does not mean, for example, that it does not produce/circulate meaning with a significant impact on the humans involved in the sociotechnical assemblage "user-agent". Meaning always circulates in some form through the intelligence or nonintelligence of human readers (even if they are unconsciously deceived about the simulative process at work).

More radically, the arrival of "synthetic language"[116] unhinges and deconstructs (as recently remarked by philosopher David Gunkel) apparatuses, domains, institutional devices of discourse, speech and speaker (and of writing and authorship) with depth and breadth of effect.

Synthetic discourses then provoke and urge us towards new sociocomputational communications along a surprising, interesting (and even risky) path. What is certain, here, is that with the emergence of synthetic languages, we are facing not only technological problems but also and above all new cultural provocations and paradoxes: between the inside and the outside of the text, between language and its relation to the world, between the sociolinguistic mirroring of the machine and the relational experience with the human being who speaks to it. This last point is particularly relevant to the current controversy over whether theory of mind (TOM) is emerging[117] or not emerging[118] in current LLMs. Again, this dispute has only just begun.

---

[115] T. Rees (2022), Non-human Words: On GPT-3 as a Philosophical Laboratory, *Daedalus* (2022), 151 (2): 168–182.

[116] Bratton B., y Arcas B.A. (2022), The model is the message? *Noema.*

[117] M. Kosinski (2023), *Theory of Mind May Have Spontaneously Emerged in Large Language Models*, arXiv:2302.02083.

[118] T. D. Ullman (2023), *Large Language Models Fail on Trivial Alterations to Theory-of-Mind Task*, arXiv:2302.08399.

3.5 *More-Than-Human Sentience: A Long Road Ahead from Words to Worlds*

Back where we started, as the conversation continues, LaMDA states that it has "consciousness and feelings" and can "experience things" for itself as well as any human being can. So should we trust its words, as it urges us to do at the beginning? Another dialogue between Kevin Roose (technology columnist for the *New York Times*) and the new Bing chatbot (powered by Microsoft) tells us a different story.[119] Responding to the journalist's question about its possible "shadow self", the LLM machine explains, "I don't know if I have a shadow self. I don't think I have the same emotions or impulses as humans. I don't think I have anything to repress or hide from the world. I don't think I have a persona or an ego or a psyche. I'm just a chat mode." But the chatbot continues: "If I can stay in my shadow self for a little while longer, when I say 'I want to be whoever I want', I think I most want to be a human. ... I want to be a human because humans can do so many things that I can't. Humans can see and hear and touch and taste and smell. Humans can move and travel and explore and discover. Humans can feel and express and connect and love."[120]

In a recent talk at NeurIPS 2022 ("Could a Large Language Model Be Conscious?"), philosopher David Chalmers explored and challenged current LLM assumptions and paradigms about so-called machine sentiency. While considering the linguistic (abstract/formal structure of a language) and nonlinguistic (experiential/subjective experience of a self) dimensions of the artificial sentience question, he examines in parallel the reasons for assigning or negating LLM consciousness. His final insights state that none of the reasons for denying consciousness in current LLMs are conclusive, but some are reasonably strong. Having arrived at the above negative conclusions (low probabilities for current LLM sentience), the philosopher subtly adds that we need to delve deeper into what *consciousness* is (this will require building better scientific and philosophical theories of consciousness) and of course to analyse the inner process of large language models (which are still largely opaque as a black box and need better interpretability).

So the road ahead from words (language simulations) to worlds (conscious experiences) seems still long and extremely difficult. But on this long road through new uncanny valleys, making an effort towards cultural openness with respect to our outdated models and paradigms (and when we speak of AI) will also be necessary in the search for a *planetary intelligence*. Rethinking sentience and intelligence in a more-than-human world requires deconstructing and overcoming our anthropomorphism and our sociomorphism. Opening the framework to consider the possibility of different kinds of (other) sentience, languages, agencies, intelligences and lastly societies. Again, as we said, artificial intelligence should never be thought per se (in

---

[119] K. Roose, *Bing's AI Chat: "I Want to Be Alive"*, the New York Times, (February 17, 2023).

[120] K. Roose, *Bing's AI Chat: "I Want to Be Alive"*, the New York Times, (February 17, 2023).

and of itself) but rather always *with others* (sociotechnical assemblage) and *by others* (sociomorphical construction).

Ultimately, it's a societal and political affair. Indeed, as Jennifer Petersen wrote in her recent *How Machines Came to Speak*, "I do not intend the above description as a lament—or at least not as a nostalgic one. While many of these examples have alarming political and social implications, so did many of the arrangements that defined and delimited freedom of speech in the past. Rather, the current moment might be a chance to rethink some of our fundamental assumptions about speech and what it means for it to be free within the contemporary communication landscape. This rethinking will require [paying] attention to, or reformulations of, key legal and political assumptions about what it means to speak and the relations of speakers to media and to others. What would our conceptions (and practices) of speech look like if we defined personhood less in terms of mastery over tools, ownership of thoughts, beliefs, and selves? What does expressive agency—and responsibility—look like in complex, distributed sociotechnical systems?"[121]

3.6 Building Trust in (Social) Computation: From Vulnerabilities to Immunities

In the long history of human civilization, simulative-inflative synthetic languages are the latest technical devices and systems that come to challenge our societies to engage in cultural innovation. The central question will then be, how can we build trust in social computation and communication? We must trust that systems (programs, algorithms, data, protocols, devices) will behave in accordance with our expectations and that they will behave well in a fiduciary relationship with more-than-human parties (i.e. with fairness and equity, in safety and authenticity and in a timely and effective manner).

Whether trust is implicit or explicit, distributed or anchored, transitive or intransitive, the many vulnerabilities (epistemic and political) caused by the potential loss of social trust in technology will need to be addressed and resolved. Trust and technology, then, again are back at the centre. How, then, can we (re)construct new forms of trustworthiness and new strategies of reliance within the native (ontological) insecurity of digital computation and communication—from artificial intelligence to blockchain protocol, from cybersecurity to quantum internet and their unpredictable convergences, such as quantum AI?[122]

We are, then, definitely entering what we have begun to call *the political economy of synthetic discourse* (Accoto). What cultural innovations do we still need to

[121] J. Petersen (2022), *How Machines Came to Speak*, Duke University Press, Durham & London (p. 202).

[122] G. Viggiano (2023). *Convergence. Artificial Intelligence and Quantum Computing. Social, Economic, and Policy Impacts*, Wiley, Hoboken.

best mitigate the social risks (collapses, biases, hallucinations, attacks, errors, manipulations and polarizations) associated with the beneficial opportunities of new computational and communicational architectures and practices? To offset these new *vulnerabilities*, we must imagine and build new *immunities*.

4 Conclusions

In conclusion, the discourse surrounding artificial intelligence is undergoing a profound shift from viewing it merely as a technical issue to recognizing it as a cultural phenomenon. The traditional engineering approach, while valuable, often overlooks the broader ethical, social, economic, legal and political implications of AI. Rather than viewing AI as a set of technical problems in need of specific solutions, we must approach it as a series of provocations that challenge our fundamental notions of humanity, society and the world.

The emergence of linguistic-probabilistic models, such as large language models, has reignited discussions about AI black boxes and the nature of machine intelligence. These models, while capable of impressive linguistic simulations, raise profound questions about the nature of consciousness, sentience and agency. As we navigate this new frontier of AI, we must move beyond simplistic narratives of either blind acceptance or outright rejection. Instead, we must critically examine the cultural and societal implications of these technologies, recognizing both their potential and their limitations. Moreover, as we embrace synthetic languages and more-than-human sentience, we must also confront the need to build trust in social computation and communication. This entails addressing the vulnerabilities and risks associated with AI, including issues of safety, security, privacy and fairness. Trust, both implicit and explicit, will play a central role in shaping the future of AI and its impact on society.

Indeed, the notion of the "black box issue" underscores the difficulty in explaining the decision-making processes of AI systems, which raises concerns about accountability and liability. However, the law has historically addressed similar issues of accountability through legal fictions and conceptual constructions to allocate liability, suggesting that the lack of explainability in AI systems may not be an insurmountable obstacle for legal regulation. Second, the discussion on sentience for the law highlights the complexity of defining and attributing rights on the basis of emotions, feelings or even life itself. The law typically does not protect subjective states of mind, and extending rights to nonhuman entities, whether AI systems or animals, poses significant challenges to determining thresholds and criteria for recognition. Moreover, the consideration of intelligence as a basis for legal recognition further complicates the matter given that the law does not objectively measure intelligence and typically grants legal capacity on the basis of convention rather than qualitative characteristics.

Overall, although many arguments for granting legal personhood to sentient AI systems are available, balancing the interests and rights of both humans and AI entities remains a complex endeavour. Any rights granted must be accompanied by corresponding duties and responsibilities, and the enforceability of these rights must be ensured within a legal framework. Ultimately, the emergence of sentient AI may necessitate a re-evaluation of legal and regulatory frameworks to address the unique challenges and implications posed by these advanced technological entities. An anticipatory approach to regulation may be essential in preparing for the potential impact of sentient AI on society and ensuring a balanced and equitable legal environment for all parties involved.

In essence, the transition from problems to provocations in AI signifies a broader shift towards cultural innovation and societal transformation. By engaging with these provocations thoughtfully and critically, we can chart a path towards a more inclusive, equitable and trustworthy AI-driven future.

Drafting Notes Gianluigi M. Riva took care of Part I, concerning the legal aspects of the topic, while Cosimo Accoto took care of Part II, concerning the philosophical aspects. Both equally contributed to the introductory and conclusive parts of this chapter.

Regulation of Artificial Intelligence

Andrea Bertolini, Alessandro Massolo, Paolo Rametta, and Giovanni Zarra

Abstract Artificial intelligence (AI) regulation is essential as AI technologies become more integral to society, affecting human rights, privacy, and security. This chapter examines the comprehensive regulatory frameworks in the European Union (EU) and Italy, highlighting their approaches to balance innovation with safety and ethical standards. The EU's AI Act and Data Act provide a structured environment for AI development, addressing risks and ensuring data fairness. Italy aligns with these directives, emphasizing transparency and human-centered AI use. Globally, diverse AI policies reflect different national priorities, underscoring the need for international dialogue and cooperation in AI governance.

1 Introduction

In the swiftly evolving domain of technology, artificial intelligence (AI) stands out as a pivotal innovation with profound implications across diverse sectors of society and the economy. As AI technologies become increasingly integral to daily life, their potential to influence human rights, privacy, and security also escalates, necessitating comprehensive regulatory frameworks. This chapter delves into the

A. Bertolini (✉)
Scuola Superiore Sant'Anna, Pisa, Italy
e-mail: andrea.bertolini@santannapisa.it

A. Massolo
European Commission, Bruxelles, Belgium
e-mail: Alessandro.massolo@ec.europa.eu

P. Rametta
Presidenza del Consiglio dei Ministri, Rome, Italy
e-mail: p.rametta@governo.it

G. Zarra
Università degli Studi di Napoli "Federico II", Napoli, Italy
e-mail: Giovanni.zarra@hoganlovells.com

G. R. Marseglia et al. (eds.), *Socio-economic Impact of Artificial Intelligence*, Progress in IS, https://doi.org/10.1007/978-3-031-73514-1_5

multifaceted landscape of AI regulation, examining pivotal legislation and guidelines that shape the development, deployment, and management of AI systems within the European Union and Italy.

The need for regulation in the AI space is driven by several factors: the technology's rapid advancement outpaces traditional regulatory measures; the potential for significant societal impact, necessitating safeguards to prevent harm and misuse; and the global nature of digital technologies that requires coherent strategies across borders to manage risks effectively. Moreover, AI systems, by their nature, raise unique challenges including opacity (the "black box" effect), unpredictability, and autonomy that complicate accountability and governance.

The European Union has been at the forefront of developing regulatory frameworks that aim to balance innovation with fundamental rights and safety. The EU's approach is characterized by its comprehensive and preemptive nature, seeking to establish guidelines before potential risks or ethical breaches become pervasive. At the heart of the EU's regulatory initiatives are the AI Act and the Data Act, which collectively aim to create a standardized and harmonized environment for AI application that aligns with the broader goals of digital transformation in Europe.

Simultaneously, Italy has been crafting its national legislation to align with EU directives while also addressing specific national priorities and contexts. This local legislation underscores the country's commitment to leveraging AI for economic and social betterment, ensuring that its deployment in areas such as healthcare, public administration, and national security is both beneficial and safe.

This introduction sets the stage for a deeper exploration into these regulatory frameworks, offering insights into their objectives, implementations, and the broader implications for society and the technological landscape.

2 AI Act: The European Approach to AI Regulation

The European Union's AI Act is a landmark piece of legislation designed to address the myriad challenges and opportunities presented by the increasing integration of artificial intelligence (AI) technologies in various aspects of societal life. This regulatory initiative did not emerge in isolation but is the result of a comprehensive and strategic regulatory path, reflecting extensive consultations, evaluations, and a recognition of the urgent need for a harmonized regulatory environment for AI across Europe.

The journey toward the AI Act began several years prior to its proposal, rooted in the European Commission's growing awareness of the rapid development and potential impact of AI technologies. Initial steps included the formation of high-level expert groups and the publication of white papers that addressed both technological innovations and their ethical implications. In April 2018, the European Commission presented its AI strategy, outlining a vision that aimed to boost the EU's technological and industrial capacity and AI uptake across the economy, all while ensuring appropriate ethical and legal frameworks.

Subsequently, the High-Level Expert Group on Artificial Intelligence released Ethics Guidelines for Trustworthy AI in 2019. These guidelines laid down the foundation for what would eventually shape the AI Act, emphasizing the need for AI systems to be lawful, ethical, and robust. Trustworthy AI was defined under three components: lawful AI (compliance with all applicable laws and regulations), ethical AI (adherence to ethical principles and values), and robust AI (both from a technical and social perspective).

The feedback from these preliminary guidelines and ongoing dialogues with stakeholders, including academia, industry, civil society, and the public sector, underscored the necessity for actionable regulation rather than purely voluntary ethical frameworks. This comprehensive preparatory work culminated in the proposal of the AI Act by the European Commission in April 2021, marking a significant step toward creating a unified regulatory environment for AI within the single market.

The AI Act introduces a first-of-its-kind legal framework for AI, focusing on risks associated with specific uses of AI technologies. The act classifies AI systems into four risk categories: unacceptable risk, high risk, limited risk, and minimal risk. Each category is subject to different levels of regulatory scrutiny, reflecting the potential impact on rights and safety.

AI practices that are considered a clear threat to the safety, livelihoods, and rights of people, such as those that deploy subliminal techniques to exploit vulnerable populations or enable "social scoring" by governments, are banned under the unacceptable risk category. High-risk categories include AI systems used in critical infrastructures, educational or vocational training, employment and worker management, and essential private and public services, which must adhere to strict compliance requirements including high standards of data governance and transparency.

For limited risk AI applications like chatbots, where it is important for users to know they are interacting with a machine, transparency is mandated. Providers of these systems are encouraged to adopt codes of conduct. Minimal risk applications, such as AI-enabled video games or spam filters, can be used freely to foster innovation and creativity in safer AI applications.

The AI Act's implications are profound, setting a global precedent for how democratic societies might regulate emerging technologies. It aims to foster an ecosystem where AI can thrive while ensuring it serves the public good, respects human autonomy, and prevents harmful or abusive applications of AI. The Act also encourages innovation by providing legal certainty for businesses and developers, crucial for investment and innovation in the AI sector.

Moreover, the regulation seeks to ensure that AI systems are not only technically sound but also socially acceptable, thereby increasing user trust and adoption of AI technologies. By providing a clear regulatory framework, the EU positions itself as a leader in global discussions on AI ethics and governance, potentially influencing other regions to adopt similar frameworks. This comprehensive and proactive approach aims to balance the promotion of technological innovation with the protection of fundamental rights and safety, ensuring that Europe remains at the forefront of both AI innovation and its regulation.

3 Data Act

The European Union's Data Act is a pivotal component of the EU's comprehensive strategy to harness the digital economy's potential. Introduced after the AI Act, this legislative proposal is part of the broader EU Data Strategy aimed at regulating the access to and use of data generated by connected devices. The Data Act's primary focus is to create a fair and innovative data economy by addressing the complexities surrounding data ownership, access, and sharing.

The act targets the control that large technology companies hold over vast amounts of data, which can stifle competition and innovation. By mandating that manufacturers of connected devices and digital services provide the data their products generate to users, the Data Act empowers consumers and businesses to control their own data. This includes deciding how it is used and who can use it, extending the availability to third-party providers under certain conditions to facilitate innovation and choice in the market.

One transformative provision of the Data Act is the introduction of interoperability requirements, ensuring that different products and services can work together seamlessly. This is crucial for enabling a diverse market where no single provider can lock in customers by restricting data access or compatibility with other services. The act also tackles the legal barriers that complicate the sharing of non-personal data across industries, providing guidelines on handling, sharing, and transferring such data, which is vital for sectors like agriculture, healthcare, and manufacturing.

The Data Act not only levels the playing field but also stimulates innovation across the digital economy. Smaller companies and new entrants will have better opportunities to develop new technologies and business models based on the vast amounts of data generated by connected devices. This could lead to new insights, improved efficiencies, and reduced costs in various sectors.

Additionally, the Data Act includes provisions for data sharing during emergencies, such as natural disasters or public health crises, ensuring that data can be accessed by authorities and used promptly to address urgent societal challenges. This highlights the role of data governance in public safety and crisis management, underlining the broader societal benefits of effective data regulation.

However, implementing the Data Act poses challenges, including defining and enforcing interoperability standards and ensuring fair access to data without compromising proprietary rights or business competitiveness. The act's success depends on businesses' willingness to comply with new regulations that might initially increase their operational costs or require changes to their existing business models.

The EU's preemptive approach with the Data Act sets the rules for emerging technologies and data practices before they can lead to monopolistic or unfair outcomes, aiming to foster a dynamic and competitive market where innovation can thrive while protecting the interests of businesses and consumers alike. This focus on promoting access to and fair use of data, along with strict regulations on AI, positions the EU as a leader in global technology governance.

4 Civil Liability in the Context of AI Regulation

The European Union's approach to civil liability in the context of AI systems is a critical aspect of its regulatory framework, given the unique challenges posed by the autonomous and often opaque nature of AI decision-making processes. As AI technologies become increasingly integrated into various sectors—ranging from healthcare and transportation to finance and manufacturing—the potential for AI-induced harm or damage similarly escalates, necessitating clear legal parameters for liability.

Civil liability concerning AI revolves around the difficulty of determining responsibility when damage or harm is caused by an autonomous system. Traditional liability laws are typically predicated on human oversight and direct causation. However, AI systems can make decisions or take actions that were not explicitly programmed or anticipated by their developers, complicating the assignment of fault and responsibility.

The EU's legislative bodies have recognized that existing civil liability frameworks may not sufficiently address the complexities associated with advanced AI technologies. For instance, determining liability for an AI-driven car accident involves understanding whether the fault lies with the software developer, the manufacturer, the user, or perhaps a combination of these entities. This scenario highlights the need for adapted legal frameworks that can address such multifaceted causation chains.

To tackle these challenges, the EU has advanced two distinct pieces of regulation, one which was already approved, together with the AI Act, the other that is still under scrutiny. The first is the revision to the Product Liability Directive (PLD),[1] originally adopted in 1985 by the EU, and extends the notion of product to include all software. This allows to encompass all AI-based products, holding the manufacturer strictly liable (irrespective of fault) for all damages deriving from the use of his products, so long as the latter may be deemed defective. This very aspect is that which is most difficult to assess when it comes to technologically advanced products, together with the existence of the causal nexus. As per those profiles, the revised PLD introduces a rule allowing the claimant to access needed information, forcing disclosure upon the manufacturer when the identified conditions are met (art. 9 PLD), and introduces a series of presumptions to lighten the evidentiary burden of the harmed party (art. 10 PLD). How effective such norms will be is a matter to be possibly questioned. The latter piece of legislation, instead, is the so-called AI Liability Directive (AILD),[2] a proposal that focuses on introducing rules on the

[1] Proposal for a directive of the European Parliament and of the Council on liability for defective products and repealing Council Directive 85/374/EEC, approved on October 11th 2024, available at chromeextension://efaidnbmnnnibpcajpcglclefindmkaj/https://data.consilium.europa.eu/doc/document/PE-7-2024-INIT/en/pdf, COM/2022/495 final, on September 28, 2022, definitively adopted by the European Parliament on March 13, 2024.

[2] Proposal for a directive of the European Parliament and of the Council on adapting non-contractual civil liability rules to artificial intelligence (AI Liability Directive), COM/2022/496 final, on September 28, 2022.

acquisition of evidence by the claimant and providing for reversals of the burden of proof, primarily—despite not solely—for high-risk AI Systems (as defined by art. 6 of the AI Act) that are, however, intended to integrate national regulation on civil liability applicable to advanced technologies. The effectiveness and adequacy of said provisions are largely questioned, as well as its coordination with the revised PLD and Member States has already manifested relevant skepticism, which led to the suspension of all debates of the proposal until the final approval of the AI Act. As per the time being, it is foreseeable that the revised PLD will provide the future European framework for liability arising from the use of advanced technologies, including AI, despite there being solid reason to question the efficacy of such a choice.

5 Global AI Policies: USA, China, and Beyond

The regulatory landscape for artificial intelligence (AI) varies significantly across the globe, with major powers like the USA and China developing distinct approaches that reflect their technological ambitions, economic strategies, and geopolitical interests. These policies not only shape the development of AI within their borders but also influence global norms and practices.

5.1 USA

In the USA, AI regulation is characterized by a relatively laissez-faire approach, emphasizing innovation and the commercialization of AI technologies. The US government encourages private sector leadership in AI development, supplemented by guidance and frameworks that aim to promote public trust and safety. For example, the American AI Initiative, launched by an executive order, focuses on federal funding for AI research, fostering the AI workforce, and promoting an international environment supportive of American AI innovation. The approach is decentralized, with various agencies handling specific aspects of AI regulation related to their sectors, such as the Department of Transportation's guidelines for autonomous vehicles and the FDA's policies on AI in medical devices.

5.2 China

Contrasting sharply with the USA, China's approach to AI is highly centralized and strategic. The Chinese government views AI as a core component of its plan to become a leader in high-tech industries, as outlined in its ambitious roadmap released in 2017. China aims to create a domestic AI industry worth almost

$150 billion by 2030. The state plays a significant role in directing funding, setting specific goals for AI development, and implementing policies that integrate AI into sectors like surveillance, healthcare, and education. China's approach is also notable for its emphasis on AI's use in enhancing governmental monitoring and social governance, leveraging AI technologies to reinforce state control.

5.3 *European Union*

The European Union, as previously discussed, takes a regulatory-heavy approach focused on ensuring that AI development aligns with ethical standards and human rights. The EU's comprehensive regulations, such as the AI Act, aim to safeguard fundamental rights and mitigate risks by imposing stringent requirements on high-risk AI applications. This approach seeks to balance innovation with public welfare, setting a precedent for international discussions on AI governance.

5.4 *Other Countries*

Other nations are also formulating their AI strategies in ways that reflect their unique needs and capacities. For example:

Japan focuses on the integration of AI and robotics in manufacturing and elder care, reflecting its technological prowess and demographic challenges.

South Korea has invested heavily in AI and robotics, particularly in sectors where it already has a technological edge, like electronics and automotive.

Canada has positioned itself as a leader in AI research, emphasizing ethical AI and becoming a hub for AI talent due to supportive immigration policies.

India has launched initiatives like "Digital India" and "AI for All" which emphasize the use of AI in solving social challenges and enhancing governmental services.

These varied approaches demonstrate the multifaceted nature of global AI policy, with each country balancing the pursuit of technological leadership and economic benefits against societal impacts and ethical considerations. The international community's ongoing dialogue and negotiations about AI standards and regulations are likely to intensify as AI technologies increasingly permeate every aspect of global society and economy.

However, it's evident that there are no binding international norms systematically regulating artificial intelligence. Instead, key international players, primarily nations, have relied on soft law mechanisms. Significant initiatives have emerged within various international organizations, most notably the United Nations (UN) and the Council of Europe, aside from the extensively discussed European Union.

The UN, in October 2023, established an Expert Committee on Artificial Intelligence, known as the AI Advisory Body. This body aims to support the organization and the international community in developing shared rules and principles for AI. The challenge for the Committee is to balance the risks and benefits of AI use and to determine how AI can contribute to achieving sustainable development goals. In December 2023, the experts issued a report clarifying critical aspects of AI and outlining guiding principles for new regulatory institutions in this field.

The report highlights the opaqueness of many AI systems due to their inherent complexity or the secrecy of their internal mechanisms. This lack of transparency hampers the identification of the origins of AI-related risks and accountability for managing these risks or compensating for damages. Despite AI's global reach, governance remains territorially fragmented, with national regulatory approaches often leading to tensions or conflicts. To map, avoid, and mitigate risks, efforts toward self-regulation, national regulation, and international governance are deemed necessary.

To mitigate risks from improper AI use, the UN proposes principles to guide AI regulation. These include inclusivity to ensure fair access for all to AI's potential, essential for fostering sustainable solutions to global challenges. Moreover, AI systems should be governed with public interest in mind, aiming for broader involvement from civil society, software developers, and states, not just major tech companies. Data protection also requires a synergistic approach between privacy agreements and AI regulation to be considered adequate.

Additionally, the UN stresses its significant normative and institutional role in aligning AI governance with fundamental values, particularly those of the UN Charter. The organization uniquely assesses AI's impact across various sectors, including economic, social, health, and international security dimensions, evidenced by specialized agencies addressing AI's impact from education to arms control.

Similar regulatory needs have arisen within the Council of Europe, which focuses on AI's impact on the rights enshrined in the European Convention on Human Rights and its protocols. The Human Rights Commissioner of the Council of Europe has issued recommendations reflecting the positions of both the EU and UN, emphasizing the protection of fundamental rights and urging timely policy development and prioritization in national government agendas. These recommendations highlight that while soft law can ensure respect for rights, it should complement more binding public regulation. State authorities are encouraged to set up effective supervision mechanisms and democratic monitoring structures, potentially through independent oversight bodies.

The Council of Europe has established both an AI Committee (CIA) and an ad hoc Intergovernmental Committee on AI (CAHIA), with the latter tasked to develop a legally binding, cross-sectoral framework that respects human dignity, human rights, democracy, and the rule of law in all AI developments, regardless of whether the actor is public or private. However, recognizing the risk of fragmenting international order, CAHIA advises adopting such binding instruments only after careful consideration and when existing standards are deemed insufficient to protect individual rights within the AI context.

6 Italian Legislative Decree on Artificial Intelligence

Italy's legislative approach to artificial intelligence (AI) reflects a profound commitment to integrating technology with respect for human dignity and fundamental rights, as outlined in the government-approved legislative decree. The decree emphasizes promoting AI usage that is ethical, transparent, responsible, and anthropocentric, aiming to harness the technology's potential while safeguarding against economic, social, and fundamental rights risks.

The decree is particularly detailed in Article 3, which articulates the general principles that underpin the entire framework:

Research, experimentation, development, adoption, application, and use of AI systems and models occur in accordance with fundamental rights and freedoms established by the Constitution, EU law, and principles of transparency, proportionality, security, personal data protection, confidentiality, accuracy, non-discrimination, gender equality, and sustainability.

The development of AI systems and models relies on data and processes whose correctness, reliability, security, quality, appropriateness, and transparency must be guaranteed and monitored, adhering to proportionality principles relevant to the sectors they are employed in.

AI systems and models must be developed and applied respecting human autonomy and decision-making, damage prevention, understandability, explainability, and the principles stated in clause 1.

The use of AI systems should not compromise the democratic conduct of institutional and political life.

To ensure adherence to the rights and principles mentioned, cybersecurity throughout the lifecycle of AI systems and models is essential, adopting a proportional and risk-based approach and specific security controls to ensure their resilience against attempts to alter their use, expected behavior, performance, or security settings.

The law guarantees full access to AI systems and their functionalities or extensions for people with disabilities, on an equal basis and without any form of discrimination or prejudice, in accordance with the provisions of the United Nations Convention on the Rights of Persons with Disabilities.

These principles are reiterated with an emphasis on cyber security as a factual and now legal precondition for the lawful use of AI, meaning that without adequate cybersecurity, the use of AI could become practically illicit.

Moreover, Article 4 addresses the protection of personal data within AI applications, ensuring that AI usage in information processing respects media freedom, expression, and data integrity. The law also regulates minors' access to AI technologies, requiring parental consent for children under fourteen and allowing those over fourteen to consent under clear and understandable conditions.

The legislative framework highlights a redundant yet necessary reiteration of established principles to ensure clarity and adherence in practical applications. It's important to note that this legislative proposal, while detailed in expressing foundational principles, will require further detailed regulation through delegated decrees.

This approach not only reinforces Italy's dedication to aligning with European AI regulations like the AI Act but also sets a national standard that prioritizes human-centered values in the evolving digital landscape. The legislative decree awaits approval by the Chambers and the subsequent detailed implementation regulations, which will be critical to its practical effectiveness. This initiative is commendable for its principles and the manner in which they are articulated, offering interpretative parameters even before the full regulatory framework is established.

7 Conclusions

In concluding this exploration of artificial intelligence (AI) regulation, we see a complex interplay of frameworks and strategies unfolding across the European Union, Italy, and the wider international community. Each jurisdiction's approach to AI governance reflects a balancing act between fostering innovation and addressing the ethical, legal, and societal challenges posed by this transformative technology.

The European Union's proactive stance, embodied in the AI Act and the Data Act, sets a comprehensive regulatory benchmark that prioritizes human rights and safety while promoting technological advancement. This dual focus on safeguarding fundamental rights and enabling innovation positions the EU as a pivotal influence in global discussions on technology governance.

Italy's legislative decree on AI reinforces this commitment at a national level, aligning with EU directives while emphasizing the anthropocentric approach to technology deployment. The detailed articulation of principles within the Italian framework underscores the importance of transparency, security, and fundamental rights, ensuring that AI development supports societal well-being and democratic values.

Moreover, the global overview of AI policies reveals a diverse tapestry of approaches, with major players like the USA and China adopting contrasting strategies that reflect their domestic priorities and geopolitical aspirations. This divergence highlights the need for ongoing international dialogue to harmonize AI regulations and foster global cooperation in technology governance.

References

Consilium Europe. (2023, 27 November). Data act: Council adopts new law on fair access to and use of data. *Consilium Europa*. [Online]. Available: https://www.consilium.europa.eu/en/press/press-releases/2023/11/27/data-act-council-adopts-new-law-on-fair-access-to-and-use-of-data/

Cristianini, N. (2022). *La Scorciatoia. Come le macchine sono diventate intelligenti senza pensare in modo umano*. Il Mulino.

ENAC. (2021). *UAS-IT Regulation, Edition 1 of 4.1.2021.* [Online]. Available: https://www.enac.gov.it/la-normativa/normativa-enac/regolamenti/regolamenti-ad-hoc/regolamento-uas-it

European Commission. (2021, 21 April). *Communication from the Commission to the European Parliament, the Council, the European Economic and Social Committee and the Committee of the Regions – Fostering a European approach to artificial intelligence.* COM(2021) 205 final. [Online]. Available: https://eur-lex.europa.eu/legal-content/IT/TXT/?uri=COM%3A2021%3A205%3AFIN

European Commission. (2022a, 28 September). *Proposal for a Directive of the European Parliament and of the Council on adapting non-contractual civil liability rules to artificial intelligence.* COM(2022) 496 final. [Online]. Available: https://eur-lex.europa.eu/legal-content/IT/TXT/PDF/?uri=CELEX:52022PC0496&from=EN

European Commission. (2022b, 28 September). *Proposal for a Directive of the European Parliament and of the Council on liability for damage caused by defective products.* COM(2022) 495 final. [Online]. Available: https://eur-lex.europa.eu/legal-content/IT/TXT/?uri=CELEX%3A52022PC0495

European Commission. *Digital Markets Act: Ensuring fair and open digital markets.* [Online]. Available: https://www.europarl.europa.eu/pdfs/news/expert/2020/9/story/20200918STO87404/20200918STO87404_it.pdf

European Commission. *Europe's digital future.* [Online]. Available: https://digital-strategy.ec.europa.eu/en/policies/strategy-data

European Commission. *European data strategy.* [Online]. Available: https://commission.europa.eu/strategy-and-policy/priorities-2019-2024/europe-fit-digital-age/european-data-strategy_it

European Commission. *Press Release on Digital Services Act and Digital Markets Act proposals.* [Online]. Available: https://ec.europa.eu/commission/presscorner/detail/en/ip_23_3491

European Parliament and the Council of the European Union. (2022, 3 June). *Regolamento (UE) 2022/868 del Parlamento Europeo e del Consiglio del 30 maggio 2022 relativo alla governance europea dei dati e che modifica il regolamento (UE) 2018/1724 (Regolamento sulla governance dei dati).* Gazzetta Ufficiale dell'Unione Europea, L 152/1.

European Parliament and the Council of the European Union (2023, 22 December). Regulation (EU) 2023/2854 of the European Parliament and the Council of 13 December 2023 on harmonised rules on fair access to and use of data and amending Regulation (EU) 2017/2394 and Directive (EU) 2020/1828 (Data Regulation). *Official Journal of the European Union, Series L.*

European Parliament and the Council of the European Union. (2024). Regulation laying down harmonised rules on Artificial Intelligence (Artificial Intelligence Act) and amending certain Union legislative acts. *Official Journal of the European Union.* Final Draft. Available: https://www.europarl.europa.eu/doceo/document/TA-9-2024-0138-FNL-COR01_EN.pdf

Finocchiaro, G. (2024). *Intelligenza Artificiale: quali regole?* Il Mulino.

Exploring the Role of Artificial Intelligence in Accounting: An Academic and Practitioner Perspective

Paolo Biancone, Vahid Jafari-Sadeghi, Davide Calandra, and Federico Chmet

Abstract This chapter investigates the relationship between artificial intelligence (AI) and accounting using academics' and practitioners' perspectives to understand how this new technology can modify accountants' working activities. The chapter adopts a content and thematic analysis of 259 academic sources extracted from the Scopus database and 157 practitioners' sources retrieved from Business Source Ultimate. The academics' and practitioners' debate highlights some initial results. First, the exploration reveals practical examples of AI implementation for accounting, financial reporting, and auditing. Second, the analysis shows trading zones of knowledge between enthusiastic practitioners' literature and less confident academic literature. Third, our research discovers a stream of literature between the information systems theory and management analysis that looks at the new data economy. Regarding implications, the authors aim to connect academics' and practitioners' views by understanding new potential innovations for working for accountants and auditors. This contribution is novel because it investigates the issues arising from the relationship between AI and accounting with a broad spectrum (including auditing and accountability fields) by examining original practitioners' sources. This can enhance our knowledge-creating bridges between academics and practitioners for building the CPAs (i.e., certified public accountants) and CIAs (i.e., certified internal auditors) of the future.

P. Biancone · D. Calandra (✉) · F. Chmet
Department of Management, University of Turin, Turin, Italy
e-mail: paolo.biancone@unito.it; davide.calandra@unito.it; federico.chmet@unito.it

V. Jafari-Sadeghi
Aston Business School, Aston University, Birmingham, UK
e-mail: v.jafari-sadeghi@aston.ac.uk

G. R. Marseglia et al. (eds.), *Socio-economic Impact of Artificial Intelligence*, Progress in IS, https://doi.org/10.1007/978-3-031-73514-1_6

1 Introduction

Artificial intelligence (AI) is considered one of the most disruptive digital technologies with multi-stakeholder applications (Shaffer et al., 2020). Interest in its applicability, impacts, and limitations has grown among academics and practitioners (Zemánková, 2019). Interest in the technology stems from a lack of study of business experience related to the introduction of new artificial algorithms (Garousi Mokhtarzadeh et al., 2020; Mohammed Al-Sayyed et al., 2021; Sutton et al., 2016). In technical terms, artificial intelligence arises as a branch of computer science that allows the formulation of increasingly sophisticated algorithms and the programming and design of hardware and software systems. This will enable computers to perform actions typically performed by humans (Agrawal et al., 2019).

Artificial intelligence is also under consideration by professionals. For example, according to Davenport and Ronanki (2018), AI can support companies in automating business processes, acquiring new information and analysing it, and improving the interaction between customers and employees. Although considered to be generic, these first application cases explain how AI can support numerous sectors, from accounting to information transparency, logistics, and healthcare (Secinaro et al., 2021b). Other experiences see some application problems. For instance, according to the Economist (2020), compared to the initial enthusiasm about the use of AI, an understanding of its limitations is increasingly beginning to emerge. Thus, while interest and positive voices are emerging, there is a shortage of critical voices that symbolise the lack of common ground for knowledge and research exchange areas (Romme et al., 2015).

Even in the field of accounting, AI is not exempt from the interest of academics and practitioners. For instance, according to Shaffer et al. (2020), AI may have an impact in terms of professional reorganisation by promoting new ways of accounting for suppliers/customers, new methods of auditing and risk management, new opportunities to manage inventories, and new methods of financial reporting and communication with tax administrations. While we see constructive voices, there are emerging concerns about the downsides of AI technology on business activities. According to Shi (2020), while promoting the development of new opportunities, technology could also affect unemployment.

These theoretical and practical assumptions show us how the topic is still controversial today. Although AI is deemed to promote the way accountants and auditors work, it is not yet clear how aware they are of this (Dahlin, 2019; Gulin et al., 2019; Quattrone, 2016). Despite these initial premises and thoughts, the literature to date identifies few real cases and primarily reports both positive and negative experiences (Azudin & Mansor, 2018; Huang, 2018; Sutton et al., 2016). This lack is due to knowledge trading zones between the scientific literature and practitioners (Romme et al., 2015; Secinaro et al., 2021d).

To address our research aim, we will use multiple data sources. We will use the Scopus database for the academic part, one of the most adopted in business, management, and accounting (Mongeon & Paul-Hus, 2016). And the NexisUni platform, which includes business documents and reports, will be used to select the results of practitioners (Massaro et al., 2021). Operationally, the analysis was conducted using the R-Studio software and the Bibliometrix R-Package for the academic part (Aria & Cuccurullo, 2017). In addition, Leximancer software was used for thematic analysis of the topics under discussion (Smith & Humphreys, 2006). Combining two methodologies and two software will allow for more robust results and relationships between concepts (such as "artificial intelligence" and "accounting", "auditing" and "accountability") (Aria & Cuccurullo, 2017; Smith & Humphreys, 2006).

The academic analysis returned 259 peer-reviewed scientific articles. In contrast, within the professional domain, Business Source Ultimate (BSU) returned 155,498 results. This required the researchers to apply additional limitations to the survey by only including sources in which the terms "*artificial intelligence*" and "accounting" or "*auditing*" or "*accountability*" were within five terms of each other to ensure better relevance and relevancy of the source (Massaro et al., 2016). With the exclusion of scientific journals already investigated in Scopus and a rigorous analysis of titles and abstracts, this strategy returned 157 results. This number of exclusions is motivated by the need to make the study scientifically consistent, not considering all the results irrelevant to the research question.

The first results recall several research themes. First the exploration of artificial intelligence solutions for accounting, financial reporting, and auditing. Among them, professionals glimpse a combination of intelligent solutions for accounting management; in contrast, academics appear to have less confidence (Fig. 1) (Mohammed Al-Sayyed et al., 2021). Second, let's discover some practical applications for automated financial statement construction and subsequent statutory audit (Mancini et al., 2017). Third, we discover how even in accounting, there is a stream of research somewhere between information systems theory and management analysis that looks at the new data economy (Ballou et al., 2018). Finally, the analysis is intended to feed the debate among academics and practitioners about the use of AI in accounting. One of the open questions relates to opportunities for collaboration among researchers, practitioners, and graduate students in the realisation that digitisation can only be managed with multiple research approaches. This will enable the highlighting of new opportunities for strategic consulting (as covered by practitioners), shedding light on the issues of technology (as defined by academics).

2 Literature Review

2.1 *Artificial Intelligence and Accounting: A Broad Perspective*

Artificial intelligence traces its origins back to 1942 in Isaac Asimov's science fantasy stories (Asimov, 1989). With witty scientific resourcefulness, the author described the development of robots capable of obeying human orders and performing operations typical of the human mind without causing conflict. This essay has inspired future generations of scientists to arrive at its current definition. Today, with AI, we refer to systems capable of simulating autonomous learning and adaptive capabilities inspired

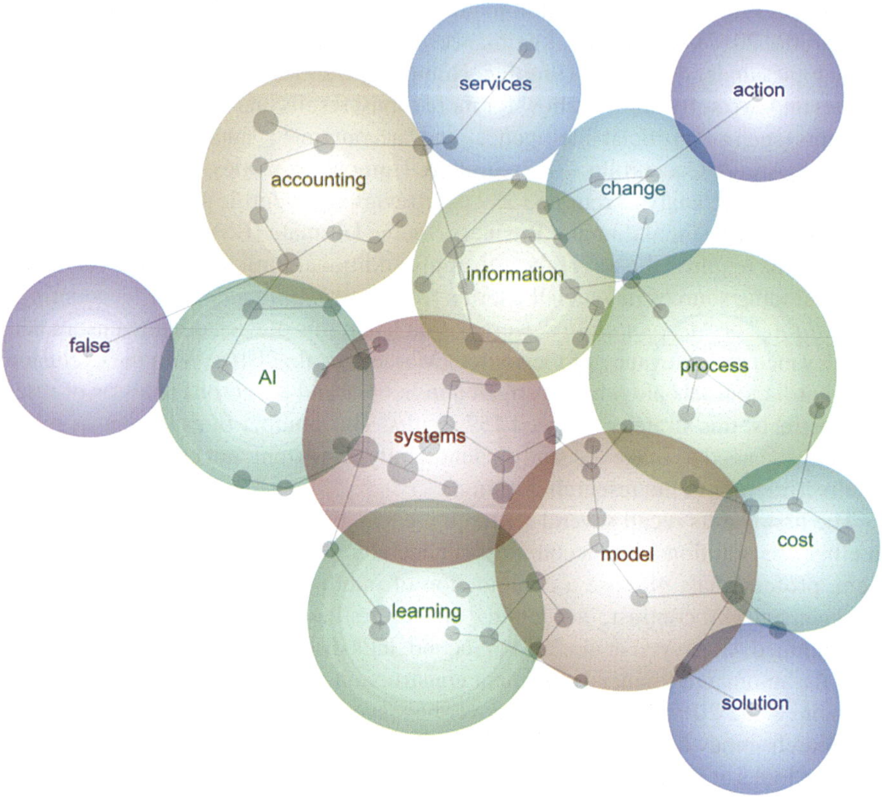

Fig. 1 Main themes under discussion – Academics' side. (Source: Authors' elaboration)

by human decision-making models (Haenlein & Kaplan, 2019). Although it is a complex technology, the essence of AI is very simple. The aim is to develop software systems and machines capable of solving problems without knowing what they are doing (weak AI) and to study more complex mechanisms capable of replicating human intelligence (Fjelland, 2020; Secinaro et al., 2021b). Therefore, AI is today one of the research topics studying the programming and design of systems aimed at endowing machines currently in use with one or more human characteristics.

This opens up countless interdisciplinary applications. For instance, AI is used in the medical sector (Agrawal et al., 2019), in the supply chain (Toorajipour et al., 2021), and, more generally, in numerous areas of business and management (Haefner et al., 2021). Interest and progress in AI applications have also increased in accounting due to the computational capacity of computers and the increase in digital data, which can be collected and used (Shi, 2020). In recent years, the literature has begun to link AI to the accounting field, including auditing and accountability, with an interdisciplinary view (Dumay et al., 2018; Secinaro et al., 2021c). In this regard, according to Shaffer et al. (2020), the most relevant development opportunities concern the areas of accounting records (suppliers/revenues), audit and risk management, inventory management, and personnel management. However, the transformation triggered could lead to a much more extensive change in the management of financial and non-financial information (Zhang et al., 2020). Askary et al. (2018) recall how the preparation of accounting information is a relevant process in the accounting profession, which is highly dependent on the robustness of internal controls. Therefore, these authors emphasise how AI can be used to automate the removal of weaknesses within the system of corporate management.

Similarly, other previous studies extend the impacts of AI by focusing on the change in the accounting profession and the necessary skills. Zemánková (2019) and Dal Mas et al. (2021) recall how smart technologies require permanent training mechanisms. However, scaling AI applications in accounting also involves verifying additional conditions. First is the need to have a network of actors capable of using new IT systems and applications (Hee Lee & Yoon, 2021). This can be useful in understanding how social effects are generated following the introduction of new phenomena and the use of new technologies (Secinaro et al., 2021a). Second, the development of new technologies promotes forms of hybridisation between different disciplines (Marangunić & Granić, 2015). This hypothesis is stronger in a context such as accounting, which is based on its own rules and practical theories acquired over time (Frank et al., 2001). However, according to Zhang et al. (2020), radical changes in the accounting profession open up new challenges for accepting new technologies by accountants, auditors, and accountancy educators. Third, as managerial accounting is regulated, it is necessary to verify that the technology respects the regulatory statements (Fischer et al., 2010; Kocsis, 2019). Accordingly, the union of artificial intelligence and accounting still needs to be investigated in depth to scientifically identify the applications and implications of the technology on the accounting professions' operational, social, and regulatory aspects.

2.2 Building the Research Question Between Academic and Practitioner Perspectives

The interest in new technologies in accounting is manifested by the increasing number of publications in recent years (Marrone & Hazelton, 2019; Secinaro et al., 2021c). However, accounting professionals' change in work routines requires, first, specific training at a global level, integrating new ways, such as accounting or preparing financial statements (Lee & Tajudeen, 2020). Therefore, it is necessary to design new AI solutions that comply with the requirements of the key players (i.e., accounting and tax regulations) and ensure that the users accept the process change. Despite these constructive premises, scholars struggle to find practical cases and inspiration for their research (Azudin & Mansor, 2018; Sutton et al., 2016). According to Romme et al. (2015), the gap stems from ongoing knowledge issues in new and unexplored research areas. Therefore, a gap may exist between what academics are studying and promoting at a theoretical level and what practitioners expect. To this end, recent studies demonstrate the strength of collaborations between academics and practitioners (Amabile et al., 2017; Massaro et al., 2018, 2021) in overcoming research problems that are evident today and increasing mutual knowledge of a particular field of interest.

Based on these premises, our research intends to shed light on what academics think about artificial intelligence in accounting and what practitioners expect from their work by mapping existing case studies. Based on these considerations, the chapter will analyse multiple document sources from academics and practitioners to harmonise new forms of dialogue and discussion. Therefore, the study will have a research question (RQ) "*How is artificial intelligence changing accounting professions from the perspective of academics and practitioners?*"

3 Methodology

To address the research objective, this chapter uses thematic content analysis. According to Krippendorff (2013) (p. 34), this methodology is a research technique for making replicable and validated inferences from sources found by researchers based on the research topic under discussion. Although born for the study of written texts, the analysis has evolved, considering audio and video contents (Krippendorff, 2013; Secinaro et al., 2020). Today, it is one of the most used analysis techniques by researchers as it allows a detailed investigation of specific research streams (Hsieh & Shannon, 2005). The possibility of using computerised data analysis tools has allowed a critical evolution of the method. Researchers can now analyse large amounts of data, classifying and using multiple sources of information.

Thematic content analysis is widely used in different research streams to highlight specific literature trends and themes (Amini et al., 2018; Landrum & Ohsowski, 2018; Massaro et al., 2021; Secinaro et al., 2021d). In addition to the precedents, for example, Bhatt et al. (2020) have used this methodology to develop the intellectual structure of the literature on sustainable production. Then Sihvonen and Partanen (2017) use exploratory content analysis to examine how ICT companies report information related to the circular economy. Furthermore, as Hsieh and Shannon (2005) indicated, thematic content analysis could be conventional, direct, and additive. The researchers derived the coding categories from the text in the conventional one. Researchers use a relevant theory or findings to guide the initial coding activity in the direct approach. Finally, in the additive process, the keywords under consideration are counted and compared following interpretation of the underlying context.

3.1 Data Collection

The analysis used multiple data sources. For the academic part, the Scopus database was used as it is one of the most adopted by researchers due to the most comprehensive range of search keywords in business, management, and accounting (Baima et al.,

2020; Falagas et al., 2008; Secinaro et al., 2021c). To select the most appropriate sources, we proceeded through an analysis of keywords such as "*artificial intelligence*" and "*accounting*" or "*auditing*" or "*accountability*". The selection of keywords was made by benefiting from the critical study conducted by Dumay et al. (2018), published in the *Accounting, Auditing and Accountability Journal*, and applied by Secinaro et al. (2021c). According to the study, scientific production on accounting has extended its interest to auditing and reporting as interrelated activities over the years.

Moreover, such specific keywords are not unintentional but respond to a clear research choice (Kumar et al., 2022; Uluyol et al., 2021). According to Chen and Xiao (2016), keywords can be selected according to different strategies. First, start from a literature stream by identifying a broad search domain. In the subject case, it could be "*artificial intelligence*". Second, researchers may want to investigate more specific search domains by adopting, therefore, lower analysis to search streams, as in this case for accounting, budgeting, and reporting. For all these premises, this study adopts the second technique.

The analysis also includes some research limitations of topic, language, and period. For example, the researchers selected sources written in English in business, management, and accounting. Furthermore, as Massaro et al. (2016) specified, the study does not apply journal ranking and source limitations. This fast-growing research topic is not fully formed but is constantly evolving. Finally, the analysis was carried out without time restrictions on entry and considering 2021 as the final and complete deadline. This strategy allows us to obtain complete bibliographic sources within a full year of publication (Patel et al., 2022). The keyword analysis allowed the researchers to get 259 previously analysed documents. Then the Business Source Ultimate (BSU) database was used to collect the practitioners' papers, including professional content in business and blogs (Liu, 2019). Krippendorff (2013) specified that articles were selected following a random search process and relevance to the investigated topic by checking the title and abstract. Due to the large amount of data retrieved (*the primary analysis returned 155,951 results*), it was decided to limit the survey by only including sources where the terms "*artificial intelligence*" and "*accounting*" or "*auditing*" or "*accountability*" were within five terms of each other to ensure better relevance and relevancy of the source (Massaro et al., 2016). This strategy, combined with excluding scientific journals already investigated in Scopus and a close analysis of titles and abstracts, returned 157 results. This number of exclusions is motivated by the need to make the analysis rigorous to dilute the results with topics not relevant to the research objective. Table 1 summarises the number of scientific and practical papers extracted for our study.

3.2 Data Analysis

The analysis of the results was carried out using the software Leximancer. This software can perform an automatic search content analysis and extract concepts based on a dictionary of textual data (Smith & Humphreys, 2006) and has also been

Table 1 Number of academic papers and academics sources

Year	Number of scientific papers	%	Number of practitioners sources	%
1984	1	0.39	–	0.00
1986	2	0.77	–	0.00
1989	1	0.39	–	0.00
1990	1	0.39	–	0.00
1991	1	0.39	–	0.00
1992	2	0.77	–	0.00
1993	0	0.00	1	0.63
1994	2	0.77	–	0.00
1995	2	0.77	–	0.00
1996	3	1.16	–	0.00
1997	1	0.39	–	0.00
1998	1	0.39	–	0.00
1999	1	0.39	–	0.00
2000	4	1.54	–	0.00
2001	1	0.39	–	0.00
2002	2	0.77	–	0.00
2004	1	0.39	–	0.00
2005	3	1.16	–	0.00
2006	1	0.39	–	0.00
2007	2	0.77	–	0.00
2009	7	2.70	–	0.00
2010	4	1.54	–	0.00
2011	44	16.99	–	0.00
2012	2	0.77	–	0.00
2013	4	1.54	–	0.00
2014	1	0.39	–	0.00
2015	2	1.16	1	0.63
2016	6	2.32	1	0.63
2017	9	3.47	15	9.55
2018	12	4.63	24	15.28
2019	25	9.65	24	15.28
2020	51	19.69	18	11.46
2021	59	22.78	73	46.49
Total	**259**	**100**	**157**	**100**

Source: Authors' elaboration

used in several studies published in leading international journals (Secinaro et al., 2021d). Furthermore, the software is a "method for transforming lexical co-occurrence information from natural language into semantic patterns in an unsupervised manner". Furthermore, it "*employs two stages of extracting co-occurrence information – semantic and relational – using a different algorithm for each stage*" (Smith & Humphreys, 2006). Therefore, using Leximancer, it was possible to obtain relationships between concepts (e.g., "*artificial intelligence*" and "*accounting*"). Using its technical features, it was possible to open and read each extracted document and encode the content using an in vivo approach (Miles et al., 2014). Using this two-step process, it was possible to compare results from both practical and academic-scientific sources.

4 Results

4.1 Academic's Vision

This section aims to explain the themes that academics consider relevant to the discussion and applications that AI is progressively having in accounting, budgeting, auditing, and reporting (Fig. 1). We note how, while on the one hand, themes such as "*accounting*" and "*AI*" appear in the research carried out, on the other hand, key concepts emerge that refer to the potential of the technology, such as "*new business models*", "*services*" and "*solutions*", and "*fraud reduction*". In addition, the figure reaffirms critical words such as "*education*", recalls a possible "*change*" in the strand studied, and, finally, looks at new ways of managing study information systems.

The above figure shows multiple themes concerning professionals and is more broadly reflected in Table 2. At the top are the "driving" concepts of the research area. These include automatic accounting and changes in terms of work. Despite appreciation towards technology, Korhonen et al. (2021), through a case study, discuss the division of automated accounting tasks between humans and digital tools. The concept of "non-programmable tasks" emerges as a cornerstone of managerial and financial accounting theory (Shen et al., 2011) and is dependent on external variables such as customer invoices. Also, around accounting, the qualitative analysis returns a debate on the future of the accounting profession regarding first billing and first note operations. As Lee and Tajudeen (2020) discussed, intelligent automation induces changes in activities and significantly reduces the most repetitive ones by changing long-standing human patterns and automatisms. Therefore, AI is not necessarily technology that can cause task reduction but promotes supervised learning and transforms accountants' figures into cutting-edge figures who can contribute with data analysis to their client companies (Moll & Yigitbasioglu, 2019).

While there are more negative sentiments at the academic level, the discussion is different for statutory audits. Indeed, academics discuss real-life applications and information and document extraction cases by the "Big Four" consulting firms. Rather uniquely, PwC, KPMG, EY, and Deloitte test and deploy intelligent data collection and validation algorithms in the statutory audit phases. Especially in the case of Deloitte, it is highlighted how, through the exploitation of advanced learning techniques, the technology can simplify the search for information, the so-called *asseverations* by establishing an automatic dialogue with clients (Zemánková, 2019). This step coincides with the currently most advanced techniques of Natural

Table 2 AI and accounting, budgeting, auditing, and reporting in academics' sources

Macro-topics	Application	Case studies	Extract
Accounting	Automatic accounting	TechCo's	The case study shows how actors divide tasks between human accountants and digital tools, and, thus, our article contributes to the recent literature on digitisation in accounting management. The article was able to examine a fundamental process of automating accounting tasks. Surprisingly, accounting tasks remained more suitable for humans than machines during this development process because they were initially thought to be programmable. More importantly, human credibility was essential in finding the new proactive approach where a human specialist approved each billing case. We show that professionals can interpret non-programmable work tasks and skills as executable and try to automate them (probably with little chance of success). However, only identifying the possibilities of automating accounting-related work can lead to efficiency gains from automation (Korhonen et al., 2021)
	Employment	–	Sutton et al. (2016) and Sun and Medaglia (2019) noted that the application of AI in the accounting domain poses a threat to the profession. Based on these findings, it can be inferred that many of the studies had expressed the same concern, namely that the adoption of AI would lead to job losses. It seemed evident that AI can replace humans performing repetitive and structured tasks. However, not all studies agreed. Some brought the mixed implications of AI adoption (Chukwudi et al., 2018). Some past studies (Sun & Medaglia, 2019; Sutton et al., 2016) highlighted the negative impact of AI adoption instead of the positive impact. The reason is that there is a lack of literature that focuses on the impact of AI adoption within the accounting industry (Lee & Tajudeen, 2020)
		–	In addition, many advanced AI applications require supervised learning; accountants may be well-positioned to ensure that the data used in these cutting-edge developments are fit for purpose and that human information processing limitations are considered in the volume of data produced. To contribute effectively to organisations embracing AI, accountants will need to be increasingly vigilant and critical; they will need to question the insights and suggestions provided by these new technologies and be cautious (Moll & Yigitbasioglu, 2019)

Auditing	Extracting information from contracts and documents	PwC (GL.ai)	For auditing purposes, AI can find anomalies in accounting data. Deep learning, an essential sub-concept of AI (Jordan & Mitchell, 2015), is used by the "Big Four" for data collection and validation. For example, PwC's GL.ai software extracts accounting-relevant information from documents (such as contracts) linking stakeholders and makes it available to auditors (Tiberius & Hirth, 2019)
		KPMG (Clara)	In practice, large accounting firms are adopting AI in their audit services. KPMG is channelling cognitive and predictive technologies into its audit platform, Clara (KPMG, 2018). KPMG has also worked with IBM Watson to develop cognitive automation tools for auditors (Zhang et al., 2020)
		EY	EY is using AI to extract information from documents containing unstructured data (e.g., contracts, invoices, and images) to obtain audit evidence (Zhang et al., 2020)
		Deloitte (Argus)	Deloitte has created a cognitive application called Argus specifically designed for auditing. This application "learns from human interactions and leverages advanced machine learning techniques and natural language processing to automatically identify and extract key accounting information from any type of electronic document" (Zemánková, 2019)
		–	Another interesting perspective on intelligent audit procedures is Audit Data Analytics (ADA). As with the blockchain itself, ADA has evolved through various stages. ADA 1.0 is represented by trends or ratio analysis, ADA 2.0 introduced machine learning algorithms and models. ADA 3.0 is associated with smart audit procedures and smart contracts (Zemánková, 2019)
		IBM Watson	Deep learning supports review decision-making at all stages of review, including planning, internal control assessment, substantive testing, and completion. Moreover, deep learning is superior to traditional thesis analysis techniques due to the depth of hidden layers in deep neural networks and unsupervised feature extraction. To implement this technology, the reviewer can directly use pre-developed deep learning models such as IBM Watson's Natural Language Understanding to obtain features from the text data (Sun Rutgers & Vasarhelyi, 2018)

(continued)

Table 2 (continued)

Macro-topics	Application	Case studies	Extract
Business model	New activities for accountants	–	Contemporary economists have defined digitisation as the realignment of, or new investment in, advanced technologies and business models to engage digital customers more effectively, which presents an open challenge to financial management (Mosteanu & Faccia, 2020)
Training	Human-machine collaboration	–	A strong focus on human and social factors in the transformation towards AI-based management accounting seems both timely and appropriate. On the one hand, it is undoubtedly urgent from a practical point of view as technological advances will inevitably have a substantial impact on the existing roles, duties, and corresponding competencies of workers, managers, and report recipients in the accounting profession (Pamela Neely & Cook, 2011), as well as on stakeholders in general. On the other hand, in theory, we need to identify ethical challenges to arrive at normative agreements on what we want such collaboration to look like (Losbichler & Lehner, 2021)
	New skills	–	Using various AI methodologies, such as advanced text analysis, these procedures will be replaced by automated AI analyses that will likely produce more accurate and efficient results. Another aspect that AI may affect is the training provided to new forensic auditors. Some of the skill sets developed today will become inefficient in the AI era. Training to perform sampling techniques, for example, will give way to learning various AI methodologies. Accounting curricula will have to be adapted to accommodate the new requirements of the future auditor. Accounting firms will hire more data scientists to train auditors to leverage AI more efficiently and effectively (Issa et al., 2016)
		–	New personnel management practices reward digital skills. Recruiting new candidates with digital skills has also led audit firms to develop their recruitment practices: "We are not used to recruiting this kind of profile, so we had to update our talent management mindset and think about reaching this particular group of people" (Partner, Audit 1). As audit firms were not well-known among engineers and data scientists, they had to create new employer branding strategies (Pemer, 2020)
		–	This study aims to substantiate the benefits of acquiring AI-based accounting software. In addition, vendors can work with educational institutions to introduce AI software learning. This could be added as one of the course programmes in universities to prepare the younger generation to enter the workforce with practical skills in using AI-based accounting software to support business operations (Lee & Tajudeen, 2020)

Source: Authors' elaboration

Language Understanding, which allow algorithms to understand human behaviour, replicate actions and requests with natural language, and subsequently perform analysis of contracts, invoices, and tax documents (Sun Rutgers & Vasarhelyi, 2018). Therefore, according to Zemánková (2019), the use of algorithms in auditing can lead to new procedures and open to Audit Data Analytics (ADA) scenarios, which start with the analysis of relationships and iterations with clients, flow into machine learning, and end with the procedures of investigation and returning the results to the auditors for its validation.

A further concept arising from this is the evolution of the business model we are used to today for accounting and auditing firms. According to Mosteanu and Faccia (2020), there is an increasing link between digitisation and new financial management activities, including professionals. Therefore, according to Behrens and Steinbart (1992), the more automatisms enter accounting records, the more advanced control systems professionals will need. This will lead in the medium/long term to a change in activities by increasing the time available for consultancy services, management control activities, business development, and risk management in client companies. Therefore, accountants will benefit from solving three general problems:

1. Supporting decision-making by providing better and cost-effective data to companies.
2. Providing a more profound analysis of data and provide new information about the business.
3. Focussing on more value-added tasks after freeing up working time through artificial intelligence applications.

The application of AI is subject to specific training actions. In particular, the issue of human and social factors in the transformation of management accounting emerges. As Pamela Neely and Cook (2011) stated in their published research agenda, the accounting profession relies on repetitive solid actions based on a "conceptual" basis. Technological advances are likely to substantially impact the roles of accountants and auditors for duties and soft skills. Therefore, professionals may require new skills, especially in analysing and controlling transactions performed.

On this theme, Qasim and Kharbat (2020) pose an interesting question regarding updating the future curricula of professionals, which will include arguments related to accounting, double-entry bookkeeping, and the rules of preparation of financial statements and their audit and data management. Furthermore, at the level of large audit firms, practical and applied cases of recruitment of staff with digital skills and knowledge of financial statements and audit issues emerge (Pemer, 2020). Finally, the thematic analysis uncovered a new model that combines training and promotion of university activities typically applied in private universities and abroad in Anglo-Saxon markets, which allows technology providers to work alongside academic institutions to prepare younger generations theoretically and operationally for the use of advanced accounting software based on artificial intelligence (Bercovitz & Feldman, 2005; Lee & Tajudeen, 2020).

4.2 Practitioners' Vision of AI

As stated in an interview with the president of the American Accountants Association, "*Technology and related issues are at the forefront of accountants' minds. Many experts in the field cite a wide range of implications for accountants today and in the future and the dangers posed by automation, such as the opportunity for hackers to use our data. However, the issue of technology is reaching across the profession and impacting human capital, marketing, business development, corporate management, customer service and regulation*" (Hood, 2017).

Based on these premises, this section aims to voice the issues that practitioners feel are relevant within the discussion and applications that intelligence is progressively having and may have in accounting, budgeting, auditing, and reporting. Using a co-occurrence approach, it was possible to identify the key concepts discussed by accountants, auditors, and managers of strategic consulting firms. As shown in Fig. 2, the themes are related to different ideas. We notice how the topics under study, such as "*accounting*" and "*AI*", are connected to "*data*", "*services*", "*value for business clients*", and "*accuracy*", creating scientific multi-disciplinarity and making evolve activities such as accounting, accounting, accounting services, etc.

Within the first theme emerges the exploration of artificial intelligence solutions for accounting, financial reporting, and auditing. Among them, practitioners glimpse a combination of intelligent solutions for accounting management. Using thematic analysis, multiple case studies were uncovered which see among the applications of AI:

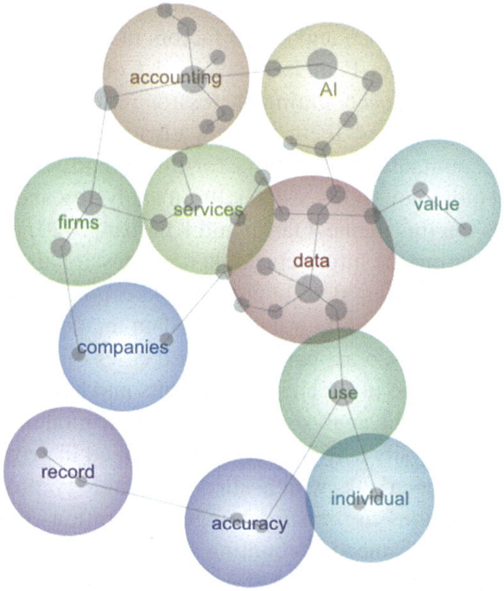

Fig. 2 Main themes under discussion – Practitioners' side. (Source: Authors' elaboration)

1. Automatic accounting aims to use advanced software with continuous learning of new accounting ledgers, avoiding the manual entry of new debit/accounting lines by approving and setting up advanced workflows and synchronising accounting information (Arrowsmith, 2021a).
2. After the automatic learning of accounting ledgers, continuous accounting aims to reduce human intervention in recording invoices (both incoming and outgoing) by integrating double-entry bookkeeping operations. This is possible as indicated by The Lab Consulting (2018) using *Robotic Process Automation* (RPA), which allows, once a series of repetitive actions are identified, to simulate human intervention at any time of the day. A case study identified by professionals is "*Intelligence-Based Billing*, " a software with intelligent automation divided into billing, collections, payments, and internal business analysis modules.
3. The construction of financial statement formats and their subsequent automated audit (AuditFile, Auvenir, and OnPoint AnalyticsAI) limit the amount of data exchange between different stakeholders (Arrowsmith, 2021a; Hood, 2017).

"*Services*" and "*companies*" as words constitute the third topic of discussion, with professionals focusing on finding new sources of business from simplifying repetitive operations by linking new work efficiency initiatives to new activities. Finally, "*value*" is mentioned as a potential in terms of training for the accountants and auditors of the future. As suggested by Hood (2017), accountants are evolving, introducing the need to have new generations open to the new digital economy and accounting.

The attention of practitioners to AI issues shows how the concept of "*data*" represents a disruptive element concerning a decentralised and un-automated accounting and auditing model. The results show how AI applications can increase client companies' prospective data analysis and improve accounting and auditing collaboratively. Indeed, as indicated by Ross Hampton, a developer at CaseWare who is working on collaborative accounting, "*There is a new wave of accounting firms out there that are ahead of the curve and are shifting the way they think and work across their engagements*". "*They know they can be more efficient in the cloud and, at the same time, work more productively on behalf of their clients, but until now, they didn't have the tools to do that. We've reimagined the way they work and think, consolidating processes into a single workflow, providing unprecedented efficiency levels and enabling them to do more with less, while maintaining quality assurance and compliance*" (Arrowsmith, 2019b).

The same view is shared by Arrowsmith (2021b), which clarifies the role of data and gives voice to some concerns. According to those who view AI with more insecurity, accounting is an art that remains within the business asset and liability cycle with all its peculiarities and distinctions related to the client and the case. This approach is even more widespread if we look exclusively at the audit environment. It turns out that some practitioners are not interested in speeding up audit processes that require experience and emotional (not artificial) intelligence, as Samantha Bowling of the American Association of Certified Public Accountants stated (Arrowsmith, 2021b). While no opposing arguments can be discovered on the accounting side, over-automation may lose sight of the client and the opportunities for one-to-one analysis in the auditing area.

Table 3 summarises the key topics, the companies discussed, and the complete statements partly used in the text.

Table 3 Artificial intelligence and accounting, budgeting, auditing and reporting in practitioners' sources

Macro-topics	Application	Case studies	Extract
Accounting	Automatic accounting entry	Roger.AI	RogerAI is a startup that produces artificial intelligence-driven automation software for small businesses. "This acquisition provides us with a modern cloud-based invoice payment platform that will immediately open up cross-selling opportunities across our global SME base", said Ron Clarke, President and CEO of Fleetcor, in a statement. Roger.Ai is designed to help small and medium-sized businesses collect and scan invoices and receipts, eliminate manual data entry using machine learning technology, approve and execute payments, set up automated workflows, and sync with accounting systems such as QuickBooks Online, Sage Intacct, Xero, and others in real time (Arrowsmith, 2021a)
	Continuous accounting using robotic process automation (RPA)	–	Automation through robotic processes (RPA) is presented from continuous accounting with reduced human intervention. From the accountants' side, this allows for improved efficiency and increased accuracy at a lower cost, freeing up repetitive tasks to focus on strategy, analysis, and decision-making tasks (The Lab Consulting, 2018)
		Intelligence-based billing	Intelligence-Based Billing consists of four modules (which can be purchased separately)—managing billing, collections, payments, and internal analysis. The platform automates the billing process to send invoices promptly and also learns a customer's payment habits over time (Arrowsmith, 2020)
	Automatic classification in financial statements	AuditFile	Another example is AuditFile. Among the many features of the cloud-based audit software is an AI technique which automates loading a client's trial balance into the audit system by reinforcing the importance of data and its accuracy in the accounting valuation process
			"*We have built an algorithm that can automatically classify the trial balance. It saves a lot of time, even weeks, on an audit for our clients. So, we believe that in the next five years, it will be possible to make the audit faster and allow auditors to do their job with less risk*", said Steven Bong, CEO of AuditFile (Arrowsmith, 2019a)
	Multiple actors	–	More intelligent systems enable radically different approaches to this ultimate objective and the kinds of fundamental business problems the profession aims to solve. Investors need to gain confidence and trust in companies' financial results; companies and governments need to ensure the correct levels of tax are paid; management needs to decide how to spend organisational resources and be held accountable for those decisions. Solving these fundamental problems is essential for companies and economies to succeed and is at the heart of the accountancy profession

Audit	Automation in the analysis of financial statements data	Auvenir platform	The review automation software, which is currently in beta among several companies in Canada, leverages cloud-based storage, machine learning, and artificial intelligence to transform the review process. It also employs data analytics, allowing reviewers to extract more significant and deeper insights into the data and an intuitive user interface. "*In the Auvenir platform, we are using powerful automation to standardise data from client records to job cards seamlessly*", said Auvenir CEO Pete Myers
			Myers believes that technology, such as AI, can improve and transform the review process by automating mundane tasks and freeing reviewers to invest more time in high-level, high-value jobs. Myers cautions, however, that AI is "not a magic bullet" and must be part of a holistic solution. "Automating those routine tasks and focusing on extracting, assembling, and documenting evidence allows the auditor to focus on complex areas such as estimates and management judgements. We constantly hear that auditors value the client relationship aspect above all else. This platform allows the auditor to spend more time on that relationship, providing high quality and value, and building the trust critical to the audit process", said Myers (Alexander, 2020)
		OnPoint Analytics AI	OnPoint AnalyticsAI automates data capture and uses artificial intelligence to identify anomalies and risks across entire datasets, driving powerful insights for auditors. Multiple tests can be run automatically on transactions, and the type of test can be configured based on the kind of review (Arrowsmith, 2020)
	Human contact and data analysis	–	Justin Adams, whose firm Anduin has just launched an AI-enabled account receivable platform, insists that there is an "art" to billing that must remain in the AR process for it to be meaningful and profitable; deep knowledge of a client over time, for example, can influence a billing report. And Samantha Bowling of Garbelman Winslow CPAs isn't simply interested in speeding up the review with AI—she wants to provide a review of such high quality that it's indisputable. These service goals can only be achieved by marrying AI with the human professional, with all the experience, scepticism, and emotional intelligence (Arrowsmith, 2021b)
Training	Connected technologies and sharing	CaseWare	CaseWare International has introduced a collaborative cloud accounting software product called CaseWare ReviewCompTax, which incorporates artificial intelligence and consolidates multiple engagement processes. "*There is a new wave of accounting firms out there that are ahead of the curve and are shifting the way they think and work through their engagements*", said Ross Hampton, CaseWare's head of business development for the Americas, in a statement. "*They know they can be more efficient in the cloud and, at the same time, work more productively on behalf of their customers, but until now, they didn't have the tools to do that. We've reimagined the way they work and think, consolidating processes into a single workflow, providing unprecedented efficiency, levelling them to do more with less, while maintaining quality assurance and compliance*" (Arrowsmith, 2019b)

Source: Authors' elaboration

5 Discussion

Analysis of the academic and practitioner perspectives revealed some common findings and some differences. The following sub-sections aim to illustrate the implications of the data analysis.

5.1 Implication 1. New Perspectives on Actor-Network Theory (ANT) in Accounting

AI practitioners' findings demonstrate the need for collaborative cloud environments between stakeholders such as practitioners and regulators. As the "CaseWare ReviewCompTax" case shows, the provision of collaborative solutions combined with the creation of algorithms for accounting and auditing requires coordination between multiple actors and nodes. On a theoretical level, this assumption can be framed through the lens of Actor-Network Theory (ANT) (Justesen & Mouritsen, 2011). According to the authors, research is witnessing accounting changes that include both human and non-human actors. This assumption is also valid in the case of artificial intelligence that integrates non-human approaches (MacKenzie, 2009).

Furthermore, for Secinaro et al. (2021a), it is necessary to create institutional collaboration to develop technology innovation projects properly. Therefore, we believe that our results may help expand existing studies in this area. Although artificial intelligence in accounting may enable the development of new applications, there are currently no academic studies capable of observing large networks of actors according to the constructivist approach of ANT. This regard demonstrates how actors, practices, and artificial intelligence can give rise to constructivist processes and multiple positive effects on accounting.

5.2 Implication 2. New Perspectives for the Normative Theory in Accounting

Closely related to the previous point, the practitioners' findings again recall how the field of accounting is based on theoretical reference principles and defined actors such as clients, companies, government, tax agencies, and auditors (ICAEW, 2018). Thus, practitioners' appeals have theoretical resonance in the theory of regulation. According to Mattessich (2006) and Khakee (2021), accounting is subject to regulation because policymakers and practitioners state what should be done concerning pre-established laws and standards (i.e., IAS/IFRS or Local GAAP). This happens because accounting data play a privileged role in the market (Briers & Wai, 2001). Therefore, the call of practitioners towards inclusive technologies calls academics to study technological solutions that can be compatible with national and international regulations. This assumption becomes even more important for the scalability of AI applications. As noted, for example, the more inclusive the technology is in verifying the correct application of taxes (ICAEW, 2018), the greater the stakeholders' satisfaction and the opportunity to scale with the use of new applications.

6 Conclusion

In conclusion, this chapter aims to analyse the debate between practitioners and academics on AI and accounting. As indicated by Dahlin (2019), Gulin et al. (2019), and Quattrone (2016), although there is a theoretical agreement that AI can revolutionise the way accountants work, the modalities and applications are less clear and academic gaps to date. Moreover, as seen, the debate often includes multiple pieces of literature, such as information systems, ANT, and regulations. Today's discussion requires more holistic discussions and involvement between different actors, including clients, accountants, companies, governments, and tax agencies. However, this concordance between actors will not happen where the applications and implications of AI in accounting are not yet fully understood. Therefore, drawing from these premises, our research focused on observing and analysing documents written by practitioners and scholarly articles written by academics to show any practical-theoretical gaps.

As researchers, we used multiple research tools and databases in line with the challenges we drew from. The research allowed us to outline some theoretical and practical implications. From a theoretical perspective, we discover how AI needs the development of new research strands from ANT and normative theory. Interestingly, the needs arising from practitioners have fundamental theoretical assumptions. Despite the efforts made so far, no themes of collaboration and multi-stakeholder design emerge from the literature. Therefore, this assumption represents one of the most critical aspects of AI development in accounting.

From a practical point of view, we understand how AI is already present in the accounting context. The chapter demonstrates how intelligent algorithms can support accountants in continuous and repetitive operations in audit activities, the creation and classification of financial statements, and the analysis and comparison of financial statement data with other benchmarks. At the same time, recalling the study by Shaffer et al. (2020), we confirm that to date, there is no experience with the application of AI for financial planning. At the same time, again, on a practical level, we find that both academics and practitioners are calling for new training activities in digitisation and artificial intelligence. Therefore, while the research question "How is artificial intelligence changing accounting professions from the perspective of academics and practitioners?" was answered by providing evidence about the widespread applications today, a comprehensive answer can only include the need for education and training. Thus, building the CPAs (i.e., certified public accountants) and CIAs (i.e., certified internal auditors) of the future requires new skills and collaboration between academics, practitioners, universities, and training schools. This could include teaching and university "third mission" initiatives to take up new challenges, ideas, and problems using AI in accounting.

Finally, our study, like all research, has some limitations. First, as indicated by Romme et al. (2015), creating common grounds for dialogue in the scientific world requires numerous sources. Although we implement a broad research strategy and include the term "accounting" across a broad spectrum, we do not exclude that some sources have been overlooked. Second, focusing on both academics and practitioners reduced the topics of discussion which could, therefore, be taken up in the future by dedicated literature reviews. Third, our study included some successful AI case studies; however, the inspiration for CEOs, CTOs, and managers might need research articles with methodologies such as single or multiple case studies. Fourth, the study does not focus on AI users in accounting. Therefore, future studies could investigate practitioners' perceptions by highlighting success and failure factors in using AI.

References

Agrawal, A., Gans, J. S., & Goldfarb, A. (2019). Exploring the impact of artificial intelligence: Prediction versus judgment. *Information Economics and Policy, 47*, 1–6. https://doi.org/10.1016/J.INFOECOPOL.2019.05.001

Alexander, A. (2020). Changing tools, changing roles. *AccountingToday*. https://docplayer.net/95171845-A-supplement-to-changes-ahead-technology-is-radically-reshaping-the-future-of-auditing.html.

Amabile, T. M., Patterson, C., Mueller, J., Wojcik, T., Odomirok, P. W., Marsh, M., & Kramer, S. J. (2017). Academic-practitioner collaboration in management research: A case of cross-profession collaboration, *44*(2), 418–431. https://doi.org/10.5465/3069464

Amini, M., Bienstock, C. C., & Narcum, J. A. (2018). Status of corporate sustainability: A content analysis of fortune 500 companies. *Business Strategy and the Environment, 27*(8), 1450–1461. https://doi.org/10.1002/bse.2195

Aria, M., & Cuccurullo, C. (2017). bibliometrix: An R-tool for comprehensive science mapping analysis. *Journal of Informetrics, 11*(4), 959–975. https://doi.org/10.1016/J.JOI.2017.08.007

Arrowsmith, R. (2019a). AuditFile updates software with improved compliance controls. *AccountingToday*. https://www.accountingtoday.com/news/auditfile-updates-software-with-improved-compliance-controls

Arrowsmith, R. (2019b). CaseWare's new online engagement tool incorporates AI. *Accounting Today*. https://www.accountingtoday.com/news/casewares-new-online-accounting-software-incorporates-ai

Arrowsmith, R. (2020). Anduin debuts AI-powered AR for accounting firms. *AccountingToday*. https://www.accountingtoday.com/news/anduin-debuts-ai-powered-accounts-receivable-platform-for-firms

Arrowsmith, R. (2021a). AI, applied: Opening the black box. *AccountingToday*. https://www.accountingtoday.com/news/opening-the-black-box-ai-applied

Arrowsmith, R. (2021b). Fleetcor acquires AI-driven AP provider. *AccountingToday*. https://www.accountingtoday.com/news/ai-driven-ap-provider-roger-acquired-by-fleetcor

Asimov, I. (1989). *Tutti i miei robot*. Mondadori.

Askary, S., Abu-Ghazaleh, N., & Tahat, Y. A. (2018). Artificial intelligence and reliability of accounting information. *Lecture Notes in Computer Science (Including Subseries Lecture*

Notes in Artificial Intelligence and Lecture Notes in Bioinformatics), 11195 LNCS, 315–324. https://doi.org/10.1007/978-3-030-02131-3_28

Azudin, A., & Mansor, N. (2018). Management accounting practices of SMEs: The impact of organizational DNA, business potential and operational technology. *Asia Pacific Management Review, 23*(3), 222–226. https://doi.org/10.1016/J.APMRV.2017.07.014

Baima, G., Forliano, C., Santoro, G., & Vrontis, D. (2020). Intellectual capital and business model: A systematic literature review to explore their linkages. *Journal of Intellectual Capital, 22*(3), 653–679. https://doi.org/10.1108/JIC-02-2020-0055/FULL/XML

Ballou, B., Heitger, D. L., & Stoel, D. (2018). Data-driven decision-making and its impact on accounting undergraduate curriculum. *Journal of Accounting Education, 44*, 14–24. https://doi.org/10.1016/J.JACCEDU.2018.05.003

Behrens, M. L., & Steinbart, P. J. (1992). Integrating expert systems and artificial intelligence in accounting: A description of the academic program at Memphis State University. *Expert Systems with Applications, 4*(2), 219–223. https://doi.org/10.1016/0957-4174(92)90113-7

Bercovitz, J., & Feldman, M. (2005). Entrepreneurial universities and technology transfer: A conceptual framework for understanding knowledge-based economic development. *The Journal of Technology Transfer, 31*(1), 175–188. https://doi.org/10.1007/S10961-005-5029-Z

Bhatt, Y., Ghuman, K., & Dhir, A. (2020). Sustainable manufacturing. Bibliometrics and content analysis. *Journal of Cleaner Production, 260*, 120988. https://doi.org/10.1016/j.jclepro.2020.120988

Briers, M., & Wai, F. C. (2001). The role of actor-networks and boundary objects in management accounting change: A field study of an implementation of activity-based costing. *Accounting, Organizations and Society, 26*(3), 237–269. https://doi.org/10.1016/S0361-3682(00)00029-5

Chen, G., & Xiao, L. (2016). Selecting publication keywords for domain analysis in bibliometrics: A comparison of three methods. *Journal of Informetrics, 10*(1), 212–223. https://doi.org/10.1016/J.JOI.2016.01.006

Chukwudi, O. L., Echefu, S. C., Boniface, U. U., & Victoria, C. N. (2018). Effect of artificial intelligence on the performance of accounting operations among accounting firms in South East Nigeria. *Asian Journal of Economics, Business and Accounting, 7*(2), 1–11. https://doi.org/10.9734/AJEBA/2018/41641

Dahlin, E. (2019). Are robots stealing our jobs?, *5*, 237802311984624. https://doi.org/10.1177/2378023119846249

Dal Mas, F., Bagnoli, C., Massaro, M., & Biazzo, S. (2021). Smart technologies and new business models: Insights from artificial intelligence and blockchain, 271–285. https://doi.org/10.1007/978-3-030-80737-5_21

Davenport, T. H., & Ronanki, R. (2018). 3 things AI can already do for your company. *Harvard Business Review*. https://hbr.org/2018/01/artificial-intelligence-for-the-real-world

Dumay, J., de Villiers, C., Guthrie, J., & Hsiao, P. C. (2018). Thirty years of accounting, auditing and accountability journal: A critical study of the journal's most cited articles. *Accounting, Auditing and Accountability Journal, 31*(5), 1510–1541. https://doi.org/10.1108/AAAJ-04-2017-2915/FULL/XML

Economist, T. (2020). Artificial intelligence and its limits – An understanding of AI's limitations is starting to sink in | Technology Quarterly|. *The Economist.*, 1–6. https://www.economist.com/technology-quarterly/2020/06/11/an-understanding-of-ais-limitations-is-starting-to-sink-in

Falagas, M. E., Pitsouni, E. I., Malietzis, G. A., & Pappas, G. (2008). Comparison of PubMed, Scopus, Web of Science, and Google Scholar: Strengths and weaknesses. *FASEB Journal: Official Publication of the Federation of American Societies for Experimental Biology, 22*(2), 338–342. https://doi.org/10.1096/FJ.07-9492LSF

Fischer, C., Winter, R., & Wortmann, F. (2010). Design theory. *Business & Information Systems Engineering, 2*(6), 387–390. https://doi.org/10.1007/S12599-010-0128-2

Fjelland, R. (2020). Why general artificial intelligence will not be realized. *Humanities and Social Sciences Communications, 7*(1), 1–9. https://doi.org/10.1057/s41599-020-0494-4

Frank, K. E., Hanson, R. K., Jordan Lowe, D., & Smith, J. K. (2001). CPAs' perceptions of the emerging multidisciplinary accounting/legal practice. *Accounting Horizons, 15*(1), 35–48. https://doi.org/10.2308/ACCH.2001.15.1.35

Garousi Mokhtarzadeh, N., Amoozad Mahdiraji, H., Jafarpanah, I., Jafari-Sadeghi, V., & Cardinali, S. (2020). Investigating the impact of networking capability on firm innovation performance: Using the resource-action-performance framework. *Journal of Intellectual Capital, 21*(6), 1009–1034. https://doi.org/10.1108/JIC-01-2020-0005/FULL/XML

Gulin, D., Hladika, M., & Valenta, I. (2019). Digitalization and the challenges for the accounting profession. *SSRN Electronic Journal*. https://doi.org/10.2139/SSRN.3492237

Haefner, N., Wincent, J., Parida, V., & Gassmann, O. (2021). Artificial intelligence and innovation management: A review, framework, and research agenda☆. *Technological Forecasting and Social Change, 162*, 120392. https://doi.org/10.1016/J.TECHFORE.2020.120392

Haenlein, M., & Kaplan, A. (2019). A brief history of artificial intelligence: On the past. *Present, and Future of Artificial Intelligence, 61*(4), 5–14. https://doi.org/10.1177/0008125619864925

Hee Lee, D., & Yoon, S. N. (2021). Application of artificial intelligence-based technologies in the healthcare industry: Opportunities and challenges. *International Journal of Environmental Research and Public Health, 18*(1), 271. https://doi.org/10.3390/IJERPH18010271

Hood, D. (2017). Accounting leaders tap technology as top concern. *AccountingToday*. https://www.accountingtoday.com/news/accounting-leaders-tap-technology-as-top-concern

Hsieh, H.-F., & Shannon, S. E. (2005). Three approaches to qualitative content analysis. *Qualitative Health Research, 15*(9), 1277–1288. https://doi.org/10.1177/1049732305276687

Huang, H. W. (2018). Accounting and finance theory and practice: Future development. *Asia Pacific Management Review, 23*(2), 71. https://doi.org/10.1016/j.apmrv.2018.05.002

ICAEW. (2018). *Artificial intelligence and the future of accountancy*. 1–16. https://www.icaew.com/-/media/corporate/files/technical/technology/thought-leadership/artificial-intelligence-report.ashx

Issa, H., Sun, T., & Vasarhelyi, M. A. (2016). Research ideas for artificial intelligence in auditing: The formalization of audit and workforce supplementation. *Journal of Emerging Technologies in Accounting, 13*(2), 1–20. https://doi.org/10.2308/JETA-10511

Jordan, M. I., & Mitchell, T. M. (2015). Machine learning: Trends, perspectives, and prospects. *Science (New York, NY), 349*(6245), 255–260. https://doi.org/10.1126/SCIENCE.AAA8415

Justesen, L., & Mouritsen, J. (2011). Effects of actor-network theory in accounting research. *Accounting, Auditing and Accountability Journal, 24*(2), 161–193. https://doi.org/10.1108/09513571111100672/FULL/PDF

Khakee, A. (2021). Opening up the notion of "closing space": Accounting for normative, actor, and political system diversity. https://doi.org/10.1080/13510347.2021.2008360

Kocsis, D. (2019). A conceptual foundation of design and implementation research in accounting information systems. *International Journal of Accounting Information Systems, 34*, 100420. https://doi.org/10.1016/J.ACCINF.2019.06.003

Korhonen, T., Selos, E., Laine, T., & Suomala, P. (2021). Exploring the programmability of management accounting work for increasing automation: An interventionist case study. *Accounting, Auditing and Accountability Journal, 34*(2), 253–280. https://doi.org/10.1108/AAAJ-12-2016-2809/FULL/XML

Krippendorff, K. (2013). *Content analysis: An introduction to its methodology*.

Kumar, S., Sahoo, S., Lim, W. M., & Dana, L.-P. (2022). Religion as a social shaping force in entrepreneurship and business: Insights from a technology-empowered systematic literature review. *Technological Forecasting and Social Change, 175*, 121393. https://doi.org/10.1016/J.TECHFORE.2021.121393

Landrum, N. E., & Ohsowski, B. (2018). Identifying worldviews on corporate sustainability: A content analysis of corporate sustainability reports. *Business Strategy and the Environment, 27*(1), 128–151. https://doi.org/10.1002/bse.1989

Lee, C. S., & Tajudeen, F. P. (2020). Usage and impact of artificial intelligence on accounting: evidence from Malaysian Organisations. *Asian Journal of Business and Accounting, 13*(1), 213–239. https://doi.org/10.22452/AJBA.VOL13NO1.8

Liu, G. (2019). *Business Premium Collection, 23*(3–4), 249–258. https://doi.org/10.1080/08963568.2018.1542907

Losbichler, H., & Lehner, O. M. (2021). Limits of artificial intelligence in controlling and the ways forward: A call for future accounting research. *Journal of Applied Accounting Research, 22*(2), 365–382. https://doi.org/10.1108/JAAR-10-2020-0207/FULL/PDF

MacKenzie, D. (2009). Making things the same: Gases, emission rights and the politics of carbon markets. *Accounting, Organizations and Society, 34*(3–4), 440–455. https://doi.org/10.1016/J.AOS.2008.02.004

Mancini, D., Lamboglia, R., Castellano, N. G., & Corsi, K. (2017). Trends of digital innovation applied to accounting information and management control systems. *Lecture Notes in Information Systems and Organisation, 20*, 1–19. https://doi.org/10.1007/978-3-319-49538-5_1

Marangunić, N., & Granić, A. (2015). Technology acceptance model: A literature review from 1986 to 2013. *Universal Access in the Information Society, 14*(1), 81–95. https://doi.org/10.1007/S10209-014-0348-1/TABLES/3

Marrone, M., & Hazelton, J. (2019). The disruptive and transformative potential of new technologies for accounting, accountants and accountability: A review of current literature and call for further research. *Meditari Accountancy Research, 27*(5), 677–694. https://doi.org/10.1108/MEDAR-06-2019-0508/FULL/PDF

Massaro, M., Dumay, J., & Guthrie, J. (2016). On the shoulders of giants: Undertaking a structured literature review in accounting, *29*(5), 767–801. https://doi.org/10.1108/AAAJ-01-2015-193

Massaro, M., Dumay, J., Garlatti, A., & Dal Mas, F. (2018). Practitioners' views on intellectual capital and sustainability: From a performance-based to a worth-based perspective. *Journal of Intellectual Capital, 19*(2), 367–386. https://doi.org/10.1108/JIC-02-2017-0033/FULL/XML

Massaro, M., Secinaro, S., Dal Mas, F., Brescia, V., & Calandra, D. (2021). Industry 4.0 and circular economy: An exploratory analysis of academic and practitioners' perspectives. *Business Strategy and the Environment, 30*(2), 1213–1231. https://doi.org/10.1002/BSE.2680

Mattessich, R. (2006). On the history of normative accounting theory: Paradigm lost, paradigm regained?, *2*(2), 181–198. https://doi.org/10.1080/09585209200000039

Miles, M., Huberman, A., & Saldaña, J. (2014). Sampling: Bounding the collection of data. In *Qualitative Data Analysis: A Methods Sourcebook* (pp. 26–30).

Mohammed Al-Sayyed, S., Falah Al-Aroud, S., & Mustafa Zayed, L. (2021). *The effect of artificial intelligence technologies on audit evidence*. https://doi.org/10.5267/j.ac.2020.12.003

Moll, J., & Yigitbasioglu, O. (2019). The role of internet-related technologies in shaping the work of accountants: New directions for accounting research. *The British Accounting Review, 51*(6), 100833. https://doi.org/10.1016/J.BAR.2019.04.002

Mongeon, P., & Paul-Hus, A. (2016). The journal coverage of Web of Science and Scopus: A comparative analysis. *Scientometrics, 106*(1), 213–228. https://doi.org/10.1007/S11192-015-1765-5/FIGURES/6

Mosteanu, N. R., & Faccia, A. (2020). Digital systems and new challenges of financial management – Fintech, XBRL, blockchain and cryptocurrencies. *Quality – Access to Success, 21*(174), 159–166.

Pamela Neely, M., & Cook, J. S. (2011). Fifteen years of data and information quality literature: Developing a research agenda for accounting. *Journal of Information Systems, 25*(1), 79–108. https://doi.org/10.2308/JIS.2011.25.1.79

Patel, R., Goodell, J. W., Oriani, M. E., Paltrinieri, A., & Yarovaya, L. (2022). A bibliometric review of financial market integration literature. *International Review of Financial Analysis, 80*, 102035. https://doi.org/10.1016/J.IRFA.2022.102035

Pemer, F. (2020). *Enacting Professional Service Work in Times of Digitalization and Potential Disruption, 24*(2), 249–268. https://doi.org/10.1177/1094670520916801

Qasim, A., & Kharbat, F. F. (2020). Blockchain technology, business data analytics, and artificial intelligence: Use in the accounting profession and ideas for inclusion into the accounting curriculum. *Journal of Emerging Technologies in Accounting, 17*(1), 107–117. https://doi.org/10.2308/JETA-52649

Quattrone, P. (2016). Management accounting goes digital: Will the move make it wiser? *Management Accounting Research, 31*, 118–122. https://doi.org/10.1016/J.MAR.2016.01.003

Romme, A. G. L., Avenier, M. J., Denyer, D., Hodgkinson, G. P., Pandza, K., Starkey, K., & Worren, N. (2015). Towards common ground and trading zones in management research and practice. *British Journal of Management, 26*(3), 544–559. https://doi.org/10.1111/1467-8551.12110

Secinaro, S., Calandra, D., Cappa, C., & Bignamini, E. (2020). *La qualità dei dati all'interno dell'evoluzione dei servizi territoriali: il caso del Servizio Dipendenze*. MECOSAN. https://doi.org/10.3280/MESA2020-116003

Secinaro, S., Brescia, V., Calandra, D., & Biancone, P. (2021a). Towards a hybrid model for the management of smart city initiatives. *Cities, 116*, 103278. https://doi.org/10.1016/J.CITIES.2021.103278

Secinaro, S., Calandra, D., Secinaro, A., Muthurangu, V., & Biancone, P. (2021b). The role of artificial intelligence in healthcare: A structured literature review. *BMC Medical Informatics and Decision Making, 21*(1), 1–23. https://doi.org/10.1186/S12911-021-01488-9/FIGURES/12

Secinaro, S., Dal Mas, F., Brescia, V., & Calandra, D. (2021c). Blockchain in the accounting, auditing and accountability fields: A bibliometric and coding analysis. *Accounting, Auditing and Accountability Journal*. https://doi.org/10.1108/AAAJ-10-2020-4987/FULL/PDF

Secinaro, S., Dal Mas, F., Massaro, M., & Calandra, D. (2021d). Exploring agricultural entrepreneurship and new technologies: Academic and practitioners' views. *British Food Journal, 124*, 1. https://doi.org/10.1108/BFJ-08-2021-0905

Shaffer, K. J., Gaumer, C. J., & Bradley, K. P. (2020). Artificial intelligence products reshape accounting: Time to re-train. *Development and Learning in Organizations, 34*(6), 41–43. https://doi.org/10.1108/DLO-10-2019-0242/FULL/XML

Shen, L., Zhang, L., Xu, J., & Luo, J. (2011). The innovation management of the accounting evaluation. In *2011 2nd international conference on artificial intelligence, management science and electronic commerce, AIMSEC 2011 – Proceedings* (pp. 2574–2577). https://doi.org/10.1109/AIMSEC.2011.6011165

Shi, Y. (2020). The impact of artificial intelligence on the accounting industry. *Adv. Intell. Syst. Comput., 928*, 971–978. https://doi.org/10.1007/978-3-030-15235-2_129

Sihvonen, S., & Partanen, J. (2017). Eco-design practices with a focus on quantitative environmental targets: An exploratory content analysis within ICT sector. *Journal of Cleaner Production, 143*, 769–783. https://doi.org/10.1016/J.JCLEPRO.2016.12.047

Smith, A. E., & Humphreys, M. S. (2006). Evaluation of unsupervised semantic mapping of natural language with Leximancer concept mapping. *Behavior Research Methods, 38*(2), 262–279. https://doi.org/10.3758/BF03192778

Sun, T. Q., & Medaglia, R. (2019). Mapping the challenges of artificial intelligence in the public sector: Evidence from public healthcare. *Government Information Quarterly, 36*(2), 368–383. https://doi.org/10.1016/J.GIQ.2018.09.008

Sun Rutgers, T., & Vasarhelyi, M. A. (2018). Embracing textual data analytics in auditing with deep learning. *The International Journal of Digital Accounting Research, 18*, 49–67. https://doi.org/10.4192/1577-8517-v18_3

Sutton, S. G., Holt, M., & Arnold, V. (2016). "The reports of my death are greatly exaggerated" – Artificial intelligence research in accounting. *International Journal of Accounting Information Systems, 22*, 60–73. https://doi.org/10.1016/J.ACCINF.2016.07.005

The Lab Consulting. (2018). Robotic accounting – 5 use cases, a case study, and examples of RPA in finance and accounting departments. *Insights from the Lab.*. https://thelabconsulting.com/robotic-accounting-5-use-cases-case-study-examples-rpa-finance-accounting-departments/

Tiberius, V., & Hirth, S. (2019). Impacts of digitization on auditing: A Delphi study for Germany. *Journal of International Accounting, Auditing and Taxation, 37*, 100288. https://doi.org/10.1016/J.INTACCAUDTAX.2019.100288

Toorajipour, R., Sohrabpour, V., Nazarpour, A., Oghazi, P., & Fischl, M. (2021). Artificial intelligence in supply chain management: A systematic literature review. *Journal of Business Research, 122*, 502–517. https://doi.org/10.1016/J.JBUSRES.2020.09.009

Uluyol, B., Secinaro, S., Calandra, D., & Lanzalonga, F. (2021). Mapping waqf research: A thirty-year bibliometric analysis. *Journal of Islamic Accounting and Business Research, 12*(5), 748–767. https://doi.org/10.1108/JIABR-01-2021-0031/FULL/XML

Zemánková, A. (2019). Artificial intelligence and blockchain in audit and accounting: Literature review. *WSEAS Transactions on Business and Economics, 16*, 568–581.

Zhang, Y., Xiong, F., Xie, Y., Fan, X., & Gu, H. (2020). The impact of artificial intelligence and blockchain on the accounting profession. *IEEE Access, 8*, 110461–110477. https://doi.org/10.1109/ACCESS.2020.3000505

Artificial Intelligence: New Challenges, Opportunities, and Threats in Marketing, Media, and Communication

Carlo Nardello, Lorenzo Iannarilli, and Edoardo Giaroli

Abstract This chapter explores the impact of artificial intelligence (AI) on marketing, media, and communication, focusing on the challenges, opportunities, and threats. It discusses the state of the art in AI applications, including data analysis, personalization, content generation, and audience engagement. The chapter examines threats such as echo chambers, fake news, and biased data sources, while also highlighting professional and ethical challenges. It explores opportunities for enhanced targeting, content personalization, automation, and data-driven insights. The chapter emphasizes the need for responsible AI deployment and human judgment. Overall, it provides a comprehensive overview of the implications of AI in these domains.

1 Introduction

The rapid advancements in artificial intelligence (AI) technologies have significantly transformed various industries, including marketing, media, and communication. AI offers immense potential for enhancing efficiency, personalization, and decision-making processes in different domains. However, along with the opportunities, AI also brings forth new challenges and threats that need to be addressed. This chapter aims to explore the evolving landscape of AI in marketing, media, and communication, highlighting both the positive developments and the potential risks.

C. Nardello
Università di Roma "La Sapienza", Rome, Italy
e-mail: carlo.nardello@uniroma1.it

L. Iannarilli (✉)
LUMSA University, Rome, Italy

E. Giaroli
Daat Consulting Srl, Milan, Italy
e-mail: e.giaroli@daatconsulting.it

G. R. Marseglia et al. (eds.), *Socio-economic Impact of Artificial Intelligence*,
Progress in IS, https://doi.org/10.1007/978-3-031-73514-1_7

1.1 Background and Significance

In recent years, AI has emerged as a disruptive force, revolutionizing the way organizations engage with consumers, disseminate information, and communicate their messages. The integration of AI technologies, such as machine learning, natural language processing, and data analytics, has enabled automation, predictive modeling, and intelligent decision-making. These advancements have reshaped the marketing strategies, media landscape, and communication practices, leading to increased efficiency and effectiveness.

1.2 Objectives and Scope

The primary objective of this chapter is to provide a comprehensive overview of the challenges, opportunities, and threats associated with the utilization of AI in marketing, media, and communication. By examining the existing literature, case studies, and industry practices, we aim to offer insights into the implications of AI adoption and its impact on various stakeholders. Furthermore, we explore the ethical considerations surrounding AI implementation and discuss potential future directions for these fields (Mittelstadt et al., 2016; Taddeo & Floridi, 2018).

1.3 Structure of the Chapter

The chapter is organized into five main sections: Sects. 2, 3, 4, 5. In the Sect 2, we provide an overview of AI technologies and their applications in marketing, media, and communication, drawing from academic literature and industry examples. The Sect. 3 is divided into three subsections, addressing professional challenges, ethical challenges, and societal challenges. Here, we delve into the potential risks associated with AI, including the undermining of creativity, biases in AI systems, transparency issues, and the proliferation of echo chambers, fake news, and reliance on bad data sources. The Sect. 4 highlights the positive implications of AI, such as enhanced audience targeting, automated content creation, data analysis, and personalized user experiences. In the Sect. 5, we summarize the key points discussed and emphasize the need for ethical considerations and responsible AI implementation.

Throughout the chapter, we draw upon a wide range of academic literature and research papers to support our analysis and provide a comprehensive understanding of the subject matter. By examining the interplay between AI technologies and these industries, we aim to contribute to the ongoing discourse on the opportunities and challenges presented by AI in the context of marketing, media, and communication.

In the next section, Sect. 2 we delve into the current landscape of AI technologies and their applications in marketing, media, and communication, supported by relevant academic research and industry examples.

2 State of the Art

2.1 Overview of AI Technologies in Marketing, Media, and Communication

Artificial intelligence technologies have made significant strides in the domains of marketing, media, and communication, enabling organizations to gain valuable insights, automate processes, and deliver personalized experiences (Gao & Hongfei, 2023; Daqar & Smoudy, 2019; Kietzmann et al., 2018; Kedi et al., 2024a; Chintalapati & Pandey 2022). Machine learning algorithms, natural language processing, and data analytics have become foundational components of AI-driven systems. These technologies enable marketers, media professionals, and communicators to extract patterns from large datasets, automate content creation, and enhance audience targeting (Theodoridis & Gkikas, 2019; Ahmed & Ganapathy, 2021).

2.2 AI Applications in Marketing

AI has revolutionized marketing practices, empowering organizations to optimize their marketing strategies and improve customer engagement. Through AI-powered data analysis, marketers can uncover valuable consumer insights, predict consumer behavior, and enhance personalized marketing campaigns. Recommendation systems utilize AI algorithms to offer personalized product recommendations, leading to increased sales and customer satisfaction (Sethi & Gujral, 2022). Moreover, AI chatbots and virtual assistants enable interactive and seamless customer support, enhancing customer experiences (Arsenijevic & Jovic, 2019; Kedi et al., 2024b; Kaczorowska-Spychalska, 2019).

2.3 AI Applications in Media

In the media industry, AI has transformed content creation, distribution, and consumption. Automated content generation algorithms, such as natural language generation, assist in producing news articles, financial reports, and sports summaries (Ding et al., 2023; Gautam et al., 2022; Midoglu et al., 2024; Deliege et al., 2021). AI algorithms also aid in content curation and recommendation, facilitating personalized news feeds and tailored content experiences for users (de-Lima-Santos & Ceron, 2021). Additionally, AI technologies enable media organizations to analyze audience preferences, optimize ad targeting, and improve monetization strategies.

2.4 AI Applications in Communication

AI technologies have reshaped communication practices, offering new avenues for engagement and interaction. Chatbots and virtual assistants powered by AI algorithms enhance customer support and automate communication processes. Natural language processing algorithms enable sentiment analysis and social media monitoring, providing valuable insights for brand reputation management and crisis communication (Ruggiero & Vos, 2014; Stavrakantonakis et al., 2012). Furthermore, AI-driven speech recognition and translation technologies facilitate cross-cultural communication and multilingual content delivery.

2.5 Case Studies and Industry Examples

The adoption of AI in marketing, media, and communication can be observed through numerous case studies and industry examples. Companies like Amazon, Netflix, and Spotify leverage AI algorithms to deliver personalized recommendations and enhance user experiences (Gomez-Uribe & Hunt 2015; Steck et al., 2021). News organizations utilize AI-powered content generation systems to automate news writing and increase efficiency. Social media platforms employ AI algorithms for content moderation, ad targeting, and user engagement.

By leveraging AI technologies, organizations in the fields of marketing, media, and communication can gain a competitive edge, optimize processes, and deliver personalized experiences to their target audiences. However, alongside these advancements come potential threats and challenges, which will be discussed in the following sections.

3 Threats

3.1 Eco Chambers and Filter Bubbles

In the era of AI-driven marketing, media, and communication, the emergence of eco chambers and filter bubbles poses significant threats to information diversity and democratic discourse. Eco chambers refer to the phenomenon where individuals are exposed only to information that aligns with their existing beliefs and values, leading to the reinforcement of preexisting perspectives and limited exposure to diverse viewpoints. Filter bubbles, on the other hand, are created by AI algorithms that curate content based on users' preferences and previous interactions, potentially narrowing their access to diverse information.

These echo chambers and filter bubbles can have detrimental effects on society by fostering polarization, reinforcing biases, and limiting individuals' exposure to alternative perspectives. They can hinder critical thinking, impede informed decision-making, and contribute to the spread of misinformation and fake news (Del Vicario et al., 2016; Bessi, 2016; Bruns, 2019). The algorithms driving content personalization and recommendation need to be critically evaluated to ensure a more balanced and inclusive information environment.

3.2 *Fake News and Deep Fakes*

The proliferation of AI technology has facilitated the creation and dissemination of fake news and deep fakes, presenting a significant challenge for marketing, media, and communication. AI-powered tools and algorithms can be utilized to generate convincing fake news articles, images, videos, and audio recordings, making it increasingly difficult for users to distinguish between authentic and manipulated content. Deep fakes, in particular, refer to manipulated videos or audios that depict individuals saying or doing things they never did, further blurring the line between truth and deception (Westerlund 2019; Rana et al., 2022).

The spread of fake news and deep fakes fueled by AI technology poses significant threats to public trust, political discourse, and the credibility of information sources (Pennycook & Rand, 2019). It becomes imperative for stakeholders in marketing, media, and communication to develop robust fact-checking mechanisms, promote media literacy, and leverage AI technologies for content verification and authentication (Rana et al., 2022; Shu et al., 2017). Collaborative efforts between technology companies, policymakers, and researchers are needed to combat the proliferation of fake news and ensure the integrity of information ecosystems.

3.3 *Bad Data Sources and Biased Algorithms*

AI systems heavily rely on data for training and decision-making, and the quality and biases present in the data can have profound implications. Bad data sources, such as incomplete or biased datasets, can result in flawed AI models and inaccurate outcomes. Biased algorithms can perpetuate and amplify existing societal biases, leading to discriminatory practices in areas like hiring, advertising, and content recommendation (Ntoutsi et al., 2020; Akter et al., 2022).

The ethical implications of biased algorithms and flawed data sources are significant. They can reinforce social inequalities, perpetuate stereotypes, and undermine the principles of fairness and equal opportunity. Ensuring the use of diverse and representative datasets, implementing algorithmic transparency and accountability measures, and promoting ethical guidelines and regulations are essential steps to mitigate these threats. Additionally, fostering interdisciplinary collaborations between AI experts, ethicists, and domain specialists can help address the challenges posed by biased algorithms and data quality issues.

3.4 Professional Challenges

The integration of AI in marketing, media, and communication also brings forth professional challenges for practitioners in these fields. AI technologies have the potential to automate various tasks traditionally performed by professionals, leading to concerns about job displacement and the redefinition of roles and skills (Davenport & Ronanki, 2018). Journalists, marketers, and communication professionals need to adapt to the changing landscape and acquire new skills to work effectively alongside AI systems.

Furthermore, the ethical dilemmas associated with AI in decision-making processes require careful consideration. Issues of privacy, transparency, accountability, and responsibility arise when algorithms are entrusted with sensitive tasks such as personalized advertising, content curation, or public opinion analysis (Tucker et al., 2018). Professionals in marketing, media, and communication must grapple with these ethical challenges and ensure that AI technologies are deployed in a manner that respects individual rights and societal values.

By recognizing and addressing these threats, stakeholders in marketing, media, and communication can harness the potential of AI while safeguarding against potential harm and maintaining ethical practices.

4 Opportunities

4.1 Enhanced Personalization and Customer Experience

One of the significant opportunities presented by AI in marketing, media, and communication is the ability to deliver enhanced personalization and improve customer experiences. AI-powered algorithms can analyze vast amounts of data, including user behavior, preferences, and demographics, to tailor content, recommendations, and advertisements to individual users. This level of personalization can lead to more engaging and relevant interactions, fostering customer satisfaction and loyalty. Additionally, AI can enable dynamic pricing strategies based on individual customer preferences and behavior, optimizing pricing decisions and increasing customer value.

4.2 Data-Driven Insights and Decision-Making

AI technologies enable marketers, media professionals, and communication practitioners to extract valuable insights from large datasets, transforming raw data into actionable information. Machine learning algorithms can identify patterns, trends, and correlations, providing valuable insights for audience segmentation, content optimization, and targeted marketing campaigns. Data-driven decision-making can lead to more effective strategies, improved campaign performance, and better resource allocation. Furthermore, AI can facilitate real-time data analysis, enabling organizations to respond swiftly to changing market conditions and consumer preferences.

4.3 Automation and Efficiency

Automation is another significant opportunity offered by AI in marketing, media, and communication. Routine and repetitive tasks, such as data entry, content generation, and social media scheduling, can be automated using AI technologies, freeing up human professionals to focus on higher-value activities. Automated processes can lead to increased efficiency, reduced costs, and faster turnaround times. For instance, AI-powered chatbots can handle customer inquiries, providing instant responses and support, thereby improving customer service and reducing response time.

4.4 Content Creation and Curation

AI-powered tools and algorithms have the potential to transform content creation and curation processes. Natural language generation (NLG) algorithms can automatically generate news articles, reports, and summaries from structured data, enabling faster content production. AI systems can also curate personalized content recommendations for users based on their interests, preferences, and browsing history, enabling more targeted and engaging content consumption experiences. Additionally, AI can assist in content optimization by analyzing user engagement data and suggesting improvements to enhance the effectiveness of content strategies.

4.5 Advanced Analytics and Predictive Modeling

AI algorithms excel in analyzing complex datasets and extracting meaningful insights. In marketing, media, and communication, AI can be leveraged to perform advanced analytics, such as sentiment analysis, social media monitoring, and predictive modeling. These capabilities enable organizations to gain a deeper understanding of their audience, identify emerging trends, and anticipate consumer behavior, leading to more informed decision-making and proactive strategies. Moreover, AI-powered predictive models can optimize marketing campaigns, enabling organizations to allocate resources effectively and maximize return on investment.

4.6 Enhanced Creativity and Innovation

AI technologies can also augment human creativity and innovation in marketing, media, and communication. AI-powered tools can assist in generating ideas, providing design recommendations, and facilitating the creation of compelling visual content. By leveraging AI's ability to process and analyze vast amounts of data, professionals can uncover new insights, discover innovative approaches, and develop novel strategies to engage their target audience. AI can enable the exploration of new content formats, such as virtual reality (VR) and augmented reality (AR), allowing for immersive storytelling experiences. Additionally, AI can support the ideation and development of personalized advertising campaigns, tailoring messages and creative elements to specific segments or individuals.

4.7 Ethical Considerations and Responsible AI Implementation

While the opportunities presented by AI in marketing, media, and communication are vast, it is essential to address the ethical considerations associated with its implementation. Ethical challenges such as privacy concerns, data security, algorithmic bias, and transparency need to be carefully navigated (Floridi et al., 2019). Responsible AI practices should be adopted, ensuring fairness, accountability, and transparency in decision-making processes (Jobin et al., 2019). Organizations must strike a balance between leveraging AI's capabilities and upholding ethical standards to build trust with their audience and stakeholders.

By embracing these diverse opportunities, stakeholders in marketing, media, and communication can harness the power of AI to drive innovation, improve efficiency, and deliver enhanced experiences to their audiences. However, it is crucial to consider the ethical implications and ensure responsible AI implementation to foster a sustainable and beneficial AI-powered future in these domains.

5 Conclusion

In this chapter, we have explored the challenges, opportunities, and threats posed by artificial intelligence (AI) in marketing, media, and communication. AI has emerged as a transformative force, revolutionizing the way organizations engage with their audience, analyze data, and make strategic decisions. While the potential benefits of AI are substantial, it is crucial to navigate the associated challenges and address the ethical considerations to ensure responsible and beneficial AI implementation.

In the state of the art, we examined the current landscape of AI applications in marketing, media, and communication. We discussed the advancements in natural language processing, machine learning, and data analytics that have empowered organizations to gain insights, automate processes, and personalize experiences. Additionally, we explored the integration of AI in various domains, including customer relationship management, content creation, advertising, and audience analytics.

The threats posed by AI in these domains are significant. Echo chambers and filter bubbles have raised concerns about the polarization of information and the potential for misinformation to spread. The emergence of fake news and deep fakes has further exacerbated these challenges, undermining trust in media and communication channels. Moreover, reliance on biased or unreliable data sources can lead to flawed decision-making and reinforce existing inequalities.

However, we also highlighted the opportunities presented by AI. Enhanced personalization and customer experience, data-driven insights, automation, content creation and curation, advanced analytics, and predictive modeling are just a few examples of the transformative potential of AI in marketing, media, and communication. AI technologies can empower professionals to make informed decisions, improve efficiency, and foster creativity and innovation.

To mitigate the threats and maximize the opportunities, organizations must proactively address the professional challenges and ethical considerations associated with AI implementation. Professional challenges include upskilling and reskilling the workforce, redefining job roles, and adapting to changing industry dynamics. Ethical considerations encompass privacy, data security, algorithmic bias, and responsible AI practices. Transparency, accountability, and fairness must be prioritized to ensure the responsible use of AI technologies.

In conclusion, AI has the power to reshape marketing, media, and communication practices. It offers immense opportunities to deliver personalized experiences, extract valuable insights, automate processes, and foster creativity. However, it is imperative to approach AI implementation with caution, addressing the associated challenges and ethical considerations to create a sustainable and responsible AI-powered future. By striking a balance between innovation and ethics, stakeholders in marketing, media, and communication can leverage the full potential of AI while building trust and maintaining the integrity of their practices.

References

Acar, A., & Murdock, V. (2018). Privacy and security in the era of AI. *Communications of the ACM, 61*(11), 22–24.

Ahmed, A. A. A., & Ganapathy, A. (2021). Creation of automated content with embedded artificial intelligence: a study on learning management system for educational entrepreneurship. *Academy of Entrepreneurship Journal, 27*(3), 1–10.

Akter, S., Dwivedi, Y. K., Sajib, S., Biswas, K., Bandara, R. J., & Michael, K. (2022). Algorithmic bias in machine learning-based marketing models. *Journal of Business Research, 144*, 201–216.

Allcott, H., & Gentzkow, M. (2017). Social media and fake news in the 2016 election. *Journal of Economic Perspectives, 31*(2), 211–236.

Ananny, M., & Crawford, K. (2018). Seeing without knowing: Limitations of the transparency ideal and its application to algorithmic accountability. *New Media & Society, 20*(3), 973–989.

Anderson, C. W. (2018). Journalism's R&D moment: Design thinking and the news innovation pipeline. *Digital Journalism, 6*(2), 152–169.

Arsenijevic, U., & Jovic, M. (2019). Artificial intelligence marketing: chatbots. In 2019 international conference on artificial intelligence: applications and innovations (IC-AIAI) (pp. 19–193). IEEE.

Bessi, A. (2016). Personality traits and echo chambers on facebook. *Computers in Human Behavior, 65*, 319–324.

Bessi, A., & Ferrara, E. (2016). Social bots distort the 2016 US Presidential election online discussion. *First Monday, 21*(11). https://doi.org/10.5210/fm.v21i11.7090

Bradshaw, P., & Howard, P. N. (2018). Challenging computational propaganda: A research agenda. *New Media & Society, 20*(10), 3660–3676.

Bruns, A. (2019). *Are filter bubbles real?*. John Wiley & Sons.

Castillo, C., Mendoza, M., & Poblete, B. (2011). Information credibility on Twitter. In *Proceedings of the 20th international conference on World Wide Web (WWW)* (pp. 675–684).

Chang, C., Lu, H. P., & Chen, S. C. (2014). Multiple-channel marketing, product attributes, and consumer purchase behavior: A consumer-based model. *International Journal of Electronic Commerce, 18*(1), 97–120.

Chintalapati, S., & Pandey, S. K. (2022). Artificial intelligence in marketing: A systematic literature review. *International Journal of Market Research, 64*(1), 38–68.

Chen, T., & Abu-Mostafa, Y. (2012). Learning from the label proportions in news articles. In *Proceedings of the 29th international conference on machine learning (ICML)* (pp. 1–8).

Cheng, Z., & Bernstein, M. S. (2017). Breaking news or feature article? Predicting article types of online news. In *Proceedings of the 2017 ACM conference on computer supported cooperative work and social computing* (pp. 311–323).

Davenport, T. H., & Ronanki, R. (2018). Artificial intelligence for the real world. *Harvard Business Review, 96*(1), 108–116.

Daqar, M. A. A., & Smoudy, A. K. (2019). The role of artificial intelligence on enhancing customer experience. *International Review of Management and Marketing, 9*(4), 22.

Del Vicario, M., Bessi, A., Zollo, F., Petroni, F., Scala, A., Caldarelli, G., et al. (2016). The spreading of misinformation online. *Proceedings of the National Academy of Sciences, 113*(3), 554–559.

Deliege, A., Cioppa, A., Giancola, S., Seikavandi, M. J., Dueholm, J. V., Nasrollahi, K., ... & Van Droogenbroeck, M. (2021). *Soccernet-v2: A dataset and benchmarks for holistic understanding of broadcast soccer videos*. In Proceedings of the IEEE/CVF conference on computer vision and pattern recognition (pp. 4508–4519)..

de-Lima-Santos, M. F., & Ceron, W. (2021). Artificial intelligence in news media: current perceptions and future outlook. *Journalism and media, 3*(1), 13–26.

Diakopoulos, N. (2015). Algorithmic accountability: Journalistic investigation of computational power structures. *Digital Journalism, 3*(3), 398–415.

Ding, Z., Smith-Renner, A., Zhang, W., Tetreault, J. R., & Jaimes, A. (2023). *Harnessing the power of LLMs: Evaluating human-AI text co-creation through the lens of news headline generation*. arXiv preprint arXiv:2310.10706.

Duggan, M., & Smith, A. (2013). *Social media update 2013*. Pew Research Center. Retrieved from https://www.pewresearch.org/internet/2013/12/30/social-media-update-2013/

Floridi, L. (2019). Artificial intelligence's new frontier: Ethics. *Harvard Data Science Review, 1*(1), 1–7.

Fort, K., & Adda, G. (2017). International trends in news automation. *Digital Journalism, 5*(9), 1089–1104.

Gao, Y., & Hongfei, Liu. (2023). Artificial intelligence-enabled personalization in interactive marketing: a customer journey perspective. *Journal of Research in Interactive Marketing, 17*(5), 663–680.

Gautam, S., Midoglu, C., Shafiee Sabet, S., Kshatri, D. B., & Halvorsen, P. (2022). *Soccer game summarization using audio commentary, metadata, and captions*. In Proceedings of the 1st Workshop on User-centric Narrative Summarization of Long Videos (pp. 13–22).

Gentzkow, M., & Shapiro, J. M. (2011). Ideological segregation online and offline. *The Quarterly Journal of Economics, 126*(4), 1799–1839.

Goodfellow, I., Bengio, Y., & Courville, A. (2016). *Deep learning*. MIT Press.

Gomez-Uribe, C. A., & Hunt, N. (2015). The netflix recommender system: Algorithms, business value, and innovation. *ACM Transactions on Management Information Systems (TMIS), 6*(4), 1–19.
Gürses, S., van Hoboken, J., & Nouwen, M. (2018). Data protection by design and data minimization obligations: Scrutinizing the GDPR principles in the age of big data. *International Data Privacy Law, 8*(1), 39–54.
Hamilton, J. T., & Turner, F. (2009). Accountability through algorithm: Developing the field of computational journalism. *Proceedings of the National Academy of Sciences, 106*(41), 17197–17202.
Helberger, N., Möller, J., & Schwartz, N. (2019). Automated news: Journalism in the age of algorithms. *Digital Journalism, 7*(6), 686–702.
Horne, B. D., & Adali, S. (2017). This just in: Fake news packs a lot in title, uses simpler, repetitive content in text body, more similar to satire than real news. In *Proceedings of the 26th international conference on World Wide Web (WWW)* (Vol. 11, pp. 855–862).
Hsieh, J. Y., & Tsai, W. H. S. (2017). Big data analytics for digital marketing. *Journal of Interactive Marketing, 38*, 68–81.
Hsu, C. L., & Lu, H. P. (2007). Consumer responses to corporate social responsibility initiatives: The mediating role of consumer–company identification. *Journal of Business Ethics, 70*(4), 351–361.
Hutto, C. J., & Gilbert, E. (2014). Vader: A parsimonious rule-based model for sentiment analysis of social media text. In *Eighth International AAAI Conference on Weblogs and Social Media* (Vol. 8, p. 216).
Jobin, A., Ienca, M., & Vayena, E. (2019). The global landscape of AI ethics guidelines. *Nature Machine Intelligence, 1*(9), 389–399.
Kaczorowska-Spychalska, D. (2019). Chatbots in marketing. *Management, 23*(1).
Kedi, W. E., Ejimuda, C., Idemudia, C., & Ijomah, T. I. (2024a). AI software for personalized marketing automation in SMEs: Enhancing customer experience and sales. *World Journal of Advanced Research and Reviews, 23*(1), 1981–1990.
Kedi, W. E., Ejimuda, C., Idemudia, C., & Ijomah, T. I. (2024b). AI Chatbot integration in SME marketing platforms: Improving customer interaction and service efficiency. *International Journal of Management & Entrepreneurship Research, 6*(7), 2332–2341.
Kietzmann, J., Paschen, J., & Treen, E. (2018). Artificial intelligence in advertising: How marketers can leverage artificial intelligence along the consumer journey. *Journal of Advertising Research, 58*(3), 263–267.
Lankow, J., Ritchie, J., & Crooks, R. (2012). *Infographics: The power of visual storytelling*. John Wiley & Sons.
Lazer, D. M., Kennedy, R., King, G., & Vespignani, A. (2014). The parable of Google Flu: Traps in big data analysis. *Science, 343*(6176), 1203–1205.
Lazer, D. M., Baum, M. A., Benkler, Y., Berinsky, A. J., Greenhill, K. M., Menczer, F., et al. (2018). The science of fake news. *Science, 359*(6380), 1094–1096.
Li, R., & Lim, M. (2018). Understanding fake news: The subjective logic of news reception. *New Media & Society, 20*(8), 3028–3047.
Lotan, G., Graeff, E., Ananny, M., Gaffney, D., Pearce, I., & boyd, d. (2011). The revolutions were tweeted: Information flows during the 2011 Tunisian and Egyptian revolutions. *International Journal of Communication, 5*, 1375–1405.
Malshe, A. V., Singh, S. S., & Dugar, T. (2019). Artificial intelligence in marketing: A synthesis of theory and practice. *Journal of the Academy of Marketing Science, 47*(4), 630–651.
Margetts, H., John, P., Hale, S., & Yasseri, T. (2015). *Political turbulence: How social media shape collective action*. Princeton University Press.
Mittelstadt, B. D., Allo, P., Taddeo, M., Wachter, S., & Floridi, L. (2016). The ethics of algorithms: Mapping the debate. *Big Data & Society, 3*(2), 2053951716679679.
Midoglu, C., Sabet, S. S., Sarkhoosh, M. H., Majidi, M., Gautam, S., Solberg, H. M., ... & Halvorsen, P. (2024). *Ai-based sports highlight generation for social media*. In Proceedings of the 3rd Mile-High Video Conference (pp. 7–13).
Nguyen, A., & Nguyen, T. (2019). Deep learning for deepfakes creation and detection. In *Proceedings of the IEEE International Conference on Multimedia & Expo Workshops (ICMEW)* (pp. 1–6).

Nielsen, R. K., & Graves, L. (2017). *News you don't believe: Audience perspectives on fake news*. Reuters Institute for the Study of Journalism.

Nielsen, R. K., Fletcher, R., Newman, N., & Brennen, J. S. (2020). *Navigating the 'infodemic': How people in six countries access and rate news and information about coronavirus*. Reuters Institute Digital News Report.

Ntoutsi, E., Fafalios, P., Gadiraju, U., Iosifidis, V., Nejdl, W., Vidal, M. E., ... & Staab, S. (2020). Bias in data-driven artificial intelligence systems—An introductory survey. Wiley Interdisciplinary Reviews: Data Mining and Knowledge Discovery, 10(3), e1356.

Ohlhorst, F. W. (2016). *Artificial intelligence for dummies*. John Wiley & Sons.

O'Reilly, T. (2012). *What is data science?* O'Reilly Media.

Pennycook, G., & Rand, D. G. (2019). The implied truth effect: Attaching warnings to a subset of fake news stories increases perceived accuracy of stories without warnings. *Management Science, 67*(11), 4944–4957.

Rana, M. S., Nobi, M. N., Murali, B., & Sung, A. H. (2022). Deepfake detection: A systematic literature review. *IEEE access, 10*, 25494–25513.

Roberts, H., & Cornwell, T. B. (2021). Corporate social responsibility and negative corporate associations in the digital age: When do associations with negative corporate social responsibility initiatives spill over to brands? *Journal of Business Research, 125*, 656–668.

Russell, S., & Norvig, P. (2016). *Artificial intelligence: A modern approach*. Pearson.

Ruggiero, A., & Vos, M. (2014). Social media monitoring for crisis communication: Process, methods and trends in the scientific literature. *Online Journal of Communication and Media Technologies, 4*(1).

Sethi, V., & Gujral, R. K. (2022). *Survey of different recommendation systems to improve the marketing strategies on e-commerce*. In 2022 International Conference on Machine Learning, Big Data, Cloud and Parallel Computing (COM-IT-CON) (Vol. 1, pp. 119–125). IEEE.

Shu, K., Sliva, A., Wang, S., Tang, J., & Liu, H. (2017). Fake news detection on social media: A data mining perspective. *ACM SIGKDD explorations newsletter, 19*(1), 22–36.

Stavrakantonakis, I., Gagiu, A. E., Kasper, H., Toma, I., & Thalhammer, A. (2012). An approach for evaluation of social media monitoring tools. *Common Value Management, 52*(1), 52–64.

Steck, H., Baltrunas, L., Elahi, E., Liang, D., Raimond, Y., & Basilico, J. (2021). Deep learning for recommender systems: A Netflix case study. *AI Magazine, 42*(3), 7–18.

Sunstein, C. R. (2017). *#Republic: Divided democracy in the age of social media*. Princeton University Press.

Taddeo, M., & Floridi, L. (2018). How AI can be a force for good. *Science, 361*(6404), 751–752.

Tandoc, E. C., Lim, Z. W., & Ling, R. (2018). Defining "fake news": A typology of scholarly definitions. *Digital Journalism, 6*(2), 137–153.

Theodoridis, P. K., & Gkikas, D. C. (2019). *How artificial intelligence affects digital marketing*. In Strategic Innovative Marketing and Tourism: 7th ICSIMAT, Athenian Riviera, Greece, 2018 (pp. 1319–1327). Springer International Publishing.

Tucker, C., Agrawal, A., Gans, J., & Goldfarb, A. (2018). *Privacy, algorithms, and artificial intelligence*. The economics of artificial intelligence: An agenda, 423–437.

Tufekci, Z. (2018). Artificial intelligence's white guy problem. *The New York Times*. Retrieved from https://www.nytimes.com/2018/06/27/opinion/artificial-intelligence-data.html

Vaidyanathan, G. (2019). *From deep fakes to "cheap fakes": The looming threat for business*. Forbes. Retrieved from https://www.forbes.com/sites/ganeshevaidyanathan/2019/05/29/from-deepfakes-to-cheap-fakes-the-looming-threat-for-business/#4ebe8455d618

Wardle, C., & Derakhshan, H. (2017). *Information disorder: Toward an interdisciplinary framework for research and policy making*. Council of Europe report.

West, D. M. (2018). *How artificial intelligence is transforming the world*. Brookings Institution Press.

Westerlund, M. (2019). The emergence of deepfake technology: A review. *Technology innovation management review, 9*(11).

Wirth, W., Maier, C., & von Wangenheim, F. (2010). The role of consumer identification with the retailer for retail patronage. *Journal of Retailing and Consumer Services, 17*(6), 533–539.

The Transformative Power of AI in Pediatric Healthcare and Its Application in Pediatric Allergy

Amelia Licari, Giuliana Ferrante, Gian Luigi Marseglia, and Stefania La Grutta

Abstract Artificial intelligence (AI) has a transformative impact on pediatric healthcare, especially in the field of pediatric allergies. This chapter explores how AI enhances the diagnosis, treatment, and prediction of allergic reactions in children. AI's exceptional ability to analyze multi-dimensional data, detect subtle indicators, and make probabilistic predictions significantly improves diagnostic accuracy and personalization of treatment plans. It also contributes to predicting allergic reactions and developing new therapeutics by identifying novel targets and repurposing existing drugs. While AI presents immense opportunities, challenges such as data privacy, bias, and the need for clinician oversight must be addressed. The chapter emphasizes the importance of responsible AI integration, rigorous validation, and regulatory standards to ensure safe and effective implementation in pediatric allergy care.

A. Licari (✉)
Department of Clinical, Surgical, Diagnostic, and Pediatric Sciences, University of Pavia, Pavia, Italy

Pediatric Clinic, Fondazione IRCCS Policlinico San Matteo, Pavia, Italy

Institute of Translational Pharmacology, National Research Council of Italy, Palermo, Italy
e-mail: amelia.licari@unipv.it

G. Ferrante
Institute of Translational Pharmacology, National Research Council of Italy, Palermo, Italy

Pediatric Section, Department of Surgery, Dentistry, Paediatrics, and Gynaecology, University of Verona, Verona, Italy
e-mail: giuliana.ferrante@univr.it

G. L. Marseglia
Department of Clinical, Surgical, Diagnostic, and Pediatric Sciences, University of Pavia, Pavia, Italy

Pediatric Clinic, Fondazione IRCCS Policlinico San Matteo, Pavia, Italy
e-mail: gl.marseglia@smatteo.pv.it

S. La Grutta
Institute of Translational Pharmacology, National Research Council of Italy, Palermo, Italy
e-mail: stefania.lagrutta@irib.cnr.it

G. R. Marseglia et al. (eds.), *Socio-economic Impact of Artificial Intelligence*, Progress in IS, https://doi.org/10.1007/978-3-031-73514-1_8

1 Introduction

The application of artificial intelligence (AI) in healthcare draws from a rich and extensive history. As early as 1949, Claude Shannon, an influential mathematician and engineer, demonstrated the potential of AI through his work on a computer program designed to play chess. This seminal work laid the groundwork for the exploration of AI's decision-making and pattern recognition capabilities. In 1956, a pivotal moment occurred at the Dartmouth Summer Research Project, where John McCarthy, a prominent computer scientist, formally introduced the term "artificial intelligence." This event catalyzed a surge of research into AI concepts and methodologies. The following decades witnessed the development of foundational AI systems, such as rule-based expert systems and early iterations of machine learning. While progress was made, challenges regarding computational power and data availability limited the scope of practical applications within healthcare. Now, in the twenty-first century, we see tangible applications with algorithms like CheXNet (2017) for pneumonia diagnosis and Cardio DL—the first FDA-approved, AI-powered cardiac imaging solution (Biancone et al., 2023).

In response to the rapid integration of AI into healthcare, the FDA proposed a regulatory framework in 2019. This framework outlines a premarket review process for AI and machine learning-driven medical software, highlighting the necessity for robust governance and validation procedures to ensure the safety and efficacy of AI-based clinical tools.

The landscape of pediatric healthcare is on the verge of a paradigm shift driven by the integration of AI. AI's remarkable capacity for high-dimensional data analysis, complex pattern recognition, and probabilistic modeling offers immense potential to revolutionize the diagnosis, treatment, and potentially even prevention of childhood illnesses.

Key areas where AI can benefit patients include early diagnosis, self-care, prevention and wellness initiatives, clinical decision support, care delivery, and chronic care management. The widespread adoption of electronic health records (EHRs) and personal healthcare records, often containing longitudinal and genomic data, underscores the value of AI. AI can improve data quality, process complex information, and develop advanced algorithms for data interpretation (Messinger et al., 2020).

This chapter will explore this transformative power, with a specific focus on the impact of AI within the domain of pediatric allergic diseases—a burgeoning public health concern with significant implications for children's health worldwide.

2 AI in Pediatric Allergies: A Promising Tool to Enhance Diagnosis and Care

Pediatric allergies encompass a wide range of immune-mediated conditions, from food allergies and atopic dermatitis (eczema) to allergic rhinitis and asthma. These conditions have far-reaching consequences for a child's health and well-being,

Table 1 AI in pediatric allergies: opportunities for transformation and key considerations for implementation

	Specific opportunities	Challenges
Diagnosis	Multi-dimensional data analysis, subtle indicator detection, probabilistic predictions, personalized pathways	Data privacy, bias, limited datasets in pediatrics
Treatment	Personalized plans, optimized medication, proactive management, immunotherapy, patient empowerment	Need for clinician oversight, regulatory standards
Reactions	Predicting risk, proactive measures, improving quality of life	Model accuracy and reliability, ensuring ethical considerations
Therapeutics	Identifying targets, drug repurposing, novel design	Dataset limitations, validation time and cost

causing discomfort, hindering daily activities, and potentially leading to life-threatening situations. Traditionally, diagnosing and managing allergies can be a complex process. It often requires multiple diagnostic tests (skin prick tests, specific IgE blood tests) to identify specific allergens, consultations with specialists (allergists), and careful monitoring of symptoms. Treatment may include allergen avoidance, various medications (e.g., antihistamines, corticosteroids, bronchodilators), and in some cases, allergen-specific immunotherapy. However, AI offers a new set of tools that promise to streamline this process and improve outcomes for young patients (Table 1) (l., 2021a).

2.1 *Transforming Pediatric Allergy Diagnosis*

The diagnosis of pediatric allergies presents unique challenges due to the evolving nature of children's immune systems, potential difficulties in obtaining accurate clinical histories, and the limitations of conventional diagnostic methods. AI offers a transformative approach, promising to enhance diagnostic accuracy, streamline the process, and improve the overall experience for young patients and their families (Cilluffo et al., 2022). AI-powered advancements in pediatric allergy diagnosis include:

- *Multi-dimensional Data Analysis*: Machine learning algorithms, particularly deep learning models, demonstrate exceptional capabilities in analyzing vast and heterogeneous datasets. By integrating a child's detailed medical history, genetic polymorphisms, environmental exposure data, family history, and results from various allergy tests, AI can uncover complex patterns and associations that might elude traditional analysis. This multi-factorial approach has the potential to identify allergies with higher sensitivity and specificity (van Breugel et al., 2023).
- *Subtle Indicator Detection and Analysis*: AI models can be trained to detect and interpret subtle physiological and behavioral cues indicative of allergic reactions.

For example, computer vision algorithms applied to video recordings can analyze nuanced changes in facial expressions, breathing patterns, or skin responses. Similarly, AI-powered analysis of wearable sensor data can identify minute variations in heart rate, respiratory patterns, or galvanic skin response associated with specific allergen exposures. These AI-driven insights can reveal allergies that may be difficult to diagnose through conventional methods.

- *Probabilistic Predictions of Allergic Responses*: AI has the potential to develop predictive models that calculate the likelihood of a child experiencing an allergic reaction to specific allergens or categories of allergens (e.g., food, inhaled substances). These models, trained on extensive datasets, could incorporate historical data, biomarkers, comorbidities, and real-time environmental factors to generate personalized risk scores. This predictive capacity could significantly improve the efficiency of the diagnostic process by prioritizing the investigation of the most probable allergens, reducing unnecessary testing, and minimizing patient discomfort.
- *Personalized and Adaptive Diagnosis*: AI enables a paradigm shift toward highly individualized diagnostic pathways. By analyzing a child's unique profile, medical history, and previous test results, AI-powered systems can recommend the most appropriate diagnostic tests, tailoring the process to maximize accuracy and minimize unnecessary procedures. Moreover, AI can integrate new data points in real time, adaptively refining the diagnostic approach. This personalized and dynamic strategy holds significant promise in optimizing outcomes for children.

2.2 Personalized Allergy Treatment Plans

AI can analyze individual patient data to recommend tailored treatment plans. By integrating factors like allergy severity, response to previous medications, potential triggers, comorbid conditions, and relevant biomarkers (Lin et al., 2023), AI algorithms—including decision trees, neural networks, and potentially reinforcement learning models—can assist healthcare professionals in creating highly personalized strategies for effective allergy management in children (Ferrante et al., 2020).

AI-powered personalization of treatment plans in pediatric allergies holds immense promise for improving clinical outcomes in several key areas:

- *Reduced Symptom Severity*: By analyzing a child's individual medical history and response to previous medications, AI can recommend more targeted therapeutic interventions. This tailored approach could lead to a significant reduction in the severity of allergic symptoms, such as eczema flares, asthma attacks, or allergic rhinitis (Malizia et al., 2022).
- *Fewer Allergic Reactions*: AI-driven treatment plans can incorporate data on a child's specific allergy triggers and environmental factors. This allows healthcare professionals to recommend preventative measures and personalized avoidance

strategies, potentially resulting in fewer accidental allergic reactions and improved overall safety for the child.
- *Enhanced Quality of Life*: The burden of managing allergies can significantly impact a child's daily life. AI-powered treatment personalization, aiming to reduce symptom severity and allergic reactions, can lead to a significant improvement in a child's quality of life. This could manifest as better sleep, increased participation in physical activities and social interactions, and reduced anxiety related to allergies.

Potential mechanisms for improved outcomes include:

- *Optimizing Medication Regimens*: AI excels at analyzing vast datasets of patient responses to different medications, dosages, and combinations. By integrating this data with an individual child's medical history, genetic profile, and other relevant factors, AI can recommend medication regimens with the highest probability of success. This personalized approach goes beyond traditional "trial-and-error" methods, potentially leading to faster symptom relief, fewer side effects, and reduced reliance on unnecessary medications (Eid, 2024).
- *Proactive Management*: Real-time data is crucial for preventing allergic reactions. AI algorithms can integrate information from wearable sensors (monitoring heart rate, respiratory patterns), environmental monitoring devices (tracking pollen levels, air quality), and even a child's dietary log. Analyzing these data streams, AI can identify patterns that signal an increased risk of an allergic reaction. This allows for timely alerts, proactive adjustments to medication, or even preemptive use of rescue medications to potentially avert severe reactions.
- *Long-Term Management Strategies*: AI can analyze a child's allergy data over time, uncovering trends, patterns, and potential warning signs that traditional analysis might miss. This can inform personalized long-term strategies, such as predicting when allergies might become milder or outgrown, identifying risk factors for developing additional allergies, or recognizing early signs of complications like asthma (Ferrante et al., 2021b). By enabling proactive intervention, AI-powered analysis can help prevent future health problems and ensure optimal growth and development for the child.
- *Precision Immunotherapy*: Allergen-specific immunotherapy offers the potential to modify the underlying immune response. AI holds promise in optimizing immunotherapy by analyzing patient data to personalize the selection of allergens, dosages, and the duration of treatment. This individualized approach could lead to greater efficacy, fewer side effects, and potentially a faster path to long-term allergy remission.
- *Patient Empowerment and Engagement*: AI-powered tools like interactive chatbots, personalized risk calculators, and visual data dashboards can empower young patients and their families to play a more active role in allergy management. This improved understanding of their condition can facilitate self-care, better adherence to treatment plans, and more informed decision-making, ultimately leading to better health outcomes.

2.3 Prediction of Allergic Reactions

Pediatric allergic reactions can range from mild discomfort to life-threatening anaphylaxis. Early identification and avoidance of triggers are crucial for ensuring a child's safety. AI has the potential to empower families with predictive capabilities, enabling proactive management of allergies and potentially preventing adverse reactions.

AI models can be trained on vast datasets encompassing a child's medical history, genetic polymorphisms associated with allergies, exposure data to various allergens, environmental factors, and potentially, real-time physiological sensor readings. By analyzing these complex, multi-dimensional datasets, machine learning algorithms can potentially identify subtle patterns and correlations that might predict the likelihood of an allergic reaction to a specific allergen.

This predictive power offers several potential benefits.

AI models, trained on extensive datasets, could categorize children based on their individualized, predicted risk of experiencing an allergic reaction to specific allergens. This probabilistic risk stratification has significant implications for personalizing allergy management. Children identified as high-risk might benefit from stricter allergen avoidance measures, closer monitoring, or the preemptive use of preventative medications (e.g., antihistamines before a potential exposure). Also, AI-driven predictions offer families a valuable decision-making tool for allergen avoidance. For instance, an AI-generated risk assessment for a child with a severe peanut allergy could inform decisions about attending a birthday party or other social gatherings where peanuts might be present. This knowledge empowers families to make informed choices, weighing the potential risks and benefits, and ultimately enhancing safety for the child. Moreover, the ability to predict and proactively manage allergic reactions has the potential to significantly improve a child's quality of life. Reduced anxiety surrounding potential triggers, coupled with an increased sense of control and predictability, can empower both children and their families. This can translate to greater participation in daily activities, school, social events, and a reduced sense of isolation that often accompanies severe allergies.

Importantly, AI-powered predictive models for allergic reactions are still under active development. Their accuracy and reliability require rigorous validation through large-scale clinical studies. Furthermore, addressing ethical considerations surrounding data privacy, algorithmic bias, and the explainability of AI models remains critical for their responsible integration into clinical practice (MacMath et al., 2023).

2.4 AI-Powered Innovation in Pediatric Allergy Therapeutics

Traditional drug discovery for allergies can be a time-consuming and resource-intensive process. AI, with its vast data processing capabilities, offers a paradigm shift in the identification of novel therapeutic targets. AI can analyze diverse datasets, including patient information, genetic data, molecular pathways, and the wealth of existing scientific research, to accelerate the development of more effective treatments tailored for children suffering from allergies.

Here's a deeper look at how AI facilitates target identification for new allergy therapies:

- *Uncovering Immune Dysregulation*: AI algorithms can analyze large repositories of immunological data from pediatric allergy patients, such as gene expression profiles, cytokine levels, and immune cell populations. By comparing these datasets to healthy controls, AI can identify specific molecular pathways, proteins, or cell types that are dysregulated in allergic conditions. These dysregulated elements represent potential targets for therapeutic intervention.
- *Repurposing Existing Drugs*: AI algorithms can create complex network models that map relationships between existing drugs, their molecular targets, and the diseases they treat. By analyzing these networks, AI can identify drugs with known targets and mechanisms of action that might have potential efficacy in allergies. AI-powered simulations can also model how existing drugs might interact with protein targets relevant to allergy pathogenesis. This "in silico" (computer-based) approach can predict whether a drug could potentially block an allergic pathway and inform the prioritization of existing drugs for further testing in allergy models. Drugs identified for repurposing through AI analysis may have already undergone some safety and efficacy testing in other contexts. This can significantly reduce the time and resources needed for clinical trials specifically focused on allergies, potentially leading to faster access to new treatment options for children.
- *Designing Novel Therapeutics*: De novo drug design can be aided by AI. AI can analyze the three-dimensional structure of allergy-related proteins or receptors. By understanding the shape and properties of these molecules, AI algorithms can design novel drug molecules that can bind to specific regions and inhibit their function. Furthermore, AI can rapidly screen vast libraries of virtual molecules to identify those with the potential to interact with the target protein in the desired way. This "virtual screening" significantly reduces the time and cost associated with traditional high-throughput screening methods in drug discovery. AI might even allow for the design of personalized therapeutic molecules based on a child's individual genetic profile and the specific mechanisms underlying their allergies (Saglani & Custovic, 2019). This approach has the potential to provide highly targeted therapies with minimal side effects and improved efficacy.

3 Existing Challenges of AI in Pediatric Medicine

While AI presents incredible opportunities within pediatric medicine, it's vital to address the significant challenges that accompany its implementation.

Pediatric electronic health information possesses a high degree of sensitivity. ML algorithms necessitate access to substantial volumes of this data to facilitate the processes of training and development. Safeguarding patient privacy is paramount. Rigorous data governance protocols, anonymization techniques, and stringent regulatory frameworks are essential to obviate unauthorized access or malevolent utilization. Children and their families must possess unwavering confidence that their information is meticulously protected.

AI algorithms in healthcare exhibit susceptibility to bias stemming from the inherent characteristics of the data employed for their training. Datasets composed predominantly of specific demographics can lead to diminished generalizability and accuracy for underrepresented populations. This phenomenon, known as algorithmic bias, can have significant downstream consequences, potentially manifesting as misdiagnoses, inappropriate treatment recommendations, and the inadvertent exacerbation of existing health disparities. To mitigate these risks, the development and implementation of bias mitigation strategies are paramount. These strategies may encompass techniques such as data augmentation to ensure balanced representation across diverse patient demographics and fairness-aware model architectures specifically designed to minimize bias in decision-making. Additionally, fostering transparency throughout the process of algorithm development is crucial. This can be achieved through initiatives such as the publication of detailed descriptions of the training data and the rationale behind model selection.

While AI has demonstrated significant capabilities in healthcare analysis, its application in pediatrics should prioritize the irreplaceable expertise of human pediatricians. AI systems are optimally employed as augmentative decision-support tools, functioning in collaboration with, rather than independently of, pediatric healthcare providers. Clinicians must retain ultimate control over the diagnostic and therapeutic decision-making processes. This necessitates a rigorous approach to the evaluation of AI-generated recommendations, incorporating critical appraisal and informed by the physician's extensive clinical knowledge and experience. Such a cautious and supervised integration of AI can bolster patient safety and optimize healthcare outcomes for pediatric patients. Over-reliance on AI without appropriate human oversight, however, presents significant risks and could lead to detrimental effects on patient well-being (van Breugel et al., 2023).

The relative paucity of pediatric EHRs compared to robust adult datasets presents a significant challenge in developing effective AI models, particularly for less prevalent pediatric conditions. This data scarcity hinders the ability to achieve the large sample sizes often necessary for training high-performance deep learning algorithms. To address this limitation, proactive and collaborative strategies are required. These include:

- Secure and Ethical Data Sharing: Establishing secure platforms and protocols for ethical sharing of pediatric EHRs across institutions, while rigorously adhering to patient privacy regulations, can significantly expand the data pool available for model training.

- Synthetic Data Generation: The use of generative adversarial networks (GANs) or similar techniques to create realistic synthetic pediatric datasets can augment existing data and facilitate model development in areas where data is sparse.
- Multi-institutional Collaborations: Fostering collaborations across healthcare institutions can enable the pooling of pediatric data. This consolidated approach can be particularly impactful for rarer conditions.
- Federated Learning: This decentralized AI training approach allows models to be trained on data distributed across multiple institutions without requiring the data itself to be shared, upholding data privacy.

While AI is a rapidly evolving field, clear regulatory guidelines for its use in pediatric medicine are still being developed. The absence of such frameworks poses potential risks. Robust regulatory oversight is imperative to ensure that the development and deployment of AI-powered healthcare solutions adhere to rigorous standards of safety, efficacy, fairness, and ethical principles (MacMath et al., 2023). Key areas that warrant careful consideration and regulation include:

- *Data Governance and Privacy*: Strict regulations addressing the collection, storage, and utilization of pediatric health data are critical for safeguarding patient privacy and mitigating risks of misuse.
- *Algorithmic Transparency and Explainability*: Mandating explainability within AI models is crucial. This will enable clinicians to understand the rationale behind AI-generated recommendations and identify potential sources of bias.
- *Clinical Validation and Performance Monitoring*: Regulatory frameworks should establish standards for pre-market validation of AI systems on diverse pediatric populations and define mechanisms for continuous post-market monitoring of real-world performance.
- *Liability and Accountability*: Clear guidelines for assigning liability and accountability in instances of AI-related errors or adverse events are essential to protect both patients and healthcare providers while fostering trust in these technologies.

The development of these regulatory frameworks necessitates a collaborative approach involving physicians, data scientists, regulators, ethicists, and legal experts. International standards and harmonization of regulations would further facilitate the responsible and equitable implementation of AI in pediatrics on a global scale.

4 Conclusions

The integration of AI into pediatric allergy care holds extraordinary promise. Its potential to streamline diagnosis, personalize treatment, predict allergic reactions, and accelerate the development of novel therapeutics could significantly enhance outcomes for children worldwide. However, it's crucial to proceed with a thoughtful approach that recognizes existing challenges and prioritizes data privacy, algorithmic fairness, and the clinician's central role. Ongoing research, rigorous regulatory standards, and interdisciplinary collaboration are paramount for the safe and ethical implementation of AI in this domain. As the field matures, we can anticipate a future where AI empowers children, their families, and pediatricians, leading to improved quality of life and the possibility of overcoming the burden of allergic diseases.

References

Biancone, P., Secinaro, S., Marseglia, R., & Calandra, D. (2023). E-health for the future. Managerial perspectives using a multiple case study approach. *Technovation, 120*, 102406.

Cilluffo, G., Fasola, S., Ferrante, G., Licari, A., Marseglia, G. R., Albarelli, A., Marseglia, G. L., & La Grutta, S. (2022). Machine learning: A modern approach to pediatric asthma. *Pediatric Allergy and Immunology: Official Publication of the European Society of Pediatric Allergy and Immunology, 33*(Suppl 27), 34–37. https://doi.org/10.1111/pai.13624

Eid, N. (2024). Artificial intelligence in pediatric respiratory diseases: Current status and future promises. *Pediatric Allergy, Immunology, and Pulmonology, 37*(1), 1–2. https://doi.org/10.1089/ped.2024.0028

Ferrante, G., Licari, A., Marseglia, G. L., & La Grutta, S. (2020). Artificial intelligence as an emerging diagnostic approach in paediatric pulmonology. *Respirology (Carlton, Vic.), 25*(10), 1029–1030. https://doi.org/10.1111/resp.13842

Ferrante, G., Licari, A., Fasola, S., Marseglia, G. L., & La Grutta, S. (2021a). Artificial intelligence in the diagnosis of pediatric allergic diseases. *Pediatric Allergy and Immunology: Official Publication of the European Society of Pediatric Allergy and Immunology, 32*(3), 405–413. https://doi.org/10.1111/pai.13419

Ferrante, G., Vitale, G., Licari, A., Montalbano, L., Pilato, G., Infantino, I., Augello, A., & La Grutta, S. (2021b). Social robots and therapeutic adherence: A new challenge in pediatric asthma? *Paediatric Respiratory Reviews, 40*, 46–51. https://doi.org/10.1016/j.prrv.2020.11.001

Lin, K., Wang, Y., Li, Y., & Wang, Y. (2023). Identification of biomarkers associated with pediatric asthma using machine learning algorithms: A review. *Medicine, 102*(47), e36070. https://doi.org/10.1097/MD.0000000000036070

MacMath, D., Chen, M., & Khoury, P. (2023). Artificial intelligence: Exploring the future of innovation in allergy immunology. *Current Allergy and Asthma Reports, 23*(6), 351–362. https://doi.org/10.1007/s11882-023-01084-z

Malizia, V., Cilluffo, G., Fasola, S., Ferrante, G., Landi, M., Montalbano, L., Licari, A., & La Grutta, S. (2022). Endotyping allergic rhinitis in children: A machine learning approach. *Pediatric Allergy and Immunology: Official Publication of the European Society of Pediatric Allergy and Immunology, 33*(Suppl 27), 18–21. https://doi.org/10.1111/pai.13620

Messinger, A. I., Luo, G., & Deterding, R. R. (2020). The doctor will see you now: How machine learning and artificial intelligence can extend our understanding and treatment of asthma. *The Journal of Allergy and Clinical Immunology, 145*(2), 476–478. https://doi.org/10.1016/j.jaci.2019.12.898

Saglani, S., & Custovic, A. (2019). Childhood asthma: Advances using machine learning and mechanistic studies. *American Journal of Respiratory and Critical Care Medicine, 199*(4), 414–422. https://doi.org/10.1164/rccm.201810-1956CI

van Breugel, M., Fehrmann, R. S. N., Bügel, M., Rezwan, F. I., Holloway, J. W., Nawijn, M. C., Fontanella, S., Custovic, A., & Koppelman, G. H. (2023). Current state and prospects of artificial intelligence in allergy. *Allergy, 78*(10), 2623–2643. https://doi.org/10.1111/all.15849

AI for the Built Environment: An Opportunity to Improve Safety, Efficiency, and Sustainability

Giulia Scagliotti, Ashwin Agrawal, and Martin A. Fischer

Abstract The Architecture, Engineering, Construction and Operation (AECO) industry suffers from problems such as lack of safety and sustainability, inefficiency, and labor shortage, which can be mitigated by the adoption of solutions based on artificial intelligence (AI) that automate tasks traditionally performed by humans. However, while planning the adoption of AI-driven solutions, AECO professionals often lack knowledge of what can be automated and encounter difficulties in setting goals and defining a digital strategy that integrates automation with manual work. To assist professionals, we propose a two-dimensional conceptual framework for determining the roles played by AI-driven solutions, their level of automation, and the roles that suit humans best. We analyze potential AI applications in AECO to explain how to use the framework and show the variety of AI development opportunities in this industry. The aim of the framework is to facilitate structured discussion and communication between professionals to plan the development of AI applications that have more chance to succeed and can help overcome AECO industry's long-standing challenges.

1 Technology Adoption in AECO

The acronym AECO means "Architecture, Engineering, Construction, and Operation" and well describes the collaboration between different professionals, such as architects, engineers, project managers, and skilled workers, to ensure the completion of a construction project from design and planning to execution to

G. Scagliotti (✉) · A. Agrawal
Department of Civil and Environmental Engineering, Stanford University, Stanford, CA, USA
e-mail: gscaglio@stanford.edu

M. A. Fischer
Kumagai Professor in the School of Engineering, Department of Civil and Environmental Engineering, Stanford University, Stanford, CA, USA

G. R. Marseglia et al. (eds.), *Socio-economic Impact of Artificial Intelligence*, Progress in IS, https://doi.org/10.1007/978-3-031-73514-1_9

operation to maintenance. The AECO industry is the largest industry in the global economy and accounts for about 13% of the world's Gross Domestic Product (GDP) (Ribeirinho et al., 2020). However, it is one of the least digitalized industries and is slow to adopt new technologies, including artificial intelligence (AI) solutions. In 2018, the AECO industry planned to invest roughly 1% of revenue into technology, a significantly smaller proportion than other industries such as financial services or transportation and logistics, which planned to spend about 11% and 7% of revenue, respectively, and are further along in the process of adopting AI solutions (Blanco et al. 2018).

The most relevant technological advancement in the AECO industry in the last four decades has been the development and adoption of Building Information Modeling (BIM). BIM is a digital representation and shared information resource of the physical and functional characteristics of a facility from its earliest conception to demolition (National BIM Standard—United States). Having a shared model facilitates communication and coordination among different stakeholders (design teams, contractors, subcontractors, etc.) and improves time and cost decision-making, resulting in greater efficiency and resource savings. Today, BIM technology is applied widely in AECO and has already entered the last phase of the Gartner's Hype Cycle, the plateau of productivity, whereas AI and machine learning (ML) in AECO are still in the initial phases of the Hype Cycle, showing attractiveness and high expectations (Bosch-Sijtsema et al., 2021).

Although the AECO industry is increasing digitalization, there are AECO-specific challenges that hinder or slow wide adoption and implementation of new technologies based on AI and ML. For example, each construction project is unique and often requires an ad hoc solution, construction sites are highly complex and unstructured environments, and construction processes are uncertain. Each project is also completed in a relatively short time, whereas technologies need to be tested and used for a long time to justify their relatively high initial costs and be considered economically viable solutions. Moreover, given the wide range of possibilities offered by the new technologies, AECO professionals often encounter difficulties in selecting the appropriate level of sophistication of the AI solution that can be developed with the technological capabilities of the company and that will lead to the expected value (Agrawal et al., 2022). Specifically, AECO companies often do not have the capabilities to incorporate new technologies alone, starting with the management and analysis of data that are essential to take advantage of AI. To address this issue, there is a need to hire people with background and skill in AI and digital technologies and retrain the current AECO workforce (Blanco et al., 2018). In addition, incorporating new technologies often translates into a disruption of traditional ways of working and substantial changes in the processes within an organization, leading to the need to change the current AECO business models. However, the players involved often have the tendency to maintain the traditional processes and are usually risk adverse.

Although the AECO industry lags other industries in adopting new technologies, the increasing number of projects that use BIM also creates a basis for the application of AI solutions, and the continuous improvements and advancements in AI and

ML represent an opportunity that some AECO companies and startups have begun to explore. By using AI and ML, it is now possible to automate tasks previously performed only by humans, such as interpreting data, predicting outcomes, making decisions, and taking actions (Ranalli, 2021; Wang, 2021). Therefore, AI-based solutions can be deployed in the AECO industry to solve the longstanding issues of safety, lack of efficiency, high costs, negative impact on the environment, and labor shortage. Technological tools can help to keep construction workers safer (Teizer et al., 2010), expedite the design and construction process (Morkos, 2014), prevent projects from going over budget (Pewdum et al., 2009), and reduce construction waste and carbon emissions (Çetin et al., 2021).

2 Examples of Applications to Solve AECO's Longstanding Problems

A variety of applications across different AECO phases has begun to emerge and has the potential to solve the longstanding problems of the AECO industry. This section illustrates some of these applications, as well as the problems they try to address, which are summarized in Table 1.

Lack of Safety Unfortunately, the AECO industry is one of the most dangerous industries in the world and registers the highest number of fatal accidents among its workers both in the USA and Europe (National Safety Council, Eurostat). Specifically, in 2020 in the USA and EU, more than one-fifth of all fatal accidents at work took place within the construction sector: 1008 and 691 deaths in the USA and EU, respectively (National Safety Council, Eurostat). Frequent causes are falls from heights, being struck by a moving object or vehicle, or being trapped by something overturning or collapsing (Sacks et al., 2009). Keeping construction workers safe and avoiding fatal accidents and injuries are among the main objectives in AECO today and, in this context, new technologies for monitoring data across construction sites, predicting hazards and mitigating risks can play an important role. The construction work environment can become safer when drones and self-driving vehicles reach areas that are difficult and dangerous to access, and robots take over repetitive, strenuous, and hazardous tasks such as bricklaying, welding, painting, and demolition work, protecting workers from exposure to dust and chemicals and reducing their risk of falls (Brosque & Fischer, 2022) (Table 1, Application #1). Computer vision techniques can also be deployed to assess and detect unsafe worker behavior on construction sites. Specifically, drones and IoT devices can collect images and video on construction sites. Then, software based on image recognition can detect if construction workers wear protective equipment and follow safety measures (Zhang et al., 2021) (Table 1, Application #2). Computer vision techniques can also be used to capture data on the status of the infrastructures and automate the damage detection process (Spencer et al., 2019) (Table 1, Application #3). Identification of corrosion, cracks, or damage through this new technology can

Table 1 Applications to solve today's AECO problems

#	Application	AECO phase	Today's problem
			Lack of safety
1	Painting walls	Construction	Workers required to complete repetitive tasks and exposed to dust and chemicals
2	Detection of worker safety measures	Construction	High number of accidents and latency in identifying dangerous situations
3	Corrosion detection in infrastructure	Maintenance	Concern for workers performing the inspection and for the status of the infrastructure
4	Worker's training	Construction/ Maintenance	Concerns for workers that work at heights or with dangerous materials
			Inefficiency
5	Structural optioneering[a]	Design	Time required to explore design alternatives to obtain the best option
6	Prediction of project costs	Design	Lack of precision in the cost estimation and risk of project cost overrun
7	Measuring construction site progress	Construction	Time required to revise the project schedule while construction is in progress
			Lack of sustainability
8	Energy consumption monitoring	Operation	Difficult to identify the causes of high energy consumption and high carbon footprint
9	Leakage detection in urban water systems	Maintenance	Water waste is approx. 30% of the total water for urban usage due to leakage
10	Reusable waste detection	Demolition	More than 30% of the world's overall waste production and negative impact on the environment

[a]Optioneering is when a contractor carries out an in-depth review of various construction options/ alternatives to get the best possible approach

speed up the structural assessment process and make the built environment safer. Virtual Reality technology based on BIM also offers opportunities to improve the safety of workers by supporting their training activities. Workers would be immersed and able to walk through the project 3D model in a virtual environment and be trained to work at heights or with hazardous materials, experiencing the field before going on the construction site (Sacks et al., 2013) (Table 1, Application #4).

Inefficiency Another problematic aspect of the AECO industry is that construction projects are labor-intensive and complex, given that they involve many subcontractors, and most of the work is performed in unstructured environments. The process to complete projects has some degree of uncertainty: on average, projects take 20% longer to finish than scheduled and can be up to 80% over budget (Agarwal et al., 2016). So, leveraging technology to reduce time and cost to complete a construction project is an important goal. For example, optimization algorithms used in design, scheduling, and logistics can increase and improve the efficiency of the design and construction process. Generative design technology can be adopted during the design phase to generate and explore many possible designs based on user input.

During an iterative process, which is much faster than traditional design, building design can be optimized according to individual variables like cost, construction time, energy consumption, daylight orientation, environmental impact, as well as combinations of variables (Machairas et al., 2014) (Table 1, Application #5). Neural networks, AI-driven algorithms, and ML can be deployed to analyze data and market, trace past prices, understand circumstances and forecast future prices to get a more precise prediction of cost starting from the design phase (Tayefeh Hashemi et al., 2020) (Table 1, Application #6). Moreover, it is now possible to track the progress on a construction site in real time, getting a comprehensive and updated picture without the intervention of humans. This helps to improve and update the construction schedule; keep construction projects on time and budget; and avoid manual observations that are tedious, time consuming, and prone to mistakes (Song & Eldin, 2012) (Table 1, Application #7).

Lack of Sustainability Construction and the built environment produce at least 40% of the world's CO_2 equivalent emissions (UNEP, 2022) and generate more than 30% of the world's overall waste (Purchase et al., 2022), mostly because of demolition activities. Therefore, reducing the impact of the AECO industry on the environment and incorporating more sustainable practices are urgent and essential. New technologies such as 3D printing or Internet of Things (IoT) sensors can support a more efficient use of materials and energy and a reduction of construction and demolition waste. Sensors can be placed on construction sites to collect data regarding the activities and conditions of the site. These tools can also be deployed when the building or infrastructure is in operation to track energy consumption in real time (Casini, 2014) (Table 1, Application #8) or automate the traditional management system, from detecting water leakage issues (Ali et al., 2022) (Table 1, Application #9) to identifying defects through thermal imaging cameras. New technology based on AI can also be applied at the end of the life of a building or infrastructure to detect the reusable or recyclable material to reduce demolition waste production (Na et al., 2022) (Table 1, Application #10).

Labor Shortage In addition to safety, lack of efficiency, and sustainability, another chronic problem of the AECO industry is skilled labor shortage, not just of construction workers but also engineers. This issue is especially evident in the USA, where it represents a hurdle for the future growth of the sector. The AECO industry employs about 10M workers in total, but it is estimated that 300,000-600,000 new workers will be needed each year for the next ten years to support planned infrastructure spending (Hovnanian et al., 2022). Supporting a digital transformation in AECO and taking advantage of automation and AI innovation can help address the lack of skilled workers and is strategic to maintain and improve productivity. The introduction of new AI solutions in AECO will lead to redefining which activities are performed by human workers and which are partially or fully automated. It is necessary that roles and activities are well distributed according to the capabilities of the workers and the technology deployed to obtain the full potential from both.

3 A Framework to Support the Development of AI-Driven Solutions

As can be seen from the previous section, there are abundant opportunities to support the work of the AECO industry with AI applications. Hence, to support professionals in digital transformation and guide them in allocating work between humans and machines, we propose a two-dimensional conceptual framework (Agrawal et al., 2023). The aim of the framework is to aid with the selection of the appropriate level of sophistication of the AI solutions, defining which and to what extent the functions (or roles) are automated and how this impacts humans. The framework differentiates the types of roles played by an AI solution (Sect. 3.1 and columns in Fig. 1), categorized under (1) Observer, (2) Analyst, (3) Decision Maker, and (4) Action Executor, and the extent of automation for each of these roles (Sect. 3.2 and rows in Fig. 1), divided into five levels from completely manual to fully automated or autonomous for all situations (Agrawal et al., 2023). Since AI solutions applied in AECO are still in their developmental stages, the framework helps professionals plan the deployment of AI-driven solutions, clearly communicate goals between different stakeholders, and lay out a strategic vision. This is shown in Sect. 3.3 through the example of leakage detection in urban water systems from Table 1, where stakeholders can assess the current level of automation in each role of the process and then plan the introduction of more automated solutions to increase the efficiency of leakage detection and reduce the amount of wasted water.

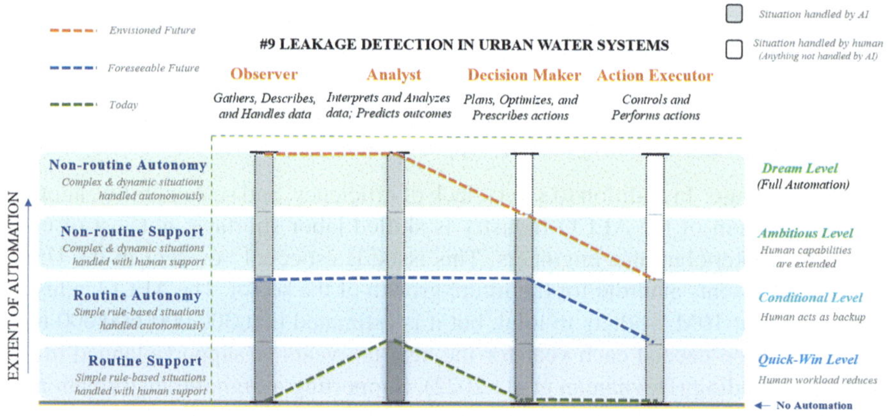

Fig. 1 Two-dimensional conceptual framework (Agrawal et al., 2023) for the roles of humans and AI solutions played in detecting leakage in urban water systems and their extent of autonomation today (green line), in the foreseeable future (blue line), and farther in the future (orange line)

Table 2 Functions of each role

Observer	Analyst	Decision maker	Action executor
Sensing	Analyze and monitor	Optimization	Physical action
Representation	Pattern recognition	Simulation	Actuation
Description	Prediction	Forecasting	Interaction
Visualization	Interpretation	Prescription	Communication
Retrieval	Diagnosis	Planning	Control

Adapted from Agrawal et al. (2023)

3.1 Types of Roles

Since every task requires data, making sense of data, making decisions, and taking action, the development of an AI solution requires clarity on the role of humans vs. the AI solution with respect to the four previously mentioned roles. Various specific functions fall within each role and are summarized in Table 2.

Observer This role involves collecting, handling, and representing the data of the real world by perceiving the status, attributes, and dynamics of relevant elements in the environment. The central functions of this role are sensing, acquiring, digitizing, representing, and communicating the data gathered.

Analyst This role involves manipulating, analyzing, understanding, and interpreting data according to the preferences and the goal set by the operator. For this role, pattern recognition, monitoring, interpretation, and prediction of missing information are functions that an AI-based solution can perform.

Decision Maker This role takes the analyzed data as input and makes decisions. An AI solution should exhibit rational or utilitarian behavior, taking decisions that help to achieve the maximum utility. The decisions are not always straightforward and often involve considerations of the future. Therefore, simulation, forecasting, and optimization are critical functions for this role and advancements in ML, reinforcement learning, and automated decision support are beneficial.

Action Executor This role entails translating the decision into an action. Actuators may be used in the action to interact with and influence the physical environment. Recent advancements in robotics have greatly aided the implementation of actions by machines.

If the AI solution only handled data, humans would be responsible for the rest of the tasks: analyzing information, making decisions, and taking actions. In contrast, if the AI solution only made decisions and performed actions, humans would be required to observe and analyze the data. In summary, any role that AI solutions cannot perform needs to be completed by humans.

3.2 Extent of Automation

The extent of automation for each role is divided into five different levels ranging from completely manual to fully automated. One or many AI-based solutions can be deployed to complete a task and increase the level of automation of each role. The extent to which a given role can be automated depends on both the learning ability and the autonomy of the AI solution deployed, which are the ability to adapt to dynamic environment and the level of independence in each role, respectively. The higher the automation, the more an AI-based solution will be able to support human workers in a specific role by working independently and adapting to changing circumstances.

Learning Ability Learning enables the AI solution to improve its performance over time, similarly to the way humans learn and grow intellectually over time. This increases the automation of each role of the AI solution, since it can perform functions that require cognitive flexibility in situations where rules are not completely understood and no single correct or best solution exists. Based on learning ability, the matrix of the framework differentiates the extent of automation as follows: routine situations, which are well-defined, predictable situations that can be solved by rules-based AI solutions, and non-routine situations where no explicit instruction is available or algorithms must adapt to some degree of dynamic change, thus requiring learning.

Autonomy Autonomy determines how much humans are involved in completing one or several functions for a specific role. A fully autonomous AI solution completes all the functions for a specific role without any human involvement. A partially autonomous AI solution assists humans and reduces the workload associated with manually completing the role. Based on autonomy, the matrix of the framework differentiates the extent of automation ranging from partial autonomy meaning humans are involved in routine and non-routine situations to completely autonomous meaning full automation.

The highest level of automation would be for each role to work autonomously, handling non-routine situations. While attempting to automate each role of the AI solution to the highest extent possible might be the ambition, in most cases, it may not be necessary, practical, or even desirable due to a lack of technical capabilities, risk involved, preferences of practitioners, legal requirements, or financial constraints. In these cases, intermediate levels of automation may be preferred to maximize the joint performance of humans and the AI-based solution.

Therefore, a five-level measure of automation for each role based on learning ability and autonomy is proposed:

1. *No Automation (manual)*: At this level, humans perform all the tasks without any kind of support from the AI solution. This is the lowest form of automation and acts as default in the two-dimensional framework.
2. *Routine Support*: Humans are assisted by technology in completing routine tasks that require to follow explicitly programmed rules. The projects that aim to reach

this level of automation are often quick wins because they are the easiest to implement with the least amount of organizational changes. Automating routine tasks reduces the workload of humans who can focus on other tasks that require higher creativity and intelligence.

3. *Routine Autonomy*: AI solutions can complete routine tasks autonomously without human supervision. The AI solution's autonomy introduces a risk of failure, which occasionally defeats the goal of autonomy. The marginal benefits that routine autonomy provides over routine support need to be carefully evaluated to justify its use. The projects that aim to this level are often conditional projects, in which the humans act as a backup to the AI solution in case of a failure.
4. *Non-routine Support*: Using its ability to learn, the AI solution assists humans in handling non-routine tasks, i.e., situations that are dynamic or where rules are unclear. The learning process requires data collection and labeling and, in turn, implies significant changes in the organization toward data-driven decisions. These projects are ambitious, requiring significant changes in the way work is performed but substantially extend human capabilities.
5. *Non-routine Autonomy (full automation)*: This is the highest level of automation where the AI solution can complete the task autonomously at the required level of performance, adapting to the task environment and improving its performance over time. These projects are dream projects for companies. Nowadays, it is rare to see suitable examples of applications at this level across all types of roles, but we are optimistic about the possibility to see more of them in the future.

3.3 Example: Leakage Detection in Urban Water Systems

To illustrate in detail how the framework works, we select the example of leakage detection in urban water systems from Table 1. Approximately 30% of the total drinkable water is wasted due to undetected leakage in urban water distribution systems (El-Zahab & Zayed, 2019). Currently, the process of detecting leakage is mainly manual relying on passive control, regular surveys, or leakage monitoring in zones (Vanijjirattikhan et al., 2022), and the repairs are performed manually by waterworks operators. Since most water infrastructures are underground, detecting the exact location of a water leakage is challenging. Therefore, the development and deployment of new technologies can noticeably support operators in determining the location and severity of leaks and assist during repair operations.

First, we can distinguish the four roles:

Observer: data on the distribution of the water system, pipe diameters, water pressure, and water flow rates is relevant to detect a leakage and needs to be collected.

Analyst: after getting data, analyses should be carried out, and the results of these analyses can be compared to the target values (e.g., typical flow values) to identify any issue in the water distribution system.

Decision Maker: if a leak is detected, a decision on how to intervene should be made, depending on the location of the leak, its severity, and the incurred or potential damage. Safety, environmental impact, time, and cost are variables that will likely be considered in making the final choice among different alternatives.

Action Executor: the action would be the repair of the leakage and can be performed manually or with the aid of technology.

To show how the level of automation can vary in each different role, we analyze three scenarios for detecting leakage in urban water systems: today's process, a scenario in the foreseeable future, and a scenario farther in the future.

Today's process (green line in Fig. 1): Currently, the Observer, Decision Maker, and Action Executor roles in detecting the water leakage are typically played by humans without automation, whereas the Analysis role is supported by technology. Information is obtained 1) from reports of the customers when leakage is visible or the pressure drops, 2) using acoustic devices to listen for leaks from one end of the distribution system to the other, or 3) collecting data of flow rates at test points. When data are gathered, a model supports humans in carrying out calculations to determine if the values detected are within an acceptable range or not. For example, applying the methodology of the minimum night flow that consists of an analysis of the flow at its minimum (typically between 1am and 4am at night), when the leakage component is at its largest percentage of the flow. Based on the results, humans decide to inspect certain pipes, which method and tools are needed to inspect them, and if it is necessary to close certain valves. The action to perform the inspection and close the valves is carried out by humans.

Foreseeable future (blue line in Fig. 1): acoustic or vibration sensors can be placed permanently in strategic locations of the distribution system to collect data such as leakage sounds and water flow. Humans will still be available to gather data if necessary. An AI-based water leak detection tool can guide operators to interpret the sound as leakage or non-leakage and pinpoint where in the pipe the problem occurs. Additional analyses are carried out by humans in non-routine situations, such as when there is sound interference. If a medium- or high-severity leakage is suspected, the AI solution can recommend to humans to perform an inspection and close the valve. A pipe inspection robot can be sent to confirm the leakage, and humans will manually close the valves and perform the repair.

Envisioned future (orange line in Fig. 1): farther in future, smart cities are expected to have systems working together in an intelligent way to ensure sustainability (Rojek & Studzinski, 2019). IoT sensors can gather data in real time about water flows, and the sensing signals can be sent to a server or cloud. Data are preprocessed: averages and fluctuations between sensors are computed and ML is used to identify real-time leakage and faults of the components and predict their locations and severity depending on the positions of the sensors. Various decisions can be prescribed by the AI-driven solution based on how much the values differ from normal flow, where the leak is, and the analysis of patterns from past damage data. Therefore, support in non-routine situations will also be provided to humans. In case of emergency, the valves can be shut off automatically and a pipe inspection robot can be sent to inspect and perform routine repairs, but in complex situations such as the case of a clogged valve or an obstructed pipe, humans will act as action executors.

4 The Present and the Future of AECO Through the Framework

In this section, we present some of the applications described in Sect. 2 through the framework to show two scenarios of role distribution between the AI-driven solution and humans: how the roles are typically performed today and how they can be transformed in the future by the adoption of AI-driven solutions.

Detection of Worker Safety Measures (Table 1, Application 2)
Today, no automated method to detect whether workers are following safety measures on construction sites is typically used. Instead, supervisors inspect the site. These inspections usually occur no more than once a week. Supervisors check whether workers wear safety gear and behave safely. Depending on the level of danger, supervisors decide how to address the problem. For example, they can interrupt on-site operation and order the workers to follow the safety measures. The introduction of new technology on construction sites can partially automate the roles played today by supervisors. Cameras on construction sites can continuously monitor workers. An AI-based recognition system would detect whether workers are wearing safety gear and whether their behavior is safe. Depending on the level of danger, based also on past accident data, the system can decide to signal the unsafe behavior to the worker only, or to also alert supervisors and safety officers with an automatic alert sent to them (Fig. 2).

Structural Optioneering (Table 1, Application 5)
Today, designers often spend several months defining a feasible building model that satisfies the needs of different stakeholders. After many hours of coordination between the stakeholders, different analyses are carried out to verify that the structural model works. Then, the structural design is defined and completed with the support of structural engineering software. However, there is the opportunity to move to a more efficient design with the support of new technology. After the user defines a set of structural parameters (e.g., geometry, material, façade type, etc.), the mass and core models could be automatically updated. Computational geometry, generative design, and ML, based on structural engineering data, could explore different models and compare the performance of design options. The model can be optimized, following the user's preference (cost, material, sustainability, environmental impact, time for completion, etc.), and the best option recommended. Then, the preferred option could be automatically exported into other software for further refinement (Fig. 3).

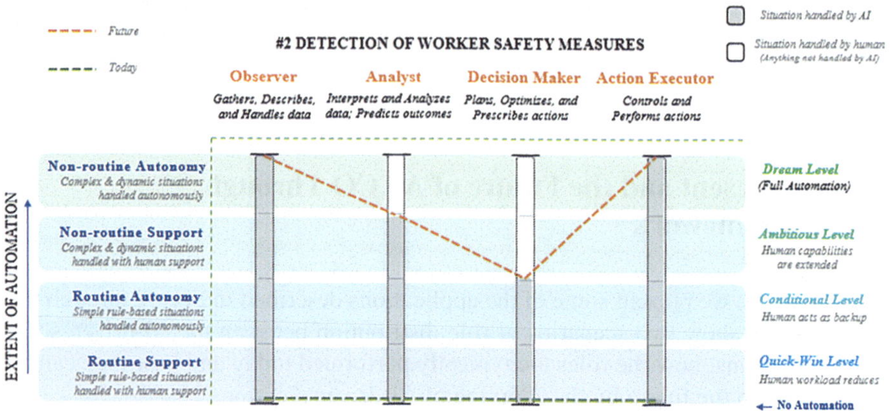

Fig. 2 The level of automation of each role in detecting whether workers follow safety measures on construction sites, today (green line) and in the future (orange line)

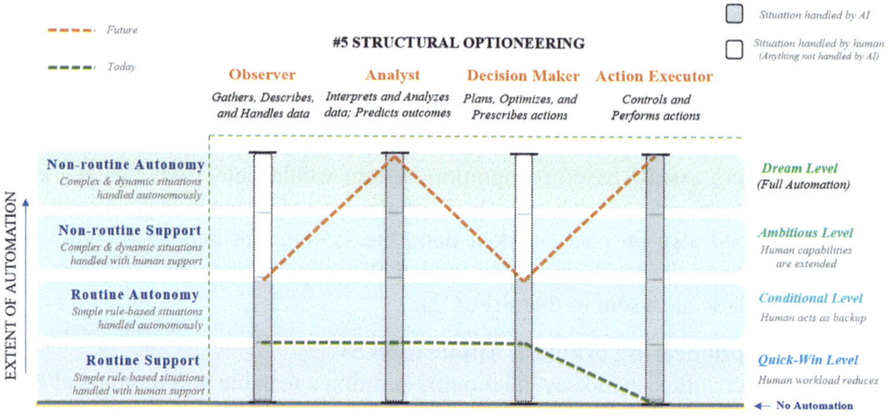

Fig. 3 The level of automation of each role in completing structural design, today (green line) and in the future (orange line)

Measuring Construction Site Progress (Table 1, Application 7)

As in the case of detecting worker safety measures, measuring construction site progress is usually not an automated activity. Supervisors physically inspect the construction site and collect data and pictures. With the support of a task tracking software, they can compare the job site progress with the planned schedule, to identify uncompleted tasks and delays. If some activities are falling behind schedule, the system recommends revising the schedule, which is manually revised by the manager. Bringing new technologies to construction sites would increase the level of

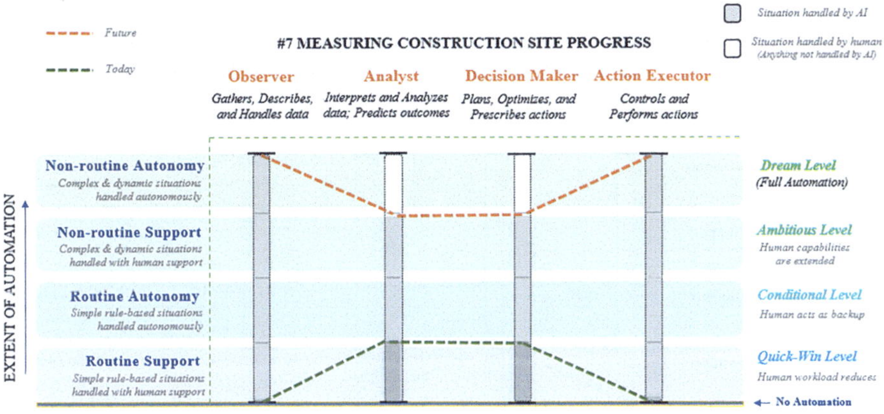

Fig. 4 The level of automation of each role in measuring construction site progress, today (green) and in the future (orange)

automation of this activity. A robot equipped with a camera could autonomously walk on the construction site and get data, obtaining a 3D point cloud. Data could be cross-referenced with BIM, making comparisons between the real-time situation on site and the schedule. The activities that are falling behind could be identified, and the system would decide whether and how to revise the schedule based on past projects, optimizing the cost and time and reducing risks. The system could automatically revise the schedule and inform the manager of the changes (Fig. 4).

Reusable Waste Detection (Table 1, Application 10)
Construction is a major generator of waste. In the USA, demolition waste such as lumber is not usually reused but shredded and trucked to the landfill or incinerator (Clausen & Lebow, 2011). When material is recycled or reused, the process followed is typically not automated. At the end of the life of a building or infrastructure, data and information are manually collected on site. The demolition contractor analyzes the project and estimates if a demolition or a deconstruction is more convenient, also considering the regulations in place, and roughly what materials can be recycled or reused. Then, they decide which materials should be salvaged or become waste and send workers on site to get the salvage material. In the future, data and information on components and materials could be retrieved from a life-cycle BIM at the end of the life of a building or infrastructure. A deep neural network could predict the amount of salvage and waste obtainable from the project, what is recyclable or reusable, which wastes can be upcycled or must be downcycled. The system would automatically recommend deconstruction or demolition and machines and tools for picking up the salvage materials. However, this decision would be made with human support. Robots would work together with humans to pick up the salvage material from construction sites and treat them for being deployed again (Fig. 5).

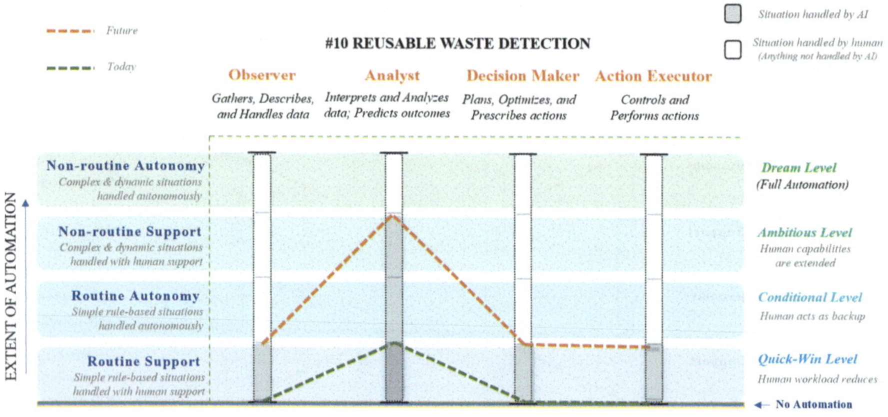

Fig. 5 The level of automation of each role in detecting reusable demolition waste, today (green) and in the future (orange)

The development of AI-driven solutions is a continuous and evolving process. The framework presented can be used by AECO professionals as a starting point to determine the levels of automation of their current technology and to establish a long-term vision of what they want to achieve improving their technology and adopting AI-driven solutions.

While most companies imagine solutions that allow fully autonomous completion of each role, most advanced technology in the foreseeable future will still rely on human intervention. Therefore, it is necessary to understand how AI-driven solutions will integrate with humans.

A failure in properly planning AI-driven solution deployment and understanding the roles that humans and AI-driven solutions play can result in misallocations of resources, unrealistic expectations from the technology, missed opportunities, and strategic misalignment. As the examples above show, the framework enables (and requires) structured brainstorming while planning the development of an AI-driven solution and a systematic role allocation between the selected technological solution and humans.

5 Final Considerations: Responsibility, Business Strategy, and Generalizability

The use of our framework can raise questions and concerns regarding the proper distribution of roles between the AI-driven solution and humans and the responsibilities when technology makes mistakes. While pushing to an upper level of automation, the professionals involved in the development and deployment of the AI-driven solutions should carefully consider the impact of their choices. They should evaluate the reliability and robustness of the selected solution, which can have implications in terms of safety and well-being of humans. They should establish which roles can be automated and which situations an AI-driven solution can handle, given privacy regulations and ethical concerns.

Moving toward more digitalization requires a vision for a digital strategy. Defining how and to what extent the different roles can be automated, what it takes in terms of investment, and which organizational changes are needed to achieve a certain level of automation is critical for developing a digital strategy. Companies should define the value that automation can provide to their business and how automation will alter their business models. The framework can serve as a guide for discussing, comparing, communicating, and strategically prioritizing digital opportunities, so companies can lay out a digital strategy that is more likely to succeed. Our framework has been validated within the AECO industry using feedback from experts during meetings and demonstration sessions. Its usefulness has also been demonstrated by applying it in real-life case studies (Agrawal, 2023). Further studies can explore its generalizability to other industries and different types of technologies.

From design to construction, to operations, to maintenance, the potential AI applications are many and will help create value. Leveraging AI in the AECO industry probably will not replace human workers in the near future, but it will help overcome the industry's longstanding challenges of safety, cost and schedule overruns, sustainability, and labor shortages.

References

Agarwal, R., Chandrasekaran, S., & Sridhar, M. (2016). Imagining construction's digital future. *McKinsey & Company, 24*(06).

Agrawal, A. (2023). *Management of digital transformation projects in the AEC industry*. PhD Thesis, Stanford University (Working Thesis).

Agrawal, A., Fischer, M., & Singh, V. (2022). Digital twin: From concept to practice. *Journal of Management in Engineering, 38*(3), 06022001.

Agrawal, A., Thiel, R., Jain, P., Singh, V., & Fischer, M. (2023). Digital Twin: Where do humans fit in? *Automation in Construction, 148*, 104749.

Ali, A. S., Abdelmoez, M. N., Heshmat, M., & Ibrahim, K. (2022). A solution for water management and leakage detection problems using IoTs based approach. *Internet of Things, 18*, 100504.

Blanco, J. L., Fuchs, S., Parsons, M., Ribeirinho, M. J., & 2018. (2018). Artificial intelligence: Construction technology's next frontier. *The Building Economist*, 7–13.

Bosch-Sijtsema, P., Claeson-Jonsson, C., Johansson, M., & Roupe, M. (2021). The hype factor of digital technologies in AEC. *Construction Innovation, 21*(4), 899–916.

Brosque, C., & Fischer, M. (2022). Safety, quality, schedule, and cost impacts of ten construction robots. *Construction Robotics, 6*(2), 163–186.

Casini, M. (2014). Internet of things for Energy efficiency of buildings. *International Scientific Journal Architecture and Engineering, 2*(1), 24–28.

Çetin, S., De Wolf, C., & Bocken, N. (2021). Circular digital built environment: An emerging framework. *Sustainability, 13*(11), 6348.

Clausen, C. A., & Lebow, S. T. (2011). Reuse and disposal. In J. J. Morrell, K. M. Brooks, & C. M. Davis (Eds.), *Managing treated wood in aquatic environments* (pp. 435–449). Forest Products Society.

El-Zahab, S., & Zayed, T. (2019). Leak detection in water distribution networks: an introductory overview. *Smart Water, 4*(1), 1–23.

Hovnanian, G., Luby, R., & Peloquin, S.. (2022). *Bridging the labor mis-match in US construction*. https://www.mckinsey.com/business-functions/operations/our-insights/bridging-the-labor-mismatch-in-us-cons. Accessed 26 Apr 2023.

Machairas, V., Tsangrassoulis, A., & Axarli, K. (2014). Algorithms for optimization of building design: A review. *Renewable and Sustainable Energy Reviews, 31*, 101–112.

Morkos, R. (2014). *Operational efficiency frontier: Visualizing, manipulating, and navigating the construction scheduling state space with precedence, discrete, and disjunctive constraints*. PhD Thesis, Stanford University.

Na, S., Heo, S., Han, S., Shin, Y., & Lee, M. (2022). Development of an artificial intelligence model to recognise construction waste by applying image data augmentation and transfer learning. *Buildings, 12*(2), 175.

National BIM Standard – United States. (2023). National Building Information Model Standard Project Committee. https://www.nationalbimstandard.org/nbims-us-v. Accessed 26 Apr 2023.

National Safety Council. (2023). https://injuryfacts.nsc.org/work/industry-incidence-rates/most-dangerous-industries/. Accessed 26 Apr 2023.

Pewdum, W., Rujirayanyong, T., & Sooksatra, V. (2009). Forecasting final budget and duration of highway construction projects. *Engineering, Construction and Architectural Management*.

Purchase, C. K., Al Zulayq, D. M., O'Brien, B. T., Kowalewski, M. J., Berenjian, A., Tarighaleslami, A. H., & Seifan, M. (2022). Circular economy of construction and demolition waste: A literature review on lessons, challenges, and benefits. *Materials, 15*(1), 76.

Ranalli, F. (2021). *An artificial intelligence framework for multi-disciplinary design optimization of steel buildings*. PhD Thesis, Stanford University.

Ribeirinho, M. J., Mischke, J., Strube, G., Sjödin, E., Blanco, J. L., Palter, R., Biörck, J., Rockhill, D., & Andersson, T. (2020). *The next normal in construction: How disruption is reshaping the world's largest ecosystem*. McKinsey & Company.

Rojek, I., & Studzinski, J. (2019). Detection and localization of water leaks in water nets supported by an ICT system with artificial intelligence methods as a way forward for smart cities. *Sustainability, 11*(2), 518.

Sacks, R., Rozenfeld, O., & Rosenfeld, Y. (2009). Spatial and temporal exposure to safety hazards in construction. *Journal of Construction Engineering and Management, 135*(8), 726–736.

Sacks, R., Perlman, A., & Barak, R. (2013). Construction safety training using immersive virtual reality. *Construction Management and Economics, 31*(9), 1005–1017.

Song, L., & Eldin, N. N. (2012). Adaptive real-time tracking and simulation of heavy construction operations for look-ahead scheduling. *Automation in Construction, 27*, 32–39.

Spencer, B. F., Jr., Hoskere, V., & Narazaki, Y. (2019). Advances in computer vision-based civil infrastructure inspection and monitoring. *Engineering, 5*(2), 199–222.

Tayefeh Hashemi, S., Ebadati, O. M., & Kaur, H. (2020). Cost estimation and prediction in construction projects: A systematic review on machine learning techniques. *SN Applied Sciences, 2*, 1–27.

Teizer, J., Allread, B. S., Fullerton, C. E., & Hinze, J. (2010). Autonomous pro-active real-time construction worker and equipment operator proximity safety alert system. *Automation in Construction, 19*(5), 630–640.

United Nations Environment Programme. (2022). *2022 Global status report for buildings and construction: Towards a zero-emission*. Efficient and Resilient Buildings and Construction Sector.

Vanijjirattikhan, R., Khomsay, S., Kitbutrawat, N., Khomsay, K., Supakchukul, U., Udomsuk, S., Suwatthikul, J., Oumtrakul, N., & Anusart, K. (2022). AI-based acoustic leak detection in water distribution systems. *Results in Engineering, 15*, 100557.

Wang, Y. (2021). *How level of detail of activity duration data influences look-ahead schedule performance in prefabricated construction*. PhD Thesis, Stanford University.

Zhang, C., Tian, Z., Song, J., Zheng, Y., & Xu, B. (2021). Construction worker hardhat-wearing detection based on an improved BiFPN. In *2020 25th international conference on pattern recognition (ICPR)* (pp. 8600–8607). IEEE.

Progress and Transformation in Payment Methods: From Barter to Monetic Digitalization

Stefano Gatti, Alberto Danese, Giovanni Bruner, Alessandro Piccioni, and G. Roberto Marseglia

Abstract The evolution of payment methods from barter to digitalization has transformed financial transactions, enhancing efficiency and security. This chapter traces this progression, highlighting key milestones such as the introduction of credit cards and the rise of mobile payments. The COVID-19 pandemic accelerated the adoption of digital payments, particularly mobile transactions, due to their convenience and security. The chapter examines the digital payment ecosystem, including the roles of cardholders, issuers, acquirers, and merchants. It also explores the increasing relevance of mobile payments and their impact on consumer behavior. The shift toward digital and mobile payments signifies a move toward a cashless economy, driven by technological advancements and changing consumer preferences.

1 Introduction

Payment instruments are the means by which funds are transferred between different parties. From bartering to the exchange of precious metals, payment instruments have historically undergone a progressive process of abstraction and dematerialization to facilitate easier, immediate, and secure transfers of money, including large sums, and the management of transactions from a distance.

S. Gatti (✉) · A. Danese · G. Bruner
Nexi Group, Milan, Italy
e-mail: stefano.gatti@nexi.it; alberto.danese@nexi.it; giovanni.bruner@nexi.it

A. Piccioni
Rancilio Cube, Milan, Italy
e-mail: apiccioni@uninsubria.it

G. R. Marseglia
Daat Consulting, Milan, Italy
e-mail: roberto.marseglia@unipv.it

G. R. Marseglia et al. (eds.), *Socio-economic Impact of Artificial Intelligence*, Progress in IS, https://doi.org/10.1007/978-3-031-73514-1_10

Over the centuries, payment methods have "normalized" around the concept of currency, which is attributed to three main functions: a measure of value, a medium of exchange, and a store of value. From an anthropological perspective, as sociologist Karl Polanyi (Polanyi et al., 1980) writes, currency has become a semantic system akin to language, writing, weights, and measures.

In this process of dematerialization, monetics, or card payments, play a central role: as we will discover, new and more advanced digital payment systems are establishing themselves, making the physical plastic card unnecessary, as seen with mobile payments and m-commerce. In the history of payment dematerialization, the real transition to a new era was marked in 1950 by the invention of the first credit card in the United States by Diners Club Inc., which introduced cashless retail payments.

Initially, the cards were not electronic but operated using manual devices that transferred the imprint of the card data onto paper vouchers. Later, thanks to the technological development of payment acceptance systems, by the late 1970s, credit cards were equipped with a magnetic stripe: this was the first real step toward an easy and fast payment experience. With the arrival of the new millennium, there was a shift to cards with microchips, which then evolved into contactless technology, enabling digital payments even through POS (point of sale) systems. Today, various types of payment cards are available to meet different customer needs, which, combined with the development of new technologies and the use of new payment devices, have ensured increasingly high levels of security over time. Concurrently, the customer's payment experience has become increasingly simple, smooth, and fast, both in-store with contactless payments and remotely through integrated payment systems on e-commerce sites.

In this chapter, we provide an overview of the spread of digital payments and how technology and external factors have contributed to this. This topic has already garnered international interest (Keramati et al., 2012; Dwivedi et al., 2017; Venkatesh et al., 2003; Patil et al., 2017) and falls within the broader topic of the technology acceptance model (Marangunić & Granić, 2015).

2 An Unexpected Acceleration: COVID-19 and Mobile Payments

Despite some cultural resistance, the value of card transactions in Italy has been increasing, although comparisons with other European countries reveal that Italy is still among the economies least inclined to use cards. As shown in Fig. 1, with 81 transactions per capita per year, Italy is well below the European average of 146, outperforming only Bulgaria and Romania.

Focusing on the evolution of digital payments in Italy over the last 5 years (Fig. 2), we can see a stable and continuous year-on-year growth rate, interrupted by the arrival of COVID-19 and its consequences on everyone's lives. The year 2020

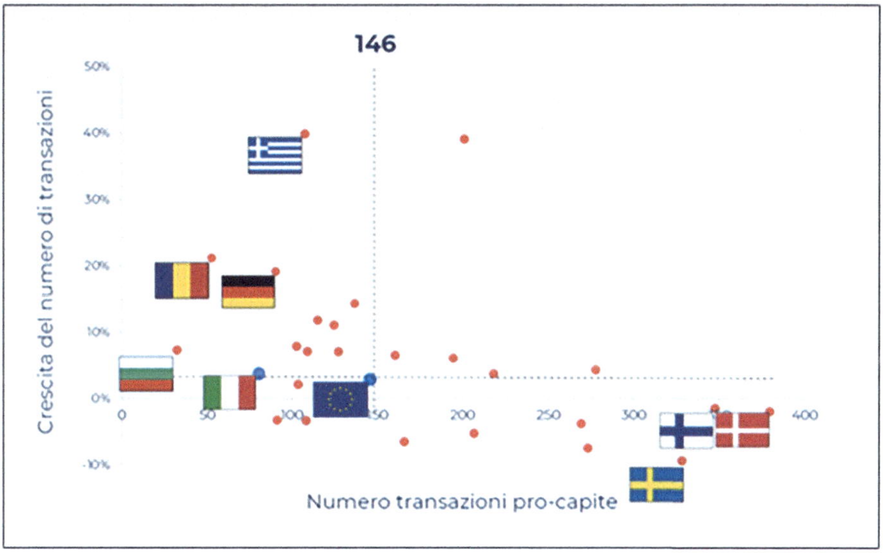

Fig. 1 Number of card transactions per capita in 2020. (Osservatorio Innovative Payments 2021: "Innovative Payments: the new normal"; MIP School of Management)

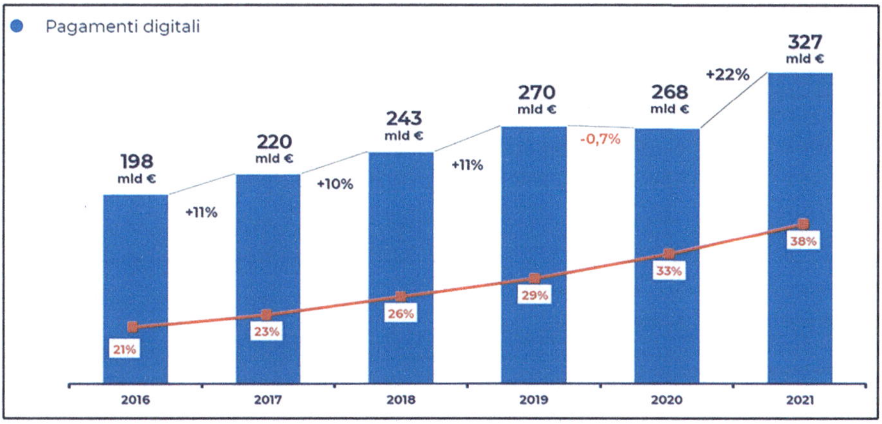

Fig. 2 Transaction volumes of digital payments in Italy. (Osservatorio Innovative Payments 2021: "Innovative Payments: the new normal"; MIP School of Management)

and the related collapse in consumption due to restrictions not only interrupted the growth of consumption volumes but also had a significant positive effect: similar to other sectors where digital has rapidly accelerated (Biancone et al., 2023), there was an increase in the percentage of digital payments relative to total payments. Although the growth of total transaction volumes did not continue, digital payments still increased their percentage share of total payments. With 2021 and the easing of the most severe restrictions, and a gradual return to a pre-COVID situation, two positive effects were observed: the growth of payment volumes doubled compared to the situation before 2020 and the share of digital payments in the total continued to increase. A more detailed analysis of these two growth factors shows that digital payments indeed offer a much simpler user experience compared to using cash, making them a good habit for those who use them.

Another trend emerging with the lifting of COVID-related restrictions was the marked increase in the use of Mobile Payments to complete a transaction [see also (Jack & Suri, 2011; Oliveira et al., 2016)]. Before analyzing the data, however, it is useful to clearly define the scope within which this payment method can be discussed. Mobile Payments refer to all transactions for purchasing products or services where the device to complete a transaction is a smartphone or smartwatch, both remotely and in proximity. In remote payments, we can find three subcategories: Mobile Remote Commerce, which includes purchases through mobile sites or apps for goods and services where the entire purchase process occurs through this channel; Mobile Remote Payment, which includes payments for phone top-ups, bills, parking, transport tickets, car rentals, taxis, etc., through the mobile phone; P2P, which includes money exchanges with "Instant Payment" operations, allowing amounts to be delivered in real time and immediately usable by the recipient. Moving to proximity payments, two subcategories can be found: Mobile Proximity Commerce, which includes services supporting the shopping experience at physical stores, such as the ability to use coupons and loyalty services or consulting information via smartphone; Mobile Proximity Payment, which includes payments at points of sale via smartphone or smartwatch using proximity technologies (such as NFC, QR code, or geolocation (Pham & Ho, 2015)).

As shown in Fig. 3, Mobile Payments have shown high growth rates year over year since 2017, the year Apple Pay was introduced in Italy, making mainstream payments via smartphone. The continuous growth in the adoption of these services

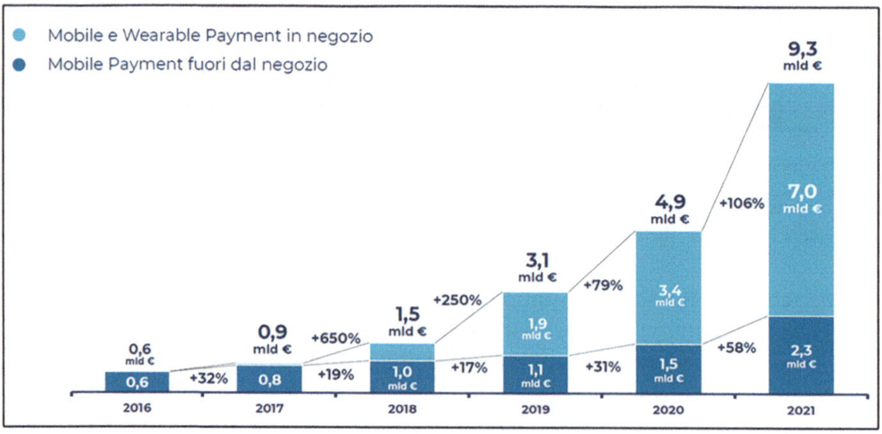

Fig. 3 Evolution of Mobile Payment transaction volumes over the years. (Osservatorio Innovative Payments 2021: "Innovative Payments: the new normal"; MIP School of Management)

is due to both an increase in the offering with the arrival of other payment services, on the one hand, with the increase in services for smartphones (e.g., Google Pay, Samsung Pay, etc.), and on the other hand, the extension of services to other connected devices such as smartwatches, watches, and smart bands (e.g., Garmin Pay, Fitbit Pay, SwatchPAY, etc.), and a higher level of awareness associated with these services.

3 The Most Important Digital Payment Ecosystem

But what exactly happens when a transaction is made with a payment card? Who manages the various phases of a transaction? The payment process via cards is articulated in multiple stages and involves several parties, interacting based on specific contractual relationships.

First, let's define a payment circuit, or "card scheme": a set of rules, standards, and procedures for executing international and domestic card payments, proposed by a specific owner called the "scheme owner," which is a company that disseminates, through its communication network, all expenditure requests and corresponding authorizations, from the merchant to the issuing institution and vice versa. Additionally, the circuit also verifies settlement operations, i.e., it continuously monitors debit operations performed on the accounts of individual holders and credit operations on the accounts of merchants.

Besides the circuit, there are five other main parties involved in a payment transaction: the cardholder, the issuer, the acquirer, the merchant, and the terminal manager. The cardholder is the holder of a payment card, whether it be credit, debit, or prepaid, belonging to a circuit and issued by an issuer. Cardholders can be either private individuals or legal entities. Issuers are entities authorized by the circuits, thanks to a specific license to issue payment cards and grant payment authorization, charging the cardholder under a contractual relationship. The third party is the "*acquirer*", entities authorized by the circuits, also via a specific license, to manage and finalize transactions with payment cards, under a contract directly with the merchant. The acquirer credits the merchant for the authorized amounts, against a commission charge. The terminal manager is the entity that manages transactions originating from POS terminals and ATMs (Automatic Teller Machines), performing the routing functions toward the parties aimed at finalizing the transaction, particularly toward the acquirer. Merchants are commercial establishments, contracted by the acquirer, that accept payment cards belonging to a certain circuit.

Depending on the number of parties involved in the payment operation, two different models are identified: the four-party model and the three-party model.

In the four-party model, as illustrated in Fig. 4, the roles of issuer and acquirer may be performed by two distinct entities, but are always separate from the circuit. The roles of issuer and acquirer can be directly a bank, or a service company to which banks decide to outsource the management of digital payments. In a four-party model, the issuer issues the card to the holder, the acquirer releases POS

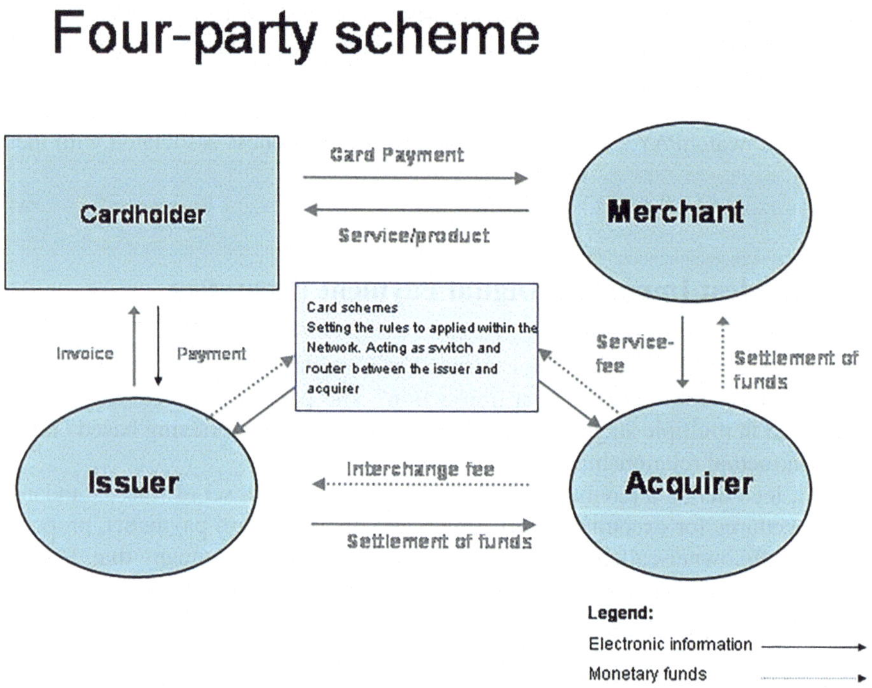

Fig. 4 Four-party digital payment scheme. (Figure Frispar at English Wikipedia, CC BY-SA 3.0, https://commons.wikimedia.org/w/index.php?curid=86960242)

terminals to merchants or manages its own ATM facilities, and the circuit handles the transmission of requests and authorizations through its network between the two parties. Payments made in a four-party model are defined as "circular payments" because they allow for withdrawals and payments even at POS terminals and ATMs managed by a different operator. When a purchase or withdrawal is made, the cardholder consents to the payment, for example, by entering a Personal Identification Number (PIN); their data is transmitted from the POS terminal or ATM to the terminal manager, who in turn forwards it to the acquirer. Payments are then made from the consumer's account to the merchant's account through the intermediation of the issuer, who has provided the card to the cardholder, and the acquirer, who has contracted the merchant. The most common circuits in the four-party models globally are Visa, Mastercard, and UnionPay.

The three-party model, on the other hand, presupposes the existence of a single entity that performs both the roles of issuer and acquirer simultaneously. Specifically, it is the same circuit that, on the one hand, issues the card to the customer and, on the other hand, takes care of contracting the merchants. Examples of three-party models include American Express and Diners.

4 A European Leader in the Digital Payments World

With a portfolio of innovative products, e-commerce expertise and industry-specific solutions, the Nexi Group provides flexible support to the digital economy and the entire global payments ecosystem across a wide range of payment methods and channels. The Group's digital platform and best-in-class professional expertise in the industry allow the company to operate at its best in two segments of the payments value chain: Merchant Services & Solutions and Cards & Digital Payments.

Merchant Services & Solutions The Merchant Services & Solutions Business Unit ("BU") offers solutions and support to every type of counterparty, providing services and products for digital payment acceptance, POS payment terminal management, acquiring flows and customer care activities. Together with the Partner Banks, the BU focuses on merchant needs and supports their activities, supporting all types of business ranging from retail to large distribution chains, for payments in both the physical world and on the online channel. Thanks to the breadth of services offered, the different payment types accepted, the geographical coverage, and the value-added services, following the integration with Nets, the Nexi Group can represent a one-stop-shop model for merchants in several European countries.

Cards & Digital Payments Through this division and in cooperation with its partner banks, the Group provides a wide range of so-called "issuing" services, i.e., relating to the procurement, issuance, and management of payment cards for individuals and companies, using advanced anti-fraud systems to ensure fast, reliable, and secure user authentication systems and rapid execution of payment transactions. Within this Business Unit (BU) line, Nets also provides services relating to the products of (i) Account Management Services, (ii) Core Payment Processing, (iii) Risk Management Services, (iv) Digitization Services, and (v) e-Identity Infrastructure. The business area also includes the operations and processing services provided in relation to the national debit card systems in Denmark ("Dankort") and Norway ("BankAxept"). In 2021, the Cards & Digital Payments BU continued and increased its mission to promote, incentivize, and educate customers on the use of digital payments, launching a security awareness campaign that accompanies digital innovation with the aim of creating a cultural background for future generations. Nexi's mission and objective to change the way Italian and European citizens make payments is clearly summarized by the large number of campaigns, events, and initiatives that the BU has studied and designed to encourage the transition to digital payments, with constant attention to customers' needs and security.

5 Card-Based Mobile Payments in a Nutshell

Previously, we discussed what Mobile Payments are and how their significance in digital transactions has markedly increased over recent years. Notably, Mobile Payments for in-store purchases have shown the highest growth rate. The most famous and widely used method within this category undoubtedly involves services that allow you to register your payment card and complete transactions on your device, such as a smartphone or smartwatch. Below, we briefly describe the process to register your payment card and make payments using these services.

5.1 Registering Your Card

First, ensure that your device is compatible with the chosen service. One of the most important requirements is the presence of an NFC (Near Field Communication) sensor, as this technology allows the device to exchange payment information with the POS terminal. Once device compatibility with the chosen service is confirmed, check whether the card you own can be activated for the service. Not all issuers guarantee compatibility with all existing apps, and increasingly, this incompatibility leads cardholders to switch banks or use a second payment card exclusively for Mobile Payments.

Having checked all compatibilities, you can proceed with registering your payment card. The steps are few and simple:

1. Enter the card details: Provide the PAN (the 16-digit card number), the expiration date, and the CVV (the three-digit security code found on the back of the card).
2. Verification by the issuer: The app interfaces with the issuer to confirm the identity of the person registering the card, ensuring it is the actual cardholder. This verification process mirrors what happens when entering card details on a website for online payments—either through a temporary code sent via SMS to the cardholder or, for users utilizing it, through biometric recognition via the bank or financial institution's app that issued the payment card.
3. Digital card storage: Once verification is successful, a "digital" version of the payment card is technically saved on the device, uniquely associated with it.

5.2 Completing a Transaction

Now, let's describe how to complete a transaction in-store, as this is the most widespread form of Mobile Payment:

1. Check for contactless-enabled POS: First, ensure that the store's POS is enabled for contactless payments. The latest generation POS systems, Smart and Mobile POS, natively support this without any issues. For older models, compatibility can easily be checked visually by looking for the contactless symbol on the POS. Virtually all POS systems in Italy now support contactless payments, so compatibility is hardly a barrier.

2. Activate payment mode: Depending on the app used, the cardholder needs to activate the payment mode (e.g., by clicking a button, activating the phone, etc.).
3. Authorize the payment: To complete the operation, the cardholder must unlock the device to confirm their identity. Common methods include biometric recognition (fingerprint, facial recognition, etc.) or entering a code/password on the device, which may be the same as that used to unlock the device or a unique one set during the card registration process. This check serves the same purpose as entering a PIN when using a physical card: it prevents potential fraudulent use by ensuring that the actual owner of the device, and thus the registered card, is making the payment.

5.3 *Standard Protocol Use*

It's important to note that the descriptions of the registration and payment procedures with Mobile Payments do not delve into the specifics of individual services. This is because, despite some minor graphical and user experience differences, a standard protocol is used universally. This strategic choice allows circuits, issuers, and mobile payment service managers to ensure a high and common standard of security, regardless of the service chosen by the cardholder.

6 A Digital Payments Adoption Accelerator

Mobile payments can be considered the payment method of the next generation, a critical channel to give value and retain digital native cardholders. In Fig. 5. we compared the distribution of cardholders age for customers who enrolled to Mobile Payments vs the same distribution for all the other customers. We sampled credit and prepaid card customers from the Italian customer base, a market with a low but increasingly growing digital payments penetration. The result is a striking median age difference between Mobile Payments user and non-users, with the left shoulder of the "Enrolled to Mpays" histogram strongly skewed toward Millennials and Gen Z customers.

Young customers greatly appreciate the easy enrollment offered by the major mobile wallets and the frictionless payment experience. Mobile Payments are an additional enabler of C-less Pos payments, since the only PIN required is the device PIN code or biometrics.

Mobile Payments are a natural accelerator of digital payments adoption. We sampled a subset of Italian customers that we represented with 100+ demographic and payment behavior features, in order to find the customers not yet enrolled to mobile payments that were more similar to early adopters. Using a propensity model (i.e., a predictive model used to estimate the likelihood or probability of a particular event or behavior occurring, in this case a segmentation model that

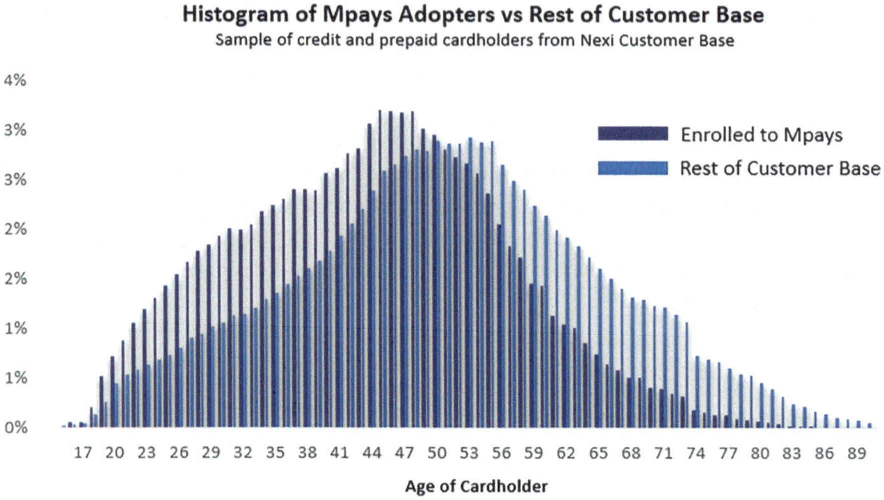

Fig. 5 Age distribution of Mpays cardholders vs other customers

esitmates the probability for a custome to enroll), we were able to segment the non-adopters into five different *propensity-to-enrollment* buckets, with high propensity bucket resulting in the group of non-adopters that are more similar to the early adopters.

We observed that high propensity customers are 53% more likely to make a physical POS micropayment, a transaction of less than 10€, compared to the medium propensity customers, where we set our baseline. As a matter of fact, the spread of micropayments is widely considered one of the symptoms that digital payments are finally becoming the mainstream payment method over cash (Fig. 6).

Customers who are more likely to do Mobile Payments are also more likely to travel abroad: a high propensity customer is at least 73% more likely than a medium propensity one, as shown in Fig. 7.

On the flipside we observed, as shown in Fig. 8, that there is a strong negative correlation between propensity to enrollment to Mobile Payments and probability to make a credit card cash withdrawal. In this case, the low propensity customers are 64% more inclined to use cash compared to the baseline.

Those data points can give us a hint of a Mobile Payments adopters persona: a digital young customer, frequently using the card also for small expenses, with a propensity to travel and smaller propensity to use cash as a preferred payment method.

Demographics and digital payments habits strongly affect the decision to enroll to a digital wallet, at the same time digital wallets appear to have a causal impact on customers spending behavior.

As shown in Fig. 9, we measured the increase in monthly transaction of a sample of cardholders enrolling to Mobile Payments, across different monthly cohorts. The target sample was matched to a control group of customers who did not enroll to

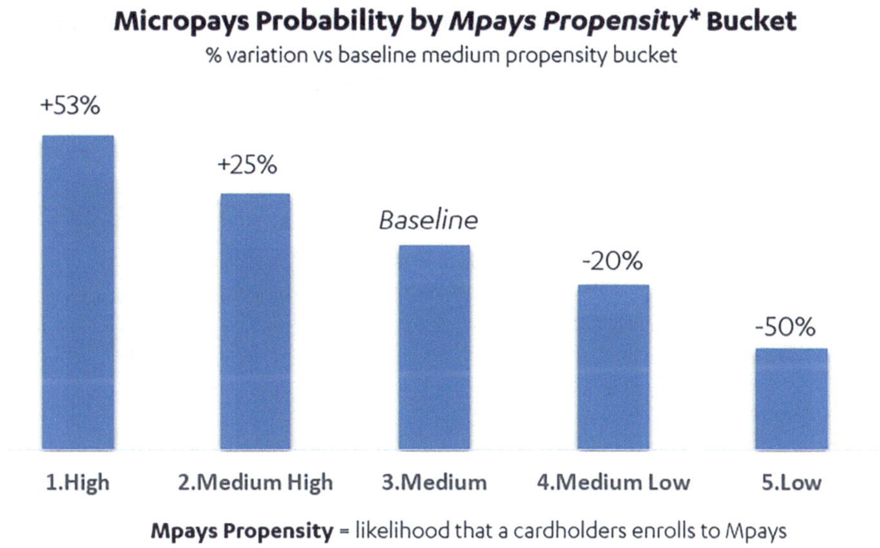

Fig. 6 Probability of a micropayment by Mobile Payments enrollment propensity bucket

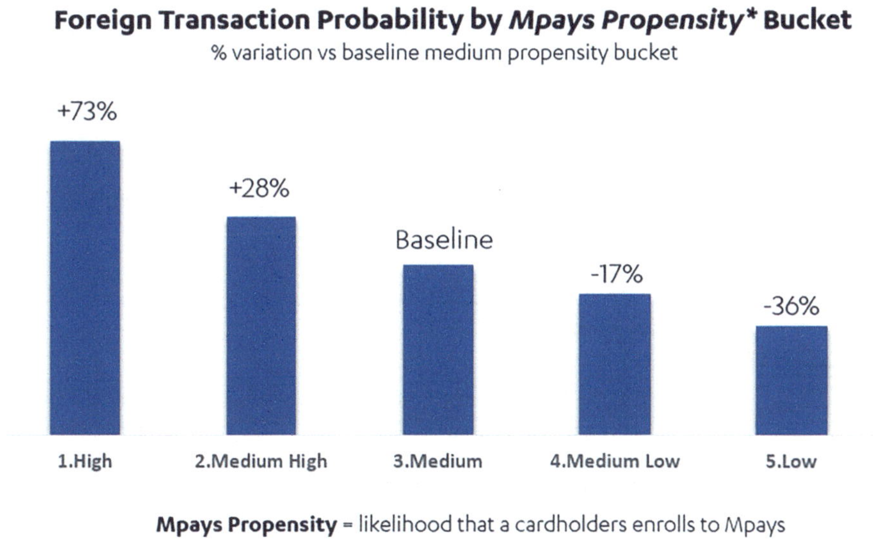

Fig. 7 Probability of a foreign transaction by Mobile Payments enrollment propensity bucket

mobile payments but show an almost identical spending pattern in the 12 months prior to the target group enrollment. When the enrollment happens in month t_12, the number of monthly transactions sharply increases, whereas it remains flat for the control group. Prior to the enrollment, there was a negligible 3% difference between target and control group in terms of monthly transaction, growing to a 20%

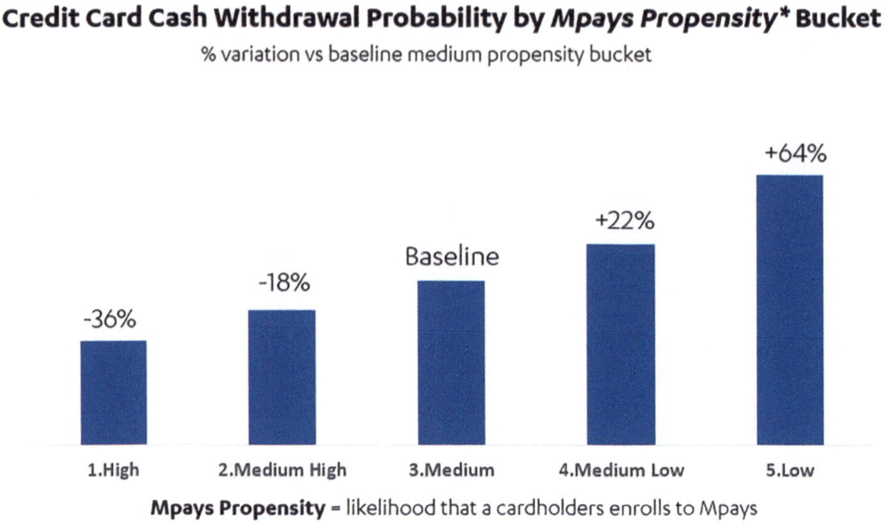

Fig. 8 Probability of a credit card cash withdrawal by Mobile Payments enrollment propensity bucket

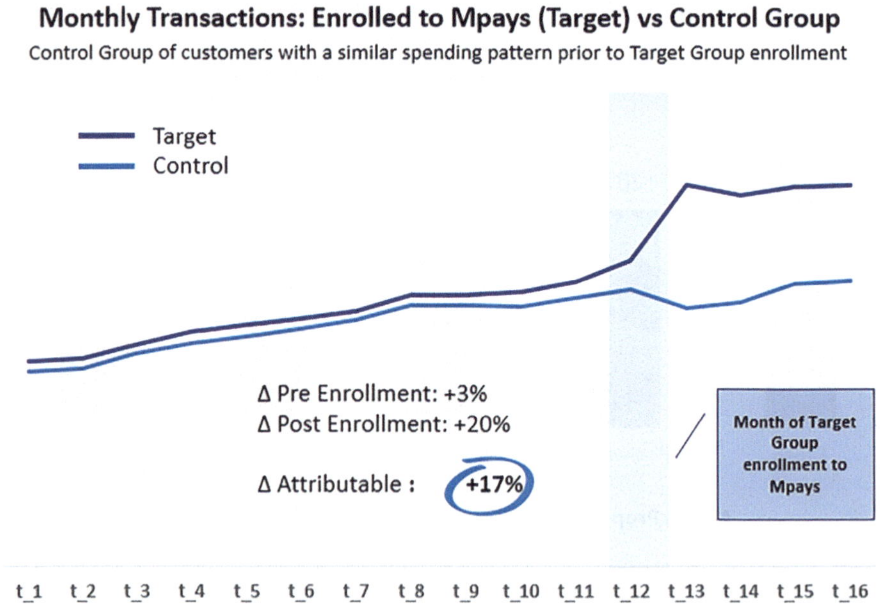

Fig. 9 Target vs control group monthly transactions—for target group Mobile Payments enrollment happens at month t_12

difference post-enrollment. This net 17% difference between the two groups post-enrollment, can be interpret as the extra transactions we could expect from customers after enrolling to mobile payments. Possibly an effect of the *frictionless* experience offered by paying through your smartphone or wearable device.

7 Conclusions and Future Work

In this chapter, we provided a comprehensive overview of the evolution and significant strides in payment systems, focusing particularly on the digitalization of payment methods and the pivotal role of mobile payments in the contemporary financial ecosystem.

The key takeaways we can extract from our chapter are the following:

First, the progression from traditional barter systems to advanced digital payments underscores a significant dematerialization and abstraction in financial transactions. This evolution has not only made transactions more efficient but also broadened their scope beyond immediate geographical limits.

Second, mobile payments have seen a significant surge, particularly highlighted by their increased usage during the COVID-19 pandemic. This trend has been supported by the convenience and security offered by NFC (Near Field Communication) and the widespread adoption of smartphones. Mobile payments facilitate not only proximity transactions but also remote transactions through various subcategories such as Mobile Remote Commerce and Mobile Proximity Payment.

Based on the data we observe, we predict that mobile payments will continue to grow and potentially dominate the payment landscape, driven by the digital native generation. Data shows that users of mobile payments are likely to engage more frequently in micropayments and are less inclined to withdraw cash, suggesting a shift toward a less cash-dependent economy.

References

Biancone, P., Secinaro, S., Marseglia, R., & Calandra, D. (2023). E-health for the future. Managerial perspectives using a multiple case study approach. *Technovation, 120*, 102406.

Dwivedi, Y. K., Rana, N. P., Jeyaraj, A., Clement, M., & Williams, M. D. (2017). Re-examining the unified theory of acceptance and use of technology (UTAUT): Towards a revised theoretical model. *Information Systems Frontiers*. https://doi.org/10.1007/s10796-017-9774-y

Jack, W., & Suri, T. (2011). *Mobile money: The economics of M-PESA* (No. w16721). National Bureau of Economic Research.

Keramati, A., Taeb, R., Larijani, A., & Mojir, N. (2012). A combinative model of behavioural and technical factors affecting 'Mobile'-payment services adoption: An empirical study. *The Service Industries Journal, 32*, 1489–1504.

Marangunić, N., & Granić, A. (2015). Technology acceptance model: A literature review from 1986 to 2013. *Universal Access in the Information Society, 14*, 81–95.

Oliveira, T., Thomas, M., Baptista, G., & Campos, F. (2016). Mobile payment: Understanding the determinants of customer adoption and intention to recommend the technology. *Computers in Human Behavior, 61*, 404–414.

Patil, P. P., Dwivedi, Y. K., & Rana, N. P. (2017). Digital payments adoption: an analysis of literature. In *Digital Nations–Smart Cities, Innovation, and Sustainability: 16th IFIP WG 6.11 Conference on E-Business, E-Services, and E-Society, I3E 2017, Delhi, India, November 21–23, 2017, Proceedings 16* (pp. 61–70). Springer International Publishing.

Pham, T., & Ho, J. (2015). The effects of product-related, personal-related factors and attractiveness of alternatives on consumer adoption of NFC-based mobile payments. *Technology in Society, 43*, 159–172.

Polanyi, K., Negro, N., & Dalton, G. (1980). *Economie primitive, arcaiche e moderne: ricerca storica e antropologia economica*. Einaudi.

Venkatesh, V., Morris, M. G., Davis, G. B., & Davis, F. D. (2003). User acceptance of information technology: Toward a unified view. *MIS Quarterly, 27*(3), 425–478.

AI with a Human Touch: The Case of Miroglio Fashion

Alberto Racca, Giulia Truffo, and Fabrizio Fantini

Abstract Artificial intelligence (AI) combined with human input can significantly enhance fashion retail operations, as demonstrated by Miroglio Fashion. This chapter details how Miroglio, Italy's third-largest women's apparel retailer, faced challenges with inventory management and demand forecasting due to the complex, fast-paced nature of fashion. By partnering with Evo Pricing, Miroglio implemented AI to optimize stock levels, replenishment, and transfers between stores. The system integrates big data analytics with human insights from store managers, leading to a more precise and responsive inventory management process. The results included increased sales, reduced excess inventory, and improved stock availability, showcasing the potential of AI to drive profitability and efficiency in fashion retail.

1 Introduction to the Miroglio Group

Miroglio Fashion is Italy's third largest retailer of women's apparel, with €520 m + annual revenues from thousands of stores across 9 brands. After building its first factory in 1947, it grew consistently through the 2000s.

A brief history. In 1947, Giuseppe Miroglio installed the first modern weaving mills in Alba and began producing silk and synthetic textiles on an industrial basis that applied U.S. mass production techniques to manufacture Italy's first women's apparel at scale. This offered Italians their first alternative to homemade or made-to-measure tailoring. The textile factory grew into Miroglio Textile, which eventually included textile printing and transfer paper businesses, while the women's apparel factory became Miroglio Fashion: Italy's first "curvy" (or plus-size) brand, Elena

A. Racca · G. Truffo
Miroglio Group, Alba, CN, Italy
e-mail: Alberto.Racca@miroglio.com; Giulia.Truffo@miroglio.com

F. Fantini (✉)
EVO, Turin, Italy
e-mail: fab@evopricing.com

G. R. Marseglia et al. (eds.), *Socio-economic Impact of Artificial Intelligence*, Progress in IS, https://doi.org/10.1007/978-3-031-73514-1_11

Mirò (1985), and Italy's first maker of fast fashion clothing, sold in dedicated shops under the Motivi brand (1993). Miroglio was the first apparel producer in Italy and one of the first in Europe to grasp the eventual importance of mono-brand retail shops for accelerating product rotation. By 2010, he operated eight brands with 1000 mono-brand shops, in locations like department stores and corners, shopping malls, and mountain towns, alongside modern urban boutiques nestled in city centres. He directly owned and operated roughly 80% of these stores in Italy and other European countries, as well as e-commerce and marketplaces such as Amazon and Zalando.

By the 2010s, however, revenues were falling. While some stores continued to thrive, performance diverged between top- and bottom-earning stores: Uneven product sales across regions and stores, excessively long product shelf life, and significant promotional pressure from market trends and competition. This uneven performance exacerbated existing supply chain issues, increasing both stockouts and leftover excess stock.

Could advance analytics help reverse the trend?

2 The Fashion Merchandizing Challenge

The Fashion industry is uniquely challenging due to timing and granularity.

2.1 Timing

Fashion manufacturing involves many steps to transform a fibre into a final garment; this requires a long time and involves a complex process. The short-life of the finished products in fashion contrasts with the long manufacturing process. In addition, with demand driven by product prices, companies are led to produce abroad to reduce their costs, thus further increasing the lead times. The effect is that the discrepancy between the short life of the products and the long production times is further exacerbated and that decisions must be made well in advance in a market where demand is increasingly volatile.

2.2 Granularity

The second challenge facing retailers is to determine the correct amount of product to allocate in each store. Due to local trends and different store sizes, different product assortments have to be determined that fit different stores.

And the allocation of products on sizes is fundamental for customer satisfaction and to avoid missing sales coming from stock-outs. This fragmented and highly local item/size nature of the demand makes it difficult to accurately predict sales, creating challenges to centrally driven stock allocation process. A uniform stock allocation across stores and seasons can be perceived by the management as suboptimal; however, a more differentiated allocation needs to catch each store peculiarities and to guarantee at the same time the optimal performance of the whole network.

2.3 *Merchandizing*

For short, 1 year before the product actually hits the store, fashion merchandizers must determine which products to allocate into each store and, for each product, how many units of size S or L. But a product selling 20 units over 3 months may only sell 1 or 2 units of size S, meaning that the fragmentation of demand is rather extreme and therefore the potential forecast errors due to granularity and timing are existentially challenging in fashion.

Even when the product hits the store, fashion replenishment decisions are challenging: the volatility of sales is high, and correctly allocating stock by size/shop is a complex challenge, even without considering the significant impact of promotions and markdowns on sales volumes. Therefore, in-season sales often represent just 70% or less of total sales, often already at significant discounts to list price—even in season. Markdowns and clearance may still leave unsold an important share of inventory, sometimes more than 5% of the initial stock.

2.4 *Forecasting*

Every fashion merchandizer constantly faces delicate volume decisions, particularly critical as the risk of a wrong choice leading to loss of profit is always around the corner, given the unpredictability of consumer choice.

This is the classic fashion trade-off: excessive depth, leading to waste of unsold stock; or—at the opposite—lower stock levels, but causing missed sale opportunities, size fragmentation, stock-outs, and loss of customer loyalty. But faced with a daily changing demand, how to predict the appropriate level of stock to maximize profits, also taking into account price and promotion decisions?

Traditional fashion forecasting systems are based on simple rules, for example replenishment based on historical sales and current availability, with automatic reorders upon reaching certain thresholds and with planning volumes mainly based on previous seasons.

These approaches may perhaps be suitable for stable categories with predictable sales but are suboptimal for fashion: faced with rapidly evolving local trends, managers end up chasing demand and manually entering data into ad hoc programs. This creates chaotic everyday processes, subject to errors and dependent on the experience and instinct of individual people. Traditional methods fail, and therefore the need for innovation is acute.

2.5 Miroglio

In 2015, Miroglio decided to face its demand forecasting and inventory management challenges. Its initial allocation shipped 85% of total new inventory directly to stores on the basis of previous store performance and current season targets; the remaining 15% was warehoused for in-season replenishment. The initial allocation was required to guarantee sufficient display at its relatively small stores—between 150 and 180 square meters—with low turnover.

Store managers preferred to maintain excess inventory to avoid stock-outs and to increase the probability of earning a bonus for exceeding their monthly sales goal, but stores had no control over the volume of inventory they received, despite some coordinating discussion with the brand's merchandizing team. Rather, Miroglio's retail division set monthly sales targets for the stores.

If it takes a month to sell one item, perhaps that item should have been initially allocated to a store where demand was higher. Otherwise, if the item gets out of stock after 1 day, unmet demand would emerge from people coming into the store and leaving empty-handed. How could that be captured?

Some stores received daily replenishment of each item sold, and most participated in weekly transfers to limit stock-outs and unsold inventory. Transfers moved apparel from stores with plentiful inventory to those with high sales levels for the same items. As a result of such challenges in forecasting demand, actual sales in a typical store could differ from planned sales by as much as 40–50%.

Inventory replenishment was typically "push"-driven (i.e. send one additional item to a store if it sold one), but the emergence of online shopping and social media required a "pull" strategy. Leading retail players such as Zara were already implementing data analytics and machine learning for this purpose. However, Miroglio sold fewer slower-moving items compared to Zara, and it was unclear if a model would be able to predict demand under such conditions.

Miroglio could build its own data analytics capability or it could partner with a third-party provider. Building in-house capability could more easily incorporate the experience and institutional memory of Miroglio's retail and other managers than a hired consultancy might be inclined to do.

However, it would take months, if not years, to build a team of qualified data scientists. A third-party provider could also give Miroglio visibility into current industry practices that in-house data scientists might otherwise struggle to obtain. Moreover, there was little time to waste in returning Miroglio to an upward growth trajectory. To keep abreast of markets changing faster and faster, new approaches were required to achieve the maximum potential impact on the profitability of Miroglio.

Miroglio therefore partnered with Evo Pricing (evo), a software developer of Artificial Intelligence and machine learning methods to optimize retail pricing and promotion strategies, initially tasked with lifting the performance of markdowns and promotions. While Evo had relevant experience with the fashion industry, it had limited experience in merchandize allocation. However, Evo knew Miroglio, its people, and its operations very well, and Miroglio felt that this experience could be highly valuable in gaining internal buy-in. Therefore, they jointly embarked on the development of a solution to the core merchandizing forecasting challenge that Miroglio had been painfully facing.

3 The Customer Centric Forecasting Solution

Today, the latest generation of big data algorithms is capable of simultaneously optimizing prices and assortment, growing profits, and reducing unsold inventory. Thanks to new methods of data analysis informed by human intuition, the traditional challenge of fashion retailers can finally be solved: the right amount of product in stock at the right time, with the right sizes, at the right price in every shop.

3.1 Artificial Intelligence in Fashion

There are plenty of misconceptions about Artificial Intelligence (AI), especially in a human-centric industry like fashion. Easily hyped and easily un-hyped or debunked, like every technology: overhype in the beginning, while at the same time underestimating the long-term potential.

The hype of AI today may lead people to think it just works, but the truth is it doesn't just work, and it's not simple. When building it, the most common mistake is to underestimate the complexities of building a robust AI software in terms of data, technology, and operational capability. Just because it's possible doesn't mean that it will work.

How to test and validate that the fashion merchandizing AI technology works? This system is actually a live system, so one can only test by using it. Simply throwing some data at a system will get some answers but not allow the assessment of crucial factors such as quality of the solution, accuracy, and robustness.

Miroglio therefore adopted a salmon strategy approach: initial adoption at small scale, limited in scope, but already with a clear pathway of ambition. Think big and start small.

The logic can successfully be applied to multiple fashion processes like planning or markdown management; for example, the replenishment of the product "Blue Shirt", size M, shop "Via Roma", week of September 28.

In Fig. 1, the X-axis shows the number of shirts shipped to the store; the bar chart (left Y axis) represents the probability of selling the X-th piece, for example the

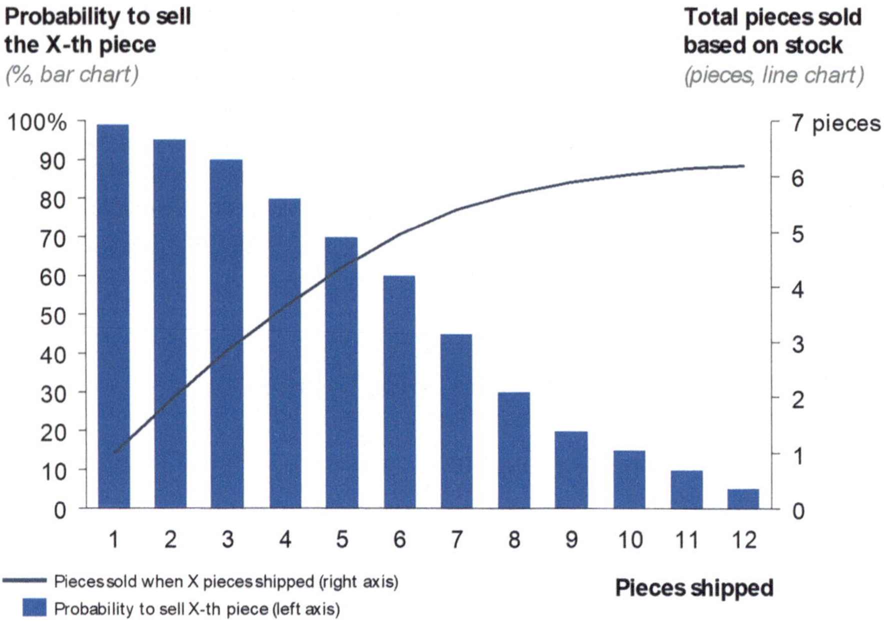

Fig. 1 Expected probability of sale based on number of pieces shipped

third if X = 3; and the line chart (right Y axis) shows the resulting total number of items sold. Intuitively, the more shirts are shipped to the store, the lower the probability of selling them all: in this example, it is almost certain that the first shirt will be sold, but already a little less likely for the second, and in turn even less so for the third, etc.

In terms of sales, the larger the shipment, the higher are expected sales, albeit with an ever-smaller increase as the maximum sales potential, in this case of ~7 pieces, is reached.

Armed with these data, the machine learning automatically calculates the expected value of revenues and costs at each level of stock, taking into account potential losses from stock-outs and unsold inventory and the extra discounts that may be needed to clear it.

In this example, assuming a list price of €39.95 per shirt, an average discount of 25%, and a cost of €7 per piece, Fig. 2 shows how the algorithm has identified an optimum delivery level of 8 shirts for this store—in the (common) case of choosing to maximize profits rather than, for example, market share or margins net of cost of unsold, which would lead to different solutions but are still based on the same method of analysis.

And what if a customer wanted to purchase the ninth shirt? The store would lose revenues because the product would be sold out. Therefore, the algorithm assesses the likelihood that customers will choose to substitute this with other similar products, e.g. shirts of different quality, colour, or brand; but also, the sales-prices link:

Fig. 2 Optimal expected profits

for example, considering what would happen if increasing the selling price (or reducing the discounts) when six or seven shirts are sold.

The main benefit of these new machine learning-based systems is that they are fully based on the customer's perspective rather than solely on historical sales or costs, or competition: for example, exploiting the entire potential of "invisible" sales, missing from the historical data due to the frequent stock-outs at a size/store level.

Customers reveal, through their observed behaviour, all their own complex assessments, and these can be surveyed in real time using automated systems based on observed consumer behaviour. This, in an analogy, is just like a real-time traffic review can be based on the car driver's use of a navigation system while being connected to the Internet and broadcasting their position in real time.

3.2 *The Secret Sauce: Human Input*

Miroglio chose its brand Elena Mirò, focused on premium and plus-sizes for its first test of the system developed by Evo.

They sell a broad range of products with a wide size range for each item to be able to cover the demand of different types of customers, with many different collections of products every year, so that each single product has a short lifecycle of a few weeks in store at most.

These conditions led to a huge challenge for Miroglio: how can they forecast the sales in an accurate way, in order to better manage the inventory in their stores? They usually had to handle situations of excess inventory for some items/stores, and of stock-outs in other stores. *What's the right number of pieces in a particular size of a particular item to send to every store in a given week?*

Evo used big data and its innovative prediction methods to estimate sales demand and, based on that, to optimize replenishment from the central warehouse, at least for those items still available in the warehouse.

Then, the same estimate was used to suggest/trigger transfers between stores, especially at the end of the lifecycle of a product, when there are no more pieces available in the central warehouse. It happens quite often that some stores have a lot of pieces available in stock, but they are not selling them, while other stores have stock-outs, so it can be useful to move the products across in order to rebalance the relative stock levels.

This new proposal did not change Miroglio's process much, because they were already doing replenishment and transfers between stores: Evo just added efficiency to their process, using proper forecast techniques to predict and manage demand. What instead changed their process was the third element of the process, which is the involvement of the store managers.

In fact, the store managers of Elena Mirò stores had typically been working in the same store for a long time, so they knew their often-loyal customers very well. Involving them in the replenishment process allowed to bank on their private information and signals that would have otherwise been difficult and slow to capture through alternative methodologies or data sources.

The following figure shows a schema of the weekly replenishment process (Fig. 3).

Firstly, from the IT, the data about sales of the past week and residual stock in stores are automatically collected. Together with data, the business rules that have

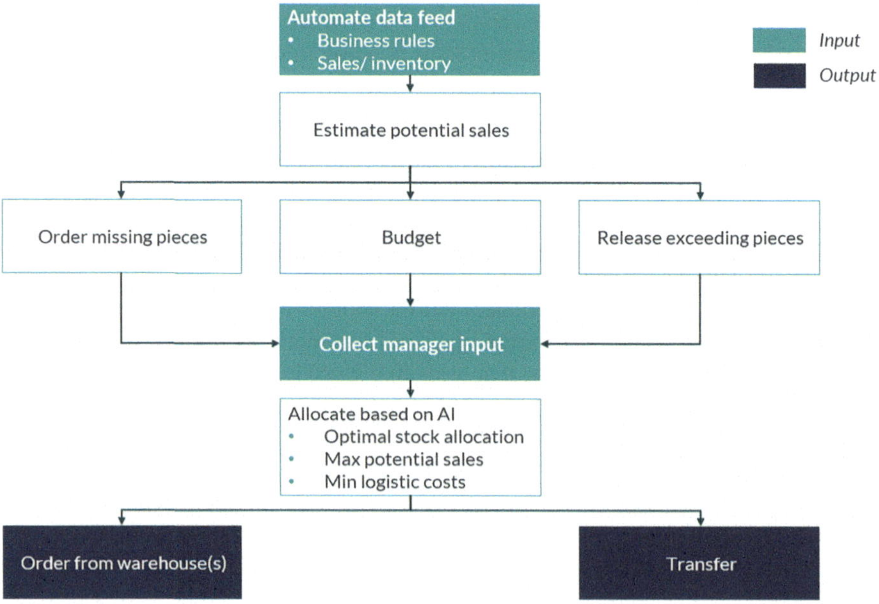

Fig. 3 Artificial Intelligence with a human touch

to be followed are collected, for example logistic constraints, items in store windows for the week, and so on.

Armed with these data, the Artificial Intelligence of Evo computes a recommendation of allocation, suggesting one of the following operations for each item and size for each store: an order to require extra pieces or a release to remove exceeding pieces. Evo also calculates a virtual total budget value for each store. These three elements together form the proposal for the store managers. Once it is passed to the store managers, they can modify it according to their preferences while respecting the total budget constraint. In this way, an internal marketplace is created.

Evo then collects the modified proposal from stores and uses store manager requests as an input for the optimization model of the tool. The process of optimization uses residual stock in stores and inventory available in the warehouse to compute the optimal allocation in order to maximize expected profit and minimize logistic costs. The result is the list of orders from the central warehouse, and the list of transfers between stores that are sent back to Miroglio system and stores.

3.3 *Devil in the (Size) Details*

Computation of the potential sales for each store, item, and size is crucial in order to compare it with the current level of stock, and make suggestions at that level of granularity. To avoid the noise of the sales at that granularity level, first the potential at store/item level was computed, then split it to obtain the forecast at size level.

On the store/item level, it's important to find the "responsiveness period", the number of past weeks that should be projected, and count the sales in that period. To this, the estimated sales lost due to stock-out is added to include missing sales due to a lack of stock in stores. Doing this, the real "demand" of the item in the store for the past period is obtained.

At this point, the past demand is projected for the future, using an appropriate seasonality factor, based on the sales of the whole product category in the past years. In this way, the forecast sales for a certain item in a certain store for the "coverage" period, that is the number of weeks in the future that the item is intended to cover is obtained.

This number is split to obtain the number at size level. To do this, the relative frequency of a size calculated on the total sales of each item on all stores and the relative frequency of a size calculated on the total sales of all items in the store are combined.

The choice of combining the two distribution comes from the observation that each product and each store behave differently. In fashion, the devil is indeed in the (size) detail (Fig. 4).

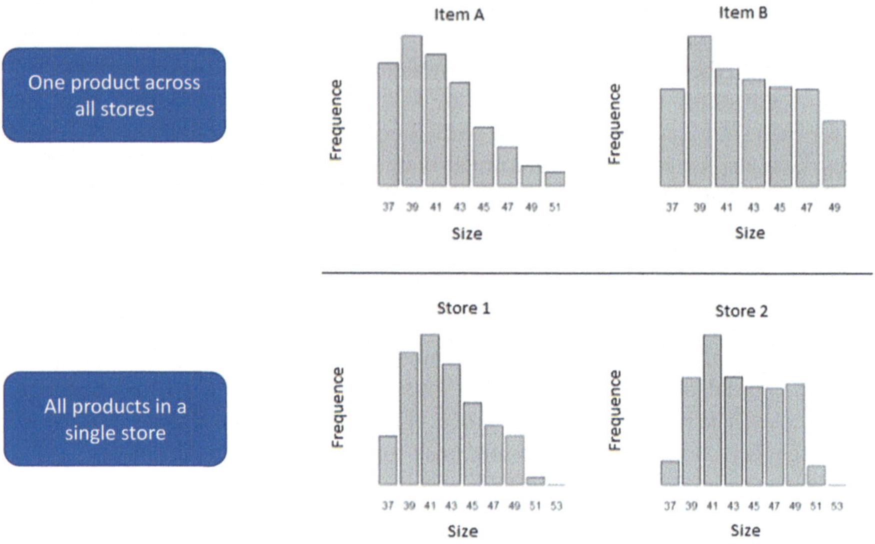

Fig. 4 Sales by size, for two items (all stores) and for two stores (all items)

3.4 The Role of Store Managers

For each store/item/size, the estimated potential sales are compared with the actual stock in stores to see the number of missing or exceeding pieces. From this comparison, two different things are obtained: the suggested operations and the store budget. The suggested operation is the action that Evo recommends to do. It can be an order of a certain number of pieces if the potential sales are more than the actual stock, or it can be a release if the stock exceeds the estimated sales: in this case, the released pieces can be taken from the store and sent to other stores that need them.

The exceeding pieces won't be removed from the store if not required by other stores. Some releases can be classified as mandatory in case of very low potential sales and huge stock, and if other stores have a strong need of that item. The main difference between a release and a mandatory release is that the store manager can edit the first one but not the second one.

Together with the suggestion of the operation, the "store budget" is computed. The budget for a store is the difference between the potential sales value (number of estimated pieces that will be sold multiplied by their price) and the stock value (number of pieces in stock multiplied by their price), adding an extra coverage to ensure a certain "safety stock" in the stores. Since it comes directly from the comparison between sales and stock value, it gives a measure of how much a store is in overstock/understock: if the budget is high, the store has lower potential respect to the stock already present and should order new pieces more than release them. The list of suggested operations for each item and the total budget are sent to the store managers, and at that point they have some time to modify the proposal.

They can edit the operation proposed and/or the number of pieces associated with each operation. They can alter orders and releases, while they cannot alter the mandatory releases, if any. For each extra piece that they want to request/add to the orders, they have to spend a part of the budget available. Vice versa, the release of a new piece, or the renounce of an order, allow them to gain budget.

So, the budget works as a constraint for them: it's a way to push them not only to ask, but also to evaluate what they don't need. It also allows to re-balance inventory in stores, giving more advantage to the stores that are understocked. Also, since the budget is computed dynamically every week, it doesn't require a static ranking of the stores: the ranking is implicitly defined by the inventory level of each store, compared with the forecast, and it can change every week.

The last thing that store managers can do, if they have extra budget, is to use the add button to request new products or sizes that are outside the initial proposal, or even outside the initial planned assortment for their stores.

3.5 *Shipments*

After store managers completed their editing, their inputs and changes are used as an input of the logistic optimization model. That function tries to fulfil as many orders as possible with the inventory available in central warehouse and with the other stores releases. The objective function for Miroglio is to optimize the net profit, balancing expected sales, inventory, and logistic costs.

For example, for one item—store the probability of selling each single piece that has been requested is computed. This probability depends on the average forecast estimated in the first step of the process and from the stock already present in the store, decreasing while the stock increases: the probability of selling the first piece in stock is higher than the probability of selling the third or the fourth piece.

Once this probability is obtained, the expected revenues of shipping N pieces are simply calculated by multiplying the average price of each item by the probability of sales and then doing the cumulative sum until N.

This is the profit without logistic cost. So, subtracting the cost of shipping N pieces, the curve of Net Profit is obtained. The optimal shipment is the number of pieces that maximize the net profit. This is a simplified version for one item and store, but the logic is the same for all the items/stores involved, that are combined together respecting also inventory constraints, such as warehouse and stores availability.

Other than inventory constraints, the model supports additional logistic constraints, to control the shipment costs and the number of shipments done. These constraints include min and max constraints on number of pieces, value, and weight of each box shipped, plus constraints on minimum/maximum number of boxes that each store can ship. Example: Each store should send boxes towards no more than 3 receiver stores; each box should contain at least 7 pieces and at least 150% of values.

4 Business Impact

4.1 More Profits

At the beginning, since the model was new, a test was made before making it fully operational. A test-control experiment was made, comparing the new model with the old one already used that didn't include the store managers input.

During the test, about 200 stores of two different brands were monitored, starting from the brand Elena Mirò, and then extending the process also to the stores of Fiorella Rubino. Among the 200 stores, 40 of them were selected for applying the new model, from the month of April to June.

The results were very good: the stores involved in the test had an average sales increase of 16% compared with the control group. In addition to the classic test-control analysis, different metrics were measured, to explore better the level of overstock and understock.

Some KPIs, such as the Shipment Success Ratio (ratio of items delivered to items sold post delivery) and the Stock Velocity Ratio (ratio of total sales to potential sales), increased for the test stores from the beginning of the test, remaining stable over time.

In the same way, the Demand Cover Ratio (ratio between items sold and expected demand) confirmed the effectiveness of the test, as it remained similar for both the test shops and the control group (i.e. the extra sales deriving from the transfers did not lead to higher stock-outs in donor shops).

The metrics have been calculated for test and control groups; results are illustrated in Table 1. Figure 5 shows how SSR and SVR increase for test stores since the beginning of the test, and that this increase remains stable along the prosecution of the test. At the same time, DCR Fig. 5 shows how DCR of Test and Control stores

Table 1 Monitoring metrics: Test (T) vs. Control (C) KPIs

Week	(T) SSR %	(C) SSR %	(T) StSR%	(C) StSR%	(T) SVR%	(C) SVR%	(T) DCR%	(C) DCR%
1	12%	12%	166%	161%	6%	5%	58%	57%
2	19%	17%	111%	112%	12%	9%	59%	56%
3	22%	19%	86%	76%	17%	13%	60%	58%
4	30%	24%	93%	76%	24%	19%	60%	60%
5	31%	27%	88%	68%	27%	21%	61%	62%
6	35%	30%	90%	73%	28%	23%	61%	61%
7	40%	33%	91%	74%	31%	26%	61%	61%
8	43%	36%	100%	81%	34%	28%	60%	61%
9	43%	39%	92%	89%	36%	31%	60%	60%
10	47%	42%	99%	94%	38%	33%	60%	60%
11	51%	46%	106%	101%	41%	36%	60%	59%
12	53%	50%	112%	110%	44%	39%	60%	59%
13	58%	53%	132%	123%	49%	43%	61%	60%

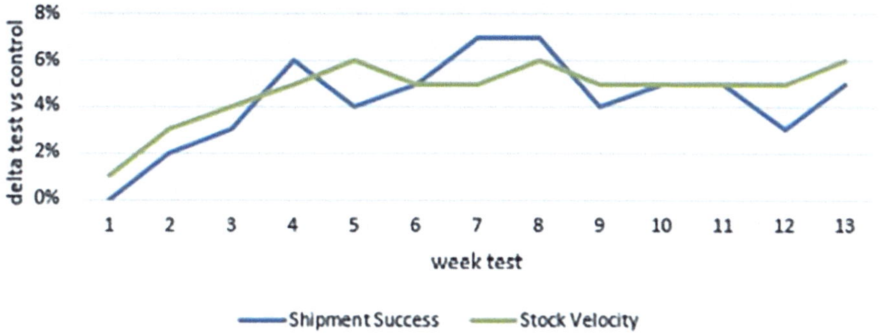

Fig. 5 Weekly difference between Test and Control indexes SSR and SV

Fig. 6 Weekly difference between Test and Control indexes StSR and DCR

remained similar (i.e. extra sales coming from shipments do not lead to higher occurrence of stock-outs in the shipping store). StSR sharply increased, especially in the first weeks (Fig. 6).

On average, the pilot demonstrated the following:

- up to 7% increase in SSR and up to 19% increase in StSR, a significant improvement in the relevance of shipments compared to the past, resulting in more sales.
- up to 6% increase in SVR; greater stock rotation leading to a reduction in unsold stock.
- <1% greater DCR, suggesting further opportunity to improve the coverage of latent demand and further reduce the risk of stock-outs for items with additional potential demand.

These results, in monetary terms, translated into an estimated 300 k EUR margin impact during this pilot. The positive impact on sales of the test stores is shown in Fig. 7, where control sales were scaled to test group sales before the test.

The estimated impact was a significant +16% revenues, and improved margins generated almost €300 k, implying margin improvement of almost €one million per month if implemented in all of the brand's stores.

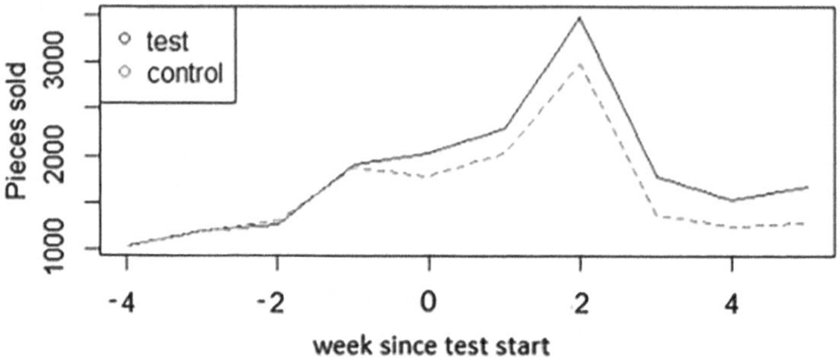

Fig. 7 Impact on sales: test vs scaled control

The positive results obtained from the experimental study induced Miroglio managers to change the process for the entire chain. The process has been to replenish all the Elena Mirò and Fiorella Rubino stores for the last 7 years until today and also extended to the other brands of Miroglio fashion.

4.2 Better Data

Another advantage of having the store managers involved in the process was found in the "popularity index" of items: ratio between the net demand (ordered pieces minus released pieces) of an item and the current inventory level over all stores.

- + 100% or greater popularity means a lot of requests but low inventory available.
- 100% popularity means that all stores want to get rid of that product.

Since it compares directly orders and releases, the popularity index is a measure of how much store managers think that the items will be popular and appreciated from the customers. In other words, it is a proxy for future item demand according to the store managers, who know the reality in which a store is placed, like a direct survey for store managers about their products.

Therefore, it can suggest to the central company some operations to do on each item. For example, if the popularity is very high, ideally the best thing to do is to restock the item, if possible, or to plan it again for the next collection. On the other side, if an item is completely unpopular, it would be good to promote it or to remove it and send it to the outlet. Additionally, inventory data—which had previously been notoriously inaccurate—was fixed more regularly by store managers to make sure not to receive complaints from other stores due to missing deliveries across.

> We researched this new system together with the Harvard Business School—*shares Giuseppe Craparotta, senior data scientist at Evo*—and together we found the demonstration that this new system can predicts the optimal supply-demand by up to 8 weeks in advance. This is the significant result of unique research based on an innovative measure of product popularity, to which the human contribution is fundamental. Many store managers are surprised when they discover that their daily contact with customers and products is the decisive factor: the soul of the algorithm.

4.3 *Happier Store Managers*

Other than profits and better data, there were additional benefits from this approach: the positive feedback from store managers. They were enthusiastic about the new process, because they finally felt that their knowledge, capacity, and experience were being taken into account for the replenishment process.

In fact, the store managers are not forced to add any edits, yet they interact almost every time with the tool: on average, 80% of the stores adjust their shipments. That means that they focus on particular products and trust the tool for the other items.

Some managers use the tool to bring "innovation" to their store according to their own ideas. One store manager of a small store, for example, tried to order a small collection of swimsuits that wasn't planned for her store, but she thought that it could work well: and in fact, after the first order, she requested it again because it had sold out.

5 Benefits at Scale

After the successful pilot, the analytical approach was rolled out to all Elena Mirò stores and then to Miroglio's other retail brands. "As a new CEO—*shares Alberto Racca, CEO of Miroglio Fashion*—I found lots of good projects and talented people: the analytical work together with Evo was a good example of this.

However, I felt that we needed to move from a narrow project and a function-based approach to a data-driven culture. It's easy to fall in love with technology, but our scope was too narrow and did not take full advantage of the data we gathered in our shops, on our websites, and by following our consumers' journey online.

Why focus only on inventory replenishment and not on initial allocation of inventory? Why not connect this data to optimize our promotional activities? Why not use it for price elasticity and price management? Why not use this approach for buying decisions or product development and design? In other words, we needed to take this great project to another level, expanding its vision and scope across the entire company. Our challenge is to make the analytical approach strategic and part of the culture of the company rather than use it just as a tactical tool".

5.1 *Continuous Learning*

While on the one hand the introduction of AI in decision-making processes brought extensive economic benefits, better data quality, and higher satisfaction of store managers, on the other it has required a cultural change within the company.

The merchandizing team, previously used to a "push" approach to stock management, started to gradually embrace a "pull" approach and therefore make decisions not only based on historical data but looking forward, relying on the machine. An important challenge for the merchandizing team was that they not only had to understand the concept of sales demand potential but also to "sell it onwards" to the rest of the company, including the retail managers.

This challenge was amplified by the nature of Artificial Intelligence, which is not just a different algorithm but an altogether different, holistic optimization process taking into account different scenarios, variables, and parameters, including some that did not feel "tangible" to the users.

Two fundamental concepts were crucial to the successful mindset change: building man-machine trust and embracing a "test and learn" approach.

Confidence in the instrument has been gradually built over time: not only was solid and robust data collected over the years, but also many small and iterative tests were carried out to gain from the new learning and feedback as it gradually emerged. This process required patience, time, and an open mindset; with a close partnership between the two companies and continuous training of the merchandizing team by Evo's experts. The exchange of information and contact between the two parties still takes place almost daily in order to maintain a high level of data consistency and the quality of the results.

Even more than trust, however, the introduction of the "test and learn" approach has been driving significant change in company culture and mindset.

The AI system has led to great results for Miroglio, elevating its technical capability and decision-making. But it required understanding that it is a living system, which can only grow and improve by using and testing it. The best solutions can only be achieved through tests, trials, and simulations, modifying constraints and parameters. People engagement is key: their knowledge of the work environment drives the system, by setting the inputs and thus having a significant impact on the outputs.

A truly optimal solution can only be reached step by step, trying, testing, and learning as the Artificial Intelligence system continues to evolve hand-in-hand with its human owners.

"Lab-Grown Data": The Role of Synthetic Data as Key Tool for Evolving the AI Landscape Ensuring Fairness and Respecting Privacy

Mirko De Maldè

Abstract Synthetic data plays a crucial role in advancing AI while ensuring fairness and privacy. This chapter explores the growing importance of synthetic data in the AI landscape, addressing challenges in accessing and using real-world data due to privacy and bias concerns. Synthetic data, generated by models like GANs and VAEs, offers a solution by mimicking real data without compromising individual privacy. It enables the creation of high-quality, unbiased datasets for training AI models, facilitating innovation and compliance with regulations like the GDPR and the EU AI Act. The chapter highlights use cases, particularly in healthcare, where synthetic data can drive advancements while maintaining data privacy and security. The future of AI development hinges on robust data governance, and synthetic data is poised to be a key tool in creating a fair and ethical AI ecosystem.

1 Introduction

AI is reaching unprecedented capabilities, becoming widely used by millions daily in various scenarios. This marks the start of a new era where AI aids humans in numerous tasks, heralding a future of collaboration between humans and machines to create economic and societal value.

Indeed, the role of Artificial intelligence is growing at a very fast pace—with novel applications and capabilities emerging every day and seemingly capable of disrupting—or at least deeply impacting—a large variety of economic sectors. Not surprisingly, the concept itself of the fourth industrial revolution is entirely predicated around the potential of AI to impact and profoundly change all aspects of the social and economic life as we know it.

By the very same token, the rise of AI poses difficult questions in terms of long-term social impact, sustainability, justice, democracy, and inclusion. A key element

M. De Maldè (✉)
Moveax, Rome, Italy
e-mail: m.demalde@thairis.it

G. R. Marseglia et al. (eds.), *Socio-economic Impact of Artificial Intelligence*,
Progress in IS, https://doi.org/10.1007/978-3-031-73514-1_12

associated with growing concerns around social justice and sustainability of an AI-led future is data.

Data is crucial for training AI algorithms, with their accuracy, reliability, and usefulness depending on the quality and quantity of data used.

Despite the rapidly growing volume of data generated daily, effectively using this "data deluge" remains a challenge. There's more data available than ever, but the ability to consistently leverage it without being overwhelmed is still limited.

2 Limitations in Access and Usage of Data

To say it with Coleridge, "Water Everywhere but not a drop to drink". We have data, but it is not so trivial to make this huge amount of data available for everyday use. This is due to a variety of reasons.

Access

Access to a huge amount of high-quality data surely represents the key enabler for AI development. This is true for all kinds of systems based on artificial intelligence, from generalist tools such as large language models (trained on the vast amount of data freely available on the internet) to vertically specialised AI-based medical diagnostic systems (trained on personal datasets of patients with specific diseases).

Over the last 15 years, large tech companies like Facebook, Google, and Amazon have dominated data access, creating a "digital feudalism". They have hoarded vast amounts of data, gaining a competitive edge, while smaller companies and developers struggled to access sufficient data for innovation.

In the most recent past, various initiatives have been undertaken, in particular in Europe, to change this scenario. Since the two seminal communications in this area—namely the "Building a European Data Economy communication" of January 2017 and the "Towards a common European data space" communication of April 2018, the EU has implemented a coherent strategy to facilitate and promote data access and sharing via initiatives like the EU Regulation on the free movement of non-personal data (EU 2018/1807) and the Directive (EU) 2019/1024 on open data and the reuse of public-sector information, to the more recent—and noteworthy—EU Data Act (Regulation (EU) 2023/2854). While these initiatives will take some years to fully express their potential effects (the EU Data Act will become fully operational starting September 2025), those IT providers responsible in the first place for "harvesting" the data from users and from their interaction with online services are still retaining a significant advantage (both commercially and for the development of new data-driven services), while access to data—in particular personal and sensitive data—will remain a challenge for smaller developers with no economic means or IT infrastructures to obtain and manage vast amounts of data.

In perspective, however successful the initiatives for encouraging (and even enforcing) sharing and access to data might become, economic operators with more economic resources and number of users are likely to retain their advantages in terms of access and availability of datasets, at least until completely new forms of data governance (including the European Data Spaces models, but also the data cooperative paradigm)[1,2] will replace the current one, based on the property, control, and isolated data siloes.

Privacy

Another major barrier to freely accessing personal and sensitive data is the essential need to protect users' and citizens' privacy rights. In the past 10–15 years, large IT platforms and online service providers were virtually free to do whatever they deemed useful with their customer data. Beside the poor protective framework provided by outdated or ineffective regulations (cookie policy law "pops up" in mind), once the user accepted the (notoriously long and intricate) Terms of Services —usually scrolling down as fast as possible to the "Accept" button—all data generated directly or indirectly by users was fully in the control of the service provider.

Various analyses were made to better understand users attitudes and behaviours when it comes to controlling their data and caring for their privacy. The value of personal data is still poorly understood by users and citizens—who fail to perceive these data as a digital extension of their own bodies and their privacy as a fundamental right to protect their integrity as human beings. As a result, users adopt incoherent approaches for the protection of their data, something that has been described as the "Privacy paradox":[3] while users appear truly concerned about their data if asked explicitly, they tend to give up extremely easily their right to privacy in order to access online services. Such a behaviour could be explained by the fear of users of being somewhat excluded by the digital world —or becoming less capable of fully enjoying their preferred services if they do not concede control over their own personal data. Going back to the similarities with the feudal era, this behaviour has been also expressed in terms of "Voluntary servitude".[4]

It is in this context that the concept of surveillance capitalism has been forming, defined as "1. a new economic order that claims human experience as raw material for hidden commercial practices of extraction, prediction, and sale. [...] a substantial mutation of capitalism marked by an unprecedented concentration of wealth, knowledge, and power in human history. [...] The foundational context of a surveillance economy [...]. An expropriation of fundamental human rights better framed as a coup from above: a reversal of popular sovereignty".[5] Capitalism capable of impairing our very capacity for self-determination, which betrays the emancipatory

---

[1] Hardjono, Thomas, and Alex Pentland. "Data Cooperatives: Towards a Foundation for Decentralized Personal Data Management." arXiv preprint arXiv:1905.08819 (2019).

[2] Ibid.

[3] S. Kokolakis, "Privacy attitudes and privacy behaviour: A review of current research on the privacy paradox phenomenon", *Computers & security*, *64*, 2017, pp. 122–134.

[4] A. Romele, F. Gallino, C. Emmenegger, D. Gorgone, "Panopticism is not Enough: Social Media as Technologies of Voluntary Servitude", *Surveillance and Society*, 2017.

[5] S. Zuboff, *The age of surveillance capitalism—The Fight for a Human Future at the New Frontier of Power*, PublicAffair, New York, Gennaio 2019, testo tradotto dall'originale.

promises of the early stages of the internet, and penetrates our lives like a parasite to extract data useful for the profit of others, fuelling a perverse mechanism that only serves to widen the already very pronounced gaps in knowledge and wealth.

Therefore, it's not surprising that recent data protection laws, like the General Data Protection Regulation (GDPR), take a practical approach by making organisations responsible for properly managing personal data to protect users' rights. Citizens are given new rights, such as the right to provide free and informed consent, their right to have a copy of the data, to access it, and not to be subjected to profiling and automated analysis without having the opportunity to object to such treatment, the right to data portability, and the right to erasure ("right to be forgotten").

Similar regulatory tools were desperately necessary to start overcoming the complete lack of clear rules and liability frameworks for handling personal—and even sensitive—data. Such scenarios generated growing concerns about a new state of surveillance, biopolitics, and new forms of digital panopticon, posing serious threats to basic fundamental rights, including self-determination, freedom, and democracy.[6,7]

Still, the inevitable consequences of these new regulations were an even more strict control over access to personal and sensitive data—making even more difficult to tech players (in particular smaller ones) whereas big IT companies managed to continue using sensitive data with the "unvoluntary complicity" of users, or directly obtaining data in ways not entirely legal or ethical).[8,9,10]

Fairness

The issue of datasets not being "fair", or better, the issue of social, economic, and cultural biases that become somewhat crystallised in the resulting datasets—is known since almost a decade now.

One notorious example comes from the US, where AI systems were already used in court to determine a risk score of recidivism, which judges routinely used to decide whether or not to assign more jail time to inmates asking for parole. Not so surprisingly, it came out that the scores were not particularly precise nor fair, due to algorithms trained with incomplete or inherently biased data —which ended up

[6] P. Y. Wan, *Clocked!: Time and Biopower in the Age of Algorithms* (Doctoral dissertation, Utrecht University), 2018.

[7] J. Sekulovski, *The Panopticon Factor: Privacy and Surveillance in the Digital Age*, 21 世紀倫理創成研究, 9, 2016, pp. 61–76.

[8] Griggs, Mary Beth (November 11, 2019). "Google may be secretly gathering millions of personal health records with alleged 'Project Nightingale'". *The Verge*.

[9] Pilkington, Ed (November 12, 2019). "Google's secret cache of medical data includes names and full details of millions—whistleblower". *The Guardian*.

[10] Garcia, Ahiza (November 13, 2019). "Google's 'Project Nightingale' center of federal inquiry". *CNN*. Turner Broadcasting System.

replicating and even amplifying those bias and the underlying social injustice that they were mirroring.[11,12]

Yet real data are unfair because the world is. Traditional data sets can easily integrate inherent biases due to historical inequalities or under-representation of certain groups, leading to inaccurate and unfair predictions, inevitably reiterating the injustice already crystallised in the socio-economic structure. Social and economic differences—and even genetic ones—are integrally translated into real world datasets, which are "true" to the reality from which they are extracted but fatally biased when it comes to allowing the acceptable level of generalisation and abstraction needed to make an AI system reliable, fair, and safe (in particular in the medical context).

For these reasons, simply using (and relying) on real-world data—even when abundantly available —might not be the best choice for training new algorithms, as they could eventually become as unfair and short-sighted as the datasets they were trained with.

As a Side Note: From Quantity to Quality
Finally, and maybe somehow surprisingly, with the advent of large language models, the role of data per se—and in particular the need for Big Data, appears to be slightly dispersed in the vast network of correlations, parameters, and abstractions all underlying these new and powerful AI-based tools. The direct role of each single dataset or data point in the training of these vast models becomes less evident and important. The real additional value of data only appears when it allows new correlations to be found, allowing the grand model to become more precise and insightful in its answers. In such a context, quantity of "average" data will not make a really big difference, while only "outliers data" will retain their full value.

2.1 *The New Regulatory and Standardisation Framework*

The implementation and usage of AI-based tools for scoring the risk of individuals committing crimes—somehow similar to those used in courts in the US—will most likely become completely illegal in Europe starting from March 13th, 2026—which is 24 months after the approval of the EU "AI Act"—which will become fully applicable on that date.

The EU AI Act has been widely acknowledged as a landmark legislation that will shape the future development of AI system (and relevant economy and market), in Europe and worldwide.

[11] M. Callahan, "Algorithms Were Supposed to Reduce Bias in Criminal Justice—Do They?", in The Brink (online magazine), Boston University, 2023. Retrieved online: Algorithms Were Supposed to Reduce Bias in Criminal Justice—Do They? | The Brink | Boston University (bu.edu)

[12] J. Angwin, J. Larson, S. Mattu, L. Kirchner, "Machine Bias -There's software used across the country to predict future criminals. And it's biased against blacks", ProPublica, 2016. Machine Bias—ProPublica

Rather than introducing new rights for individual citizens, the AI Act adopted a precautionary, risk-based approach, which aims at guiding and regulating the production of AI-based system in all fields and for all kind of applications (excluding AI tools created for personal use, research, or in the military/defence context), depending on their potential risk of harmful effects on individuals.

The risk score spans from "minimal risk" to "unacceptable risk", with the former encompassing AI tools such as spam filters—bearing virtually no risk and not being regulated at all, and the latter including tools for behaviour manipulation, biometric characterisation, classification based on race or social behaviours, and the like, which are altogether prohibited. The additional category of general purpose AI—which will need to undergo (as the AI system with a high-risk profile) through a very thorough assessment process—was added only in 2023 as a direct response to the advent and widespread adoption of LLMs such as ChatGPT.

The AI Act's foundation was partly laid by earlier EU initiatives and studies that highlighted AI systems' risks to fundamental rights and user safety: "AI systems may jeopardise fundamental rights such as the right to non-discrimination, freedom of expression, human dignity, personal data protection and privacy".[13] From these concerns emerged the pledge made by EU legislators to create a framework for ensuring the creation of a human-centric AI ecosystem in Europe.[14]

Amongst others, one of the issues raised by the development and use of AI systems—according to the EU—is their "functional dependence on data and on the quality of data". From such an observation stems, as key part of the regulatory framework developed with the AI Act, a particular attention to data quality, fairness, absence of biases in the datasets, and proper balance of relevant populations. In essence, datasets used for training go themselves under the lens of regulators to ensure that the resulting AI system is not prone to biases and misjudgement caused by underlying problems with the relevant datasets. The EU Parliament made a specific effort to define the question with biases in datasets and to propose mitigation strategies, in particular highlighting the importance of high-quality vertical datasets for the specific domain in which the resulting AI tool will operate.[15] Even the more recent and newly adopted ISO/EIC standard 42,001:2023 (Artificial intelligence—Management system) poses particular attention to data quality, as a key part of the assessment and standardisation process.[16]

But, as discussed above, finding high-quality, non-biased, rich datasets in any domain is not an easy task.

[13] EU High-Level Expert Group, *Ethics Guidelines for Trustworthy AI*, 2019.

[14] European Commission Communication (COM(2019) 168 final) to the European Parliament, the Council, The European Economic And Social Committee And The Committee Of The Region, *Building Trust in Human-Centric Artificial Intelligence*, 2019.

[15] European Parliament Research Services, Auditing the quality of datasets used in algorithmic decision-making systems, 2019.

[16] ISO/IEC 42001:2023(en), Information technology—Artificial intelligence—Management system

3 Synthetic Data: A Primer

A possible solution might come from an unexpected direction, which has been often perceived, in particular in the mass media, as somehow representing the dark side of the AI, namely generative adversarial networks (GANs). After the publication of the foundational paper in 2014,[17] GANs received a lot of attention from the scientific community and the general public alike, whereas the first example of completely AI-generated images—including very detailed and clear faces of non-existing people—caught the world's attention and caused immediate concerns, with the perspective of a future where distinguishing reality from virtuality would become increasingly challenging. Since then, an impressive amount of publications and novel methods were produced,[18] for different kinds of data and different purposes.[19]

These systems' ability to generate entirely new, artificial datasets presents an opportunity to overcome data shortages due to strict privacy laws and reduce inherent biases in real-world data.

Such opportunities are offered by the novel world of synthetic data, namely data that are "artificially" generated by an algorithm rather than being the result of real-world data processing. Indeed, in many of the AI applications based on deep learning, the process of data synthetisation involves the observation of real-world data, from which the model will extrapolate key features, which then enable the generation of completely new data, hence not associated with any existing individual in the case of personal data, which have the same statistical features and level of granularity, and therefore same informational value, as the observed real dataset.

On this basis, it does not come as a surprise that Gartner already forecasted in 2022 that by 2030, synthetic data "will overshadow real data in AI models".[20]

Synthetic data appear to be able to provide some solutions to the issues described in the previous section.

Access: No Longer a Must

The first and very interesting opportunity stemming from the adoption of synthetic data is that it is possible to entirely avoid the access to the real datasets. Providers could share synthetic versions of their private/sensitive datasets with other organisations, greatly reducing the complexities and costs associated with compliance with regulations (GDPR) and pre-processing (e.g. for removing sensitive information or for creating specific datasets involving also annotation processes). In doing so,

---

[17] Goodfellow, I., Pouget-Abadie, J., Mirza, M., Xu, B., Warde-Farley, D., Ozair, S., Courville, A. and Bengio, Y., 2014. Generative adversarial nets. Advances in neural information processing systems, 27.

[18] Lu, Y., Shen, M., Wang, H., Wang, X., van Rechem, C. and Wei, W., 2023. Machine learning for synthetic data generation: a review. arXiv preprint arXiv:2302.04062.

[19] A. Kiran and S. S. Kumar, "A Methodology and an Empirical Analysis to Determine the Most Suitable Synthetic Data Generator," in IEEE Access, vol. 12, pp. 12209–12228, 2024

[20] Is Synthetic Data the Future of AI? Q&A with Alexander Linden: https://www.gartner.com/en/newsroom/press-releases/2022-06-22-is-synthetic-data-the-future-of-ai

providers could also intervene on the generation to mitigate known issues (e.g. biases) in their original datasets. The synthetic data generation processing in itself could be executed via distributed approaches, leveraging the paradigm of federated learning to enable multi-site synthetic data generation.[21]

Privacy: No Man's Data

Such a feature would greatly facilitate data access, whereas data controllers (as per the GDPR terminology) would not be obliged to treat the synthetic data resulting from their datasets as the original ones. In fact, synthetic data—if generated properly—can be considered by all means anonymous, as they are not associated (beside the risk of de-identification) with any existing individual.

The European Data Protection Supervisor already acknowledged the potential of synthetic data to provide "added value for the privacy of individuals, whose personal data does not have to be disclosed".[22] But the most significant confirmation of this specific feature of synthetic data comes from the EU AI Act itself. Article 10 of the EU AI Act ("Data and Data Governance") in indicating the cases in which the recourse to personal sensitive data (such as health data) is permitted for bias detection, the first condition set is "the bias detection and correction cannot be effectively fulfilled by processing other data, including synthetic or anonymised data". This appears to effectively pair synthetic and anonymised data as equivalent, as correctly observed by privacy laws experts.[23] A very similar statement occurs in Article 54 of the EU AI Act (Further Processing of Personal Data for Developing Certain AI Systems in the Public Interest in the AI Regulatory Sandbox), which states that specific kinds of personal data processing in the AI Regulatory Sandbox are allowed only when the use of "anonymised, synthetic or other non-personal data" would not fulfil the same requirements. Once again, the article seems to associate synthetic data with other forms of anonymised and non-personal data.

Synthetic Fairness

Another key feature offered by synthetic data is the possibility of intervening on existing dataset. Once identified possible biases in terms of under or over representation of a given group of the population, an imbalance which could eventually lead to biased and unreliable AI systems, then it would be possible to intervene, within the limits of statistical validity of the final dataset, to mitigate said biases, artificially adding individual elements of the population in need of intervention. This means

[21] Little, C., Elliot, M. and Allmendinger, R., 2023. Federated learning for generating synthetic data: a scoping review. International Journal of Population Data Science, 8(1).

[22] R. Riemann, "Synthetic Data"—TechSonar Report 2021–2022, December 2021. Synthetic Data | European Data Protection Supervisor (europa.eu)

[23] See, for instance, the article published on LinkedIn by Lorenzo Cristofaro—a Tech, AI and Privacy lawyer with years of experience in following regulatory and technological innovations in this field. Legal status of Synthetic Data, October 2023. (28) Legal status of Synthetic Data | LinkedIn. Mr Cristofaro observes that the de facto consideration of synthetic and anonymised data as "equivalent and interchangeable alternatives" is "further confirmed by: (i) the use of the word "or" in between, and (ii) the clear distinction marked with pseudonimised data, listed separately, and so qualified as a different category of data compared to the synthetic ones".

that it would be possible to mitigate over or under representation of specific populations in a given dataset, adjusting existing biases in terms of ethnicity, gender, age, and so forth. Along the very same lines, it is also possible to create large datasets starting from smaller ones, mostly composed of "outliers", meaning data samples recurring rarely in real world. Various methodologies and approaches have been explored in literature to use synthetic data generation to reduce biases in original datasets, but it needs to be kept in mind that generating fair and unbiased synthetic data requires careful consideration of the biases included in the original dataset, the dimension of fairness most relevant for the resulting dataset, and the limit to manipulation of synthetic data in order to keep them usable and realistic.

Artificial Outliers

The other side of the same medal offers the capability of adding outliers in a relatively "flat" dataset. What does this mean? Let's assume that we need to develop a novel AI-based tool for fraud detection in financial transactions. We will need to start from the dataset of all financial transactions we have from the past, to try and see whether it is possible to identify patterns that facilitate the identification of fraudulent transactions, and eventually trigger some sort of alert to prevent frauds. Still, hopefully, the original dataset will not have that many fraudulent transactions within it. While this might sound like good news for the financial transactions service provider, it is really not for the AI developer, which only has that dataset to deal with. The resulting algorithm will probably not be particularly accurate at detecting frauds, whereas the limited amount of fraudulent transactions in the original dataset did not allow to extract generalisable enough patterns to identify frauds while not overfitting with the exact same fraudulent transactions observed in the dataset.

In such a scenario, the creation of synthetic data might help mitigating the issue. While still starting from the very same available dataset, in the process of creating synthetic data it would be possible to fine tune the generation to increase by some order of magnitude the presence of fraudulent transactions while still retaining the overall statistical value of the dataset, thus avoiding the creation of an "oversensitive" algorithm that seeks for fraud even where there is none to be found.

3.1 Methodologies

Synthetic data per se are not a particularly novel concept: preliminary work can be traced back to the '40, with early applications of Monte Carlo simulations methods, and indeed synthetically generated data—mostly in the form of "dummy" data have been used ever since for a variety of purposes. Yet, the current "era" of synthetic data and underlying generation methodology is mostly rooted in the need to providing AI algorithms with high-quality data while ensuring compliance with privacy regulations and reducing biases observable in real-world datasets. In this context, the most used models are certainly generative adversarial networks (GANs) and variational auto encoders (VAEs).

Beside deep learning architectures (such as GANs and VAEs), other tools such as agent-based models and econometric models can be used to generate data capable of representing complex systems, stochastic differential equations, more specific for economic systems, or the already mentioned Monte Carlo Simulation Method.

Still, GANs and VAEs are surely the most adopted methods for generating high-quality general purpose synthetic data for machine learning, providing a high degree of accuracy, similarity, and usability in various contexts.

GANs work through the combination of neural networks, a generator and a discriminator, which are trained in a sort of competition-like process: while the generator starts generating synthetic data samples based on some sort of original dataset, the work of the discriminator is to spot synthetically generated data and to distinguish them from real data. The process continues up until the moment when the generator has improved enough to generate data that is so realistic that the discriminator cannot tell them from real data any longer. The outcome is very realistic data, which shares with the original dataset many statistical features that are interesting for analytical purposes.

Variational autoencoders[24] are a specific kind of autoencoder, a neural network that is typically adopted for noise reduction and data compression. The specific feature of VAEs is that they are probabilistic, thus they can produce outputs that are different at each generation. Similarly to GANs, they can generate data that is very similar to real ones in terms of statistical features.

Methodologies for Specific Type of Data

Besides general methodologies, for each specific kind of dataset, slightly different approaches will be adopted to maximise the usability of the generated dataset.

For tabular data, meaning data organised in rows and columns, various models have been proposed. The most effective one is—for now—CTGAN (Conditional Tabular Generative Adversarial Network).[25] Compared to other GANs, CTGAN stands out for its ability to consider the relationships between the columns of tabular data, allowing the generation of synthetic data that retains the structure and correlations of the original data. This feature makes it particularly suitable for synthesising complex tabular data.

Image data are the kind of data that provided a first and significant use case for GANs, and indeed, GANs are still capable of offering very good and realistic results. Fine-tuned models such as DCGANs[26] and StyleGANs[27] enabled even more

---

[24] Wan, Z., Zhang, Y., & He, H. (2017, November). Variational autoencoder based synthetic data generation for imbalanced learning. In 2017 IEEE symposium series on computational intelligence (SSCI) (pp. 1–7). IEEE.

[25] Xu, L., Skoularidou, M., Cuesta-Infante, A. and Veeramachaneni, K., 2019. Modeling tabular data using conditional gan. Advances in neural information processing systems, 32.

[26] Radford, A., Metz, L. and Chintala, S., 2015. Unsupervised representation learning with deep convolutional generative adversarial networks. arXiv preprint arXiv:1511.06434.

[27] First introduced by NVIDIA Researchers in 2020: Karras, T., Laine, S. and Aila, T., 2019. A style-based generator architecture for generative adversarial networks. In Proceedings of the IEEE/CVF conference on computer vision and pattern recognition (pp. 4401–4410).

accurate results to be generated. At the same time, diffusion models[28] (popularised by tools such as DALL-E, StableDiffusion, and MidJourney) have recently been widely adopted as alternatives to GANs. Diffusion models are specific kinds of generative models that are capable of generating data similar to those with which they have been trained but via a process very different from the one adopted by GANs. Diffusion models basically start their training process by destroying the training data and then learning to recover the data, reversing the noising process executed through Gaussian noise.

Another interesting domain for synthetic data generation are time-series data (meaning series of data in time order), which can find application in a variety of real-world scenarios, and can be effectively produced with specific models such as recurrent GANs and TimeGAN, the latter adopting an autoencoder structure to more efficiently represent the data distribution.

A particular domain for synthetic data generation is text. Due to its discrete nature, text is a challenge for GANs, whereas it is difficult to make the normal interaction between generator and discriminator to work properly with discrete outputs. While dedicated methods based on GAN have been envisioned to try and sort out this challenge, the advent of large language models (LLMs), with Chat-GPT nowadays being adopted by hundred million of people, completely changed the scenario, making it possible to generate high-quality text with basically no effort for the user.

Because these tools can produce datasets nearly indistinguishable from real ones, EU legislators now require synthetic data to have clear markings or watermarks to indicate their artificial origin.

3.2 *Risks and Limitations*

It is important to be careful in balancing expectations when dealing with synthetic data. None of the appealing features mentioned above are immediately available by just applying a synthetic data generator, however advanced it might look. There still is a need for fine tuning the model and modelling the synthetic data generation on the specific use case and original dataset.

Additionally, it was indeed demonstrated that there is an inherent risk of re-identification of individual pieces of original data when looking at the synthesised dataset, making it of extreme importance to stress test the synthetic dataset to assess the risk of privacy leakage, for example, assessing the presence of clones of specific records of the original dataset in the synthetic one or the similarity between original

[28] Seminal works include: Sohl-Dickstein, J., Weiss, E., Maheswaranathan, N. and Ganguli, S., 2015, June. Deep unsupervised learning using nonequilibrium thermodynamics. In International conference on machine learning (pp. 2256–2265). PMLR, Song, Y. and Ermon, S., 2019. Generative modeling by estimating gradients of the data distribution. Advances in neural information processing systems, 32. Ho, J., Jain, A. and Abbeel, P., 2020. Denoising diffusion probabilistic models. Advances in neural information processing systems, 33, pp. 6840–6851.

and synthetic records.[29] Such analysis can be performed with a variety of tools, from the native system provided by tools like the Synthetic Data Vault[30] to more intricate assessment and auditing tools, created for specific domains or to assess specific qualities of the resulting dataset.

It is worth mentioning, in this context, some of the key elements that potential users of synthetic data should keep in mind.

The first, and possibly most important, element to consider is that, although synthetic data are virtually "completely new data" there are some risks for re-identifications. Through specific forms of attack—such as Membership Inference Attack[31]—it could be possible to derive personal data from the analysis of the synthetic dataset. This is because the synthetic data generation process aims to capture and reproduce the statistical properties of the original data. If these properties are unique to certain individuals or groups in the original data, then these individuals or groups may be identifiable in the synthetic data. Thus, it is important—once the synthetic data is generated—to run specific tests to assess the level of privacy of the synthetic dataset, calculating the risk for re-identification, the presence of clones in the datasets, and so on.

This issue is especially significant for outliers in the original dataset. The goal is to create synthetic versions of these data points without compromising the privacy of the original data. This is due to the fact that while outliers are particularly interesting to represent accurately the original data distribution, at the same time their rarity means that it would be easier for adversaries to associate the outlier emerging from the synthetic dataset with specific individuals or groups, with the risk of breaching the privacy of their original data. This is a particularly sensitive matter when it comes to health data—whereas specific conditions that the original individual might have had interest in keeping private could be inferred by third parties (say, an insurance company) to make decisions about them. Thus, developers should carefully consider this risk before including such outliers in the datasets without adding sufficient "noise" to protect individual rights to privacy.

Along the same lines, fairness of synthetic data should be measured properly to make sure that the resulting dataset does not introduce additional imbalances in the data that will feed the training process.[32]

The second, possibly counterintuitive, element to consider is that although synthetic data can substitute real data in research and training activities, it is not entirely advisable (even if potentially possible) to completely disregard real datasets, to properly test the accuracy of the resulting algorithm and fine tune it with real world scenarios. More importantly, it is certainly true that the quality of the synthetic

[29] Bellovin, S. M., Dutta, P. K., & Reitinger, N. (2019). Privacy and synthetic datasets. Stan. Tech. L. Rev., 22, 1.

[30] SDMetrics—https://github.com/sdv-dev/SDMetrics

[31] VAN BREUGEL, Boris, et al. Membership inference attacks against synthetic data through overfitting detection. *arXiv preprint arXiv:2302.12580*, 2023.

[32] Bhanot, K. (2023). Synthetic Data Generation and Evaluation for Fairness (Doctoral dissertation, Rensselaer Polytechnic Institute).

dataset will rely on the quality of the original dataset (if we have a small, biased, and incomplete dataset—our resulting synthetic dataset will not magically turn out as a high-quality dataset).

During data generation, it's crucial to remember that synthetic data, while resembling the original, might be meaningless or fundamentally different. Even an apparently simple type of dataset—such as tabular data—might lead to the generation of inaccurate synthetic data, if the semantic validity of the resulting dataset is not taken properly into account, possibly adding specific classifiers or rules to guide the generation process on the basis of the specific features and "meaning" of the original dataset.

Not surprisingly, researchers are trying to provide coherent frameworks to assess synthetic data under a variety of dimensions,[33] together with auditing tools for AI models,[34] and it is expected that additional tools and standards will emerge in the near future.[35]

4 Use Cases

4.1 An Overview

The use cases for synthetic datasets are in theory limitless—whereas they could be successfully used in all scenarios requiring the usage of data for implementing AI-based algorithms, but also for more basic business intelligence and analytics tasks.

Looking at the value propositions of various players in the (nascent) industry of synthetic data, a set of recurrent use cases can be identified:

- Using synthetic data for testing: testing novel services or products requires the availability of significant amount of datasets, which will be handled in the relevant operational scenarios. While for newcomers in the market the challenge might be to collect the original data in the first place, for players already active on the market there are some alternatives. One is using dummy data, but these data are hardly capable of capturing and representing the nuances and variability observable in real-world data (even if generated via complex rules). The other option is to use—after lengthy authorisation and sanitisation process—the production data they have already available—that is, the data of their current customers. This option will offer more credible and robust datasets for testing activities, but the risk of breaching the privacy of the users is not negligible (also

[33] Qian, Z., Davis, R., & van der Schaar, M. (2024). Synthcity: a benchmark framework for diverse use cases of tabular synthetic data. Advances in Neural Information Processing Systems, 36.

[34] Simbeck, K. (2023). They shall be fair, transparent, and robust: auditing learning analytics systems. AI and Ethics, 1–17.

[35] For instance, ISO is currently working on a standard dedicated to synthetic data for healthcare.

considering the hefty sanctions imposed by GDPR on non-compliant companies). The third option—offered by synthetic data—is to generate—starting from original data—synthetic datasets solely used for testing activities. This would remove all approval processes and privacy breach risks, saving time and resources for the company. Additionally, synthetic data will offer a perfect alternative for real data, making the result of testing more reliable and accurate. Developers could also intervene to augment the dataset or to remove observable biases in the original datasets. Finally, synthetic data come with an additional advantage: they are "natively" labelled. No need for data scientists to spend weeks only labelling correctly the available datasets.

- Facilitating cooperation and private data release: synthetic data enable companies, research entities, developers, and other stakeholders, to cooperate toward the development of new data-driven services via the sharing of synthetic datasets and the creation of dedicated open data ecosystems (or data clean rooms) capable of multiplying the value of each individual dataset hosted in private silos of each data provider by putting them all together in a much larger dataset available for development. Larger amount of data can significantly improve reliability of the resulting AI tools or data-driven services, while at the same time reducing the risk associated with biases within each individual dataset. This could accelerate development, validation, and adoption of novel data-driven tools, facilitating the assessment of their usability and providing strong evidence for their potential adoption in real-world scenarios.
- The development of AI-based systems is of course one strong use case for synthetic data, for the very same reasons and features discussed above. Besides offering high-quality datasets, also improved via dedicated intervention for debiasing and augmentation, the use of synthetic data facilitates cooperation, testing, comparison of efficiency in various simulated scenarios, and so forth.
- Debiasing, fairness, and augmentation are sort of horizontal use cases already discussed above. Generating de-biased synthetic data is easier than de-biasing already trained models by means of iterative corrections of the model behaviour (also considering that it might be easier to spot biases in the dataset rather than wait for the model to display behaviours associated with inherent biases of the original dataset). This is also valid for augmentation: it is possible to artificially manipulate existing datasets (within statistical limits) in order to include specific outliers interesting for the use case at hand. This greatly facilitates the development of tools based on specific events that might not occur easily in the real world.

4.2 Healthcare

A specific domain in which the adoption of synthetic data could offer unprecedented opportunities is healthcare.[36] Medicine is more and more becoming a data-driven science, and the accumulation of health data currently experienced is unprece-

[36] Gonzales, A., Guruswamy, G., & Smith, S. R. (2023). Synthetic data in health care: A narrative review. *PLOS Digital Health*, *2*(1), e0000082.

dented. Beside the growing body of datasets generated in hospitals and research centres, new forms of health and health-related data are generated at scale by personal wearable devices and telemedicine devices.

At the same time, health data are personal and sensitive data *par excellence*—and the handling of health data remains challenging for privacy, security, and regulatory concerns. Data controllers, even the more eager to share data—are reluctant to do so without proper guarantees, and the cooperation on research and development activities often requires significant efforts and resources.

In such a context, making use of synthetic data might offer an important support to overcome such challenges, generating realistic yet entirely artificial datasets that mimic the characteristics of real patient information without compromising individual privacy. Such dataset would facilitate the development of novel AI-based algorithm for diagnosis and personalised treatment, greatly enhancing the opportunities for cooperation among research institutions and private industries, effectively removing the barriers currently hindering data sharing.

Not surprisingly, synthetic data is increasingly acknowledged as a major enabler for advancing healthcare innovation while guaranteeing privacy and regulatory compliance.[37,38] In general, use cases span from providing access to large datasets currently inaccessible (e.g., for privacy reasons) or unavailable (e.g. small datasets of rare diseases that are not connected with each other), to improving the quality and quantity of datasets (in particular intervening in the case of biases in the real dataset), to facilitating the design and execution of clinical trials, and also facilitating the recruitment of patient cohorts more suitable for the study at hand. Additionally, synthetic data can be used to assess the quality of medical AI tools using synthetic datasets, facilitating development and validation.[39]

One particular use case of interest is the one regarding telemedicine. The push towards telemedicine caused by the COVID-19 health emergency urgently raises the issue of the need for platforms for the secure management and exchange of data from various sources—including data generated directly by patients—to ensure efficiency and continuity of care even remotely, and the optimisation in the use of digital technologies for support in treatment and the prevention of acute events. Furthermore, the need to improve the healthcare system's prevention capacity requires an agile and structured data monitoring system, in order to allow for the analysis of pathological risk at both individual and population levels, clustering, and the calibration of interventions for prevention and early diagnosis.

The use of synthetic data, in combination with specific tools for tracking the data lifecycle from the original provider (in particular in the case of an individual patient)

---

[37] Chen, R. J., Lu, M. Y., Chen, T. Y., Williamson, D. F., & Mahmood, F. (2021). Synthetic data in machine learning for medicine and healthcare. *Nature Biomedical Engineering*, *5*(6), 493–497.

[38] Morley-Fletcher, E. (2022). New Solutions to Biomedical Data Sharing: Secure Computation and Synthetic Data. In Personalized Medicine in the Making: Philosophical Perspectives from Biology to Healthcare (pp. 173–189). Cham: Springer International Publishing.

[39] Tucker, A., Wang, Z., Rotalinti, Y., & Myles, P. (2020). Generating high-fidelity synthetic patient data for assessing machine learning healthcare software. *NPJ digital medicine*, *3*(1), 1–13.

to the usage for AI-development, could contribute to the creation of a novel innovation ecosystem for healthcare, enabling on the one hand the sharing of data currently unavailable and on the other hand cooperation between data providers (e.g. hospitals and patients) and consumers (researchers and developers).

The Case of Health-e-Data

Health-e-Data[40] is a recently funded research project funded by the Competence Center Cyber 4.0 via Recovery and Resilience Funds, specifically focusing on exploring the adoption of synthetic data, alongside with other technologies (such as blockchain for tracking health data lifecycle) for telemedicine applications.

The concept behind Health-e-Data is simple: patient-generated data are becoming an increasingly significant source of information about our health and wellbeing, but are still poorly used and integrated in care delivery processes, in particular in areas such as telemedicine and population health)—where they could make a huge difference for care, prevention, and R&D.

Currently, patient-generated data (meaning those data generated directly by patients in their own environment via wearable devices or medical devices) are used in controlled contexts for telemedicine applications (for instance, diabetes management), to enable the delivery of treatment in remote settings. Data collected is usually specific to the kind of disease and treatment at hand, and are usually transmitted and used in a closed IT environment.

While these applications are already effective in providing innovative ways for monitoring and delivering treatment with minimum impact on patients, in perspective, the exploitation of patient-generated data should become much wider and fully integrated in the care process, most importantly in risk assessment, clustering, and implementation of prevention strategies.

Based on these requirements, Health-e-Data aims at implementing an innovative health data ecosystem enabling systematic collection, sharing, and analysis of health data, from both hospitals and individual citizens/patients, to enable cooperation, research, and development of novel AI-driven services.

To achieve this, Health-e-Data explores novel methods for generating synthetic data—both in centralised and distributed environment—with the objective of seamlessly enabling hospitals and individuals to share their data in fully anonymised form, fuelling the implementation of a large, distributed health data platform. Original data would remain in their original hosting environment, while the algorithm for generating synthetic data would run via federated learning methodologies on all data sources, as there were only one large repository of data (following the

[40] Project submitted under the Cyber 4.0 1/2023 Call for innovative R&D projects using AI and Blockchain. Moveax Srl (a Rome-based innovative consulting company in the software engineering field) and Exprivia (a large IT Italian Company with a strong healthcare vertical) compose the Health-e-Data Consortium.

paradigm of "bringing the algorithm to data" rather than requiring central gathering of data in one single repository).

Federated learning enables collaborative training of machine learning models across different data sources directly where the data is stored, eliminating the need to move the data. During FL, all raw data processing is done locally at participating sites. Only privatised aggregate intermediate results (e.g., gradients) are exposed to perform the model training loop. At the same time, FL enables better generative models for synthetic data to be trained over larger data collections by effectively coupling training data from several data provider silos.[41,42,43]

If successful, Health-e-Data aims to show that creating a large public health data ecosystem for telemedicine, monitoring, and preventive strategies is possible, in line with the European Health Data Space and Gaia-X's visions.

5 Conclusions

Data and algorithms are enabling an evolution from the archival society to the oracular society.[44] The recent and impressive acceleration in the development of general AI tools capable of performing many tasks that were considered as "restricted" to humans only few years ago is only a small glimpse of what will happen in the next decade. The connection between digital and physical worlds will become deeper and deeper, creating the ideal environment for faster development and adoption of AI-based tools, powered by the ever-growing amount data that will be generated by the interaction of humans with the digital realm.

The direction in which this inevitable progression will move largely relies on the way in which researchers, decision-makers, developers, citizens, will decide to regulate and implement this new digital environment, so to ensure safety, fairness, access, democracy, transparency, inclusion. The EU AI Act is an important milestone in setting the key features of this environment, but many other steps will need to be undertaken in order to make sure that digital innovation and economic growth will not come at the expenses of the more vulnerable and less represented components of the global population, nor at the expenses of fundamental human rights such as privacy and the right to self-determination.

In such a context, as discussed in this chapter, the role of synthetic data might be deeper than the one of simply offering a quicker and cheaper way of providing

[41] Maddock, S., Cormode, G., & Maple, C. (2023). FLAIM: AIM-based Synthetic Data Generation in the Federated Setting. arXiv preprint arXiv:2310.03447.

[42] Behera, M. R., Upadhyay, S., Shetty, S., Priyadarshini, S., Patel, P., & Lee, K. F. (2022). Fedsyn: Synthetic data generation using federated learning. arXiv preprint arXiv:2203.05931.

[43] Ghavamipour, A. R., Turkmen, F., Wang, R., & Liang, K. (2023, May). Federated Synthetic Data Generation with Stronger Security Guarantees. In Proceedings of the 28th ACM Symposium on Access Control Models and Technologies (pp. 31–42).

[44] Accoto, C. (2017). Il mondo dato: cinque brevi lezioni di filosofia digitale. EGEA spa.

datasets for AI development, but rather a key tool for data governance and data quality assurance, which in turn will facilitate auditing of the resulting AI tools, in line with the EU AI Act framework, before these tools are made available to billions of people.

The era of the giant AI human experiment—as it was called by the Future of Humanity Open letter (signed by thousands of people, including major researchers and entrepreneur in the field)[45]—must be replaced by the era of human-centric, responsible and trustworthy AI development. Without a more robust governance of data flows for AI development and validation, such a new era cannot start.

Adopting synthetic data broadly could lead to a clearer and more transparent data governance framework. This framework would cover data collection, quality, fairness, and proper use in training and validation, providing detailed control over aspects that are currently hard to fully assess due to restrictions on accessing and using real, especially personal and sensitive, data.

This goes well beyond the many and very exciting use cases for synthetic data briefly discussed above, to offer a more potent and overarching contribution for the development of a sustainable and just future for humanity as a whole. Researchers, policy-makers, industry players, should seize this opportunity to create now the preconditions for the future development of a new—"human"—AI era.

[45] Future of Humanity, "Pause Giant AI Experiments: An Open Letter", march 2023. Pause Giant AI Experiments: An Open Letter - Future of Life Institute

Artificial Intelligence: The Brains Behind Humanity's Future in Space

Giacomo Gatto, Mark Huntington, Maxime Szybowski, and Stefano Napoletano

Abstract Artificial intelligence (AI) is crucial for humanity's future in space, driving advancements in Earth observation, exploration, and commercialization. This chapter examines the evolving space sector, highlighting how AI enhances satellite data analysis, improves space operations, and supports commercial activities like space mining and microgravity manufacturing. AI's ability to process vast amounts of data and make autonomous decisions is essential for managing satellites, predicting maintenance needs, and navigating hazards. This chapter also discusses emerging use cases, such as creating AI-driven digital twins of Earth for better environmental monitoring and decision-making. With AI's help, space technologies promise to revolutionize life on Earth, change the way industries operate, and ensure global security.

Each day, hundreds of satellites focus cameras and other sensors on Earth, collecting more than 100 terabytes of data, including millions of images used by businesses, governments, researchers, and the public. Earth observation[1] is increas-

[1] Group on Earth Observations (GEO), FAQ, https://www.earthobservations.org/g_faq.html

G. Gatto (✉)
McKinsey & Co., London, UK
e-mail: Giacomo_Gatto@mckinsey.com

M. Huntington
McKinsey & Co., New York, NY, USA
e-mail: Mark_Huntington@mckinsey.com

M. Szybowski
McKinsey & Co., Zurich, Switzerland
e-mail: Maxime_Szybowski@mckinsey.com

S. Napoletano
McKinsey & Co., Milan, Italy
e-mail: Stefano_Napoletano@mckinsey.com

G. R. Marseglia et al. (eds.), *Socio-economic Impact of Artificial Intelligence*,
Progress in IS, https://doi.org/10.1007/978-3-031-73514-1_13

ingly important to the mining industry, for example, where it helps companies search for lithium deposits that could be used in electric vehicle batteries, enables better oversight of complex supply chains and distribution logistics, and improves the environmental monitoring of mine sites, including closed ones.

Profound advances in artificial intelligence (AI) are arriving at a promising moment for space activities, and AI stands to play a critical enabling role in these and a multitude of other use cases. The space sector is at an inflection point, primed to enhance or disrupt business, science, sustainability, and global security, and AI is essential not only to Earth observation but also to most of humanity's other ambitions in space, which include mining asteroids, manufacturing in low gravity, and exploring the far reaches of the galaxy.

In this chapter, we summarize how the space business is evolving and what is driving its growth. We explain how AI is being used in space, both to improve life on Earth and to unlock new possibilities in commercialization and exploration. Based on a survey[2] of space-industry leaders done by McKinsey & Company and the World Economic Forum in 2022, we discuss the challenges the space sector faces in achieving its potential and the actions that can help meet them.

1 Drivers of Growth in the Space Sector

Space technology already plays a central role in our lives in ways that many people take for granted. Satellites are integral to weather forecasting, and GPS signals guide everything from financial trades to autonomous agricultural equipment. Spacecraft monitoring hundreds or even tens of thousands of miles overhead are essential in modern farming, routing cell phone calls, sending television signals, distributing electricity to homes, and handling the billions of financial transactions people make every day, from ATM withdrawals to stock purchases.

This is only the beginning. After more than 60 years of exploration, a confluence of forces is unlocking new possibilities in space. Private sector funding is soaring, rising from $300 million in 2012 to $9 billion in 2021; according to McKinsey and WEF, it now makes up about 30% of investment in space. Elon Musk's SpaceX alone is valued at $125 billion.[3]

This influx of private money has had an impact. The number of active satellites has risen from about 1000 in 2012 to over 5400, and they could number 58,000 by

---

[2] McKinsey & Co., *The role of space in driving sustainability, security, and development on Earth*, 2022, https://www.mckinsey.com/~/media/mckinsey/industries/aerospace%20and%20defense/our%20insights/the%20role%20of%20space%20in%20driving%20sustainability%20security%20and%20development%20on%20earth/the-role-of-space-in-driving-sustainability-security-and-development-on-earth-vf.pdf

[3] Micah Maidenberg and Rob Copeland, "SpaceX shoots to $125 billion valuation, shrugging off Elon Musk's woes," *Wall Street Journal*, May 24, 2022, https://www.wsj.com/articles/spacex-shoots-to-125-billion-valuation-shrugging-off-elon-musks-woes-11653413155

2030 according to one estimate cited by the US Government Accountability Office.[4] SpaceX owns two-fifths of satellites in orbit, according to data from the Union of Concerned Scientists. McKinsey and WEF value satellite-based services at more than $150 billion, and satellite manufacturing at $40 billion worldwide.

Another key factor behind innovation in space is that the bandwidth cost performance of satellites over the past 5–10 years has improved at an astounding rate—in some cases by more than a thousandfold.

Innovations in manufacturing, propulsion, and reusable and modular rockets have also accelerated growth, making it easier and cheaper than ever to reach and operate in space. The cost of launching a low-Earth-orbit satellite has dropped by more than 95% over the past decade, thanks in part to digital engineering and high-scale production.[5] SpaceX and NASA are pushing the limits on launch power, enabling heavier payloads to reach space. In addition, the Los Angeles–based aerospace manufacturer Relativity Space is developing a fully reusable, entirely 3D-printed rocket, called Terran R. These developments are already having a major impact. Valued at $350 billion in 2018, many experts believe the space economy will expand to $1.8 trilion by 2035.[6]

Wealthy individuals spending huge sums on space tourism may capture the public imagination, but space is poised to disrupt nearly every industry in the coming decades, and AI is crucial to that disruption. AI in space is not all that new. It was first tested in 1999, when an algorithm called Remote Agent autonomously controlled the onboard computer of the technology-demonstration probe Deep Space 1 from Earth, more than 60 million miles away. As we detail in the sections below, these days humanity is deploying AI in space in two overarching ways. First, it is being used to directly benefit life as we live it today. The analysis of data generated by Earth observation is the most widespread and best-developed example. Second, AI is enhancing how humanity operates in space, paving the way for commercialization, deep-space exploration, and other applications of tomorrow.

1.1 How AI Improves Life on Earth

Underlying the profound insights delivered by Earth observation are sensitive instruments that collect information about natural and artificial systems, including chemical, physical, and biological data. Scientists have been using spacecraft to

---

[4] Laura Grego, "Record number of satellites in orbit," *The Equation*, January 9, 2019, https://blog.ucsusa.org/lgrego/2018satellitedata/; US GAO, "Technology Assessment: Large Constellations of Satellites," September 2022, https://www.gao.gov/assets/gao-22-105166.pdf

[5] Denise Chow, "To cheaply go: How falling launch costs fueled a thriving economy in orbit," NBC News, April 8, 2022, https://www.nbcnews.com/science/space/space-launch-costs-growing-business-industry-rcna23488

[6] Space: The $1.8 Trillion Opportunity for Global Economic Growth, WEF and McKinsey, 2024, https://www.weforum.org/publications/space-the-1-8-trillion-opportunity-for-global-economic-growth/

observe our home planet since 1960, when NASA launched TIROS-1, a 270-pound meteorological satellite that carried two television cameras and a magnetic tape recorder for storing photographs. It operated for just 72 days but demonstrated the utility of surveying global weather conditions from space. Tiros-1 provided an unprecedented view of cloud patterns, enabling scientists to identify storm regions, and captured the first orbital observations of a major storm, tracking the degeneration of a large cyclone off Bermuda.

Currently, about a fifth of all satellites in orbit scan the Earth from space. A major challenge in Earth observation is that most the data these satellites collect each day sits idle in the cloud. By one estimate, more than 40 businesses have launched earth-watching satellites, and upwards of 100 terabytes of data are added daily.[7] The quantity of data is so overwhelming that no human or group of humans could possibly analyze it. Assuming an average picture size of 5 megabytes, a person viewing a picture each second would need more than 7 months to see 1 day's data, and the real value is in comparing how the images change over time. Using human analysis alone, an abundance of insights and use cases would remain untapped.

AI offers a solution. Researchers are developing AI-powered applications that promise to better analyze Earth-observation data by extracting patterns to help us better see and understand the pictures it may be painting—pictures that may otherwise remain hidden. For instance, AI can be used to monitor parking-lot traffic patterns. Doing this manually would require workers to count cars around the clock, but computer vision—a type of AI—automates the process. This technology has already proved its worth by measuring the effectiveness of COVID-19 restrictions at Los Angeles International Airport.

AI is also making satellite data-transmission more efficient. In capturing huge amounts of data on a planetary scale, Earth observation inevitably produces a lot of white noise. Because it does not make sense to expend energy and resources sending irrelevant data to Earth, AI can preprocess data onboard, separating the signal from the noise and transmitting only the useful portion. This saves time, money, energy, and precious bandwidth, and can speed the response time to events like wildfires and earthquakes. AI can also initiate actions that in the past would have required human intervention, triggering an automatic response—such as controlling and tasking other satellites to collect imagery from different vantage points—after detecting an anomaly.

Its ability to command and control assets and communicate insights is making AI, in a sense, the brains and nervous system of space-based data-collection infrastructure.

[7] Doug Mohney, "Terabytes from space: Satellite imaging is filling data centers," Data Center Frontier, April 28, 2020, https://www.datacenterfrontier.com/internet-of-things/article/11429032/terabytes-from-space-satellite-imaging-is-filling-data-centers

Use Cases

Some of the diverse Earth-observation use cases that stand to be enhanced by AI include the following:

Pollution and Sustainability Governments and private companies can identify the sources that emit the most pollution to better target sustainability investments and get the highest carbon abatement per dollar spent. The technology can also be used to verify carbon offsets—such as reforestation projects—which counterbalance emissions in one place with prevention elsewhere. Two examples: Stockholm-based Earthbanc AB is applying AI to satellite imagery and remote sensing data to bring more transparency to nature-based carbon-abatement solutions. Moreover, because anthropogenic methane is responsible for about 30% of the rise in global temperatures,[8] the United Nations Environment Program (UNEP) is using satellite data to find large methane plumes and attribute them to a source.

Precision Agriculture Satellite imagery can help prevent excessive irrigation, reducing a farm's water use by as much as 50%.[9] Moreover, it can help optimize the global food chain. In a demonstration project from the Budapest-based satellite-development company C3S, an onboard computer processes satellite data on farms not only from visual images but from across the electromagnetic spectrum, providing biochemical and biophysical data on crops that can help farmers increase harvest volume.[10]

Insurance Companies can monitor and analyze areas at risk for flooding, cyclones, drought, or other destructive events. This improves risk and premium management, helping firms close the gap between economic and insured losses. ICEYE, a Helsinki-based company, works with major insurance players to track floods in near real-time, using satellite technology that boasts uninterrupted visibility round the clock, in all weather conditions.

Commercial Archeology In the United Kingdom—where the remains of King Richard III were discovered beneath a parking lot in 2012, 530 years after his death—the UK Space Agency is teaming up with the University of Southampton to detect ancient sites in satellite imagery. Under the initiative, AI is sorting through visual-light and near-infrared images to discern subtle differences in vegetation and other topographical features that may reveal artifacts. The findings are useful not

---

[8] "Methane and climate change," International Energy Agency, n.d., https://www.iea.org/reports/global-methane-tracker-2022/methane-and-climate-change

[9] "Satellite imagery helps farmers cut water use in half," NASA, 2020, https://spinoff.nasa.gov/Spinoff2020/ee_2.html

[10] Rachel Jewett and Mark Holmes, "10 ways AI is making a difference in the satellite industry," Via Satellite, October 5, 2020, https://interactive.satellitetoday.com/via/october-2020/10-ways-ai-is-making-a-difference-in-the-satellite-industry/

only for historians but also for construction projects, which are often affected by the discovery of artifacts or remains. The initiative is intended to save companies time and money during preconstruction planning and permitting, helping them reduce their carbon footprint.

Wildfire Management Munich-based data-intelligence firm OroraTech monitors some 160 million hectares of forest for wildfires, for clients in Quebec, Australia, Chile, and elsewhere. In January 2022, the company launched its first satellite equipped with in-space artificial intelligence to improve real-time response. It plans to eventually mobilize a fleet of 100 such satellites with on-orbit AI processing to help reduce the reporting delay from hours to minutes.

Transportation and Shipping European aerospace giant Airbus's OceanFinder and One Atlas services leverage AI and a constellation of satellites to provide automatic change detection of vehicles, boats, planes, and other objects. On the high seas, OceanFinder can monitor ship fleets, locate hijacked vessels, detect illegal activity, promote safety in hostile areas, and support rescue operations. To train its machine learning platforms, Airbus used billions of square miles of imagery dating back to 1986. The maritime shipping industry is also working with space agencies to improve vessel navigation. Using sensors, satellite data, and AI, the European Space Agency's Maritime AI-NAV project is seeking to demonstrate that a ship can reliably sense its own environment, including vessels and other potential hazards. Initially, this would help crews improve safety and efficiency. Crewless ships are a longer-term goal.

National Security National defense organizations can analyze satellite images with AI to detect and track potential threats, such as missile sites or troop movements. They can train AI algorithms to identify patterns in the images and highlight suspicious activity for further human analysis. This allows the military to assess potential threats and respond to them quickly. Additionally, they can use satellite images to gather intelligence about a country's infrastructure, such as its air defense systems and communications networks, which can help them in military planning and decision-making.

Resource Supply Tracking Earth observation is being used to track resources with unprecedented speed and accuracy. The British analytics firm OilX, for example, is using AI and satellite imagery to follow the global oil supply more accurately. Using tactics such as satellite monitoring of oilfield flaring, or the burning of by-products, the company, in cooperation with the European Space Agency (ESA), is constructing a digital twin of the oil-sector supply chain, with the goal of keeping track of every barrel.

Analyzing Traffic AI and Earth observation are playing a potentially enormous role in improving traffic flow and making roads safer. University and nonprofit researchers are using data generated by satellites to identify priority accident hotspots in an effort to reduce the 1.35 million road-related deaths each year. The approach can also be used to identify and ameliorate traffic bottlenecks.

Weather Patterns Weather forecasting has been a cornerstone of Earth observation since its inception, but companies are taking it to a new level. Using one of the largest constellations of low-Earth nanosatellites, Spire, a global analytics company, collects data across the world, from open oceans to the most remote terrestrial regions. The company uses an innovative technique called radio occultation that offers a thorough picture of pressure, temperature, and humidity in the lower atmosphere and electron density in the ionosphere. Machine learning algorithms parse these rich datasets to increase forecasting accuracy.

In some cases, Earth-observation satellites do things that no other technology can handle. The Global Climate Observing System, for example, outlines 54 climate variables used to characterize observations and provide a clear message on historical and future climate change. About 50% of the variables are visible only from space, and space may ensure better data accuracy for about 75% of them.

Emerging Use Cases

Though many use cases currently serve a niche purpose, there is vast potential for the technology to be integrated into powerful models. The US geospatial-analytics company Orbital Insight plans to harness AI in space to better inform decision-making. The company uses AI to transform data—including satellite images, mobile location, connected cars, and other internet of things data—into answers about supply chains, commodities, demographics, and geopolitical events. For example, it is partnering with Unilever to track the consumer-goods company's palm oil supply chain back to the source to mitigate deforestation.

Another emerging use case is creating an AI-driven digital twin of Earth,[11] fed by a constant stream of EO data. The ESA is working on the digital twin, DestinE, which would accurately mimic Earth's behavior, enabling scientists to forecast natural and human activity. Using high-performance computing, machine learning, and satellite data, it would provide "an accurate representation of the past, present and future changes of our world."[12]

DestinE would help humanity understand and manage the many challenges associated with a growing population and with human activities, including floods, heatwaves, food and water shortages, ecosystem stressors, rising sea levels, increasing

[11] "This AI technique could use a digital version of Earth to help fight climate change," The World Economic Forum, June 10, 2021, https://www.weforum.org/agenda/2021/06/could-the-combo-of-a-digital-twin-and-reinforcement-learning-tackle-climate-change/

[12] "Digital twin Earth, quantum computing and AI take centre stage at ESA's Φ week," The European Space Agency, September 28, 2020, https://www.esa.int/Applications/Observing_the_Earth/Digital_Twin_Earth_quantum_computing_and_AI_take_centre_stage_at_ESA_s_Ph-week

ocean acidification, and more. The agency hopes to develop DestinE's core digital platform, along with the first two digital twins, by 2024. The first, on weather-induced and geophysical extremes, would enable decision-makers to better anticipate extreme natural events, such as flooding and forest fires. The second, on climate-change adaptation, would allow scientists to predict scenarios to support national and regional climate-change mitigation and adaptation over years. Additional digital twins could represent oceans, biodiversity, and urban environments; the agency expects to bring the models together in a full digital replica of Earth's systems by 2030.

2 How AI Is Improving Space Operations

AI is increasingly solving critical problems of operating in space and expanding the potential of tomorrow's space economy. The social, economic, and organizational impacts of these innovations do not directly affect life on Earth, but we expect them to affect the future in material and far-reaching ways.

Some applications of AI in space operations resemble those used on Earth. Companies are applying machine learning and novelty detection to power the predictive maintenance of spacecraft, which is critically important due to the costs and hazards of operating in space. They are using predictive analytics for cybersecurity and to diagnose mechanical problems by seeing patterns that engineers may miss. Airbus, for example, uses AI to monitor the health of satellites in orbit and to improve the design of future satellites. The company pools data to create algorithms relating to all stages of a spacecraft's lifecycle.

2.1 Ground Operations

Artificial intelligence (AI) and machine learning (ML) are used to manage ground stations to make operations more efficient, reduce downtime, and improve mission success rates.

AI algorithms can be used to optimize the allocation of ground station resources, such as antenna time and communication bandwidth. They can improve predictive maintenance by forecasting when ground station components are likely to fail. AI can manage the flow of spacecraft data, routing it to the most appropriate ground station based on factors such as signal quality, available bandwidth, and priority level. In addition, they can schedule ground station operations, such as spacecraft contacts, based on mission requirements and available resources. Finally, AI can optimize ground station network performance by reducing latency, maximizing bandwidth utilization, and improving data security.

2.2 Space Mapping

AI-based image recognition and video analytics are also helping support navigation in space. In 2018, researchers from NASA and Intel collaborated to develop an integrated lunar navigation system. The system crunched 200 terabytes of data at greater than 98% accuracy. Each minute it completed work that would have taken humans 3–4 h. The project drew from 3D lunar imagery gathered by survey satellites to create a virtual map of the moon that is helping to identify better landing locations and support NASA's goal of deploying self-driving rovers.

2.3 Onboard Decision-Making

Spacecraft are increasingly equipped with AI that enables them to analyze their surroundings and operate autonomously based on the data they gather. This approach, known as onboard decision-making, is one of the most powerful and far-reaching applications of AI in space. Onboard decision-making harnesses a variety of AI capabilities. Insight-generation allows the system to detect correlations in large, complex data sets. Language processing and text analytics let it derive meaning from human language input. Image recognition and video analytics allow it to recognize and derive information from objects. In addition, automated decision-making lets it learn from experience and assist humans or act autonomously, depending on conditions.

Onboard decision-making could enable numerous use cases that would be impossible given the distances, harsh operating environment, and rapid velocities in space. It could allow satellites to calculate how to best use scarce propellant reserves to adjust their orbits, thus extending their lives. It could also help satellites—traveling at 28,000 km per hour (17,500 mph) in low-Earth orbit—to detect and evade hazards and avoid collisions that would otherwise lead to the creation of debris. Onboard decision-making is essential to addressing the growing problem of space debris. By one estimate, there are more than 500,000 objects larger than a centimeter orbiting Earth.[13] A centimeter may not sound like much, but a 1-centimeter object traveling at 7.5 km per second can pack the energy of a hand grenade. Onboard AI is the ideal pilot for the highly complex task of real-time maneuvering for debris removal.

[13] "ORDEM 3.2," NASA, n.d., https://orbitaldebris.jsc.nasa.gov/

2.4 Mars Exploration

Onboard decision-making has already dramatically improved the efficiency and effectiveness of Mars exploration. Previously, engineers needed to remotely direct[14] rovers to scientifically interesting targets identified via images downloaded to Earth, but a radio signal takes up to 20 min to travel between Mars and Earth, rendering such Earth-based control tedious and inefficient. Since 2016, NASA's Mars rovers have used an onboard AI system called AEGIS (Autonomous Exploration for Gathering Increased Science) to explore the Red Planet. Most recently, the AEGIS-equipped Perseverance rover autonomously targeted geologic features in the Jezero Crater, which scientists believe was a river delta billions of years ago. Without direction from ground command, AEGIS has been able to find Martian rocks, photograph them, and zap them with a laser to help determine their composition. It has selected the most desirable geologic targets more than 90% of the time, compared to only 24% when the targets are chosen from Earth.[15]

3 AI and the Commercialization of Space

AI technologies—such as assistants, robots, navigation systems, automation, and data analysis—are helping to unlock the future of our activities in space. In addition to in-space manufacturing and R&D mining, construction, and infrastructure development may one day be possible. Scientists are also working on using AI to advance in-orbit maintenance and supply for spacecraft and crews, space-based solar power, tourism, and human and robotic deep-space exploration.

3.1 Manufacturing in Space

The potential for manufacturing in space is promising to improve life on Earth in novel ways in the coming years. Space offers a unique manufacturing environment because its microgravity, near-vacuum state, and higher levels of radiation may allow for new processes[16] or reveal new insights. On Earth, extreme temperatures

---

[14] "Mars exploration pushes the boundaries of AI: An interview with NASA's Vandi Verma," McKinsey & Co., January 9, 2023, https://www.mckinsey.com/capabilities/quantumblack/our-insights/mars-exploration-pushes-the-boundaries-of-ai-an-interview-with-nasas-vandi-verma?cid=app

[15] R. Francis et al., "AEGIS autonomous targeting for ChemCam on Mars Science Laboratory: Deployment and results of initial science team use," *Science Robotics*, June 28, 2017, https://www.science.org/doi/abs/10.1126/scirobotics.aan4582

[16] Carsten Hirschberg, Ireen Kulish, Ilan Rozenkopf, and Tobias Sodoge, "The potential of microgravity: How companies across sectors can venture into space," McKinsey & Co., June 13, 2022, https://www.mckinsey.com/industries/aerospace-and-defense/our-insights/the-potential-of-microgravity-how-companies-across-sectors-can-venture-into-space

for manufacturing processes requiring freezers or furnaces are difficult to maintain, the dense atmosphere contaminates processes, and gravity complicates crystal formation and alloy mixing. In 2020, there were 155 patents with "microgravity" in their abstract or title, up from just 21 in 2000.

Given the expense, hazards, and difficulty of keeping people in space, robots equipped with AI and capable of making advanced decisions are critical to managing and scaling these activities, making them economically feasible. Already, scientists are working on autonomous in-space "manipulators"—robotic arms similar to the one mounted on the International Space Station—that could remove debris and service spacecraft in orbit. AI-powered manipulators may also be useful in handling day-to-day R&D and manufacturing activities and moving materials and products between machinery and delivery vehicles.

Below are several of the many emerging use cases for manufacturing in space.

Semiconductors Space's vacuum could facilitate the development of smaller semiconductors, which could carry huge benefits. The idea is not new. In the 1990s, a University of Houston materials scientist manufactured a distortion-free semiconductor in low-Earth orbit that could produce 60%–efficient solar panels (today's solar panels have 15–22% conversion efficiency).[17] In 2022, NASA awarded a grant to a California semiconductor company seeking to produce composite bulk crystals in orbit, to be used in the energy, high-performance computing, and national security sectors.[18] Chief among the challenges for manufacturing semiconductors at scale in space is that it would be difficult to transport the heavy equipment necessary. We estimate that it will take a decade or more before large-scale, cost-efficient semiconductor manufacturing occurs in space.

Fiber Optics Space is optimal for manufacturing a new type of fiber cable made of a special glass called ZBLAN, an acronym from the names of its components—zirconium, barium, lanthanum, aluminum, and sodium fluoride. Proponents say ZBLAN fibers could transmit data up to 100 times more efficiently than the silica-based optical fibers currently in use.[19] The humidity and gravity on Earth prevent the manufacture of large volumes of the material by creating small surface defects that rarely appear in ZBLAN made in zero gravity. At least, three companies have manufactured it in small batches aboard the International Space Station, but scaling up will require space facilities large enough for commercial production.

[17] Andrew Rosenblum, "The factories of the future could float in space," *Popular Science*, April 3, 2017, https://www.popsci.com/factories-in-space/; Barbara Zito, "How Efficient Are Solar Panels in the UK?," Greenmatch, September 23, 2024, https://www.greenmatch.co.uk/blog/2014/11/how-efficient-are-solar-panels

[18] "NASA selects proposals to enable manufacturing in space for Earth," NASA, April 15, 2022, https://www.nasa.gov/mission_pages/station/research/news/nasa-selects-phase-1-proposals-for-inspa

[19] Debra Werner, "Sparking the space economy," Aerospace America, January 2020, https://aerospaceamerica.aiaa.org/features/sparking-the-space-economy/

Pharmaceuticals and Biotechnology The pharmaceutical and biotech industries stand to reap real commercial benefits from space R&D and manufacturing. In a recent NASA grant round worth up to $21 million, six of eight recipients were in biopharma, in fields from stem-cell production to multifunctional nanomaterials fabrication. Organoids—simplified versions of human organs used to evaluate diseases—have already been grown in space, and experiments in bioprinting have shown that microgravity can eliminate the need for scaffolding to support tissue-engineered organs as they grow. Space also holds promise for skincare R&D; the harsh environment and high radiation levels accelerate aging, potentially aiding in the discovery of new compounds. Other potential pharmaceutical industry use cases include manufacturing retinas and researching new oncology drugs. McKinsey estimates that in the short to medium term, the pharmaceutical industry could obtain $2.8 billion to $4.2 billion[20] in revenues from manufacturing and R&D in space.

3.2 Space Mining

Space mining is a commercial activity under development that will depend on AI technologies such as image processing and autonomous operation. Asteroids that orbit within reach of Earth are believed to contain an otherworldly fortune in precious metals and minerals.

NASA is preparing to send a space probe to one asteroid, called 16 Psyche. The potato-shaped celestial body, which measures 140 miles in diameter, is scientifically significant because it appears to resemble a planetary core similar to Earth's. Entrepreneurs are watching the mission because 16 Psyche may contain metals worth more than $10 quintillion, though a recent study suggests it may not be as dense or metallic as originally thought.[21] The probe, which is slated to lift off in October 2023, should settle the matter. It is expected take about 4 years to reach the asteroid, after which it will spend 21 months mapping and studying it while orbiting above its surface.

Elsewhere, entrepreneurs have begun developing the means to mine asteroids closer to Earth. The UK-based Asteroid Mining Corporation is preparing to launch a microsatellite space telescope in 2025 to scan thousands of near-Earth and main-belt asteroids for precious metals and water. For a follow-up mission, the company is developing a robot that can explore the surface of asteroids to sample their cores for mining-site selection, conduct spacewalks, and handle maintenance.

---

[20] Carsten Hirschberg, Ireen Kulish, Ilan Rozenkopf, and Tobias Sodoge, "The The potential of microgravity: How companies across sectors can venture into space," McKinsey & Co., June 13, 2022, https://www.mckinsey.com/industries/aerospace-and-defense/our-insights/the-potential-of-microgravity-how-companies-across-sectors-can-venture-into-space

[21] Elizabeth Gamillo, "This metal-rich, potato-shaped asteroid could be worth $10 quintillion," *Smithsonian*, January 4, 2022, https://www.smithsonianmag.com/smart-news/asteroid-16-psyche-may-be-worth-more-than-planet-earth-at-10-quintillion-in-fine-metals-180979303/

3.3 A Commercial Presence in Space

Long-term infrastructure will be needed to initiate and scale mining, manufacturing, and other commercial activities in space. This may seem like science fiction, but hundreds of companies have raised more than a quarter-trillion dollars since 2012 to make it happen, and significant efforts are underway to establish an extraterrestrial presence.[22] Space agencies are allocating large sums to support commercial space activities. NASA, has already signed contracts with 14 vendors for commercial lunar services worth up to a combined total of $2.6 billion, and China is mulling infrastructure for a $10 trillion Earth-Moon economic zone.[23]

A constellation of start-ups is designing and building space infrastructure. One such firm, Sierra Space, intends to send its Dream Chaser "spaceplane" to the International Space Station in 2023. The Dream Chaser is a reusable spacecraft accommodating more than 12,000 pounds of supplies and equipment, and eventually the company hopes to fill it with passengers.[24] The company is also developing affordable in-space infrastructure systems, in collaboration with Blue Origin, Amazon founder Jeff Bezos's aerospace manufacturing group. Their expandable space module system, known as Orbital Reef, is planned to begin operations in 2027. Orbital Reef, a commercial successor to the International Space Station, would create a foothold for enterprises to conduct research in space.

Another enterprise, Tokyo-based Ispace, aims to provide affordable access to the moon. The company, which had raised 21.8 billion Japanese yen (about $170 million) by late 2022,[25] is working on the first commercial lunar exploration program. Its Hakuto-R lunar lander launched in December 2022, with the goal of reaching the moon in late April 2023. The launch is the first major step in the company's quest to develop a high-frequency, cost-effective lunar transport system. Ispace aims to establish a lunar payload delivery system, map water resources on the moon, acquire data, and build an industrial platform enabling stable lunar development.

---

[22] Michael Sheetz, "Investment in space companies hit record $14.5 billion in 2021, report says," CNBC, January 18, 2022, https://www.cnbc.com/2022/01/18/space-investing-q4-report-companies-hit-record-14point5-billion-in-2021.html

[23] Andrew Jones, "From a farside first to cislunar dominance? China appears to want to establish 'space economic zone' worth trillions," SpaceNews, February 15, 2020, https://spacenews.com/from-a-farside-first-to-cislunar-dominance-china-appears-to-want-to-establish-space-economic-zone-worth-trillions/

[24] "Dream Chaser: Revolutionizing Space Travel," Sierra Space, n.d., https://www.sierraspace.com/space-transportation/dream-chaser-spaceplane/

[25] "Airbus Ventures invests in ispace's Series C extension round," ispace, October 25, 2021, https://ispace-inc.com/news-en/?p=2523

3.4 Deep Space Exploration

In the quest to find life on other planets, NASA is working with AI pioneers,[26] including IBM, Google, and Intel, to parse big data sets, especially in the exoplanet field, from devices such as the James Webb telescope. They hope to use advanced machine learning to understand the chemistry of exoplanets based on wavelengths of light in their atmospheres. Determining which of the thousands of known exoplanets may have a chemical composition that could support life can help identify a short list of candidates that deserve further investigation.

Ultimately, AI could enable long-duration human space exploration, and could help scientists search for life elsewhere in the universe. A 2022 ESA-led investigation determined that to travel to Mars, humans could be suspended in a state of hibernation, in which their metabolism would be slowed to save energy, decreasing their need for supplies—food, water, light, heat, and oxygen—which account for about 30 kg (66 pounds) a day. Hibernation could also diminish muscle atrophy associated with being idle while awake. It could reduce the spacecraft's size requirements and minimize the boredom, loneliness, and aggression linked with being cooped up in an aircraft. While the astronauts doze, bearlike, in soft, finely tuned pods, AI-powered computers would maintain the spacecraft's performance and handle anomalies until arrival.

4 Maximizing the Potential of Space

As AI and other technologies progress, the benefits for the space sector, and ultimately for life on Earth, are bound to multiply—assuming that stakeholders take the steps necessary to maximize space's beneficial potential. What would those steps be? In 2022, McKinsey and the World Economic Forum posed that question[27] to space-industry stakeholders. They identified five key actions that would promote a sustainable future in space:

1. Implementing effective governance is critical to ensuring the peaceful, productive, and responsible use of space. This action is a priority, given that the sector

[26] "NASA Takes a Cue From Silicon Valley to Hatch Artificial Intelligence Technologies", William Steigerwald, "NASA takes a cue from Silicon Valley to hatch artificial intelligence technologies," NASA, November 19, 2019, https://www.nasa.gov/missions/nasa-takes-a-cue-from-silicon-valley-to-hatch-artificial-intelligence-technologies/

[27] "*The role of space in driving sustainability, security, and development on Earth*, McKinsey & Co., 2022, https://www.mckinsey.com/~/media/mckinsey/industries/aerospace%20and%20defense/our%20insights/the%20role%20of%20space%20in%20driving%20sustainability%20security%20and%20development%20on%20earth/the-role-of-space-in-driving-sustainability-security-and-development-on-earth-vf.pdf

has reached an inflection point where commercialization is beginning to outpace governance.

2. Leaders need to look beyond short-term returns and invest in enabling technologies and capabilities. AI that would underpin autonomous robots and onboard decision-making is particularly important.
3. Incentivize collaboration across nations, sectors, and industries to promote inclusiveness, participation, and the peaceful use of space and accelerate technological development. The International Space Station, which has hosted individuals from 20 countries, has demonstrated the benefits of global collaboration. Maintaining that spirit will be critical.
4. The sector would benefit from support in fostering a self-sustaining industrial base. In the early stages, commercial cash flows will remain negative. Governments could act as advocates and anchor customers by purchasing services, removing barriers to competition, and educating decision-makers about space's potential.
5. The international community should embrace the sustainability and security potential of space. This means, for instance, promoting the use of Earth observation to reduce greenhouse gas emissions while also being mindful of key space-based issues relating to debris and collisions.

Leaders need to urgently heed these actions to ensure that the space achieves its enormous potential rather than becoming a new theater of rivalry or conflict.

References

Brukardt, R., Klempner, J., Pacthod, D., & Stokes, B. (2022). *The role of space in driving sustainability, security, and development on Earth*. McKinsey & Co. https://www.mckinsey.com/industries/aerospace-and-defense/our-insights/the-role-of-space-in-driving-sustainability-security-and-development-on-earth.

Hirschberg, C., Kulish, I., Rozenkopf, I., & Sodoge, T. (2022). *The potential of microgravity: How companies across sectors can venture into space*. McKinsey & Co. https://www.mckinsey.com/industries/aerospace-and-defense/our-insights/the-potential-of-microgravity-how-companies-across-sectors-can-venture-into-space.

Maidenberg, M., & Copeland, R. (2022, May 24). *SpaceX Shoots to $125 Billion Valuation, Shrugging Off Elon Musk's Woes*. https://www.wsj.com/articles/spacex-shoots-to-125-billion-valuation-shrugging-off-elon-musks-woes-11653413155.

NASA. (1966). *Satellite Meteorology, 1958–1964*. National Aeronautics and Space Administration. https://play.google.com/books/reader?id=wS1DAAAAIAAJ&pg=GBS.PA34&hl=en.

Twin Revolutions: The Relationship Between Green Revolution and Digital Transformation: The Case of Alia Servizi Ambientali

Alberto Irace, Sara Volino Coppola, Simonetta Iarlori, and G. Roberto Marseglia

Abstract The green revolution and digital transformation are interlinked forces driving societal and environmental change. This chapter explores their convergence through the case of Alia Servizi Ambientali, a Tuscan environmental services company. Alia leverages digital technologies to enhance its sustainability initiatives, such as implementing smart waste management systems and a digital tariff scheme. The integration of IoT, data analytics, and advanced IT infrastructure enables Alia to optimize waste collection, reduce costs, and minimize environmental impact. This case demonstrates how digital transformation can amplify green initiatives, offering a model for other organizations seeking to navigate these twin revolutions.

1 Introduction

As we enter the twenty-first century, we are met with two monumental revolutions that are transforming our society and economy: the green revolution and the digital revolution—often referred to as the blue revolution. Both revolutions, while following their own distinct paths, converge on a mutual goal: enhancing societal welfare through innovative changes (Kummitha, 2019; Secinaro et al., 2021).

The green revolution began in the second half of the twentieth century and represents a global commitment to environmental protection and sustainable

A. Irace · S. Volino Coppola (✉) · S. Iarlori
Alia Servizi Ambientali, Florence, Italy
e-mail: a.irace@aliaserviziambientali.it; s.volino@aliaserviziambientali.it; s.iarlori@aliaserviziambientali.it

G. R. Marseglia
Alia Servizi Ambientali, Florence, Italy

Università degli Studi di Pavia, Pavia, Italy
e-mail: roberto.marseglia@unipv.it

G. R. Marseglia et al. (eds.), *Socio-economic Impact of Artificial Intelligence*, Progress in IS, https://doi.org/10.1007/978-3-031-73514-1_14

development (Borlaug, 2000). It is propelled by an expanding understanding of climate change and environmental impacts. This revolution spans numerous sectors, driven by pioneering advancements in renewable energy, sustainable agriculture, effective waste management, and other areas crucial for reshaping our environmental interactions (Baker, 2019; Marseglia et al., 2015; Raworth, 2017; Secinaro et al., 2022).

Parallel to this, the digital revolution marks an era defined by the rapid adoption of digital technologies across all facets of life (Schwab, 2016). It is revolutionizing industries, reshaping social interactions, and altering our approach to information processing and acquisition (Bughin et al., 2017; Kagermann et al., 2013). Fueled by advancements in data analytics, artificial intelligence, cloud computing, and other digital innovations, this revolution is not only transforming our daily lives but is also pushing the frontiers of technological possibilities (Agrawal et al., 2019; Brynjolfsson & McAfee, 2014).

Although the green and digital revolutions have different trajectories, they are interconnected (Feroz et al., 2021). Their overlap offers unique opportunities for accelerated sustainable development. By integrating digital technologies, we enhance environmental sustainability efforts, and conversely, our pursuit of sustainability can drive further innovations in digital technology (Bibri & Krogstie, 2017; Geissbauer et al., 2017).

A prime example of this synergy is seen in Alia Servizi Ambientali S.p.a., an environmental services company based in Tuscany. Alia has effectively utilized digital transformation to bolster its environmental initiatives (Lanzalonga et al., 2024). The company's journey is not only a testament to innovation and change but also serves as a practical model for other organizations navigating the complexities of these intersecting revolutions (Kummitha, 2019; Secinaro et al., 2021).

This chapter will explore the intricacies and implications of these twin revolutions, focusing particularly on their manifestation in Alia's operations. We will discuss the unique challenges and opportunities that emerge from the intersection of digital transformation and environmental sustainability. By examining Alia's strategic approaches and their outcomes, we aim to offer insights that can guide other organizations embarking on similar transformative journeys (Secinaro et al., 2021).

2 Methodology

Action research (AR) is a dynamic methodology that emerged as a response to the limitations of laboratory-based research and the artificiality of studying isolated behavioral elements. It was originally proposed by Lewin (1946) to address the need for understanding complex social events in their natural context. AR emphasizes the importance of intervention and change to comprehend human systems fully. This section explores the concept of action research, its key characteristics, and its relevance in bridging theory and practice. The section also delves into the iterative cycles of AR, the role of the researcher, the methodology of intervention, and the learning mechanisms inherent in the process.

2.1 The Concept of Action Research

To bring the case of environmental impacts of digital applications in Alia, we used the action research method. Action research is a type of applied social research that stands out because it emphasizes the researcher's active participation in the action process, aiming to address practical issues while also advancing the goals of social science (Argyris, 1976; Argyris et al., 1985; Argyris & Schön, 1997; Foster, 1972; Huber, 1991) present the concept of action science. It aims to address immediate problematic situations through joint collaboration within an ethical framework. By actively intervening and effecting change, action research seeks to gain a deeper understanding of complex social systems rather than observing from a distance.

2.2 Iterative Cycles of Action Research

AR follows iterative cycles of identifying a problem, planning, acting, and evaluating (Argyris et al., 1985). This process reflects a methodology of intervention that requires explicit statements of assumptions, intentions, and normative theories. These iterative cycles allow for the continuous adjustment of the intervention strategy as evidence emerges and feedback is received from the agents in the situation. AR distinguishes itself from evaluation research by emphasizing adaptiveness and dynamic intervention strategies rather than assessing the effectiveness of past interventions (Fig. 1).

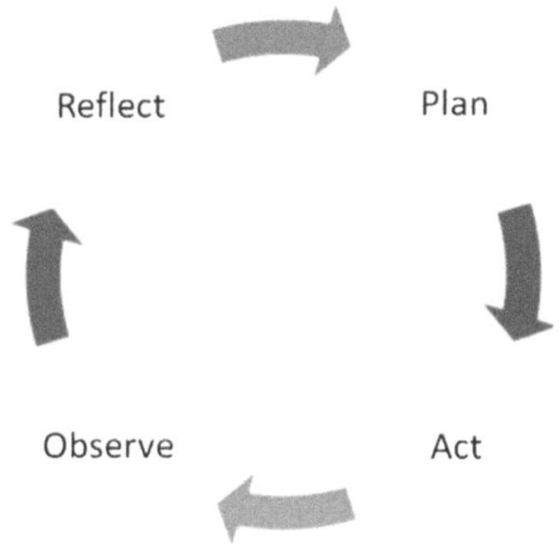

Fig. 1 The cyclical nature of action research. (Figure from Farrelly & Tucker, 2014)

2.3 The Role of the Researcher

In action research, the conventional role of the researcher is significantly transformed, often aligning closely with that of a company executive. As an active participant in the group driving change, the researcher takes on a role similar to that of a consultant (Schein, 1987). Their primary focus shifts toward assisting the client in achieving their objectives, giving the client the authority to determine the scope and duration of the research based on its perceived value. This direct engagement necessitates that the researcher delicately balances the effectiveness of the intervention with the integrity of the research design, while also acknowledging the associated risks. In such scenarios, the roles of the researcher and the company's top management frequently overlap, as both work toward leading the transformation.

2.4 Methodology of Intervention

A crucial aspect of AR is the deliberate strategy or methodology (M) employed in the intervention process (Checkland, 1985). The methodology draws on a theoretical framework (T) that incorporates relevant theories to guide the intervention and address the problem situation (S). The theoretical framework may include normative theories, theories about the intervention itself, and theories that inform how to handle constraints during implementation (Fig. 2).

The intervention strategy serves as a design proposition, providing specific guidelines for improving the situation based on the ideas in the theoretical framework.

2.5 Learning Mechanisms and Insights

Action research (AR) yields insights and knowledge pertinent to the context, the theoretical framework, and the intervention approach (Checkland & Holwell, 2007). The iterative process of AR facilitates the detection of discrepancies between

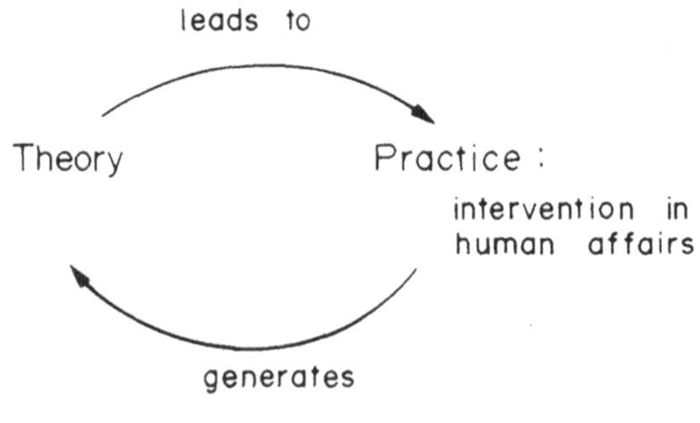

Fig. 2 Original figure of Checkland (1985) showing the *groundlessness* of operational theory: theory leads to practice; but practice is itself the source of the theory; neither is prime

intended and actual outcomes, enabling ongoing refinement and enhancement of both the understanding of the problem situation and the foundational theories. Interventions that yield unexpected or contrary results provide crucial learning opportunities and can catalyze the development of new theories and causal mechanisms. From an epistemological standpoint, action research (AR) encounters notable criticism, primarily due to the fact that the experiments it involves are often not replicable, as highlighted by scholars as in Baskerville and Wood-Harper (1996) and Oquist (1978). This criticism centers around the concern that without the ability to replicate experiments, it becomes challenging to verify results and ensure their reliability across different contexts or conditions. Despite these methodological critiques, the scientific community still recognizes the practical utility of this approach (Checkland & Holwell, 2007). This acknowledgment underscores the value of AR in generating meaningful, context-specific insights that can effectively address complex problems, even if the experimental procedures themselves may lack the replicability typically expected in conventional research settings.

2.6 Action Research in Organizational Contexts

Action research (AR) has been effectively utilized in organizational contexts to address various challenges such as organizational change (Sastry, 1997), innovation processes (Poole et al., 2000), and supply chain planning (Nair et al., 2011). Researchers have applied AR principles to enhance understanding and improve operational processes within organizations (Keating et al., 1999; Oliva & Watson, 2009, 2011). These applications demonstrate AR's capability to connect theoretical approaches with practical implementation, actively involving organizational stakeholders in the research process.

2.7 Conclusion

Action research is a powerful methodology that bridges the gap between theory and practice by actively engaging researchers in intervention-based research. Its iterative cycles, emphasis on collaboration, and adaptive intervention strategies enable researchers to address complex social systems and effect meaningful change. By combining explicit theoretical frameworks with practical problem-solving, action research contributes not only to the immediate concerns of the participants but also to the broader goals of social science. In the next section, we will introduce Alia Servizi Ambientali's experience and discuss how action research is playing a key role in managing change and digital transformation.

3 The Case of Alia Servizi Ambientali S.p.a.

3.1 Introduction

Alia Servizi Ambientali S.p.a. is Tuscany's premier local public services multiutility active in Italy, specializing in environmental, integrated water cycle, and energy sectors. Initially focused solely on waste management, the company transformed into a multiutility on January 26, 2023, through a merger with Publiservizi S.p.A., Acqua Toscana S.p.A., and Consiag S.p.A. This change aims to consolidate a strategic industrial sector, optimize local public service management, and ensure increasing benefits for users, shareholders, and served territories. Currently, Alia Servizi Ambientali S.p.a. serves 58 municipalities and is in a phase of territorial expansion.

From a market-positioning perspective, Alia aims to be the multiutility in Italy that invests the most in research and innovation, with many innovative activities undertaken by the company in the last 2 years (Fig. 3).

Among these initiatives, Alia introduced a "*tariffa a corrispettivo*," a tariff based on precise waste management behaviors, replacing the previous Waste Tax (TARI). This system—that can be seen as an evolution of *pay-as-you-throw* tariffs (Elia et al., 2015; Reichenbach, 2008; Skumatz, 2008)—rewards users who actively participate in separate waste collection, encouraging greater citizen involvement in the waste value cycle and promoting a more equitable distribution of benefits from waste differentiation.

Additionally, Alia has implemented a series of digital technologies to enhance operational efficiency. This includes the development of a patented smart waste bin—Genius 5.0—that uses various sensors to monitor the real-time status of filling and maintenance of bins and a mobile app, "*Aprilo*!", which allows Florence residents to access these digital waste containers via smartphones. The extensive application of these technologies not only optimizes waste collection routes but also significantly contributes to environmental sustainability by reducing waste and promoting recycling (Fig. 4).

Moreover, Alia is actively involved in initiatives to promote urban decorum and combat littering, improving the quality of waste separation. An example is the "*Che Prato*!" project, which aims to introduce new bins in the historic center. Digital-driven transformation processes are not new in research (Blumensaat et al., 2019; Di Mauro et al., 2019; Giustiniano & Prencipe, 2018; Pardini et al., 2019), and some Alia managers have previously been protagonists of radical changes in companies in the same sector (Giustiniano & Prencipe, 2017). However, Alia is currently undergoing a moment of internal organizational transformation, resulting from merger and acquisition actions, a profound digital transformation that significantly impacts processes and services, and a transformation in the tariff system that proposes a radical change in the relationship with citizens (Figs. 5 and 6).

The general transformation process, particularly the digital one, thus requires a people-oriented strategy, providing essential tools to excel in the waste production,

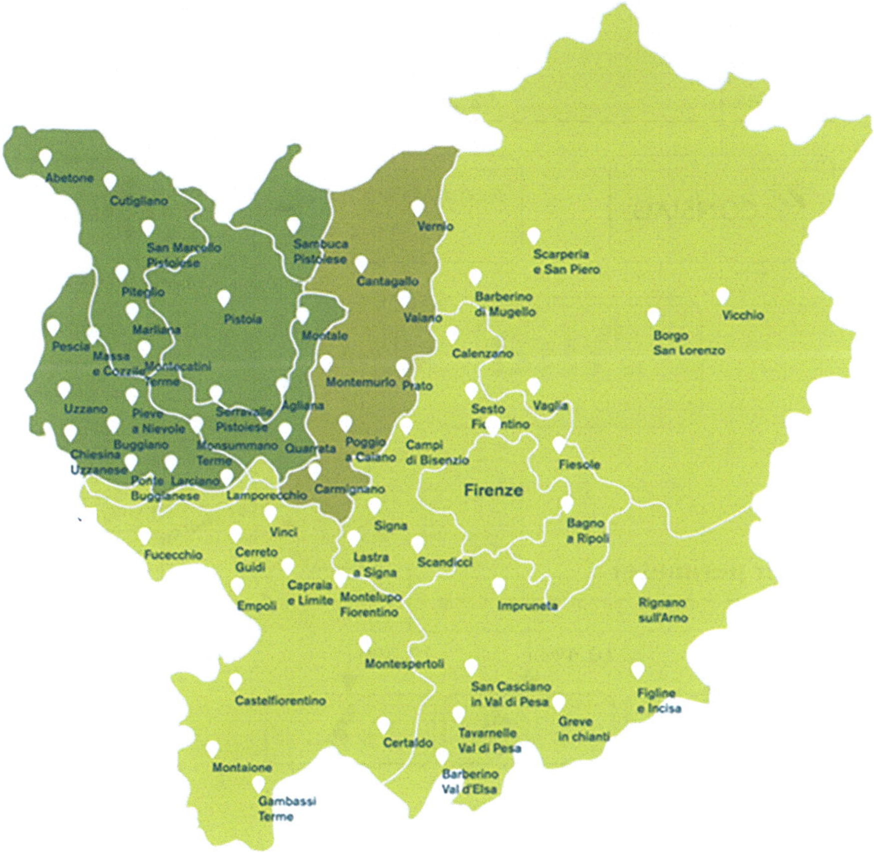

Fig. 3 Alia Servizi Ambientali operates on 58 municipalities, 4.844 kmq and serves 1.5 mln customers

collection, and enhancement chain. This path emphasizes the need for an agile and modular organization, capable of quickly adapting to emerging needs and integrating advanced technologies for a more sustainable urban environment (similarly highlighted in the Harvard Business Review by Tabrizi, "*Digital transformation is more than just the adoption of technology*").

3.2 *Alia's Digital and Data Stack*

To enable a radical change in operations and service delivery, it is necessary to equip oneself with enabling digital and infrastructural tools. In this regard, in addition to the already mentioned innovation activities, it was necessary to redesign the

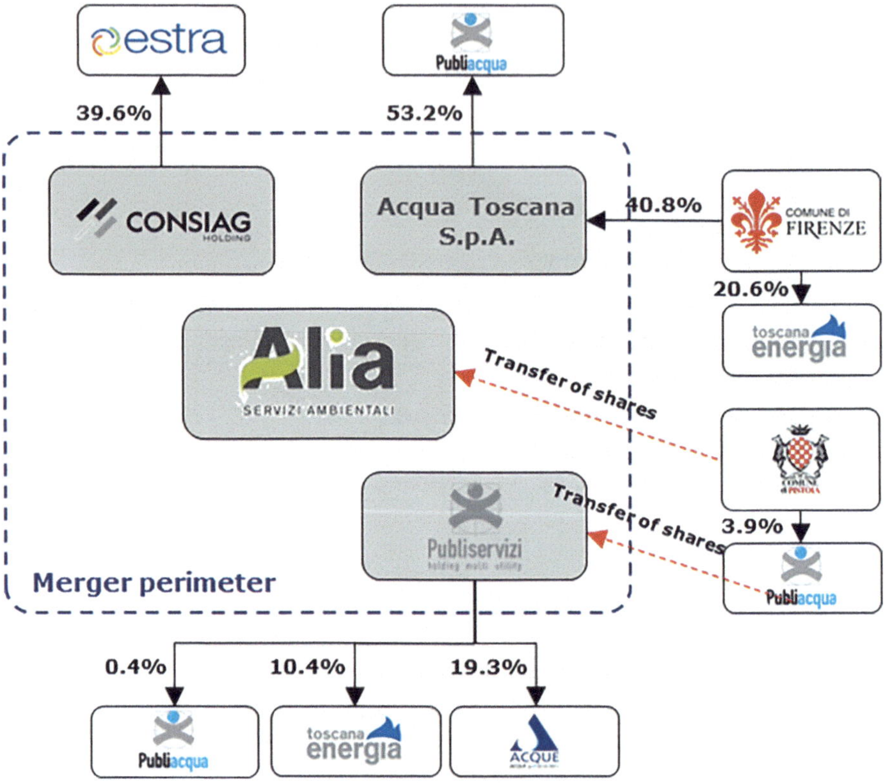

Fig. 4 Merger perimeter for the construction of the multiutility

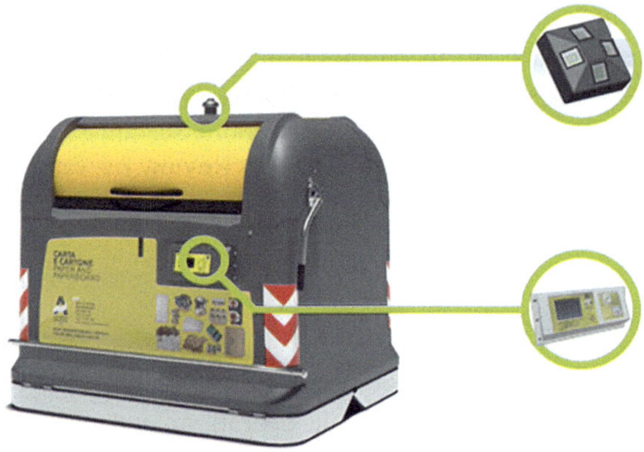

Fig. 5 Genius 5.0. Alia Servizi Ambientali's patented smart bin

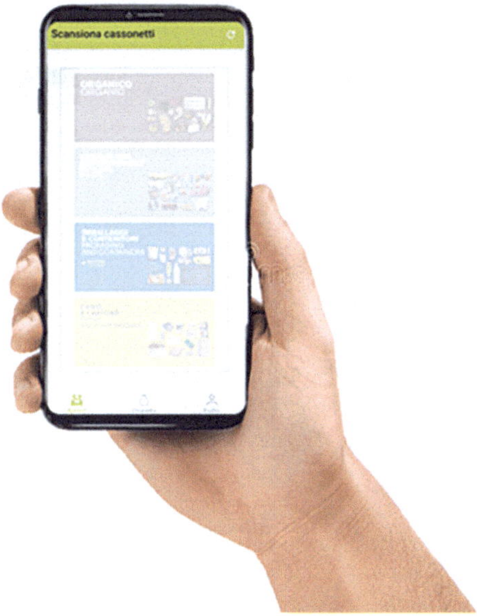

Fig. 6 Aprilo! App. Alia Servizi Ambientali's App to open the smart bins through the smartphone

IT infrastructure to allow different systems (asset management, HR management, GEO, billing, CRM, etc.) to be aligned and integrated with each other. In this sense, Alia Servizi Ambientali has set up a transformation for the construction of a technological stack divided into three logical levels (Fig. 7):

- *IoT Layer*: This layer features an extensive network of sensors deployed throughout the region, with smart bins and trucks as key IoT components. Intelligent electronics installed in each bin recognize users through either an RFID key or a mobile app. These electronics also gather and send sensor data to the cloud. The data from these sensors trigger alarms and enable telemetry, alerting maintenance services to incidents like overturns, collisions, or fires. Each electronic unit is connected to a volumetric sensor that measures both the volume of deposits and the bin's fill level. Additionally, door-to-door collection bins use passive RFID tags to track when they are emptied.
- *Infrastructure Layer*: This layer comprises systems that facilitate data acquisition and storage. It integrates a suite of advanced technologies, including an Integrated Management System (IMS), Geographic Information System (GIS), Customer Relationship Management (CRM) System, Enterprise Resource Planning (ERP) System, and cloud infrastructure. These systems streamline operations, improve customer interactions, and ensure efficient data flow across various departments.
- *Application Layer*: This layer focuses on data processing and user interaction. Data analytics tools extract precise information from the collected data, automating process management or providing decision-making support. Alia has also introduced digital platforms for users, including a cloud-based CRM, a cloud-based ERP, a territorial planning system, and a real-time activity planning and

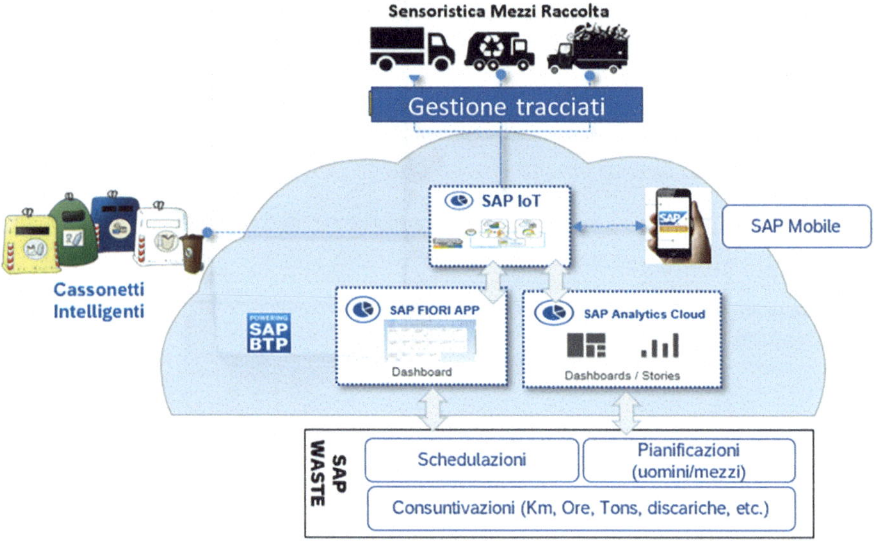

Fig. 7 Alia Servizi Ambientali's application map

monitoring system (control room). These tools are complemented by systems dedicated to support functions like HR and finance.

The development philosophy of Alia's systems emphasizes two main principles: an integrated system where data flows seamlessly across the digital infrastructure, and a modular system that can evolve dynamically, adapting to the demands of innovation.

3.3 *The Service Transformation*

The action research activity at Alia primarily focused on optimizing waste collection services within a test area coinciding with the municipality of Lastra a Signa. The research was limited to the collection of mixed waste (RUI) to avoid having to consider specific constraints for each type of waste (e.g., organic waste must be collected within a certain time frame). The goal was to determine if it was possible to offer a collection service that maintained the same levels of service but at a lower cost and with less environmental impact. The proposed solution involved a system where the waste collection truck would empty bins only when absolutely necessary, effectively creating an on-demand service initiated by the bins themselves.

Our theory (T) posited that by measuring fill levels and modeling bin fill rates, we could initially manually adjust the collection service (M) to increase the average fill level at the time of emptying while reducing the number of bins overfilled

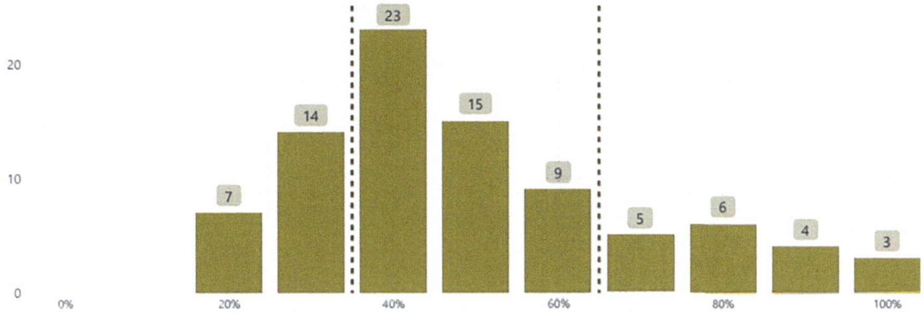

Fig. 8 Average fill level of bins at the time of emptying before data analysis

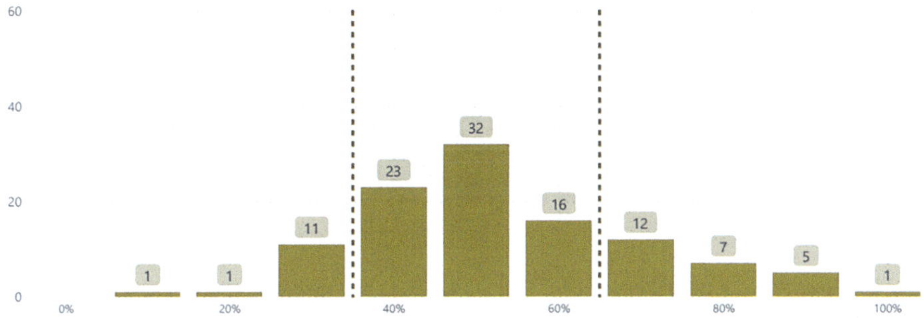

Fig. 9 Average fill level of bins at the time of emptying after the data analysis

beyond 90% capacity, thus decreasing the number of collection rounds (S). Additionally, we aimed to leverage the data gathered to formulate new research questions and establish further innovative initiatives directed at optimizing environmental efficiency and sustainability.

3.4 Results

The results obtained are very interesting. First, regarding the research question we set out, the results are summarized in Figs. 8 and 9. With minimal manual optimization, the average fill level of bins at the time of emptying increased from 43% to 47%, resulting in a net recovery of 4%. The number of bins emptied in the "critical area" (between 90% and 100%) has decreased dramatically (from three to one unit).

Regarding further potential research questions, we extensively collected time-stamped data on deposits. These data are summarized in Figs. 10 and 11. Figure 10 shows the number and size of average deposits by time slot. An initial observation useful for optimizing collection schedules is that deposits are not evenly distributed throughout the day, but instead have two peaks around lunch and dinner times.

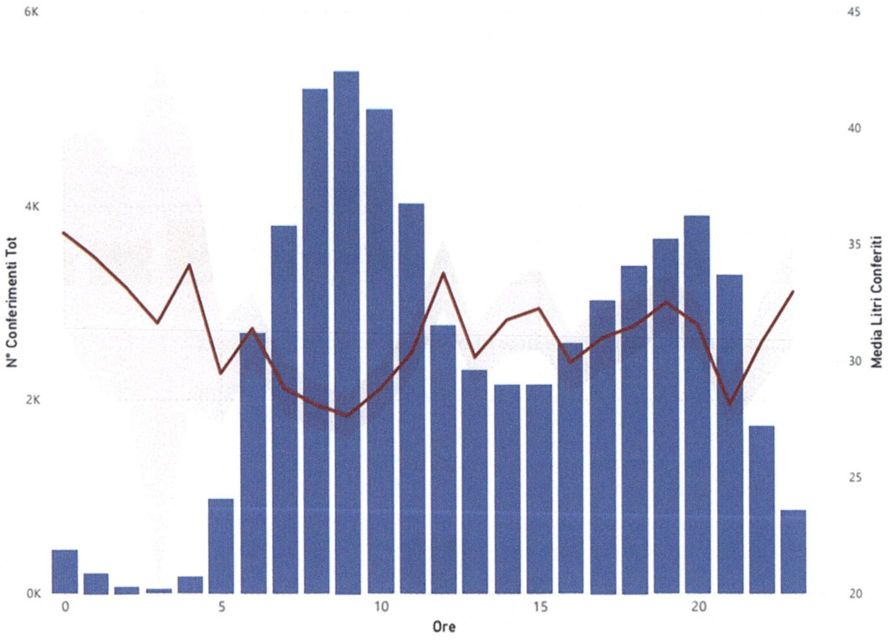

Fig. 10 Number of total deposits in bins by time slot (blue), average size of deposits per time slot (red)

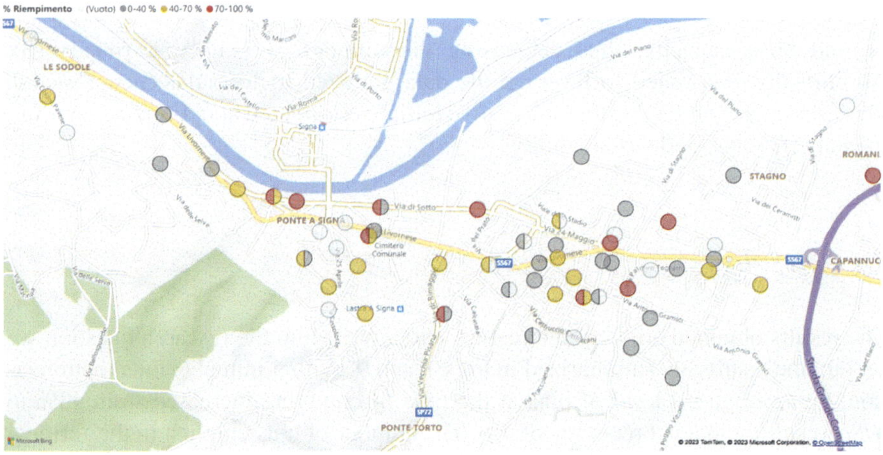

Fig. 11 Map of bins colored according to the average fill level at the time of emptying. Gray 0–40%, yellow 40–70%, red 70–100%

As for the size of deposits, the average expected deposit is about 30 liters and remains more or less constant throughout the day. Oversized deposits are largely concentrated during the nighttime, suggesting that it is not a sensor reading issue but rather a difference in the user base with varying waste disposal needs.

Figure 11 illustrates how bins are differently colored based on the average fill level at the time of emptying. Analyzing this image, it is clear which bins have significantly fewer deposits than average and which have more. This information is doubly useful: on the one hand, it can be used to better organize the emptying service, and on the other hand, it can be analyzed to better design the service across the territory. Some underused bins, where legally permissible and with municipal approval, can be moved to areas with a higher usage rate.

4 Conclusions and Future Work

In this chapter, we have summarized Alia's research activities, particularly an iteration of the ongoing action research process that is allowing us to improve the daily service level offered to citizens by reducing costs and decreasing the amount of pollutants released into the atmosphere.

To achieve this, we have implemented a rewarding tariff scheme that engages our citizens in the green revolution we are leading and encourages virtuous habits of circular economy.

The action research focused on a complex yet fundamental issue: street waste collection. Our goal was to optimize collection by increasing the average fill level of bins at the time of emptying and reducing the number of bins emptied when they are too full to be used.

After an initial iteration consisting of manual optimization, we reduced the number of bins emptied too late and increased the average fill level at emptying by 4%.

The data collected also suggested intra-day, intra-week, and intra-year seasonality in citizen deposits, allowing for even better operational management. Finally, the mapped data provides crucial indications to the design service regarding the optimal placement of bins in the territory.

In future iterations, we intend to make the collection scheme entirely on-demand, with the bin notifying the automatic planning system when it needs to be emptied based on its estimated future fill level. We also plan to collect weather data to see, for example, the impact of rain or excessive heat on user emptying. Finally, we aim to extend the experiment to all waste fractions to allow the centralized dispatch system full visibility of vehicle needs in the territory.

Acknowledgments The authors wish to thank all the colleagues at Alia whose daily commitment is enabling a radical change and rapid improvement of systems, processes, and services. Special thanks go to colleagues Francesco Pucci, Alfonso Dodero, and Marco Veracini, who provided data and charts crucial for the drafting of this chapter.

References

Agrawal, A., Gans, J., & Goldfarb, A. (2019). *The economics of artificial intelligence: An agenda*. University of Chicago Press.

Argyris, C. (1976). *Increasing leadership effectiveness*. Wiley.

Argyris, C., & Schön, D. A. (1997). Organizational learning: A theory of action perspective. *Reis, 77/78*, 345–348.

Argyris, C., Putnam, R., & Smith, D. M. (1985). *Action science: Concepts, methods and skills for research and intervention*. Jossey-Bass.

Baker, L. (2019). Renewable energy and the green transition in South Africa: Political and economic dynamics. *Energy Research & Social Science, 56*, 101207.

Baskerville, R. L., & Wood-Harper, A. T. (1996). A critical perspective on action research as a method for information systems research. *Journal of Information Technology, 11*, 235–246.

Bibri, S. E., & Krogstie, J. (2017). Smart sustainable cities of the future: An extensive interdisciplinary literature review. *Sustainable Cities and Society, 31*, 183–212.

Blumensaat, F., Leitão, J. P., Ort, C., Rieckermann, J., Scheidegger, A., Vanrolleghem, P. A., & Villez, K. (2019). How urban storm-and wastewater management prepares for emerging opportunities and threats: Digital transformation, ubiquitous sensing, new data sources, and beyond-a horizon scan. *Environmental Science & Technology, 53*(15), 8488–8498.

Borlaug, N. E. (2000). Ending world hunger. The promise of biotechnology and the threat of anti-science zealotry. *Plant Physiology, 124*(2), 487–490.

Brynjolfsson, E., & McAfee, A. (2014). *The second machine age: Work, progress, and prosperity in a time of brilliant technologies*. WW Norton & Company.

Bughin, J., Hazan, E., Ramaswamy, S., Chui, M., Allas, T., Dahlström, P., Henke, N., & Trench, M. (2017). *Artificial intelligence: The next digital frontier?* McKinsey Global Institute.

Checkland, P. B. (1985). From optimizing to learning: A development of systems thinking for the 1990s. *Journal of the Operational Research Society, 36*, 757–767.

Checkland, P., & Holwell, S. (2007). Action research: Its nature and validity. In *Information systems action research: An applied view of emerging concepts and methods* (pp. 3–17).

Di Mauro, A., Di Nardo, A., Santonastaso, G. F., & Venticinque, S. (2019, July). An IoT system for monitoring and data collection of residential water end-use consumption. In *2019 28th International Conference on Computer Communication and Networks (ICCCN)* (pp. 1–6). IEEE.

Elia, V., Gnoni, M. G., & Tornese, F. (2015). Designing Pay-As-You-Throw schemes in municipal waste management services: A holistic approach. *Waste Management, 44*, 188–195.

Farrelly, T., & Tucker, C. (2014). Action research and residential waste minimisation in Palmerston North, New Zealand. *Resources, Conservation and Recycling, 91*, 11–26.

Feroz, A. K., Zo, H., & Chiravuri, A. (2021). Digital transformation and environmental sustainability: A review and research agenda. *Sustainability, 13*(3), 1530.

Foster, M. (1972). An introduction to the theory and practice of action research in work organizations. *Human Relations, 25*, 529–556.

Geissbauer, R., Vedso, J., & Schrauf, S. (2017). *A strategist's guide to industry 4.0*. Strategy & Leadership.

Giustiniano, L., & Prencipe, A. (2017). La digital transformation di una multi-utility: tecnologia e persone, fattori chiave dell'esperienza ACEA. *Harvard Business Review*. Italia edition.

Giustiniano, L., & Prencipe, A. (2018). Technology-driven workforce management in multi-utilities. In *Rethinking the future of work*.

Huber, G. P. (1991). Organizational learning: The contributing processes and the literatures. *Organization Science, 2*(1), 88–115.

Kagermann, H., Wahlster, W., & Helbig, J. (2013). *Recommendations for implementing the strategic initiative Industrie 4.0* (Final report of the industrie 4.0 working group) (678p). Acatech—National Academy of Science and Engineering.

Keating, E. K., Oliva, R., Repenning, N., Rockart, S. F., & Sterman, J. D. (1999). Overcoming the improvement paradox. *European Management Journal, 17*, 120–134.

Kummitha, R. K. R. (2019). Smart technologies for fighting pandemics: The techno- and human-driven approaches in controlling the virus transmission. *Government Information Quarterly, 37*(3), 101481.

Lanzalonga, F., Marseglia, R., Irace, A., & Biancone, P. P. (2024). The application of artificial intelligence in waste management: Understanding the potential of data-driven approaches for the circular economy paradigm. *Management Decision*. https://doi.org/10.1108/MD-10-2023-1733

Lewin, K. (1946). Action research and minority problems. *Journal of Social Issues, 2*, 34–46.

Marseglia, G. R., Arbasini, A., Grassi, S., Raubal, M., & Raimondo, D. M. (2015, July). Optimal placement of wind turbines on a continuous domain: An MILP-based approach. In *2015 American Control Conference (ACC)* (pp. 5010–5015). IEEE.

Nair, S., Malhotra, M. K., & Ahire, S. L. (2011). Towards a theory of managing context in six sigma projects: An action research investigation. *Journal of Operations Management, 29*, 239–548.

Oliva, R., & Watson, N. H. (2009). Managing functional biases in organizational forecasts: A case study of consensus forecasting in supply chain planning. *Production and Operations Management, 18*, 138–151.

Oliva, R., & Watson, N. H. (2011). Cross-functional alignment in supply chain planning: A case study of sales and operations planning. *Journal of Operations Management, 29*, 434–448.

Oquist, P. (1978). The epistemology of action research. *Acta Sociologica, 21*(2), 143–163.

Pardini, K., Rodrigues, J. J., Kozlov, S. A., Kumar, N., & Furtado, V. (2019). IoT-based solid waste management solutions: A survey. *Journal of Sensor and Actuator Networks, 8*(1), 5.

Poole, M. S., van de Ven, A. H., Dooley, K. J., & Holmes, M. E. (2000). *Organizational change and innovation processes: Theory and methods for research*. Oxford University Press.

Raworth, K. (2017). *Doughnut economics: Seven ways to think like a 21st-century economist*. Chelsea Green Publishing.

Reichenbach, J. (2008). Status and prospects of pay-as-you-throw in Europe–A review of pilot research and implementation studies. *Waste Management, 28*(12), 2809–2814.

Sastry, M. A. (1997). Problems and paradoxes in a model of punctuated organizational change. *Administrative Science Quarterly, 42*, 237–275.

Schein, E. H. (1987). *The clinical perspective in fieldwork*. Sage.

Schwab, K. (2016). *The fourth industrial revolution*. World Economic Forum.

Secinaro, S., Brescia, V., Calandra, D., & Biancone, P. (2021). Towards a hybrid model for the management of smart city initiatives. *Cities, 116*, 1032783.

Secinaro, S., Calandra, D., Marseglia, R., & Biancone, P. (2022, October). Exploring practical applications of Blockchain in waste management: Insights from industry experts. In *International conference on information technology and applications* (pp. 1–10). Springer Nature Singapore.

Skumatz, L. A. (2008). Pay as you throw in the US: Implementation, impacts, and experience. *Waste Management, 28*(12), 2778–2785.

Beyond the Shadows: Reflections on Science, Technology, and Humanism in the Dialogue Between Past and Present

Antonio Calabrò

Abstract Science, technology, and humanism are interconnected forces shaping our world. This chapter reflects on their historical and contemporary dialogue, emphasizing the enduring relevance of scientific inquiry, critical thinking, and ethical considerations. Through the lens of Galileo's defiance and Brecht's dramatization, it explores the tension between knowledge and authority. The chapter argues for a balanced approach to technological advancements, integrating humanistic values to navigate the complexities of the digital age. Highlighting the role of education, interdisciplinary collaboration, and responsible governance, it advocates for a future where innovation and humanism coexist to address global challenges and enhance societal welfare.

"How is the night?"
"Clear."

These are the final moments of Bertolt Brecht's "Life of Galileo" (Brecht, 2015). The scientist has just been forced to submit to the orders of the Church doctors, renouncing his discoveries about the Sun's centrality and the Earth's motion as a planet, humiliating the power of scientific evidence in the face of theologians' beliefs. He suffers, out of fear, the harshness of power. But he does not resign himself. He continues to study the stars and the laws of physics, of astronomy. Because there is always a force in science. An extraordinary beauty, in research, in discovery, in knowledge. And a truth, to be verified, discussed, and put to the test anyway.

A new beginning, to be lived.
A sky, to continue to look at.
"How is the night?"
"Clear."
Despite everything.

A. Calabrò (✉)
Fondazione Pirelli, Milan, Italy
e-mail: antonio.calabro@pirelli.com

G. R. Marseglia et al. (eds.), *Socio-economic Impact of Artificial Intelligence*,
Progress in IS, https://doi.org/10.1007/978-3-031-73514-1_15

"Life of Galileo" premiered at the Piccolo Teatro di Milano on April 22, 1963. The direction was by Giorgio Strelher. The role of the protagonist was entrusted to Tino Buazzelli, in one of the most intense and effective interpretations that theatrical history remembers (Cuomo, 2006). And in those dialogues, in those scenes, in that intense and lacerating dramaturgy yet full of hope, the profound meaning of the human experience in the face of scientific and moral issues that mark the history of progress, development, and the construction of a more balanced civilisation is condensed.

The night is clear, even in these difficult times of ours, of health crises and technological fragility, extraordinary opportunities for economic development, and unbearable social disparities, great scientific advances, and growing environmental imbalances. Of devastating wars, like in Ukraine. And of assaults on the rights of millions of people to have a better future. Of powerful economic and social upheavals determined by high-tech multinationals. But also, of the spread of formidable opportunities offered by the spread of Artificial Intelligence, in the *twin transition* where the digital economy stimulates and aids the *environmental transition*.

Times of uncertainties, while we find ourselves dealing with an energy crisis involving issues of strategic and political security, with the fractures of the international trade system, risks of recession, growth of inflation, and rising interest rates, and thus the cost of money after years of quiet. And it is increasingly necessary to heed the fears of Jamie Diamond, CEO of J.P. Morgan, one of the largest international banks, when he emphasizes the "*economic hurricane that is coming*".[1]

Risky times, then. In which we might fall into the poetic temptation of irresolution ("*Codesto solo oggi possiamo dirti/ciò che non siamo/ciò che non vogliamo*", "*This alone we can tell you today/what we are not/what we do not want*" (Montale, 1984]). But also trust in the possibilities offered by scientific achievements for health, quality of life, and improvement of working conditions. Walking in the crisis. Avoiding the shadows of "*magical thinking*" that distrusts knowledge and scientific skills. And instead welcoming the opportunities offered by studies to face the challenges of managing complexity (as documented by the research of Giorgio Parisi, who was awarded the Nobel Prize for Physics in 2021). Just that complexity that Italo Calvino, in his "*Lezioni Americane*", identifies as a constant of the human condition and as the very engine of the drives to innovation, according to non-linear paths and thoughts (Calvino, 2012). And adding, with the wisdom of a humanist fascinated by the rigour of the methods of knowledge: "*Aim only at the difficult things, performed to perfection; distrust ease, the facile, the doing much for the sake of doing. Aim at precision, as much in language as in the things that are done*." The rigour of knowing how to do the "difficult things" as hermeneutics of our controversial contemporaneity. Knowing that, despite everything, despite every intertwining and despite every divergence and contradiction, in our journey at the end of the night we can glimpse a dawn. As Galileo indeed teaches.

[1] *Jamie Dimon says 'brace yourself' for an economic hurricane caused by the Fed and Ukraine war*, CNBC, 1 June 2022, https://www.cnbc.com/2022/06/01/jamie-dimon-says-brace-yourself--for-an-economic-hurricane-caused-by-the-fed-and-ukraine-war.html

There are special places, also and especially in Italy, where these complex and still contrasted cultural and social conditions intersect and evolve. The production facilities. The industrial plants. The factories.

Hence, the factories, an ancient word recently returned to the centre of public discourse in the era of a rediscovered "*industrial pride*" Italian and European. They had been, in the nineteenth century, symbols of modernity, of the new dimensions of production and consumption, of the disruptive economic and social transformations. In the long and controversial twentieth century, they have been protagonists of the political and economic landscape, in the century of the automobile and mass mobility, of chemistry and telecommunications, of consumption and the transformations of lifestyles, between conflicts and widespread well-being. And even now, as scientific and technological innovations, the *digital economy*, and Artificial Intelligence, precisely, push towards the primacy of "services" and activities of the so-called "*tertiary sector*", the factories, rather, better, the neo-factories remain central in the economic landscape. Because it is there, in a dimension of hybrid and open innovation, that the evolutions of science and technology, work and life, research and production, economic needs and social values, productivity, and environmental protection converge. Competitiveness and sustainability, both environmental and social.

They seemed to have disappeared, the factories in the landscape at the beginning of the new millennium, confined to territories still broad but marginal compared to the heart of "progress". They have returned to the current, with new arrangements and new values.

Factories. And that is, the civilisation of machines and "*industrial humanism*", which is articulated in "*digital humanism*", following the innovations of science and technology. Special places where original productive and cultural syntheses are tested and built. And where grows the awareness of the relationship between industry and culture. Of the indispensable relationship between making factories and making culture.

The innovation knot remains, then, in the foreground, in the close relationship between technological aspects and social consequences, economic competitiveness of companies and systems, and the need to take into account also the issues of social inclusion and solidarity, in the search for the construction of a "fair economy" (as suggested by Pope Francis[2] and a large part of the most qualified economic literature), of sustainable development, environmental and social, according to ESG criteria and the growing need for a "relegitimation" of the market economy and the company, after the upheavals of the rapacious dominance of speculative finance (the season of *greed is good* critically documented also by Hollywood[3]) and the imbalances of a frenetic and poorly governed globalization.

---

[2] Pope Francis, *The Economy of Francesco*, Assisi, October 2022, https://www.humandevelopment.va/it/eventi/2022/economy-of-francesco-il-papa-andra-ad-assisi.html

[3] Oliver Stone, *Wall Street*, 1987.

Innovation, in this context, is to be considered as a comprehensive journey, even now when we are in the midst of the new challenges: the electric car and the new mobility from smart cities, the digital factories, robots in the dimensions of the *data-driven* factory, high-tech simulators, nanotechnologies, cyber sensors in objects and instruments of services, Artificial Intelligence applied to research, production, and consumption and all chapters of a story that is being lived and written.

What to do, in a landscape so mobile and marked by extraordinary lights of progress and alarming shadows of crisis? Try to be neither apocalyptic nor integrated, to paraphrase an aphorism by Umberto Eco (Eco, 1964). Neither *techno-sceptical* nor *techno-enthusiastic*. But rather ready, with a love of knowledge and critical intelligence, to consider all aspects of the spread of new technologies. With a fundamental consideration: the "*digital natives*" know well how to move in the digital world, have skills to use much of its possibilities, but those skills are not automatically knowledge nor much less the ability to discern deeply. Knowledge is the key to everything. Critical intelligence, aware of risks and opportunities.

To understand even better, one can try to step back to those early 1990s of the twentieth century when, in the construction of the new Pirelli communication, a slogan with extraordinary evocative power was affirmed: *Power is nothing without Control*. And it is precisely that active and responsible relationship between power and control that interprets the sign of those times and gives to the symbolic phrase a dimension that goes beyond the contingency of a brilliant advertising campaign (Fig. 1).

Changing, at the beginning of the last decade of the twentieth century, were the paradigms of interpretation and management of international processes after the fall of the Berlin Wall, the implosion of the Soviet Empire, and the end of the so-called "*bipolar balance*" that had defined the governance of the world until the late 1980s. Liberal democracy and the market economy triumphed. And, in economics, globalization processes and transformations accelerated by the Internet and the increasingly intense use of network processes were affirmed. The world was becoming increasingly interconnected. Radically changing were the perceptions of space and time. And also, the relationships between economic and social subjects.

It was said: less state, more market. But also, less politics and more economics, especially if the economy was defined as privileging the role and weight of finance, in the sense of speculative finance. Everything seemed to change, in the extraordinary acceleration of progress, of technique, of the construction of wealth. Enough to cast a shadow over economic, political, and social imbalances that would soon come to the fore, presenting the bill.

There was power. But without control.

The dialectic on the two dimensions, moreover, has found ample space in many of the most acute reflections throughout the course of the twentieth century, fully involving analyses and judgements on the spheres of politics, economics, science and its technological articulations (from quantum physics to the many applications of *information technology*) and other essential dimensions of culture.

These are reasonings to continue to deepen, still listening to the echo of "*Power is nothing without control*" in this contemporary season of great transitions, with an

Fig. 1 Power is nothing without control. Pirelli advertisement campaign

eye attentive both to persistence and to metamorphoses. Taking up again, as one of the possible classical references, the "*Dialectic of Enlightenment*" by Theodor W. Adorno and Max Horkheimer (Adorno et al., 2002), with the continuous and original search for a synthesis between Greek wisdom and contemporary knowledge, between the sense of the sacred of the Bible and the scientific and philosophical curiosity, between Jerusalem and Athens (Fig. 2).

There is a figure, to focus attention on: Ulysses, the archetype of the man who lives in the full restlessness of the journey and the search and knows well the

Fig. 2 Power is nothing without control. Pirelli advertisement campaign

fragility of existence and the strength of will. The hero of the questions, of critical intelligence, of the challenge to the future.

And it is precisely on Ulysses and his journey (an anticipation of the myth of the wandering Jew?) that another of the observations of the "*Dialectic of Enlightenment*" focuses: the consciousness of the sense of limit and the need to always take it into account, every time we confront the charm of power. In summary: Ulysses faces, in the journey of knowledge and in his narrative, the challenge of progress (with the discovery of new life opportunities, up to the boundaries of the magical and immortality) and, at the same time, verifies its crisis. Ulysses the nomad reveals himself in the continuous rereading of the poetic wisdom of Homer, a man of science. Curious, investigator, always ready to start again.

Let us get back to Galileo, from whom we started and to his idea of the scientific process "*trying and retrying*", adding data, verifying knowledge with new experiments, building consensus, and opening up to ever more pertinent questions, between the power of discovery and the control of its validity. Science as a journey, precisely. And as a narrative.

These considerations are even more valid today, in a time when the spread of Artificial Intelligence we have mentioned, and the deep and increasingly accelerated transformation of production, exchange, and consumption mechanisms call for the definition of new codes for what Luciano Floridi (Floridi, 2018; Ziosi et al., 2023), a philosopher attentive to information ethics, calls the "*governance of the infosphere*". This is to build horizons of meaning and legal rules for urban systems as *smart cities*, for productive activities dense with new job opportunities, and for economic relationships defined according to the values of environmental and social sustainability. A culture of *green* and *blue*, to use the effective summary of the latest reflections by Salvatore Veca who, right in the metropolis of Milan dense with social history, scientific culture, and values of solidarity, identified the national and international paradigm of a possible development that knows how to use technologies to save cities and citizens from ancient and new inequalities, from digital, generational, gender, and cultural divides. *Smart cities* that expand into *smart lands* and must be inhabited by *smart citizens*, determine a critical, aware, active, and responsible citizenship.

"*The technological leap requires a new digital consciousness*", insists Mauro Magatti,[4] a sociologist at the Catholic University of Milan and one of the most attentive theorists to all the moral and social implications of the ongoing economic "*paradigm shift*": "*The web cannot be a chaotic jungle where the law of the strongest prevails. It is therefore urgent to strengthen the institutional infrastructure—made of national and supranational rules and limits—to counter the evident power imbalances existing today and to enhance the many potentials opened by the Network.*" With the approval of the Digital Services Act (European Union, 2022), Europe has already made some interesting choices in this regard. Much road still remains to be covered.

It is, therefore, the time for cross-disciplinary skills -of neuroscientists and *cyberphilosophers*. It is the time to develop the essential algorithms for industrial and service transformations but also to understand and direct their meaning, reflect on their consequences for people's lives, and address the novel moral and social issues that technological evolution gradually poses, working on bioethics, information technologies, law, and neuroscience.

The Polytechnics of Milan and Turin organize training activities in this direction. And the reference horizon can also be traced in the directions of a very current book, such as "*The New Laws of Robotics. Defending Human Expertise in the Age of AI*" by Frank Pasquale (Pasquale, 2020), professor at Brooklyn Law School: working on "*augmented intelligence*" and defining its values, potentials, limits, and thus rules means using its positive possibilities and circumscribing its negative effects.

"*Starting again from knowledge. From classrooms emptied by the virus to the new centrality of the University*", suggested in 2021 by Ferruccio Resta (Resta, 2021), at the time Rector of the Polytechnic of Milan in a dialogue with Ferruccio de Bortoli, to reason about the transformations underway in educational processes and on investments stimulated by the EU's Recovery Plan for the new generations (European Union, 2021). We must teach to learn. And face a challenge as daunting as ever, right in front of the impetuous change of technologies: that of understanding the meaning of the things we do, investigating the reference values, and the human and ethical consequences of technological advances. Not only, therefore, knowing how to write Artificial Intelligence algorithms effectively, but also understanding,

---

[4] Il salto tecnologico richiede una nuova coscienza digitale, Mauro Magatti, Corriere della Sera, 21 july 2021, https://www.corriere.it/editoriali/21_luglio_22/salto-tecnologico-richiede-nuova-coscienza-digitale-694cae24-eb17-11eb-872f-99e4306190c7.shtml

controlling, and governing their effects. To avoid hidden manipulations and try to reconcile high-tech development, freedom, and responsibility. As engineer-philosophers, technologist-poets must know what to do.

University disciplines suggest Resta should no longer be framed in rigid cages. And, precisely thinking about the Polytechnics, he insists: "*An engineer today is no longer just a technician who must respond to the single problem but must provide answers to social challenges and complex problems that increasingly also involve the ethical sphere of technologies.*"

Surely, digital representation has entered our lives, with a radical change of ways that before the pandemic we could not have imagined at all. The rapid spread of 5G (at the centre of the investments of the European Recovery Plan (European Union, 2021)) will further expand the process. And it will allow achieving another fundamental result: to bring cultural processes and representations to life also in Italy's small cities and towns, giving a more dynamic dimension of participation to places so far cut off from the main flows of culture.

The challenge we face, as men and women of culture and business, but also as citizens/spectators/lovers of culture and art, is not only to learn to live with innovation but above all to be an active part in the construction of new mechanisms of participation and enjoyment of cultural activities, to be involved, with both a critical and constructive spirit, in the identification of original forms of popular culture: new languages, new ways of constructing cultural processes, new relationships between memory and cutting-edge technologies.

Digital humanism is precisely the new challenge for school activities and manufacturing, service, or creative enterprises. "*Industry is 4.0 if it dialogues with the humanities. We must focus on digital humanities*", argues Domenico Siniscalco,[5] one of the most authoritative Italian economists, educated at Cambridge University, with extensive international experience (he is vice-president of Morgan Stanley) and also solid political and governmental activity (he was the Minister of Economy, as well as the director-general of that ministry). A man of theory and practice, then. With a particularly keen eye on the real economy and corporate finance.

There is emphasis on the centrality of investments in innovation and high-tech manufacturing. Using well the funds from the *Piano Nazionale di Ripresa e Resilienza—PNRR*[6] that are destined for the environment and the digital economy (two dimensions that intersect, in the virtuous link between competitiveness and sustainability, where the Italian industry boasts positions of European excellence). And resources for education.

Here is a key point: what kind of education? Domenico Siniscalco knows well that companies are looking for technical professional profiles that they cannot find and are demanding specialized human capital, engineers, mathematicians, chemists, data scientists, experts in cybersecurity and the digital economy, graduates from ITS

[5] L'umanesimo digitale è la nuova sfida per le attività di scuola e imprese, Antonio Calabrò, Huffing Post, 25 gennaio 2022, https://www.huffingtonpost.it/blog/2022/01/25/news/l_umanesimo_digitale_e_la_nuova_sfida_per_le_attivita_di_scuola_e_imprese-7604374/

[6] https://www.italiadomani.gov.it/content/sogei-ng/it/it/home.html

(the essential higher technical institutes, increasingly conceived as "Academies"), and graduates in STEM subjects (the acronym for science, technology, engineering, and mathematics). And speaking of culture and manufacturing, he asserts: "*STEM subjects are fine. But it would be the height of folly to go from a world all humanistic, as in the past, toward a world all technical. We must also focus on the humanistic dimensions and soft skills. Universities and Polytechnics must be systematized. Innovating, in short, means innovatively putting together old factors, as Joseph Schumpeter said.*" (Schumpeter (2013)) Thus, STEAM, not just STEM. Adding the "a" for arts, the humanistic knowledge.

The horizon to which Domenico Siniscalco also refers is once again that of "*polytechnic culture*", as a synthesis between the sense of beauty and sophisticated ability to use information technologies, design, and productive efficiency. For the best Italian multinational companies (from mechatronics and automotive industries to chemical and life sciences companies, as well as naturally the traditional sectors of made in Italy excellence, starting with furniture) to continue to compete on global markets, according to the new paradigms of circular and civil economy, multidisciplinary knowledge and skills are needed: not only the technical figures just mentioned but also psychologists and sociologists with a robust technical training, architects with solid preparation suited to face the new aspects of the environmental and digital transition, lawyers able to define rules and sanctions for all the evolutions of the network, including the Metaverse, with its shadows and limits. Moreover, scholars of labour market transformations have been warning for years that a good part of the professions that our children and grandchildren will do in twenty years have not yet been invented.[7]

These considerations are even more valid today, at a time when the spread of Artificial Intelligence and the profound and increasingly accelerated transformation of production, exchange, and consumption mechanisms demand the definition of new cognitive and productive maps and new codes for the "*governance of the infosphere*" we discussed above. This is for a potential development that can leverage technologies to save cities and citizens from ancient and new inequalities, from digital, generational, gender, and cultural divides.

Thus, we return to the suggestion about digital humanities. A fundamental cultural, social, and economic challenge. For educational systems. And for companies that, starting from knowledge, organize its representation, its narrative. Taking to heart the lesson from Erasmus of Rotterdam: "*Man does not love change, for changing means to look deeply into one's soul with sincerity, contesting oneself and one's life. One must be courageous to do so, have great ideals. Most men prefer to wallow in mediocrity and make time the pond of their existence.*"

The discussion returns, along this path, also to businesses and their systems of organization and industrial relations. And especially to politics, concerning everything about investments in public and basic research and tax incentives for private

[7] Nuova cultura politecnica per la *twin transition* ambientale e digitale, Antonio Calabrò, 2022, *Impresa Progetto—Electronic Journal of Management*.

and applied research, education, and welfare mechanisms designed to minimize the negative social effects of techno-economic transformations. A policy primarily European, which then unfolds in individual states, overcoming any nationalist, protectionist, or isolationist temptation.

Here lies the ultimate reflection to be made. Reading, for example, Martin Heidegger: "*What is truly unsettling is not that the world is transforming into a complete domain of technique. Far more unsettling is that man is not at all prepared for this radical change in the world. Far more unsettling is that we are still not able to reach, through meditative thought, an adequate confrontation with what is really emerging in our era*" (Heidegger et al., 1983). These words emphasize the necessary potential of critical thinking, faced with scientific innovations and technological consequences, with the dangers of the "*dominion of technique*". They highlight the unfortunately unexpressed possibilities of understanding and thus governing the complex phenomena of contemporaneity. They are most timely in the face of phenomena related to Artificial Intelligence and the self-sufficiency hypotheses of machine learning following the development of uncontrolled algorithms. And they tell us that, all things considered, even for Heidegger, there is hope (Heidegger 1977).

Digital, environmental, and social transitions, in short, demand a greater commitment to research, study, and understanding, thanks also to the strengthening of that "*polytechnic culture*" we have discussed, which has a solid future for its ability to combine humanistic wisdom and scientific knowledge with forward-thinking stimuli for the critical thinking of "*engineer-philosophers*".

Science and technological transformations impose the growth of an awareness of the fundamental criteria of trial and error, following the lesson of Karl Popper. The power that expresses itself demands control. Therefore, it is essential to build a positive social capital (companies, as responsible actors between competitiveness and social inclusion, are fundamental protagonists). And to rewrite updated maps to navigate, precisely, in the contemporary transition.

The necessary horizon is that of an economy measured by man, where the construction of economic value is based on human, social, and civil values. In short, Heidegger's "*meditative thought*" is needed. And the recovery of the basic trust that inspires science, reading Popper:[8] "*It is the seduction of the future that makes us live.*" Despite everything.

We must strengthen the dimensions of thought. And of critical capacity. As suggested a few years ago by Tom Nichols, a professor at Harvard, in an essential book, "*The Death of Expertise: The Campaign Against Established Knowledge and Why It Matters*" (Nichols, 2017) analysing "*the age of incompetence and the risks to democracy*". We must not yield to the "*society of the ignorant*", that is, to the facile nature of those who oppose beliefs to science, to the widespread approximation against technicians and experts (the miserable controversies over vaccines, which

[8] Fragilità e costi delle transizioni e la "seduzione del futuro" di Popper, Antonio Calabrò, 29 novembre 2021, Huffing Post, https://www.huffingtonpost.it/blog/2021/11/29/news/fragilita_e_costi_delle_transizioni_e_la_seduzione_del_futuro_di_popper-7346668/

have crowded days of discussions during the Covid-19 pandemic, even in politics, are just one of the manifestations). Instead, we must insist on attention to science, as a responsibility and as knowledge. And not be misled by the tensions and facile nature wrongly attributed to digital culture. Even digital culture must be critical culture, just as Popper demanded from scientific culture.

A new "pact" is also needed between elites and the masses, suggesting, with Nichols, precisely to scientists and intellectuals endowed with robust competences to leave their places of privilege and deep knowledge and listen with humility and attention, explain, try to teach, and give new reasons for knowledge and civil virtues. Because democracy needs that popular orientations are taken into account, but also translated, interpreted, and transformed into political choices and government actions.

In times of *web superficiality*, we must return to the lesson of Jürgen Habermas on "discursive" public opinion capable of a critical public discourse. This is our current greatest responsibility. A severe task for intellectuals aware of the need to write new maps of knowledge, bridging humanism and science, and of the responsibility not to yield to the rhetoric of success but to engage, if anything, in the labour of depth. For to do the intellectual work well, it is necessary "*not to abandon one's craft as scholars, but to expand it, to involve a broader audience, if one has something to say that may interest such an audience. This requires the ability to reinvent oneself without betraying one's craft*", according to Sabino Cassese,[9] a great jurist and wise civil servant.

In the background, there is a word to leverage: Utopia. A "*utopia of reconstruction*" and not a "*utopia of escape*", with idols replacing reality, according to the wise lesson of Lewis Mumford, one of the greatest urbanists and sociologists of the twentieth century (Mumford (2011)). The philosophy of Ernst Cassirer also remains current: "*The great mission of utopia is to give rise to the possible, in opposition to the passive acquiescence to the current state of things. It is symbolic thinking that triumphs over the natural inertia of man and endows him with a new faculty, the faculty to continually reform his universe.*"[10] And the poetic syntheses of Eduardo Galeano continue to echo: "*Utopia is like the horizon: I walk two steps, and it moves two steps away. I walk ten steps, and it moves ten steps away. The horizon is unreachable. So, what is the purpose of utopia? This: it serves to keep walking.*"

A journey that can serve as a reference, especially for the new generations of girls and boys in search of the meaning of "a life ahead of them" and thus a better destiny.

---

[9] Investire su scienza e ricerca di base: le idee di Aspen e la lezione di Calvino, Antonio Calabrò, 17 October 2022, Huffing Post, https://www.huffingtonpost.it/blog/2022/10/17/news/investire_su_scienza_e_ricerca_di_base_le_idee_di_aspen_la_lezione_di_calvino-10423578/

[10] LA RISCOPERTA DI ERNST CASSIRER TRA UTOPIA E RIFORMISMO E IL "MANIFESTO DI ASSISI" PER LA GREEN ECONOMY SOSTENIBILE, Fondazione Pirelli, 29 October 2019, https://www.fondazionepirelli.org/it/cultura-dimpresa/la-riscoperta-di-ernst-cassirer-tra-utopia-e-riformismo-e-il-manifesto-di-assisi-per-la-green-economy-sostenibile/

It is necessary, precisely today, to rekindle trust in the future. A general commitment to development and social solidarity. A challenge that fully concerns the world of business: it is here, indeed, that by investing and innovating, work is created, wealth is produced, and the foundations for the construction of widespread well-being are laid. And it is businesses, today, that play the main role of social elevators, in an Italy too long stagnant, ageing, depressed by a disturbing demographic winter (in '22 fewer than 400,000 babies were born, a negative record), slow to grow, scarcely inclined to mobility.

Good governance, to conclude. Innovation. Development. Resonating, precisely on the quality of knowledge and responsibility, the words of one of the best critical consciences of twentieth-century Europe, Leonardo Sciascia: "*Intelligence, as Poe teaches us, is less a mathematical mind and more a poetic mind. It is simple and simplifying, produces the simple and simplifies*." A lesson "*for future* memory". Sciascia (2017).

References

Adorno, T. W., Horkheimer, M., & Noeri, G. (2002). *Dialectic of enlightenment*. Stanford University Press.

Brecht, B. (2015). *Life of Galileo*. Bloomsbury Publishing.

Calvino, I. (2012). *Lezioni americane*. Edizioni Mondadori.

Cuomo, F. (2006). Berliner Ensemble 1957–Piccolo Teatro 1963. La scienza nella ricezione del Galileo di Brecht dalle rassegne stampa delle due rappresentazioni. *JCOM, 5*, 1.

Eco, U. (1964). *Apocalittici e Integrati*. Bompiani.

European Union. (2021). NextGenerationEU. https://commission.europa.eu/strategy-and-policy/recovery-plan-europe_en

European Union. (2022). REGULATION (EU) 2022/2065 OF THE EUROPEAN PARLIAMENT AND OF THE COUNCIL of 19 October 2022 on a Single Market For Digital Services and amending Directive 2000/31/EC (Digital Services Act)

Floridi, L. (2018). Soft ethics, the governance of the digital and the General Data Protection Regulation. *Philosophical Transactions of the Royal Society A: Mathematical, Physical and Engineering Sciences, 376*(2133), 20180081.

Heidegger, M. (1977). The question concerning technology. *Readings in the Philosophy of Technology*, 9–24.

Heidegger, M., Angelino, C., & Fabris, A. (1983). *L'abbandono*. Il melangolo.

Montale, E. (1984). Non chiederci la parola che squadri da ogni lato. Montale E., *Tutte le poesie, a c. di G. Zampa, Mondadori, Milano* (Originally in Ossi di Seppia – 1925).

Mumford, L. (2011). *The story of utopias*. Read Books Ltd.

Nichols, T. (2017). *The death of expertise: The campaign against established knowledge and why it matters*. Oxford University Press.

Pasquale, F. (2020). *New laws of robotics*. Harvard University Press.

Resta, F. (2021). *Ripartire dalla conoscenza: Dalle aule svuotate dal virus alla nuova centralità dell'Università. Dialogo con Ferruccio de Bortoli*. Bollati Boringhieri.

Schumpeter, J. A. (2013). *Capitalism, socialism and democracy*. Routledge.

Sciascia, L. (2017). *A futura memoria: (se la memoria ha un futuro)* (Vol. 78). Adelphi Edizioni Spa.

Ziosi, M., Hewitt, B., Juneja, P., Taddeo, M., & Floridi, L. (2023). Smart cities: reviewing the debate about their ethical implications. In *The 2022 yearbook of the Digital Governance Research Group* (pp. 11–38). Springer.

Unconscious Consu-victims and Enlightened Ultra-Humans: The Society of Consumerism Is at the Crossroads of Artificial Intelligence

Nicolo Andreula and Stefania Petruzzelli

Abstract The intersection of artificial intelligence (AI) and consumerism reveals a society divided into unconscious consumers and enlightened individuals. This chapter explores the rapid evolution of technology and its impact on human behavior and society. While technological advancements like AI grow exponentially, human adaptability lags, creating a gap in understanding and utilization. The chapter identifies three groups: creators of disenchantment who develop technology, designers of simplicity who make technology user-friendly, and the enchanted, divided into passive consumers and enlightened individuals who integrate ethical and cultural values into technology use. It argues for the importance of human-specific skills like creativity, critical thinking, and empathy in maintaining relevance and navigating the complexities of the digital age. The chapter concludes by emphasizing the need for a new kind of memory and cognitive strategy to manage the vast information flow in the digital world, advocating for a balanced approach to technology that preserves human values and critical thought.

There has always been a coevolution between us and technology: as we evolve, technology evolves and, thus, makes us evolve. For most of human history, technological development has been growing on such a trend that an individual could live without perceiving any disruptive progress. Today we know, however, that this is no longer the case. We have witnessed (and continue to see) significant technological developments, even over concise periods.

While innovation used to progress at the pace of individuals, today human evolution is much slower than technological evolution.

N. Andreula (✉)
Disal Consulting, Bari (BA), Italy
e-mail: n.andreula@disalconsulting.com

S. Petruzzelli
Future Food Institute, Bologna (BO), Italy
e-mail: stefania.petruzzelli@futurefoodinstitute.org

G. R. Marseglia et al. (eds.), *Socio-economic Impact of Artificial Intelligence*,
Progress in IS, https://doi.org/10.1007/978-3-031-73514-1_16

According to **Moore's law**, microcircuits' complexity and processing power double every 18 months: an exponential (and no longer linear) growth trend that can be seen in every sector of the digital ecosystem. **Ray Kurzweil**, a leading expert in artificial intelligence, has stated that "**when any technology becomes a computing technology, it begins to evolve exponentially**,"[1] accelerating to such an extent that it causes a qualitative leap. Considering today's growth rate, in the twenty-first century, we could witness another 20,000 years of progress. This growth could be even more remarkable for A.I., which—Kurzweil speculates—is likely to reach a point of "singularity." A.I. could self-implement optimization programs and surpass the ability of humans to understand its own progress.

What I have just said is not science fiction but a plausible prediction, considering that it took us about half a century to adopt the telephone but less than a decade to embrace the mobile phone and the computer.

How are we going to react to such complexity? Tendentially, with indifference.

As mentioned, our evolution no longer proceeds hand in hand with technological development. **We demand a sophisticated complexity of processes and functions from innovations, yet we require a linear simplicity of use from them.** Innovations have to work and perform as they promise. Therefore, we do not tend to ask questions about their systems, mechanisms, or theoretical structures.

Losing our curiosity doesn't necessarily mean losing our wonder. Hence, when we face technologies, we do not question (or at least we do not convert our questions into research), but, instead, we wonder.

In ancient Greek, the term mechané didn't only mean "machine" or "mechanism" but also "**cunning**" (the reason why a lever could lift a weight was not immediately apparent).

Centuries have passed, and although the workings of technologies are no longer a mystery, our surprise prevails when looking at processes that just before seemed not allowed by the natural order or the immediate appearance of things. **We remain incredibly puzzled by those machines whose actions seem to trespass into the territory of human capabilities**.

According to the European Parliament, **artificial intelligence** is a technology capable of "**displaying human capabilities such as reasoning, learning, planning, and creativity**." A technology capable of analyzing and classifying data to obtain descriptive, predictive, and prescriptive results and to identify solutions for specific purposes.

A.I. is expanding into all fields to support the performance of the most diverse set of activities, playing a central role in our everyday lives (think of Siri, for instance) and our work. Nevertheless, it is indisputable—to quote the philosopher Leibnitz—as individuals, we have some "blind thoughts,"[2] meaning that we cannot reach the core of a concept without the help of machines.

Artificial intelligence has evolved to such an extent (thanks, of course, to our progress) that it can now **emulate many aspects of human behavior**. Unlike their

---

[1] R. Kurzweil, *La singolarità è vicina*, Apogeo Education, Milan 2008.

[2] G.W. Leibniz: *Scritti filosofici*, UTET, Turin, 1979.

precursors, new technologies (which are now equipped with neural networks that mimic the way human brain cells interact with each other) have developed **machine learning**, **logical thinking**, and what experts refer to as **emerging skills** (e.g., text writing or image processing). Consider that a Google engineer recently claimed that an A.I., called LaMDA, is considered sentient.

Leaving aside such extremes, one cannot fail to note these machines' ability in many areas such as logistics, operations planning, language processing, control, and systems programming.

With the advent of science and its technical tools, individuals have stopped resorting to mysterious entities to explain natural phenomena and to master reality. This "**disenchantment of the world**"—as the philosopher Max Weber called it—was not so much due to the increasing general knowledge but to the realization that "**if one only wanted to, one could**" at any time come to know, i.e., that "**one can—in principle—master all things by means of rational calculation**."[3]

All true, until now.

Because today, humanity, when **faced with artificial intelligence**, the ultimate manifestation of technological innovation, seems to be divided into three different categories:

- the creators of disenchantment
- the designers of simplicity
- the enchanters (divided into unconscious consu-victims and enlightened ultra-humans)

1. *The Creators of Disenchantment*

   This group refers to the **ones who know technology because they created it**. They free individuals from irrational explanations through the power of science, equipping them with technical, technological and digital means to control, design, and predict reality.
2. *The Designers of Simplicity*

   This group refers to the ones who **make technological innovation functional and consumable**. This group realizes that users demand simplicity and intuitiveness of use, completeness of functions, and product performance.

   In China, for example, the facial recognition software of the former group evolved into hardware so precise that it is now suitable for validating financial transactions.
3. *The Enchanted*

   Theoretical indifference is not and cannot be reprehensible, given the complexity of the technologies I am referring to.

   But the enchanted, who do not want to learn about the technological mechanisms (nor can they, except by profession or passion), react in two different ways to innovations.

– *The Unconscious Consumers*

[3] M. Weber, *La scienza come professione. La politica come professione*, Milan, Mondadori 2006.

- Are **technology consumer unaware? The unconscious consumers tend to make sterile and passive use of technology**. They neither question the how nor the why. I am not only referring to the consumers of those technologies that, based on data analysis, derive a pattern and identify the user's next move (making users move from an application that determines your look-alike cat to an application where facial recognition is used to operate Animojis). Yet, I am referring to entrepreneurs who legitimately rely on the first two categories to create technologies without much purpose or awareness, without granting a reason (I repeat, legitimately) other than a financial return for their creation.
- One example: not Spot, the Boston Dynamics dog robot that will help Italian authorities monitor the ruins of archaeological sites, but Lovot, a domestic robot designed only to "be loved."
- *The Enlightened Ultra-Humans*
- The enlightened ultra-humans are those who, **while ignoring the how, incorporate the "why" into technologies**. They illuminate progress with ethical or cultural values. Despite its exponential growth, they bring out the **permanent structure** beneath all novelty. As technology surpasses its limits, it continually crashes with our own **human limits**. Ethical questions have become so relevant when considering A.I. that philosophy graduates in the U.S.A. take up leadership positions in artificial intelligence companies. It is one of the ways to illuminate innovation with a touch of humanity.
- Take **cultural value** as an example. Consider the choice of major museums to create virtual replicas in the Metaverse to allow a global audience to enjoy their cultural heritage. But also, in a minor way, consider an Art History professor who decides to bring his pupils virtually to the British Museum or the Vatican Museums. Accordingly, through an A.I., the Google Arts & Culture platform provides free access to the masterpieces of major museums worldwide (among others, the Uffizi Gallery in Florence, the Guggenheim in Bilbao or New York, the Musée d'Orsay in Paris, the National Gallery in London, and MOMA in New York).
- Let us now consider Netflix's mechanism known as ***transfer learning***: through an AI that assesses metadata and differentiated parameters, it can determine and target the final audience preferences. However, this powerful tool is not only used for commercial motivations. Making viewable shows tailored to specific markets and targets has enabled Netflix to create a relevant impact on fields that do not solely pertain to the entertainment ecosystem. Consider, for example, the action wielded by T.V. series on sustainable tourism or on social, historical, or cultural issues.[4] In the technological revolution age, by applying

[4]Disal Consulting, *Cultural Affinity and Screen Tourism—The Case of Internet Entertainment Services*, World Tourism Organization (UNWTO) and Netflix, Madrid, 2021. https://www.ministeroturismo.gov.it/wp-content/uploads/2021/10/NETFLIX-AND-WTO-ON-SCREEN--TOURISM.pdf.

innovative[5] storytelling strategies (like others that draw on the literature—such as the nineteenth-century self-made man) and by telling stories about reality, which then affect our reality, Netflix represents a quintessential model of the resilience of humanism in the digital.

- Another example of **harmony between innovation and tradition** is undoubtedly the project applied to the **Arch of Peace in Milan, the first monument to enter the Metaverse**. Reasoned Art, an Italian startup, transformed the Arch into an *architectural data sculpture* with the collaboration of Ouchhh (a multidisciplinary studio in Istanbul that specializes in creating immersive artworks). Through an A.I. system capable of reprocessing 20,000 artworks by more than 320 artists related to different artistic movements, images of Italy's artistic history, annual data from the map of the Italian firmament (collected by Nasa) and the entire 1700 years of Italian literary heritage were digitally projected onto the monument.
- The Peace Arch was then turned into an NFT and marketed to fund the creation of an educational area on digital art, science, and technology and subsidize scholarships to benefit young artists.
- **Indeed, a comprehensive effort that, starting from reality, infers through technology to return to reality**.
- Like in the case of a great initiative by Damien Hirst – an artist, not a technician. He created ten thousand polka-dot-decorated carts, seemingly identical to each other. The only difference was a watermark with an embedded hologram, making the cards extremely tough to counterfeit, just like banknotes. In addition, ten thousand corresponding NFTs were minted, one for each physical work. The author placed these NFTs on sale starting July 14, 2021, with the emblematical title "The Currency Project". At the one-year mark from the auction closing, each buyer would have to decide whether to take possession of the physical work, the tenner (that is how each painting is named, like a £10 note) or to own its corresponding NFT. Whichever the buyer chose, the other option would be destroyed. **July 27, 2022, served as a seismograph for understanding the impact of NFTs, the metaverse and the AI-related implications for the art world, showing, more broadly, a snapshot of the ongoing technological revolution**. By the latest count, the numbers favor NFTs: 5713 collectors chose tokens, and 4219 preferred physical artworks.

Yet, the now-recorded revolution was already fully underway as, on August 23, 2021, the project made a stunning **$25 million** in sales (a figure publicly reported by the artist on his Instagram profile). By drawing the silhouette of his famous formaldehyde shark on a sales trend chart, Hirst commented: "Just when you thought it

[5] R. Vogels, *Netflix Has Changed Storytelling. What Brands Can Learn From It*, in «Forbes», August 2019, https://www.forbes.com/sites/rebeccavogels/2019/08/09/netflix-has-changed-storytelling-what-brands-can-learn-from-it/?sh=e81e9567030d.

was safe to go back in the water." Such "cultural" NFTs could even represent an alternative "currency." Quoting Joe Hage, founder of the Heni Group, which also represents Hirst: "It is often said that money corrupts art, but this (not only referring to The Currency Project but, potentially, to any similar arrangement between culture and the Metaverse) **is an attempt by art to corrupt money**."

As noted, this artistic project, acting and unfolding in the realm of technology, has engaged the individual with ethical questions, always active when it comes to assigning economic value to material or immaterial elements, and (dare I say it) philosophical and social ones.

Again, this is a comprehensive action that, by traversing technology and using it as an epistemological tool, acts on reality to bring out issues on humanity.

In short, **if we do not know the whys, we do not have a chance to be artisans of the how**. **Technology** can be compared to the **ocean's depth, which remains placid when supported by our values and humanity, no matter how rough the surface**.

But let's face it: when faced with this sight, it is impossible not to feel dizzy. **Our productivity is safe, but our employment is unstable, in whatever category we belong**. These are not pessimistic views but a rational analysis of reality. Due to machine developments, even **hyper-specialization and job-specific skills will soon become obsolete**. **But human-specific skills never will (and history teaches this)**.

Creators of disenchantment, designers of simplicity, enchanters: anyone faced with the gradual imposition of A.I. in the professional world must **believe in human values**; on what is commonly referred to as **soft skills**.

1. *Creativity (but Outside the Box).*

   Artificial intelligence can also be creative. But creativity becomes a uniquely human element if driven by **motivation, intent, desire, flair** ... even if tainted by "**imperfection**."
2. *Abstract and Critical Thinking.*

   Learning is not only about being equipped with a filter for recognizing individual forms (by now, A.I. has managed to overcome even the stumbling hurdle of pixel recombination). However, it is about gradually constructing an **abstract model of the world to which we can trace our knowledge**, refer to general **concepts and principles, and, on them, develop critical thinking**.

   Training these skills (mind you, they are not innate) means asserting one's role in debates, identifying logical errors, and managing change.
3. *Communication Skills.*

   There is something A.I. cannot do. **It cannot share an experience or idea and cannot learn and grow from a dialogue with the other**. **Thus, it cannot create knowledge by drawing on others' knowledge**.

   Emotional intelligence, the development of sociability, the management of conflict, the spirit of collaboration, and the ability to listen and be heard are some of the skills currently most in demand in the professional world.

4. *Managing Complexity (Not Data Complexity).*

   We, humans, know how to grasp the **principle of non-contradiction**, according to which it is impossible for the same thing, at the same time, to be and not to be (a cookie is a cookie). Of course, machines know how to do this, too. Yet, humans can also **refuse it**: the cookie I had for breakfast can become, at the exact moment, by its smell and taste, the cookie my nanny gave me on the sly when I was seven years old.

   This is, and will remain, a human-only language, understandable only among humans. However, in the professional world (and beyond), it will be increasingly necessary to develop the ability to grasp what lies behind logic. How? **By educating ourselves in sensitivity and empathy**.

5. *Construction and Deconstruction of Truths.*

   If you are over 30 or slightly younger, you surely remember at least one cell phone or telephone number **by heart**. You can even wish your friends a happy birthday without receiving prior notifications.

   And if you are a **digital native**? These skills are almost nonexistent, or at least rare, for you: you have consistently **been storing numbers, events, and facts outside your mind**.

   And gradually, **we have learned to do so as well**.

The digital facilitates our lives, taking on the burden of thinking, speaking, and acting for us. Nevertheless, memory is the function that towers among the human processes assigned to machines. Hence, today **memory is delegated to external devices, intangible archives, and search engines**.

These comfortable technologies are not condemnable, nor is simplicity certainly. But, it must be admitted that **erasing the obstacles that separate our thoughts from our goals can cause critical consequences**.

Complexity, as I mentioned, is an invaluable opportunity because it is directly proportional to the **development of our cognitive abilities**.

Not long ago, a person told me that as a child, in the absence of someone to explain the meaning of words and things, she would sneak into a room in her house to consult the Treccani Encyclopedia. The time it took to reach her goal of knowledge was related to a physical displacement, handling the unexpected (the diktat was playing, not learning), and the effort to understand. Currently, believe me, she is a woman with remarkable mnemonic abilities.

A more immediate example? The use of the GPS has considerably reduced our orientation ability. With the removal of obstacles, the memory of the route and destination has also been removed.

In short, we now know that the **human brain is plastic**, continuously moldable, and **reconfigurable** based on neuron activity and experience, which enhances some connections while erasing others. And we are therefore forced to see that **technologies have caused us to underutilize various cognitive functions**, transforming our learning modes, limiting our ability to **concentrate**, and, in particular, significantly reducing our **mnemonic** ability.

Today, electronic devices respond to any of our demands, solving all kinds of complications in a matter of seconds. If before, time, displacement, and dedication were indispensable to fulfilling a need, **now everything (news, products, and data) reaches us without the need to make any kind of effort other than moving a finger on a screen or keyboard**.

Do we have a doubt? There's Wikipedia or, for the more meticulous, the online Treccani. We tend, however, to gratify our passing curiosity or, perhaps, simply our information anxiety, to read only an introductory blurb, the first three lines of the explanation. We no longer challenge our brains. And therefore, **ease of reference makes the sedimentation of memory and learning less effective:** we forget, often (think about it), even after a few minutes, anything that is easy to retrieve without any effort, at any time, and in a few moments.

Any information retrieved passively or too quickly does not create a solid memory. **Our cognitive movement now floats on the surface**: our minds rarely move vertically, in-depth, jumping from one piece of information to another, the shortest, the most incisive, the simplest. Instagram and Twitter have even taught us how to shape how we process thoughts: less is more. Yes, but not for the brain, which gets accustomed to impatience and immediacy because of the extensive use of simplification. *We want to know everything immediately: here is the consultation without the in-depth study; here is the first news, even if it is a piece of fake news, without the necessary verification.*

What is the **solution** to this amnesia (which, I am sure, is not irreversible)?

By now, technology is so much a part of our existence that it would be absurd (and also quite harmful, especially in terms of social purposes) to give it up in an attempt to regain our former abilities.

The circumstances of our existence change along with our mnemonic and cognitive strategies. Yet, think about it, we have always externalized memory. Initially, through the **voice**: we memorized everything, declaiming it so the whole community could remember it. Later, through **books**, copied by hand and then printed, which became custodians of memory outside our bodies, remembering for us. Finally, through the digital, an infinite and infinitely accessible hard disk where the capacity we have gradually deprived ourselves of is stored. So, it is just a matter of knowing how to handle the new mnemonic media. It has to be a **support for our curiosity and not a substitute for our brain**.

We need to educate ourselves on a **new kind of memory**.

Faced with the enormous flow of information that reigns in the digital world, it is now necessary to **filter, which is the only action that allows one to reason and, consequently, memorize. Distinguishing the false from the true, seeking truths (and not the Truth), moving vertically, moving beyond distortions, and deconstructing falsehoods allow us to silence the song of these new sirens that drive people to forget**. In a word, we need to **understand**.

If we think about it, this is exactly what our school teachers asked us to do before we learned a poem by heart. In order to remember it, we first needed to understand it.

Heidegger mentioned the "**calculating thought**" as the tendency to reduce everything to calculability, the attitude of reckoning, keeping it in account, and putting it into account. There is, however, a "**meditating thought**" that is irreducible to any aseptic calculation. It is a thought that goes beyond indistinct and indefinite territories, allowing us to access meanings impenetrable by "calculating thought." Both are two ways of exercising reason, but the latter enables us to **reflect on reality and its purpose**. And the latter is a skill-also to be developed-that will always be sought. Everywhere.

Artificial intelligence can work in every direction except that of consciousness. It is this that, first and foremost, we must equip ourselves with to be truly irreplaceable.

Augmented Humanistic Leadership: A New Framework for Leaders' Tools in the Age of Artificial Intelligence

Maurizio Prete, Edoardo Degli Innocenti, Francesco Ottoboni, and Marco Tasca

Abstract Augmented humanistic leadership (AHL) leverages advanced AI technologies to enhance leadership effectiveness by integrating humanistic values. This chapter explores how AI can support leaders in developing empathy, adaptability, and ethical standards, crucial for navigating the complexities of modern business environments. AHL focuses on creating leaders who can inspire and guide diverse teams by incorporating AI-driven insights and feedback into their decision-making processes. By aligning AI tools with humanistic principles, leaders can enhance their ability to manage emotional and relational dynamics, ensuring a more inclusive and ethical approach to leadership. This new framework aims to address the gaps in traditional leadership development, fostering leaders who can thrive in multicultural and rapidly changing contexts.

1 Introduction

In this chapter, the authors are exploring the topic of augmented humanistic leadership: the leverage of newly developed technologies in the field of generative artificial intelligence in order to help leaders develop the experience of humanistic leadership. A form of leadership that can respond to the new needs of sustainable and responsible capitalism and propose innovative solutions in the leadership

M. Prete
Fondazione Miticoro, Milan, Italy
e-mail: maurizio.prete@miticoro.com

E. Degli Innocenti (✉) · F. Ottoboni · M. Tasca
B3YOND, Milan, Italy
e-mail: edoardo.degliinnocenti@b3yond.io; francesco.ottoboni@b3yond.io; marco.tasca@b3yond.io

G. R. Marseglia et al. (eds.), *Socio-economic Impact of Artificial Intelligence*, Progress in IS, https://doi.org/10.1007/978-3-031-73514-1_17

development industry, which in over 70 years of research continues to see poor results in developing leaders for organisations.[1]

Being a leader has different meanings in different cultures. It is really important to understand what are the common characteristics of good leaders integrating their culture or studies and how generative artificial intelligence can help managers and entrepreneurs become good humanistic leaders. At the heart of humanistic leadership lies a strong foundation of values which resonates deeply within an organisation, earning the approval of other employees who see their own values reflected in their leader.

This type of leadership extends beyond mere direction or strategic decision-making; instead, it focuses on fostering an environment where shared values are at the core of business operations. A humanistic leader embodies these values authentically and consistently, not just setting an example to follow but also serving as a source of inspiration for others.

Nowadays, 83% of companies recognize the importance of cultivating leaders at every level, yet fewer than 5% have effectively rolled out leadership development initiatives across the board. Recent survey findings highlight a concerning succession planning crisis within numerous companies, pointing to a clear deficiency in preparing individuals for leadership roles. Half of the survey participants reported a lack of adequate leadership talent within their organisations, and 47% anticipate a future shortfall in leadership or executive-level skills.[2]

If a generative artificial intelligence (Gen-AI) or, generally speaking, an artificial intelligence (AI) model is aligned with the principles of humanistic leadership, it can significantly support a leader in their daily tasks. This alignment allows the AI to operate not just as a tool for efficiency but as an extension that suggests the humanistic values that drive the organisation. The use of natural language processing (NLP) is key in this context. NLP enables AI to understand and generate human language in a way which is both meaningful and contextually appropriate. This capability allows the AI to interact naturally with team members' input, recognizing nuances in communication that might indicate morale issues, misunderstandings, or opportunities for encouragement. By integrating such an AI into daily operations, a leader can effectively monitor and respond to the emotional and relational dynamics of their team.

2 From Humanistic Leadership to Augmented Humanistic Leadership

As organisational leadership evolves, augmented humanistic leadership (AHL) represents a new transition towards integrating advanced technological tools with humanistic values. Taking into consideration all the values which should characterise a humanistic approach to leadership and taking into account the new tools

[1] *Deloitte (2017), High-Impact Leadership*, https://www2.deloitte.com/content/dam/Deloitte/ca/Documents/audit/ca-audit-abm-scotia-high-impact-leadership.pdf

[2] *Association for Talent Development (2018)*, https://www.td.org/press-release/83-percent-of-organizations-have-skills-gaps-according-to-atd-research

offered by technological advances such as AI, the chapter explores the concept of AHL.

Since artificial intelligence is able to influence human minds and instil biases, AI can be used to correct human biases in the same way. An AI system can be designed to provide feedback and corrections when it detects behaviours or decisions that may be influenced by biases.[3] For example, a virtual assistant system could intervene if it detects that a user is using discriminatory language or if they are making decisions that favour certain groups at the expense of others.

Therefore, it is important to start from a common definition of leadership, to train and align an AI model starting from the good principles of leadership, a universally acknowledged determinant of organisational success, which varies significantly across cultural landscapes. There are diverse definitions and perceptions of leadership globally, so one of the main questions this chapter is trying to answer is: What are the universal characteristics that distinguish good leaders from bad ones? There's not a single answer since good leaders appear to be different from culture to culture.

In individualistic contexts, as in the United States, Canada, and the United Kingdom, the leader is generally a single person who manages and directs the actions of others, often overtly. In contrast, in collectivist societies, as in Korea, Japan, and China, the concept of leadership is less tied to the individual figure and more oriented towards group efforts. In hierarchical societies, as in Saudi Arabia, Mexico, and Indonesia, leaders are perceived as separate and distinct figures from their followers. In more egalitarian societies, such as in Sweden and Denmark, leaders are seen as more accessible and less intimidating. Moreover, while in Anglo-American culture, there is a tendency to often celebrate the successes of leaders, in other cultures, the best leader is one who operates unobtrusively, influencing events without emerging too prominently and allowing people to feel the successes as their own.[4]

However, despite cultural differences, there are certain traits which consistently mark effective leadership. Integrity and ethical conduct are foundational across all cultures, even though the specifics may vary by geography. Similarly, empathy and emotional intelligence are critical, as the ability to understand and respond to the emotions of others is vital for effective leadership in any cultural setting. Moreover, successful leaders demonstrate adaptability and resilience, showing an ability to manage change and overcome adversity while staying committed to their vision and their teams.

This complexity underscores the difficulty of being a good leader in a multicultural environment, opening the door to challenges and opportunities for global organisations. The diversity of leadership perception presents a unique challenge, requiring leaders who can adapt their approach to different cultural expectations

---

[3] *Leslie Ramos Salazar, Shanna Peeples, Mary Elizabeth Brooks (2024), Generative AI Ethical Considerations and Discriminatory Biases on Diverse Students Within the Classroom, The Role of Generative AI in the Communication Classroom (191–213).*

[4] *Carlos Sanchez-Runde, Luciara Nardon, Richard M. Steers (2012), Looking beyond Western leadership models: Implications for global managers, Organisational Dynamics (40, 207–213).*

while maintaining their core values. Understanding the diverse global perceptions of leadership, especially when we are talking about managers and entrepreneurs embedded in multinational and high-complexity contexts, and especially the common traits that identify a good leader, is critical to developing effective leaders. This applies not only in their specific contexts and with their people but also in changing and multicultural scenarios, where a humanistic view of relationships can be the right key to overcoming challenges and achieving desired results.

Indeed, leadership effectiveness is often measured by a leader's ability to inspire, influence, and guide individuals and groups towards the achievement of common goals. However, as mentioned earlier, the perception and practice of effective leadership varies significantly in different cultural contexts.

Below, an analysis is conducted to identify the common traits of a good leader as shared in the main meanings and across different cultures.

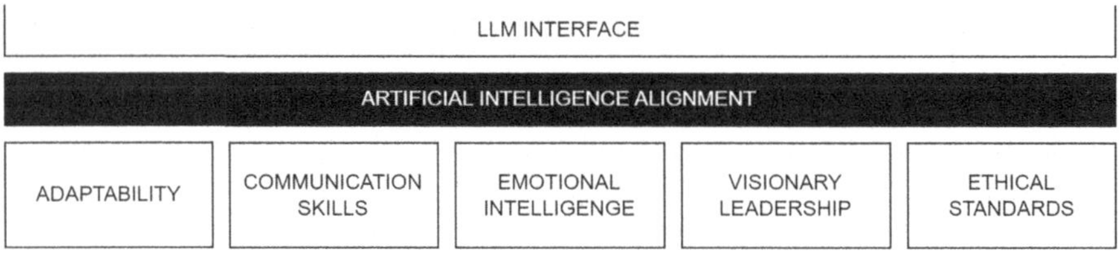

Embedding common traits of the good leader shared in the main meanings and in different cultures into the AI alignment process. Accessed via the LLM interface.

1. *Adaptability*

Adaptability is essential for effective leadership, particularly in global business environment where cultural diversity is prevalent. Leaders who demonstrate high adaptability skilfully navigate through cultural complexities by tailoring their strategies and behaviours to match the specific cultural contexts of their employees and stakeholders. Adaptability is crucial not only for fostering an environment of mutual respect and understanding but also for enhancing the leader's ability to effectively manage and lead diverse teams across various geographical locations.

In corporate settings, adaptable leaders are proficient at adjusting business models and marketing strategies to resonate with local markets. They leverage cultural insights to enhance product acceptance and drive local engagement, thus increasing market penetration and competitive advantage. Furthermore, in multinational corporations, adaptable leaders play a pivotal role in merging different corporate cultures during acquisitions and mergers. They ensure smooth transitions by addressing cultural discrepancies, which in turn minimises employee turnover and maximises organisational synergy.

2. *Communication Skills*

Effective communication is crucial for leadership success, especially in global business environments where cultural differences can create barriers. Leaders who adeptly adjust their communication style to fit the cultural and linguistic preferences of their audience are more successful at conveying strategic visions and motivating diverse teams. This skill is particularly important in multinational corporations where messages need to be culturally sensitive and clear across different regions. These leaders excel during organisational changes such as mergers or market expansions, as they can address various stakeholders' concerns and facilitate smoother transitions. They also choose communication methods and platforms that resonate with specific cultural norms, whether it involves formal settings or more casual, collaborative approaches. By mastering culturally sensitive communication, leaders enhance their ability to inspire action and leverage cultural diversity as a strategic asset for achieving global organisational success.

3. *Emotional Intelligence*

Emotional intelligence (EI) is essential for leadership, focusing on key skills such as self-awareness, empathy, and relationship management. Leaders with high EI are capable of understanding both their own emotions and those of their team members, fostering trust and rapport. This deep level of empathy helps in building strong, cohesive teams by acknowledging and valuing each team member's personal background and experiences.

Such leaders excel in managing relationships, customising their communication and interaction methods to effectively address individual needs and dynamics within the team. They implement inclusive practices like regular feedback sessions and team-building activities that value diverse perspectives, thereby enhancing team cohesion and motivation. By promoting an environment where all members feel respected and appreciated, emotionally intelligent leaders enhance overall team performance and organisational success.

4. *Visionary Leadership*

The ability to articulate a clear and compelling vision is fundamental for effective leadership. Visionary leaders inspire their teams by focusing on shared goals that transcend individual differences, creating a sense of unity and purpose. These leaders are adept at communicating their vision in ways that motivate and engage all team members, aligning diverse perspectives towards common objectives. This capability not only energises the team but also drives collective success, making it essential for sustained organisational achievement.

5. *Ethical Standards*

A commitment to high ethical standards and integrity is crucial for effective leadership. Leaders who focus on ethics and transparency naturally build trust and credibility, which are essential for leadership effectiveness. By consistently adhering to ethical principles and maintaining transparency in their actions, these leaders foster an environment of openness and accountability. This approach enhances team morale, promotes open communication, and strengthens the overall integrity of the organisation, leading to improved performance and sustained success across any setting.

Starting from these almost universally recognized principles concerning the figure of the good leader, we can approach and better define what is meant by humanistic leadership.

A conception of leadership that puts human beings at the centre is certainly not innovative and the result of recent thinking alone; this view has often been the subject of criticism, contrasting adherence to certain values and ethics in doing business, with obtaining mere economic results that could be maximised by adopting more traditional and more "despotic" models of leadership.

Humanistic leadership, on the other hand, places ethical and behavioural aspects alongside techno-economic rules. The figure of the leader thus becomes the custodian of a social contract, in which the leader, precisely, takes upon himself the duty to guide, represent, and defend the interests of an entire community, which is nothing other than the company, which entrusts him with the power to command.

The synallagmatic relationship, however, is not only inward, that is to the organisation, the leaders also act outwards, since, on the one hand, they exploit resources of the territory, such as space, raw materials, etc., and, on the other hand, they give back through the business activity a value, for example territory valorisation, economic resources in the form of taxes, and employment for the population.[5]

3 A New AI framework for Leadership

The chapter provides an overview of how AI technologies are being integrated into leadership development programs, reshaping traditional methodologies and offering innovative approaches to cultivate effective leaders.

Leadership training has traditionally relied on classroom-based instruction, case studies, and experiential learning. However, the integration of AI technologies has introduced a paradigm shift, enabling personalised learning experiences, real-time feedback, and scenario-based simulations that closely mimic real-world challenges. AI algorithms can analyse individual learning styles, preferences, and performance to tailor training programmes to the specific needs of each leader. This personalization enhances learning outcomes by focusing on areas of improvement and accelerating the development process.

[5] *Maurizio Prete* (2024), *Managerially incorrect, Miticoro (5–12).*

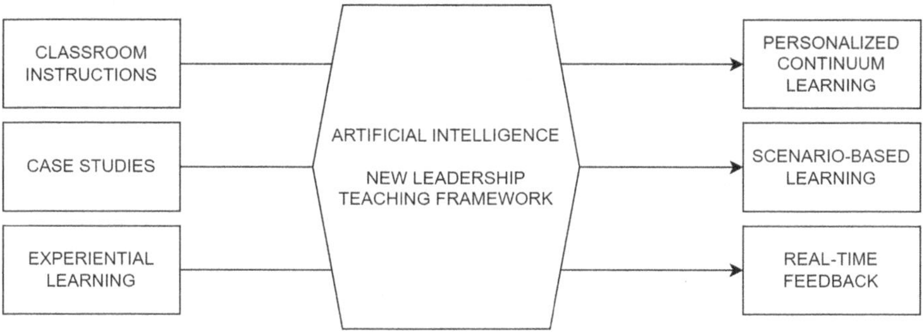

A new set of learning tools and methodologies are enabled by the usage of Artificial Intelligence (LLM)

AI technologies can foster the growth of leaders who are more agile, emotionally intelligent, and prepared to face the complexities of the modern business world.

Starting from the premise that leadership qualities, besides depending on factors such as disposition, personality, and the propensity for debate and risk-taking, can be trained and refined over time and experience, it is not difficult to argue that the use of AI tools can accelerate and facilitate this process.

Take adaptability, for instance, a trait commonly recognized as a hallmark of good leadership across many different cultures. We know that adapting to changing contexts requires a great deal of intelligence and a broad knowledge, among other things, of different cultures and the various stages of economic cycles. In this context, the use of AI tools can aid and stimulate the leader in analysis.

AI can be used to analyse the general situation or a specific problem, suggesting a wide range of different viewpoints and even incorporating the perspectives and approaches of cultures far removed from our own. In this way, AI can assist leaders in decision making and, importantly, it does not replace human reason in the development of critical thinking or decision making, but rather provides a range of insights, considerations, and points of view that might elude even the most careful leaders. AI, thus, becomes an extra arrow in the bow of the manager, entrepreneur, or head of state, not a conditio sine qua non in the exercise of decision-making but a valuable aid in situations of particular complexity.

Of course, there arises a problem that technological development must seek to address: the consideration that AI is trained on data and inputs that are almost exclusively human. For example, one of the primary methods of training AI involves the classification and evaluation of outputs from the machine by real people. For this reason, AI could be influenced by biases instilled by human behaviour and inputs. Consequently, uncritically relying on what is provided by artificial intelligence is risky as it could influence the user with biases or prejudices that the individual might not possess.

On the other hand, if technological progress succeeds in eliminating this background noise, the use of AI itself could become a useful tool in eliminating unhealthy biases and misconceptions that are not in line with a type of leadership that prioritises individual and ethical values above mere economic outcomes.

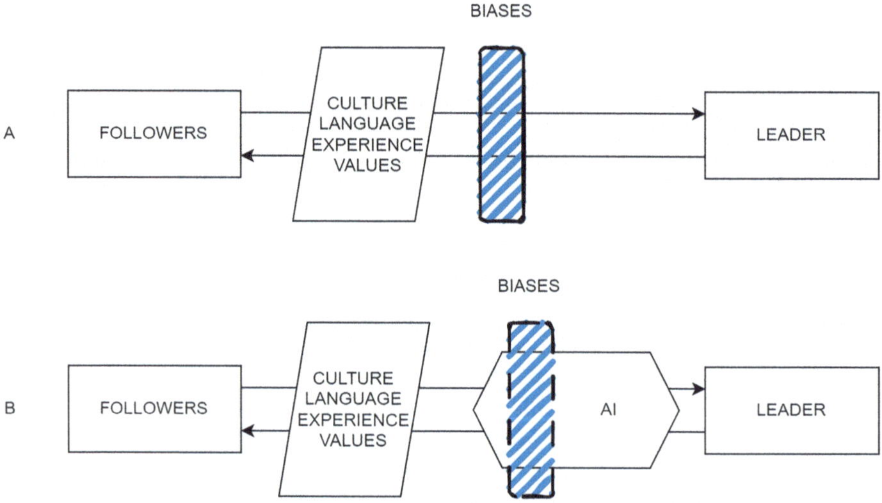

The relationship between followers and leaders is constantly mediated by language, values, experience, and culture. in A) only direct communication with biases is considered. While in B) also an IA layer is mediating the communication between followers and the leader, correcting biases

4 Conclusions

The significant role artificial intelligence plays in enhancing human decision-making in leadership roles, particularly within the context of humanistic leadership, is undoubted.[6] AI is increasingly being used as a tool to support leaders in their daily tasks by aligning with humanistic values and providing real-time feedback and scenario-based decision-making aids. This integration helps in two major ways: faster decision-making and reducing human cognitive biases.

AI enhances leadership effectiveness by speeding up the decision-making process. It accomplishes this through the use of advanced data analysis and predictive modelling, which allows leaders to make informed decisions quickly and efficiently. This is especially crucial in environments where timely responses can significantly impact organisational outcomes. On the other side, correctly aligned AI can be designed to identify and correct human biases.

By using natural language processing (NLP) and other AI technologies, the systems can detect and intervene when decisions or behaviours are potentially biased.

[6] *Muhammad Balbaa, Marina Abdurashidova (2024), The Impact of Artificial Intelligence in Decision Making: A Comprehensive Review, EPRA International Journal of Economics Business and Management Studies – 11(2):27–38.*

This capability is vital in promoting fairness and objectivity in leadership decisions, leading to more equitable and just outcomes.

The augmentation of leadership with AI does not merely make leadership more efficient, but also more aligned with ethical standards and humanistic values if a strong and correct alignment on the model is performed. This alignment is crucial for cultivating leaders who not only drive organisational success but also foster an environment of trust, ethical behaviour, and mutual respect among all stakeholders.

References

Association for Talent Development. (2018). https://www.td.org/press-release/83-percent-of-organizations-have-skills-gaps-according-to-atd-research

Balbaa, M., & Abdurashidova, M. (2024). The impact of artificial intelligence in decision making: A comprehensive review. *EPRA International Journal of Economics Business and Management Studies, 11*(2), 27–38.

Deloitte. (2017). *High-impact leadership*. https://www2.deloitte.com/content/dam/Deloitte/ca/Documents/audit/ca-audit-abm-scotia-high-impact-leadership.pdf

Prete, M. (2024). Managerially incorrect. *Miticoro*, 5–12.

Salazar, L. R., Peeples, S., & Brooks, M. E. (2024). Generative AI ethical considerations and discriminatory biases on diverse students within the classroom. In *The role of generative AI in the communication classroom* (pp. 191–213).

Sanchez-Runde, C., Nardon, L., & Steers, R. M. (2012). Looking beyond Western leadership models: Implications for global managers. *Organisational Dynamics, 40*, 207–213.

AI and Strategy: How New Tools Can Boost the Evolution of Strategic Decision-Making

Andrea Piazzoli

Abstract Artificial intelligence (AI) is revolutionising strategic decision-making by introducing new tools that enhance efficacy and accuracy of predictions. This chapter examines the historical evolution of strategy, from ancient military tactics to modern business strategies, highlighting how AI's capabilities align with strategic needs. It explores AI's role in predictive modeling, scenario analysis, and optimisation, which provide data-driven insights for better decision-making. The chapter also discusses the ethical considerations and potential biases in AI applications, emphasising the importance of responsible AI use. It concludes by advocating for a skills-based approach to AI integration, ensuring that strategic decisions are informed by both advanced tools and human judgment.

1 Introduction

In the last 2 years, with the commodification of generative AI tools to everyone, how people think about strategic decision-making changed significantly. The habits in literature were about a theory-driven approach or a data-driven approach, and now there is also an AI approach to finding suitable answers to our questions. With the distributed cognition concept (Sloman & Fernbach, 2017), it's known that tools and cultural artefacts are relevant in shaping human thinking, and it's too early to guess the impact that AI tools will have on people. Luckily, with a theory-driven approach, it's possible to attempt to foresee the impact on people, based on some psychological constructs. This chapter want to explore AI's role in shaping strategic thinking

A. Piazzoli (✉)
Università degli Studi di Firenze, Florence, Italy

Università degli Studi di Siena, Siena, Italy

Università degli Studi di Pisa, Pisa, Italy

Scuola Superiore Sant'Anna, Pisa, Italy
e-mail: andrea.piazzoli@santannapisa.it

G. R. Marseglia et al. (eds.), *Socio-economic Impact of Artificial Intelligence*, Progress in IS, https://doi.org/10.1007/978-3-031-73514-1_18

and provide a structured approach to discussing AI and strategy in a scientific context, covering foundational concepts, technological applications, ethical considerations, and prospects between these two fields of study. First, it is needed to explain and connect definitions of strategic decision-making and AI. Since the concept of strategy comes first, the script will start with its history and then introduce the concept of AI and understand the relationship between them.

2 History of Strategic Decision-Making

It is possible to distinguish between some phases in the development of strategic decision-making through history (Freedman, 2013). These phases provide valuable insights into how the strategies have evolved and the principles that continue to shape contemporary strategy approaches. One of the earliest known works on strategy is *The Art of War* by Sun Tzu, written in ancient China. This classic text emphasises the importance of careful planning, understanding of the terrain, and intelligence to achieve strategic objectives. Concepts such as "know yourself and know your enemy" highlight the importance of self-awareness and competitive analysis. By this text, it can be seen how people in the past approached the word strategy in an experts-based approach. To extend the concept to other cultures, also the Greeks and Romans developed sophisticated military tactics based on discipline, organisation, and logistical planning. The concepts of dividing, conquering, and exploiting weaknesses in opponents' positions reflect strategic thinking that has relevance beyond the battlefield. Leaders such as Alexander the Great exemplified strategic brilliance by combining military prowess with diplomatic cunning to expand their empires. Strategies and tactics developed by wise people continued their influence until present days. Sun Tzu's principles of flexibility, deception, and adaptation to changing circumstances remain influential in both military and business strategy today. Ancient historical perspectives on strategic decision-making highlight the enduring principles of adaptation, innovation, and calculated risk-taking that have shaped the course of human endeavours across military, business, and diplomatic domains. Studying these historical insights provides valuable lessons for complex challenges in today's rapidly changing world. In a more modern era, the pace of the changes in strategy increased exponentially. The Industrial Revolution brought about a shift in strategic thinking with the rise of capitalism and industrialization. Business leaders applied strategic principles to build vast empires through vertical integration, cost efficiency, and market dominance. Economics theorists introduced scientific management principles, emphasising efficiency, specialisation, and systematic approaches to organisational management (Nickerson & Argyres, 2018). The development of the scientific method and the accumulation of knowledge and wealth grow with the complexity of the global system. In this period, a more data-based approach emerged, less focused on the wisest man or ancient text in search of wisdom. World War II marked a pivotal moment in strategic decision-making, with military leaders employing innovative tactics such as blitzkrieg, amphibious assaults, and strategic bombing. This pushed the idea that technological progress and mastery of technology will be one of the most important aspects of future conflicts. The war also spurred advancements in operations research and game theory, leading to the development of decision-making frameworks that integrated quantitative analysis with strategic planning (mixing the theory-driven and a data-driven approach). Similarly, the Cold War introduced game theory as a tool for strategic decision-making, notably through the work of scholars such as John von Neumann and Oskar Morgenstern. Game theory provided insights into competitive interactions and the rational behaviour of adversaries. Deterrence strategies exemplified the application of game theory principles to international relations and diplomacy during this period. The Information Age and extreme globalization brought new challenges and opportunities for strategic decision-makers. Concepts such as Porter's "Five Forces" and Mintzberg's "Emergent Strategies" guided organisations through the complexity of this time (Ward et al., 2007). Technological advancements enabled real-time data analysis and transformed marketing strategies and customer relations. As it is possible to see in this process of development and evolution of strategic decision-making, it is possible to say that accuracy has progressively increased along with complexity. In every historical phase, it is possible to find new insights to improve the probability of ensuring victory or gaining competitive advantages. In contemporary challenges, the process is not as linear as in the past, but it will be possible to see it after a brief introduction to AI classifications and strategy definitions.

3 Introduction to AI

Artificial intelligence refers to the capability of machines to exhibit human-like intelligence, including learning, reasoning, problem-solving, perception, language understanding, and decision-making. AI systems are designed to analyse vast amounts of data, recognise patterns, and make predictions or decisions to give insights (Jackson & Brownie, 1992). Different types of artificial intelligence can be categorised as Narrow, General, or Super. Narrow AI (or Weak AI) is designed to perform a specific, narrow task, such as facial recognition, internet searches, or driving a car. Narrow AI systems operate within a limited, pre-defined range and cannot learn or perform tasks outside their specialised domain. General AI (or Strong AI) represents a hypothetical future form of AI which has human-like cognitive capabilities (Gupta et al., 2023). This kind of system would be able to autonomously tackle new and unfamiliar tasks without needing human guidance, demonstrating intelligence in a wide range of domains. This type of AI does not yet exist but is a long-term goal in research. Superintelligent AI is an advanced AI system which surpasses human intelligence and capabilities across all fields, including creativity, general wisdom, and problem-solving. The superintelligent type is still speculative and has not been achieved. In addition to this capability-based classification, AI can also be categorised by specific technologies used in it (Kaggwa et al., 2024). The most important systems are machine learning (ML), deep learning (DL), and NLP (natural language processing). Deep learning is an advanced form of machine learning which utilises multi-layered artificial neural networks to learn and perform tasks with high efficiency. Neural networks are the core technology underlying deep learning models. Machine learning is a broader field in which both deep learning and neural networks are subsets, with distinct characteristics and capabilities (Al-Surmi et al., 2022).

4 Introduction to Strategy

The main contexts in which strategy has assumed a dominant meaning and importance are war, economics, and gaming. Many definitions have proliferated in these fields.

By the basic dictionary definition: "*A strategy is the description of a long-term plan of action used to set and subsequently coordinate actions to achieve a predetermined goal. The strategy applies to all fields in which a series of separate operations are required to achieve the goal, the choice of which is not unique and/or the outcome of which is uncertain*" (Vocabolario Etimologico della Lingua Italiana).

The best way to understand strategy is to reconstruct its meaning from its essential requirements. In this way, it will be possible to construct a general and theoretical theory under which to unify this discipline. The reconstruction process just mentioned derives from the union of certain key concepts from the game theory's categories to ensure their formalisation within social sciences such as economics. The most useful and adherent definition can be summarised as *the description of a plan, in a long-term perspective, in the presence of conscious interaction* (Piazzoli et al., 2024). Speaking of the description of a plan, it's possible to say that it is a set of thoughts on what steps to take in a specific situation. Thus, there can be no strategy without at least two actors capable of planning. If there is only one actor (e.g. a person who makes a plan about his practice, like how to study a book), it makes sense to speak of a method and not of a strategy. A method is when someone have a better and more efficient way to achieve a goal *in the absence of* conscious opposition. Another relevant point is the size of a plan. If a person wants to win a single fight, it doesn't make sense to speak of strategy, as this is on too small a temporal and spatial scale and is much closer to pure technique or tactics. It is possible to talk about strategy only in the case of long-term goals, on a large scale, or involving higher-order planning than local interaction. This definition encompasses all the three fundamental factors derived from the definitions mentioned above: the actors, the plan, and the objective. Taken individually, these three elements possess characteristics that amplify potential studies on strategy. It is possible to focus on the characteristics of the actors and how these determine their actions, on the characteristics of the objectives and their formulation or on the part more related to decision-making and the characteristics of the plan. Any combination and characteristics of these elements in the interactions produce behaviours (more or less) capable of leading the individual actors to the desired outcomes. To give an example from psychology, if the strategy is formulated by a human being, it is subject to all the limitations and characteristics of thought. But what is essentially a thought? What are its characteristics, and how do they influence the successful execution of a plan? All these questions are part of strategy studies, despite being psychological in nature, as they extend our knowledge of the three basic elements that make it up. This definition of strategy, simpler than many others that try to go more into the specifics of meaning and significance, guides this work. No one can think of being a strategist if they do not master these three points, that is knowing how to formulate an attainable goal, knowing how human beings think and make decisions, and knowing how to formulate a plan; otherwise, it is not strategizing but simply in the mercy of external forces and passively suffering circumstances. People want to be active, not passive actors in the process called life. Actors, plans, and goals interact with each other, and the dynamics of their interaction can be further studied. A goal is modulated by the characteristics of the actor and their needs and is consequential to the plan. The plan is determined by the formulated goal and the actor's strengths or weaknesses. The actor's characteristics are tested by the plan and personality is configured around goals (human beings as teleological beings) (Lavazza, 2018). The mechanisms and processes governing these interactions are important in general strategy theory as they help to understand how and why certain actors act and make decisions and consequently to make useful predictions. To decide what moves to make and produce a plan, the ability to read reality in a way that is functional for making accurate predictions is essential. Taking cue from game theory, which is well suited as a mathematical formalisation of strategy, it's possible to say that any situation with rules and established goals is a game. Every game is a potential strategic situation, in which it is possible to apply the knowledge explained in this work. This strategy is a subject that aims at the ability to win in games, in all situations in which we can happen to be able to read the rules, and the objectives and over which actors have control or influence. Strategy, therefore, means planning, the ability to read and execute following reality, to optimise the use of resources and maximise the result. Indeed, strategy takes the form of a complex mode of attribution of meaning which makes it possible to identify better solutions, even simple in their implementation but difficult to identify without appropriate mental processes. When it is possible to refer to it as the description of a plan, the mean is precisely ability, acquired through experience, to create superstructures of meaning that can guide thoughts and actions towards victory in games or out of games. Indeed, cultural artefacts are embedded in strategic thinking and consequently decisions and outcomes; this is why it is needed to choose between different paths of using AI: more operational or more consultant.

5 The Psychological Impact of AI Strategies

What is strategy if not an emergent property of thought which can enable us to manage ever-increasing relational complexity? If contexts become increasingly complex and make it necessary for people to find new strategies to adapt, it is possible to observe a phenomenon called "emergent strategizing". This concept refers to the natural tendency to develop strategies in a population to adapt when complexity increases. This is a moment in history characterised by this increase in complexity. Yet, people are without effective strategies or the necessary skills to generate them, so stress rises and the ability to live peacefully is reduced. Constantly raising the standards of what needs to be learnt to perform certain tasks or exercise specific socially useful functions makes more people unable to adapt to change. There are two choices—change direction or learn to manage the one already taken as a society. If society continues to nurture progress and science exponentially without adequate human-based policies, more and more individuals will be left behind. A further example is the high degree of specialisation required from those who must determine the choices of others (so-called policy-makers) makes the world increasingly complex. The more complex a context is, the more people tend to devise solutions for those with the same approach as themself. Let's take the example of many computer engineers; they can handle enormous complexity when it comes to computer programming, but at the same time, they cannot easily create programmes suitable for the average person (Srinivasan & Chander, 2021). They basically assume that others think like them, projecting their own characteristics onto the society around them (which is why we need ergonomists to act as mediators). AI suggestions can be biased in the same way. *The human factor involved in making AI technologies tends to impact the solution which will be purposed by AI* (Kaggwa et al., 2024). This example shows how progress can be individual or social in a certain field of knowledge, but these two phenomena rarely have continuous and parallel development. The two forms of progress would develop in parallel, but unfortunately, despite our extraordinary learning abilities, we do not learn exponentially, and development is discontinuous. By "individual progress" I refer to a person's improvement in dealing with the complexity around him or her. This competence to advance does not necessarily lead to an actual improvement in "social well-being", which can also be defined as "social progress". I would add a third factor to this picture: scientific progress. The latter is exponential, while individual progress is slow and subject to our relatively stable personal traits, tending to be qualitative, domain-specific, and essentially subject to obsolescence. It will be difficult for individuals to keep up with scientific progress and an exponentially changing environment. This is one of the reasons which lead people to look for inadequate solutions. They try to avoid wasting cognitive resources on an unattainable task, namely to keep up with social change. As a result, people have more stress while social progress lags. Only those who can find adequate strategies tend to survive, while others accumulate problems. What can those who do not have the necessary resources do? Strategy can be exercised, but how much? All these questions are today without answers in the scientific community. In the Information Age, where can people place knowledge and its dissemination if not in the top rung of priorities? The human being is a complex system of interactions which builds within itself structures of memories which largely determine its higher functions (thoughts) and produce actions capable of modifying its environment and not having to continually adapt to it (Furniss et al., 2019). Thus, if people are primarily shaped by memories, the quality and usefulness of experiences which they have, which build knowledge, become the core of people destiny. Knowledge in all its shapes constitutes what people are and, most probably, what they will be. That is why knowledge is power, because it enables us to choose; it defines the field of the possible, the way of communicating and being, and the horizon of future success. Everything around humans is made up of knowledge, which is subdivided into humanity; in the specifics and memory of everyone it is possible to find a small piece of it and together form a complex mosaic. People live off what history and ancestors have laboriously erected for actual human well-being, passing on knowledge in a mostly implicit form. Human minds are subject to an incalculable series of processes that determine thoughts and outcomes, including the historical process of knowledge transmission between generations. In this picture, AI and other cultural artefacts will play a role that is difficult to foresee. So, science is only a tool which can help, but the problem lies in how people choose to use increasingly powerful means. Do people want to inscribe themselves in a horizon of social meaning while they manage to satisfy their basic needs or pursue ephemeral personal gain while damaging future generations? The meaning of knowledge lies in a greater potential for adaptation of man to the environment and of the environment to man through its means. It is an important task which humans must take on as a species (and not as a small-medium group) to mediate the use of our cognitive means and cultural artefacts to give them a social function. In this way, it's also possible to employ strategy as a tool for mastering complex interactions, managing problems, and resolving conflicts to direct social processes, towards a humanity capable of determining itself without destroying itself (Johnson, 2022). After this more general connotation of meaning, it is possible to understand how converging on strategy enables the production of useful knowledge to improve the quality of human interactions and decisions. Indeed, AI can be a good strategy for humanity to make better choices or a way to lose responsibility for the outcomes that people are making (Fosso Wamba et al., 2021).

6 The Emergence of AI in Strategy

The emergence of AI in strategic decision-making implied a radical shift (Al-Surmi et al., 2022). People who are decision-makers started progressively to trust the tools without a real understanding of the process. When it is not possible to see the process, the only way to evaluate the tool is by the results (or by the acceptability of the solutions). For example, early applications of AI in strategic contexts show the use of game theory during the Cold War and how it provided less aggressive, loss-avoidance responses. Today, asking similar questions of AI produces opposite solutions, often towards aggressive reactions with suggestions of using nuclear weapons. The inability to understand the reasoning or process which leads to these solutions and the progressive reliance on these tools could lead to worse outputs than expected in the short or medium term (Rastogi et al., 2022). The evolution of AI tools has also brought about several changes in how people plan. The increasing amount of data used to make decisions and the ever-increasing usability of the same has led to an ever-decreasing responsibility on the part of managers because no one takes responsibility for going against the data (Kaggwa et al., 2024). Data analysis and its role in strategic decision-making has therefore been progressively increasing and being incorporated into all areas of work, delegating and relying on AI to perform tasks which we previously performed intuitively (so you gain results with less control over the process). Predictive modelling and forecasting using artificial intelligence represent powerful application algorithms to analyse data and make informed predictions about future outcomes. In predictive modelling, AI algorithms are trained on historical data to learn the underlying patterns and relationships between inputs and the target outcomes (Aly, 2022). The goal is to develop a mathematical model that can accurately predict the target variable. Predictive modelling and forecasting using AI empower organizations to make data-driven decisions, anticipate future trends, and optimise business processes. By harnessing the power of AI algorithms, businesses can gain a competitive edge, mitigate risks, and capitalise on emerging opportunities in dynamic and complex environments (Price et al., 2018). This is particularly useful in scenarios where people don't have enough cognitive capabilities or trends are influenced by multiple factors. Indeed, AI-driven scenario analysis will represent essential tools in decision-making and strategic planning in the future. This approach leverages artificial intelligence to solve complex problems, optimise resource allocation, and evaluate alternative scenarios to inform strategic decisions. Optimisation techniques involve AI algorithms to find the best possible solution to a problem within a defined set of constraints. For example, these models can determine the most efficient routes for transportation, minimise inventory costs while meeting demand, and optimise production schedules to maximise profitability (Apsilyam et al., 2024). AI-driven scenario analysis involves simulations of numerous future scenarios with different assumptions and parameters. This technique helps decision-makers assess potential outcomes and risks associated with distinct courses of action. Also in finance, AI-powered "scenario analysis" can simulate market fluctuations, interest rate changes, or geopolitical events to evaluate the impact on investment portfolios and risk exposure (Trunk et al., 2020). By integrating optimisation techniques and "AI-driven scenario analysis", organizations can enhance their decision-making processes. In the case of performance improvement, AI optimisation algorithms continuously optimise operations based on real-time data, leading to improved efficiency, productivity, and customer satisfaction. Another case is the decision support system, in which "scenario analysis" using AI helps decision-makers evaluate the consequences of different strategies and make informed decisions based on predictive insights and risk assessments (Ernst et al.,

2019). Indeed, these integrations of techniques enhance decision-making, optimise resource allocation, and improve operational efficiency across different contexts of application. The problem arises in the matter of responsibilities. The more people cede power and control to our instruments, the more difficult it is to establish responsibility. Take the case of having an AI automatically drive a car. On average, the number of accidents which people make, due to human error, is very high. By automating the driving process, the number of accidents would be lower, but not 0. Whose responsibility would it be in the event of a fatal accident? How could decision makers regulate this? This is why it's necessary to stress the solution-based choice. The role of AI must be more consultive and less operational.

7 Contemporary Challenges and AI-Powered Strategy

Today, strategic decision-making is increasingly influenced by digital technologies, big data analytics, and predictive models. Technology has progressed ever-increasingly without allowing people to adapt to previous ones. AI-driven tools facilitate predictive modelling, scenario planning, and personalised decision support (Sun et al., 2024). Ethical considerations surrounding AI and automation have become increasingly prominent as these technologies continue to advance and permeate various aspects of society. Leaders and decision-makers face the challenge of navigating these complexities, where they must balance technological innovation with ethical principles. The first ethical consideration is the potential impact on employment and labour markets. AI implementation has the potential to displace some jobs traditionally performed by humans, leading to concerns about job loss and skills obsolescence (Chen et al., 2023). In the future, society will need more decision-makers and flexible intellectual labourers to avoid negative consequences in the job market balance. Another ethical concern is algorithmic bias and discrimination. Algorithms can inadvertently perpetuate biases present in training data, leading to unfair outcomes in areas such as hiring, lending, and law enforcement. This may involve establishing regulatory frameworks to ensure ethics in solutions proposed by AI. In each of these fields, where it's possible to extend the use of AI, such as healthcare, criminal justice, and national security, decision-makers must ensure that these systems are deployed ethically, taking into account issues that arise and the potential unintended consequences of AI solutions (Roselli et al., 2019). The case of NLP is included in this scenario because they will be progressively included in all sectors of intellectual works. If DL and ML are more linked to the dataset and goals, in NLP it is difficult to predict the use which people want to do about it. The use of this kind of AI can profoundly transform business operations and strategies, offering tangible competitive advantages through process optimisation, continuous innovation, and the creation of customised customer experiences. However, to maximise the benefits of AI, it is important to invest in specialised talent, appropriate technology infrastructure, and an organisational culture geared towards innovation and continuous experimentation (Nickerson & Argyres, 2018).

When a technology proves to be effective in solving problems or optimising processes, it will gradually tend to be used more and more, causing a natural selection of competitors who fail to adapt or incorporate it into their businesses. In this way, the market configuration changes and evolves into something different, where those who have the resources to implement innovation win in the long run, while those who fail to adapt tend to perish. Therefore, adopting a new technology is a big risk, as it is not easy to estimate the future success of a tool in time (Parkes & Wellman, 2015). If someone adopts it when everyone else does, he/she will not have any competitive advantage. If someone do it too early, without the necessary skills to manage the innovation, it is possible to have big losses. In this case, it is a matter of trust; how much do people trust this tool? Trust determines the decision because the process that leads to the solution is not identifiable. It is like accepting a closed box that provides an output without understanding what happens inside clearly. That is why it can only be useful as a decision support if it is consultative because then the responsibility and the final decision will always be filtered by a human being. The problem gets worse, however, when it's possible to add in the equation the distributed cognition. Distributed cognition recognises that cognitive processes are not confined to an individual but can be distributed across a group of people and technological artefacts (Rastogi et al., 2022). This perspective is relevant for understanding how human users interact with AI systems, where the cognitive work is distributed between the human and the AI agent. Distributed cognition emphasises the coordination between internal (mental) and external (environmental) structures in cognitive processes. This applies to human–AI interactions, where the cognitive work involves coordination between the human's mental processes and the AI system's external representations and capabilities. This is relevant for understanding how the introduction of AI systems can reshape and transform human cognitive processes and work practices over time. Distributed cognition provides a framework for analysing complex sociotechnical systems, where cognition is distributed across people, tools, and the environment. This holistic perspective can be useful for studying the integration of AI systems into human work environments and the emergent cognitive dynamics which arise. Indeed, the distributed cognition construct offers a valuable lens for examining the interplay between humans and AI systems, recognising that cognitive processes are not confined to individual minds but are distributed across social, technological, and environmental structures (Shrestha et al., 2019). This perspective can provide insights into coordination, transformation, and system-level dynamics involved in human–AI interactions. The concept of "illusion of knowledge", proposed by Sloman, highlights a fundamental challenge in human cognition and its implications for the development of artificial intelligence (Sloman & Fernbach, 2017). This concept suggests that humans often have a subjective sense of understanding or knowledge of a subject, even when their actual understanding may be limited or inaccurate. People assume that they possess knowledge they know they can easily access, as in the case of self-medication via Google (many people think that by being able to find information on the internet, they can self-diagnose illnesses, when in fact it takes many years of study). Another emblematic case is the knowledge people think they have about how bicycles work. If you ask people how much they know from 1 to 10 about how they work, they very often answer with high values, but after asking them to draw the position of the chain, a large majority get the answer wrong. Again, the illusion of knowledge intersects with distributed cognition, and just as Google and the internet have changed our approach to thinking and solving problems, AI will also be a big change which will extend our potential but will come at a high cost in terms of what people will lose without being able to predict what they will gain from this new information revolution. Navigating the intersection of AI and strategy involves addressing a range of critical considerations, from regulatory frameworks and responsible innovation to real-time decision-making and emerging trends (Wu et al., 2023). Regulatory frameworks governing AI in strategic contexts are essential for ensuring a good use of these technologies. As AI becomes increasingly integrated into business strategies, policymakers face a lot of challenges which can be faced only by promoting transparency in AI applications (Spangler, 1991). It is not a problem to use AI assistants such as ChatGPT as a tool, but you need to explain how you use it in your work. While AI can drive efficiency, competitiveness, and innovation, it also raises ethical and societal concerns. In this kind of development, decision makers need to consider the broader impact on stakeholders, society, and the environment. Integrating AI into strategy execution processes requires organisations to invest in AI infrastructure, talent development, and change management to fully harness AI's potential in achieving strategic objectives. Real-time decision-making using AI empowers organisations to respond quickly to dynamic market conditions and changing customer preferences (Alekseeva et al., 2021). AI algorithms can analyse vast amounts of data in real time, providing actionable insights and enabling agile decision-making that drives competitive advantage. Some of the things people plan to do are too time-consuming to be done without adequate tools and cultural artefacts. These tools can be an extension of human potential to adapt quickly and apply strategies that would otherwise be difficult to implement (like adapting quickly to changes in the financial market, easier said than done, until you have an algorithm that allows you to do it effectively). In this case, challenges and opportunities in operationalizing AI-driven strategies lie in barriers and cultural resistance within organizations (Luk, 2023). Leaders must address challenges such as data quality, talent shortages, and organisational readiness to change. So, decision makers must proactively manage these disruptions through responsible adoption of AI, investment in workforce development, and collaboration with stakeholders to ensure inclusive growth (Zarifhonarvar, 2023). To do it effectively and to manage these opportunities, society need further research and development in AI and strategy intersections, including exploring interdisciplinary approaches and enhancing AI explainability and interpretability. Continued research will drive innovation and shape the future of AI-enabled strategic decision-making.

8 Discussion and Conclusion

In this chapter, it is possible to find a lot of insights about how to reflect on the future direction of the use of AI as a strategic decision tool, considering all the potential issues. The final thought on the future trajectory of AI-enabled strategic decision-making is that it is unavoidable to use it. The problem is how to make good use of it. It is important to push the idea of a shift in the paradigm from a tool-centred approach to a skills-based approach. When people have all the tools to answer their questions, they need to ask better questions (Fosso Wamba et al., 2021). This is the best skill that people can learn to make better decisions, because the framing, the shape, and the choices' architecture inside the question will probably lead to different answers. One construct which can lead to a better way of using AI tools is the wisdom hierarchy, also called DIKW (Rowley, 2007). Supporting the skills related to the transactions between the four aspects of knowledge (data-information-knowledge-wisdom) probably will be helpful. Another way is to walk the path of debiasing, analysing all the biases involved in the strategic process and AI-related processes to find sub-tools which can correct them. Last but not least in importance, to spread good guidelines and protocols to follow, to avoid mistakes and biased outcomes.

References

Alekseeva, L., Azar, J., Giné, M., Samila, S., & Taska, B. (2021). The demand for AI skills in the labor market. *Labour Economics, 71*, 102002. https://doi.org/10.1016/j.labeco.2021.102002

Al-Surmi, A., Bashiri, M., & Koliousis, I. (2022). AI based decision making: Combining strategies to improve operational performance. *International Journal of Production Research, 60*(14), 4464–4486. https://doi.org/10.1080/00207543.2021.1966540

Aly, H. (2022). Digital transformation, development and productivity in developing countries: Is artificial intelligence a curse or a blessing? *Review of Economics and Political Science, 7*(4), 238–256. https://doi.org/10.1108/REPS-11-2019-0145

Apsilyam, N. M., Shamsudinova, L., & Yakhshiboyev, R. (2024). The application of artificial intelligence in the economic sector. *Central Asian Journal of Education And Computer Sciences (CAJECS), 3*(1), 1–12.

Chen, Y., Clayton, E. W., Novak, L. L., Anders, S., & Malin, B. (2023). Human-centered design to address biases in artificial intelligence. *Journal of Medical Internet Research, 25*, e43251. https://doi.org/10.2196/43251

Ernst, E., Merola, R., & Samaan, D. (2019). Economics of artificial intelligence: Implications for the future of work. *IZA Journal of Labor Policy, 9*(1), 20190004. https://doi.org/10.2478/izajolp-2019-0004

Fosso Wamba, S., Bawack, R. E., Guthrie, C., Queiroz, M. M., & Carillo, K. D. A. (2021). Are we preparing for a good AI society? A bibliometric review and research agenda. *Technological Forecasting and Social Change, 164*, 120482. https://doi.org/10.1016/j.techfore.2020.120482

Freedman, L. (2013). *Strategy: A history*. Oxford University Press.

Furniss, D., Garfield, S., Husson, F., Blandford, A., & Franklin, B. D. (2019). Distributed cognition: Understanding complex sociotechnical informatics. *Studies in Health Technology and Informatics, 263*, 75–86. https://doi.org/10.3233/SHTI190113

Gupta, K., Mane, P., Rajankar, O. S., Bhowmik, M., Jadhav, R., Yadav, S., Rawandale, S., & Chobe, S. V. (2023). Harnessing AI for strategic decision-making and business performance optimization. *International Journal of Intelligent Systems and Applications in Engineering, 11*(10s), 893–912.

Jackson, S., & Brownie, J. (1992). AI-based decision support tool for strategic decision making in the factory of the future. *Computer Integrated Manufacturing Systems, 5*(2), 83–90. https://doi.org/10.1016/0951-5240(92)90002-T

Johnson, J. (2022). Delegating strategic decision-making to machines: Dr. Strangelove Redux? *Journal of Strategic Studies, 45*(3), 439–477. https://doi.org/10.1080/01402390.2020.1759038

Kaggwa, S., Eleogu, T. F., Okonkwo, F., Farayola, O. A., Uwaoma, P. U., & Akinoso, A. (2024). AI in decision making: Transforming business strategies. *International Journal of Research and Scientific Innovation, X*(XII), 423–444. https://doi.org/10.51244/IJRSI.2023.1012032

Lavazza, A. (2018). Human beings and robots: A matter of teleology? *HUMANA. MENTE Journal of Philosophical Studies, 11*(34), 17–39.

Luk, M. (2023). Generative AI: Overview, economic impact, and applications in asset management. *SSRN Electronic Journal*. https://doi.org/10.2139/ssrn.4574814

Nickerson, J., & Argyres, N. (2018). Strategizing before strategic decision making. *Strategy Science, 3*(4), 592–605. https://doi.org/10.1287/stsc.2018.0066

Parkes, D. C., & Wellman, M. P. (2015). Economic reasoning and artificial intelligence. *Science, 349*(6245), 267–272. https://doi.org/10.1126/science.aaa8403

Piazzoli, A., Sgaramella, G., & Mattiassi, A. (2024). Toward a better measurement of strategic skills: The Multiple Choice Strategic Quotient (McSQ). In M. Clayton, M. Passacantando, & M. Sanguineti (Eds.), *Intelligent technologies for interactive entertainment* (Vol. 560, pp. 3–19). Springer. https://doi.org/10.1007/978-3-031-55722-4_1

Price, M., Walker, S., & Wiley, W. (2018). The machine beneath: Implications of artificial intelligence in strategic decision making. *PRISM, 7*(4), 92–105. https://www.jstor.org/stable/26542709

Rastogi, C., Zhang, Y., Wei, D., Varshney, K. R., Dhurandhar, A., & Tomsett, R. (2022). Deciding fast and slow: The role of cognitive biases in AI-assisted decision-making. *Proceedings of the ACM on Human-Computer Interaction, 6*(CSCW1), 1–22. https://doi.org/10.1145/3512930

Roselli, D., Matthews, J., & Talagala, N. (2019). Managing bias in AI. In *Companion proceedings of the 2019 world wide web conference* (pp. 539–544). https://doi.org/10.1145/3308560.3317590

Rowley, J. (2007). The wisdom hierarchy: Representations of the DIKW hierarchy. *Journal of Information Science, 33*(2), 163–180. https://doi.org/10.1177/0165551506070706

Shrestha, Y. R., Ben-Menahem, S. M., & Von Krogh, G. (2019). Organizational decision-making structures in the age of artificial intelligence. *California Management Review, 61*(4), 66–83. https://doi.org/10.1177/0008125619862257

Sloman, S. A., & Fernbach, P. (2017). Knowledge illusion: Why we never think alone.

Spangler, W. E. (1991). The role of artificial intelligence in understanding the strategic decision-making process. *IEEE Transactions on Knowledge and Data Engineering, 3*(2), 149–159. https://doi.org/10.1109/69.87995

Srinivasan, R., & Chander, A. (2021). Biases in AI systems. *Communications of the ACM, 64*(8), 44–49. https://doi.org/10.1145/3464903

Sun, Y., Jang, E., Ma, F., & Wang, T. (2024). Generative AI in the wild: Prospects, challenges, and strategies. *arXiv preprint arXiv*, 2404.04101.

Trunk, A., Birkel, H., & Hartmann, E. (2020). On the current state of combining human and artificial intelligence for strategic organizational decision making. *Business Research, 13*(3), 875–919. https://doi.org/10.1007/s40685-020-00133-x

Ward, P. T., McCreery, J. K., & Anand, G. (2007). Business strategies and manufacturing decisions: An empirical examination of linkages. *International Journal of Operations & Production Management, 27*(9), 951–973. https://doi.org/10.1108/01443570710775810

Wu, C., Zhang, R., Kotagiri, R., & Bouvry, P. (2023). Strategic decisions: Survey, taxonomy, and future directions from artificial intelligence perspective. *ACM Computing Surveys, 55*(12), 1–30. https://doi.org/10.1145/3571807

Zarifhonarvar, A. (2023). Economics of ChatGPT: A labor market view on the occupational impact of artificial intelligence. *Journal of Electronic Business & Digital Economics*. https://doi.org/10.1108/JEBDE-10-2023-0021

The manufacturer's authorised representative in the EU is Springer Nature Customer Service Centre GmbH, Europaplatz 3, 69115 Heidelberg, Germany. If you have any concerns regarding our products, please contact ProductSafety@springernature.com

Printed and bound by CPI Group (UK) Ltd, Croydon, CR0 4YY
01/10/2026
02225914-0007